International Management

International Management

THEORY AND PRACTICE

Paul N. Gooderham
NHH – The Norwegian School of Economics, Norway

Birgitte Grøgaard
University of Calgary, Canada

Odd Nordhaug
NHH – The Norwegian School of Economics, Norway

Edward Elgar
Cheltenham, UK • Northampton, MA, USA

Published by
Edward Elgar Publishing Limited
The Lypiatts
15 Lansdown Road
Cheltenham
Glos GL50 2JA
UK

Edward Elgar Publishing, Inc.
William Pratt House
9 Dewey Court
Northampton
Massachusetts 01060
USA

A catalogue record for this book
is available from the British Library

Library of Congress Control Number: 2012954987

MIX
Paper from
responsible sources
FSC® C018575
FSC
www.fsc.org

ISBN 978 1 78100 438 8 (cased)
      978 1 78254 622 1 (paperback)
      978 1 78100 439 5 (eBook)

Typeset by Servis Filmsetting Ltd, Stockport, Cheshire
Printed by MPG PRINTGROUP, UK

Contents in brief

Full contents

Authors and contributors

Authors

Paul N. Gooderham is Professor of International Management at NHH – The Norwegian School of Economics in Bergen, and Research Director at SNF – The Foundation for Social Science and Business Research. His research interests are concentrated on international and comparative management. Since 1994 he has been a member of Cranet, the largest comparative HRM research network in the world. He has published numerous articles in journals such as *Journal of Management Studies; Journal of International Business Studies; Strategic Management Journal; Human Relations; Management International Review; International Journal of Human Resource Management; European Journal of Industrial Relations*, and *Administrative Science Quarterly.*

Birgitte Grøgaard is an Assistant Professor at the University of Calgary. Her research focuses on international strategic management and multinational enterprises. Her research is published in outlets such as the *Journal of International Business Studies; International Business Review; International Studies of Management and Organization; Thunderbird International Business Review*, and Edward Elgar Publishing's *Handbook of Research on International Strategic Management.*

Odd Nordhaug is Professor in Administrative Science at NHH – The Norwegian School of Economics. His research interests comprise international and comparative management, HRM, organization theory and knowledge management. For more than two decades he has been a member of Cranet, the largest comparative HRM research network in the world. He has authored and co-authored more than 50 books and published extensively in international research journals, such as *Administrative Science Quarterly; Human Relations; Human Resource Management Review; Management International Review; Human Resource Management; International Studies of Management & Organization; Journal of Portfolio Management; International Journal of Human Resource Management; European Journal of Management; Employee Relations; Management Revue*, and *Scandinavian Journal of Management.*

Contributors

Jean-Luc Cerdin is a Professor of Human Resource Management at ESSEC, France.

Katya Christensen has had various managerial roles in Scandinavian multinational companies.

Fang Lee Cooke is Professor of Human Resource Management and Chinese Studies at Monash University.

Elizabeth Cotton is a Senior Lecturer at Middlesex University Business School.

Richard Croucher is Professor of Comparative Employment Relations at Middlesex University Business School.

Thomas H. Davenport is the President's Distinguished Professor of Information Technology and Management at Babson College and a Senior Advisor to Deloitte Analytics.

Malte Dous was a Research Associate at the Institute of Information Management at the University of St. Gallen. Afterwards he joined the Boston Consulting Group.

Martin Gjelsvik is Head of Research at the International Research Institute of Stavanger.

Atle Jordahl is a senior consultant at AFF – The Administrative Research Institute at NHH – The Norwegian School of Economics.

Sveinung Jørgensen is an Associate Professor at HIL – Lillehammer University College.

Lars Jacob Tynes Pedersen is an Associate Professor at NHH – The Norwegian School of Economics.

Vasilisa Sayapina is a doctoral fellow at NHH – The Norwegian School of Economics specializing in the area of diversity within multinationals.

Jill Thorlacius has a business degree from the University of Calgary. She works in the financial sector in London.

Sven C. Voelpel is Professor of Business Administration at Jacobs University.

Leighton Wilks is a doctoral candidate at the University of Calgary focusing on ethics and sustainability in multinationals.

Michael Zhang is a Reader at Nottingham Trent University Business School.

Introduction

There has been an explosive growth in the number of multinational companies (MNCs). Their contribution to the global economy is such that no student of business or economics can or should avoid thinking seriously about this phenomenon. In this book, we identify some of the most crucial challenges facing managers of MNCs. Most of these challenges are unique to MNCs. We chose to explore these challenges using an interactive approach whereby theory and rich-cases are juxtaposed. A core belief underlying this book is that theory is best understood by relating it not to short, 'tidy' cases but to 'baggy' cases that stretch the sense-making ability of the reader. Each of chapters 2 to 11 offers not only a theoretically grounded presentation of a particular aspect of international management but also a case culled from the real world of international management that serves to illustrate the theory.

The book is primarily targeted at master students undertaking courses in international management, MBAs and advanced bachelor students. However, the theoretical overview of international management provided by the text will make it a useful reference book for academics while the interaction between theory and case makes for a text that will also be relevant for practitioners.

The first part of the book, chapters 1 to 4, introduces the MNC and key drivers for strategic decision making. More specifically, Chapter 1 defines the MNC and discusses why firms typically choose to internationalize. We examine the role of MNCs in contemporary society and we challenge stereotypical perceptions of globalization. A brief overview of challenges facing managers of MNCs is also provided. Chapter 2 provides an overview of common operating methods and ownership forms that managers choose when they decide to enter and operate in foreign markets. A central point in Chapter 2 is the more recent research focus on MNCs' tendencies to combine multiple operating and ownership forms in foreign markets. The case in Chapter 2 illustrates such complexities by describing the internationalization of a European MNC in the Chinese market. Chapter 3 reviews key internationalization motives and the most common strategies and structures pursued by multinationals. We conclude this chapter by discussing changes over time and the increased focus on MNCs as learning networks. The case following Chapter 3 describes strategic challenges facing an MNC that is attempting to change from a very decentralized organizational form with autonomous geographically spread units to a radically more integrated form. Chapter 4 identifies common internal and external risks facing managers of multinational organizations. We discuss how these risks affect strategic decision making. The case attached to Chapter 4 illustrates how the same MNC faces different risks and challenges when entering different foreign markets.

The next part of the book, chapters 5 to 8, identifies fundamental managerial challenges when engaging in cross-border business activities. Chapter 5 introduces multiple dimensions of distance and discusses how these distances may affect the firms' success when entering foreign markets. The concept of cultural distance and how this can be measured has been highly debated over the past decades. We offer an overview of the key approaches to identifying and measuring cultural distance and identify some of the strengths and limitations of each approach. The case attached to Chapter 5 links the discussion of distance with the challenges of managing a diverse workforce. Chapter 6 discusses the nature of international or cross-national human resource management (HRM) as compared to domestic HRM, followed by the presentation of a model for cross-national HRM. We introduce a model for strategic international HRM that emphasizes that when MNCs design HRM systems for their subsidiaries they invariably will have to consider host country culture, socio-economic conditions and institutional constraints. Furthermore, in analysing the transfer of HRM to subsidiaries it is critical to distinguish 'genuine' transfer from other outcomes. In certain settings a subsidiary may experience a pronounced tension between host country and parent company expectations. The case study attached to Chapter 6 describes how a Norwegian bank attempts to implement an HRM development concept and method derived from the United States. The case points to the importance of institutional as well as cultural differences and the need to 'translate' organization and management practices when these are transferred from one institutional setting to another. Chapter 7 focuses on competence development within MNCs and the challenges of transferring knowledge across organizational and national borders. We introduce a typology for classifying competencies and present a framework for analysing knowledge transfer and sharing within MNCs. The framework highlights the importance of social capital for successful cross-border knowledge transfer. The case following Chapter 7 describes how an MNC successfully implemented its comprehensive knowledge-sharing system which has been identified as best practice in its industry. Chapter 8 deals with expatriation and repatriation, a common feature of most MNCs, particularly those exhibiting either an ethnocentric or geocentric approach to the staffing of their subsidiaries. The purpose is to provide an overview of the various roles expatriates fill and to examine factors that are associated with widespread use of expatriates. Furthermore, it deals with the importance of thorough selection and recruitment processes as well as relevant training programs preparing the personnel selected for expatriation. We also emphasize the importance of a successful repatriation process. The case linked to Chapter 8 is that of a leading global luxury brand conglomerate, LVMH – Louis Vuitton Moët Hennessy. It deals with career development through expatriation and international mobility across the conglomerate's five main world zones: France, Europe, the Americas, Pacific Asia and Japan.

The next part, chapters 9 to 11, focuses on the importance of operating in a responsible manner and securing legitimacy for the organization. For these chapters, we have drawn on the expertise of leading scholars within the field. In Chapter 9 it is argued that the recent growth in the number of MNCs, along with their increased economic and political power, strongly accentuates their ethical, social and environmental responsibilities. The purpose is to illuminate and discuss the challenges that stem from these responsibilities. We address the challenge of 'doing well by doing good' and discuss how firms should strategically target their external involvement to create responsible win–win opportunities for the firm and the communities in which it operates. The case attached to Chapter 9 illustrates how an MNC evolved over time from being the target of criticism to a sustainability leader. Chapter 10 discusses how labor regulations affect MNCs and the role of global labor unions. This chapter offers a definition of global industrial relations, an overview of global union organizations, and key instruments for regulating employment relationships at a global level. The chapter concludes by addressing how and why MNCs engage in dialogue with these global union organizations. The case attached to Chapter 10 explores potential mutual benefits of such relationships. In light of the increasing role of internationalization of firms from emerging markets, Chapter 11 focuses on the case of China. The internationalization of Chinese firms has received extensive media attention, including the fear of Chinese government influence. We address the driving forces and main forms of internationalization of Chinese firms and some of the opportunities and constraints these firms face. The case attached to Chapter 11 describes the internationalization of major Chinese firm and links the discussion to managerial challenges in foreign subsidiaries located in markets with high levels of institutional and cultural distance.

Finally, the closing chapter contains a discussion of future challenges facing managers of MNCs. First, we address the issue of whether the increased importance of competencies and networks means a shift of paradigm in the conceptualization of MNC managerial challenges. If so, we will witness the increasing focus on agile organizations. The second managerial challenge that is discussed regards the dynamics of strategy and structure and the implications this has for managing human resources. It is argued that it requires a new type of individual who not only is capable of tolerating change but who is actively seeking it. Hence, the third challenge we review is the challenge MNCs face in respect to global staffing. The fourth challenge that MNCs must confront is related to legitimacy and sources of meaning. We will argue that the long-term survival of MNCs depends on their ability to create meaning for their employees and that this can only be achieved through acquiring and maintaining their legitimacy and keeping high standards of ethics and sustainability. Finally, the rise of MNCs from emerging markets creates a shift towards a 'multi-polar' world where the power and loci of competence, technology and capital flows are shifting. This poses a challenge for scholars within international management as it may necessitate changes in internationalization strategies and business models.

1

Setting the scene: the multinational company

1.1 Introduction

This book is concerned with the managerial and learning challenges that multinational companies (MNCs) have to grapple with as they seek to develop and utilize organizational resources and capabilities that are necessary for achieving success beyond their countries of origin. The purpose of this chapter is to present a broad introduction to the MNC. We discuss MNC characteristics and address why international management is an increasingly critical area of study for business students. We provide an overview of the role MNCs are playing in the globalization of business and examine the question of how global MNCs actually are. We point out that most MNCs have strong national identities and that top management is often lacking in terms of diversity. In particular we emphasize that MNCs are far from guaranteed success. They are 'playing away from home' where they have to overcome various 'liabilities of foreignness'.

1.2 What is an MNC?

'Although many theoretical and operational definitions of the (MNC) have been proposed, none has become standard' (Aggarwal et al., 2011: 558). Definitions of the MNC can be broadly divided into those with a relatively narrow scope and those whose scope is very much broader. The narrow definitions emphasize ownership and day-to-day control whereas the broader definitions move beyond these criteria and employ influence. An example of the narrow definition is the working definition of the MNC used by Bartlett and Beamish (2011). They categorize firms as MNCs if they meet both of two qualifications. The first qualification specifies that for a firm to be regarded as an MNC it has to have substantial direct investment in foreign countries. The second stipulates that it is engaged in the active management of these foreign assets whether this involves the production of goods or of services. In other words simple ownership of foreign assets is not sufficient to be classified as an MNC. Instead entities such as hedge funds that limit themselves to ownership would be classed as investors and not as MNCs. One shortcoming of this definition is that it does take into account that some investors are substantially more active than others in terms of their oversight and support of management. This raises the question of at what point this would count as active management. Those employing the narrow definition have no firm answers to this question.

Another shortcoming of the type of definition that Bartlett and Beamish employ is that some firms exert substantial influence over firms in other countries without having any ownership or any day-to-day management control. For example a firm may enter into a sourcing agreement with a foreign firm and as part of that agreement insist not only on certain employment conditions but also the right to engage in monitoring to ensure that these conditions are being met. Or a firm may sponsor a research agenda that it has defined at a foreign university for an extended period of time. Cases of this kind have given rise to broader definitions of the MNC that go beyond ownership and day-to-day control. For example Cantwell et al. view the MNC as:

> a coordinated system or network of cross-border activities, some of which are carried out within the hierarchy of the firm, and some of which are carried out through informal social ties or contractual relationships. Thus an MNC is not defined solely by the extent of the foreign production facilities it owns, but by the sum total of all of its value-creating activities over which it has a significant influence. These activities may involve foreign sourcing of various intermediate inputs, including the sourcing of knowledge, as well as production, marketing and distribution activities. (2010: 569)

Dunning and Lundan (2008) caution that once one moves from control to influence as a criterion for determining the boundaries of a firm, 'one opens up a Pandora's box'. MNCs may not only influence suppliers but they may exert influence on retailers and even competitors. As such setting the boundary of the MNC becomes highly problematic. For this reason, while we acknowledge the shortcomings of the twofold substantial foreign direct investment and active management of these assets definition of the MNC, for pragmatic reasons this is the definition we employ in this book and make the assumption that MNCs own and control resources in foreign subsidiaries. While the topics discussed in this book are of high relevance to organizations that fit our definition of an MNC, it is also important to note that firms often combine multiple operating modes and ownership structures when internationalizing, as discussed in Chapter 2. The topics and challenges discussed in this book are thus not limited to substantial foreign direct investment as they may also influence other operating modes and ownership structures.

1.3 Why study 'international' management?

Unlike management of domestic companies, international management involves learning to cope and even thrive with different forms of distances. In his CAGE framework Ghemawat (2001) distinguishes four types of distance that MNC managers have to be sensitive to: cultural, administrative, geographic and economic. Ghemawat argues that cultural and administrative distance ('C' and 'A') often have greater impact on doing business. Cultural distance is not just language. It also refers to more subtle features such as social norms and values that determine how people interact with one another. A management style that works well in one culture may be unacceptable in another. Culture is also about taste and deep-seated preferences. A product that is a success in one country may be rejected in another. In India Hindus do not eat beef and Muslims do not eat pork, so there are neither beef nor pork byproducts in any McDonald's restaurant in India. With the high number of vegetarians in India, about half of the menu at McDonald's in India is vegetarian and McDonald's first vegetarian-only restaurant in India will open in 2013 (CBC, 2012).

Administrative distance is partly about learning to deal with being an outsider and therefore exposed to discrimination. In general governments are patriotic and seek to protect their 'national champions'. Likewise a country's natural resources are often regarded as part of a national heritage. In Venezuela in 2007 President Hugo Chávez's government nationalized an Exxon Mobil oil project in the country. For foreign oil or mining companies, being nationalized or exposed to windfall taxes is a persistent anxiety. Overcoming administrative distance is also about learning to deal with the institutions and legal systems in the host country. Trade agreements generally reduce such distances. North (1990) refers to institutionalized constraints and regulations as the 'rules of the game'. These have to be learned.

Geographic distance ('G') refers to geographical differences that affect the costs of transportation and communication. This is of particular importance to companies that depend on a high degree of coordination and mutual understanding. Physical distances within or between countries are most often emphasized when assessing transportation costs. However, many other geographic differences are also important to consider such as differences in time zones, climate and topography. Economic distance ('E') makes it difficult to replicate a business model that works well in one context (for example a developed country) in a country where country-level economic characteristics are significantly different (for example in a developing country). When Vodafone entered the Indian mobile telephony market in 2007 it was very conscious of just how challenging it would be to operate in a market where tariffs are much lower than in developed markets. Arun Sarin, Vodafone's then chief executive stated:

> frankly, we are going to learn as much from India as we are going to take to India. Like we have said in the past, prices there are two and a half US cents a minute, and they make a 35 per cent margin. How do you do that? Our prices in Europe are 13, 14, 15 euro cents, and we make a 40 per cent margin. Their cost structure is very low. The question is what can we learn about how to run a scale business [with] 35m customers, and have that low a cost structure? (*Financial Times*, 2007)

Economic distances can also arise from differences in the cost and/or quality of various resources such as natural, financial or human. Differences in infrastructure and information are also key elements of economic differences that impact both transportation and communication costs.

The topics discussed in this book will have a particular focus on cultural distance and what we will refer to as institutional distance (rather than administrative distance). The ability to handle these forms of distances is the essence of international management.

1.4 Why do firms internationalize?

Over 40 years ago Hymer raised the question of why MNCs existed at all given that they are 'playing away from home' both in national and cultural terms, assuming that domestic companies have 'the general advantage of better information about their country: its economy, its language, its laws and its politics' (Hymer, 1960/1976: 34). However, while in 1969 there were 7,000 MNCs, by 1992 this had expanded to 37,000 and in 2008 to 82,000 (UNCTAD, 2010). These 82,000 MNEs had some 800,000 foreign affiliates (Dunning and Lundan, 2008).

The dominant understanding of why MNCs exist is labeled 'internalization theory'. It has a pronounced focus on cost efficiency. Internalization theory plays a central role in Dunning's (1981, 2009) eclectic paradigm ('OLI'), which proposes that firms will seek operational control of assets abroad, that is engage in foreign direct investment (FDI),[1] when three conditions are met. The first is that of 'ownership advantages' ('O'): the firm has superior assets (for example technology, managerial competence, marketing capabilities or privileged access to resources) that can be exploited. These advantages are also often termed firm-specific advantages (FSAs). In order for the MNC to take advantage of such assets in foreign markets, they must be transferrable (that is non-location-bound, NLB) FSAs, meaning that they also add value when exploited outside of the MNCs home market. The second condition is referred to as 'location advantages' ('L'): the firm benefits from localizing certain activities in the foreign market. Firms may for instance prefer to locate production outside the home country to realize lower factor costs, circumvent trade barriers or because it is considered to be desirable to be close to key suppliers or important markets. The third condition that must be met for a firm to engage in FDI is that it must perceive 'internalization' ('I') of assets as the most advantageous organizational form. In other words after a cost–benefit calculus the firm concludes that it prefers to set up and own a foreign subsidiary rather than relying on a contractual agreement with a foreign firm. Thus the assets are transferred across national boundaries within the firm's own organizations rather than through contractual agreements with foreign-based enterprises.

The cost–benefit calculus firms make will, according to internalization theory, involve trying to calculate different forms of opportunism. On the one hand, establishing and monitoring external contracts can be both challenging and costly in terms of negotiations, monitoring, and communicating to ensure that commitments are fulfilled. Can the firm trust a contractual partner with for example its technology? On the other hand, does the firm have the resources to meet the governance costs involved in running a foreign subsidiary? One particular governance cost is that of monitoring the foreign unit.

> When company headquarters have problems in evaluating the performance of the foreign unit, they incur measurement costs. Such costs can manifest themselves as time spent on controlling delivered services from the foreign subsidiary, time and money spent on accounting issues, and extra travel expenses to control working effort. (Tomassen and Benito, 2009: 294)

Another example of a governance cost is the 'bonding' cost. Time and resources have to be spent on developing personal ties with the foreign unit and on developing a common company culture. The choice of organizing the assets through markets, hierarchies or some combination of the two is thus based on an attempt to optimize anticipated costs.

A very different view of why firms become MNCs is to be found in what is labeled 'evolutionary theory' (Kogut and Zander, 1993, 1996).

Whereas the focus on cost efficiencies and market failures in internalization theory assumes that bounded rationality and opportunism influences decision making (Verbeke, 2003), evolutionary theory emphasizes knowledge transfer as central for value creation. Like internalization theory, evolutionary theory accepts that some firms have ownership advantages. However, it argues that any key ownership advantage held by firms comprises 'tacit' knowledge embedded in social relationships. Knowledge of this kind cannot be readily packaged and licensed to other firms. It can only be transferred through cooperation and this is much more readily achieved within the firm rather than between firms. This is because unlike the market, the firm is a setting that allows for repeated interactions by individuals and groups over time. This facilitates the development of common identities and understandings that greatly improve communication and therefore learning. Evolutionary theory challenges the notion that firms are internalized markets viewing instead them as 'social communities' that unlike markets support the transfer and sharing of tacit, socially embedded knowledge. It is this 'firm advantage' that explains why MNCs decide to create foreign affiliates and not market failure. As Forsgren puts it:

> In [this] perspective, therefore, the decision to carry out a foreign direct investment does not reflect the difficulty of negotiating a contract with a potential foreign counterpart, but difficulties in detaching a capability from the firm itself . . . In this sense, the multinational firm is perceived to be one big happy family compared to [internalization theory] . . . The cheaters and shirkers of internalization theory are substituted by altruistic individuals with no intention to maximize their own interests at the cost of the organization as a whole. (Forsgren, 2008: 69–70)

As the quote illustrates, the issue of opportunism has been debated with some critics dismissing its relevance or assuming internalization theory focuses merely on costs rather than value creation. As an extension of this debate, Verbeke and Greidanus (2009) introduce bounded reliability as an additional behavioral assumption that captures many of the inherent challenges MNCs face. Verbeke and Greidanus suggest that although economic actors may not intentionally act opportunistically, their reliability is uncertain due to benevolent preference reversal associated with reprioritization or over-commitment. Internalizing transactions by establishing foreign units is therefore in many cases considered a superior choice than executing them across markets. In other words, the potential for 'market failure' is an important component in explaining MNCs.

1.5 The globalization of business

On a global basis, it has been estimated that the sales of foreign affiliates may account for as much as half of world GDP (Dunning and Lundan, 2008). MNCs generate about half of the world's industrial output and account for about two-thirds of world trade. About one-third of total trade (or half of the MNC trade) is intra-firm. MNCs are particularly strong in motor vehicles, computers and soft drinks, having on a global basis 85 per cent, 70 per cent and 65 per cent of these markets, respectively. In some countries they are the dominant manufacturing presence. As Figure 1.1 shows, in 2006 affiliates of MNCs accounted for about 80 per cent of Ireland's manufacturing output; and it exceeded 50 per cent in the Slovak Republic, Hungary, Belgium, the Czech Republic and Canada. A substantial proportion of manufacturing in the United Kingdom, Sweden and the Netherlands is also accounted for by MNCs. All the indications are that the level of production undertaken by foreign-owned manufacturing will continue to rise.

Source: OECD (2009).

Figure 1.1 Share of affiliates under foreign control in national manufacturing turnover, 2006

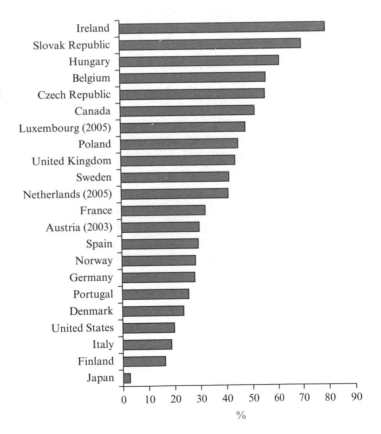

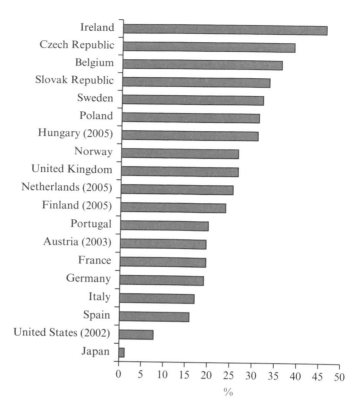

Source: OECD (2009).

Figure 1.2 Share of affiliates under foreign control in national services turnover, 2006

Manufacturing employment under foreign control generally follows the same pattern as turnover although the share in total employment is lower because FDI is more capital- than labor-intensive (OECD, 2009). Thus, for example, in Ireland FDI accounts for about 45 per cent of employment in manufacturing and about 25 per cent in the United Kingdom. For Japan it is negligible.

In services, the share of turnover under foreign control is generally lower than in manufacturing. As Figure 1.2 indicates, for Ireland it is about 45 per cent, and in the Czech Republic, Belgium, the Slovak Republic, Sweden, Poland and Hungary it is around 30 per cent. Like manufacturing, Japan is also the country with the smallest proportion of national services turnover accounted for by FDI. Services employment under foreign control generally follows the same pattern as turnover but is lower. Thus, for example, in Ireland FDI accounts for about 25 per cent of employment in services and about 15 per cent in the United Kingdom. Like manufacturing, in Japan employment in services under foreign control is negligible (OECD, 2009).

The advantages of becoming a global player in manufacturing are more obvious than for service-based firms. In the case of the former the value chain can be divided across many locations. Parts of the manufacturing process can be located to low-cost countries, while R&D can be located in a region with specialized competencies with its costs spread across many markets. In the case of service firms, much of the value chain has to be generated locally: that is, there is little in the way of opportunity to centralize activities to low-cost locations. To a greater or larger degree services have to be tailored for each client unlike, for example, pharmaceuticals, which can be mass-produced. Sharing advanced knowledge is also more problematic. In manufacturing companies it can be made available through patented technologies or unique products. In service companies it has to be transferred from country to country through learning processes. Nevertheless, with increasing liberalization the share of services in FDI has risen significantly.

While in the 1970s the proportion of the inward FDI stock in the world accounted for by services was about one quarter, by as early as 2002 it had risen to about 60 per cent (UNCTAD, 2004). Particular growth areas were within telecommunications, utilities, investment banking, business consulting, accountancy and legal services. One conspicuous example is Accenture, the management consultancy, technology services and business process outsourcing company. In 2012 it had a staff of over 240,000 employees across 54 countries (Accenture, 2012). Another is the accountancy company PricewaterhouseCooper (PwC). In 2012 it had offices in 771 cities across 158 countries that employed around 170,000 people (PwC, 2012). In addition, the emergence of the less conspicuous new services such as software, back-office services, call centers and data entry have also contributed to the relative growth of services in FDI.

At the start of the new millennium the major recipients of FDI were the USA and the European Union (EU), with Germany, the United Kingdom and the Benelux countries figuring particularly strongly. During the period 1986–2000 the typical annual average FDI growth rate was in the range of 20 to 30 per cent. For 1999 and 2000 over three quarters of global FDI inflows went to the developed world partly because of intense cross-border mergers and acquisitions activity.

Despite setbacks such as the financial crisis in 2008, the long-term flow of FDI is one of inexorable increase. However, by the end of the first decade of the new millennium it was apparent that the new powerhouse of FDI was the rise of emerging economies such as Brazil, India, China and Russia (often referred to as the BRIC countries). By 2010 developing and transition economies attracted half of global FDI inflows (UNCTAD, 2010). Among developing economies China was by far the most important recipient of FDI.

Even when one excludes Hong Kong, China was the second largest FDI recipient after the USA in 2009. Inflows of FDI into China were nearly as large as inflows to the other three BRIC countries combined.

Another aspect to the rising importance of the emerging economies is that in 2010 developing and transition economies also invested one quarter of global FDI outflows. Again China was a key player. In 2010 outward FDI from China had increased from about $15bn in 2004 to more than $220bn. However, China still accounts for only 1.2 per cent of total world FDI, about the same as Denmark. Though this is higher than that of other emerging markets such as Brazil and India, it is only about one-twentieth that of the USA (*Financial Times*, 2011a). Furthermore, much of it is very local. Hong Kong accounts for nearly 70 per cent of mainland China's outward FDI stock and other parts of Asia for about 9 per cent. Europe and North America account for a mere 6 per cent of its stock (Peng, 2011). Peng (2011: 8–9) concludes that any notion 'that China is "buying up the world" . . . is disconnected from reality and unsubstantiated by facts'. In other words, Chinese MNCs such as Lenovo and Huawei are exceptions in a world in which MNCs from North America, Japan and Western Europe continue to dominate. However, as we will point out in the next section, this dominance is decreasing.

1.6 How global are MNCs?

How global are MNCs? The Uppsala internationalization process model of the firm (Johanson and Vahlne, 1977) emerged from observing how Swedish firms developed into MNCs. It argues that firms internationalize incrementally. Firms begin with ad hoc exporting, and as learning takes place sales agents are replaced by foreign sales organizations and then production. It further argues that firms prefer to start their internationalization in culturally proximate markets where the psychic distance is low (for example low perceived difficulties in understanding the foreign market). Firms enter foreign markets that resemble their domestic markets and which are therefore more easily understood. Moving beyond neighboring markets is gradual. The implication of the Uppsala theory is that most MNCs are regional rather than global.

Focusing on global sales penetration rather than sourcing or production, Rugman (2001) also argues that most MNCs are region bound. His starting point is that the 'triad' economies – the EU, the USA and Japan – have long accounted for the bulk of global FDI. Rugman's (2001) analysis indicated that of the world's largest 500 MNCs in 1999, a total of 434 were from the triad and this percentage had remained fairly constant over the past decades.

Rugman and Verbeke (2004) argue that the problem faced by many MNCs is that they sell innovative products that stem from high investments not least in knowledge development. Although these products are protected by patents and brand names, in reality rivals in other parts of the triad create equivalent products more rapidly than they can develop distribution capabilities throughout the triad. Consequently most MNCs trade within their respective immediate region, NAFTA, the expanded EU and Asia. Rugman and Verbeke (2004: 6) were only able to identify nine MNCs in the Fortune 500 that were 'unambiguously "global", with at least 20% of their sales in all three regions of the triad, but less than 50% in any one region'. The exceptions were IMB, Sony, Philips, Nokia, Intel, Canon, Coca-Cola, Flextronics and LVMH. Although they identified a number of bi-regional MNCs, such as McDonald's, Toyota and Unilever, nearly 90 per cent of MNCs are home region oriented. They further observed that most large MNCs average 80 per cent of their sales in their home region.

Furthermore, MNCs generally have large portfolios of purely domestic assets. Even the largest MNCs have on average nearly half of their total assets in domestic assets whereas for many smaller MNCs the proportion is substantially larger. In the final analysis, 'if firms have exhausted their growth in their home region of the triad and still go into other regions, they then face (inter-regional) foreignness and other additional risks by this global expansion' (Rugman, 2005: 1). As few firms are capable and willing to bear these costs and risks, they are destined to compete within their home regions. Rugman concludes that:

> There is no evidence for globalization, that is, of a system of free trade with fully integrated world markets. Instead the evidence on the performance and activities of multinational enterprises demonstrates that international business is triad-based and triad-related. . . . European, North American and Asian manufacturing and service companies compete viciously for market share, lobbying their governments for shelter and subsidies. (2001: 10)

Proponents thus argue that the world's largest MNCs operate mostly within their home regions, that very few are global, that the global strategy is a myth (Collinson and Rugman, 2008) and that the CEOs of MNCs should, 'encourage all (of their) managers to think regional, act local – and forget global' (Rugman and Hodgetts, 2001: 341).

However, the regionalization thesis does have its critics. For example Osegowitsch and Sammartino (2008) agree that sales are the decisive indicator of firm-specific advantages: international sales reflect international customers' judgment about the attractiveness of the firm's goods services and ultimately the strength of the FSAs. However, they view the thresholds used by Rugman and co-authors as arbitrary. Why, they ask, set the home-region threshold to 50 per cent? They re-test Rugman's data using different cut-offs and find that the conclusions are far from robust, with a significant share of firms attaining bi-regional or global status. They also observe that longitudinal analysis shows that large firms increasingly are extending their sales beyond the home region. Aggarwal et al. (2011) are even more critical. They employ a classification system that goes beyond triad countries to include all countries in the world, which does not apply activity thresholds and which supplements sales with subsidiaries. Their findings indicate that the vast majority of the 100 largest G7 firms operate beyond their home regions. Nevertheless, while most are trans-regional, only 3 per cent of these firms have truly global sales, although 13 per cent have global subsidiaries.

A different type of challenge to the regionalization thesis is the revisited version of the Uppsala model. Johanson and Vahlne (2009) argue that regional bias in firm internationalization has weakened significantly. Increasingly it is not psychic distance but outsidership in relation to relevant networks that is the source of uncertainty. Insidership in networks of business relationships provides a firm with an extended knowledge base thereby enabling it to identify opportunities and to overcome the liability of outsidership. Firms go abroad based on their relationships with important partners who are committed to developing the business relationship and this may take them to much more distant markets than assumed by the original Uppsala model. Hence:

> We do believe that the correlation between the order in which a company enters foreign markets and psychic distance has weakened. Some companies and individuals have acquired more general knowledge of foreign environments, and perhaps this instils in them greater confidence in their ability to cope with psychic distance. (Johanson and Vahlne, 2009: 1421)

One obvious indicator of weakening regionalization is the increased share of global inward FDI experienced by emerging economies and not least China. In 2000 this share was 20 per cent. In 2010 it had increased to just over 50 per cent. US and EU MNCs are increasingly 'lured by these countries' fast growing markets as much as lower wages' (*Economist*, 2011a: 59). For example in 2000 emerging markets accounted for 22 per cent of all purchases of motor vehicles. As Figure 1.3 indicates, in 2010 this had risen to 52 per cent. In other words, FDI in emerging economies is not just a matter of sourcing or production. Sales are also increasingly important, as illustrated in Figure 1.4.

Source: *Economist* (2011a).

Figure 1.3 Emerging
economies' world share

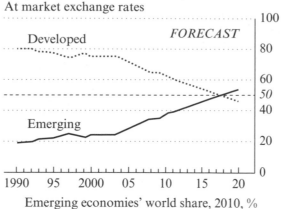

Crossed roads

Economies' share of world GDP, %
At market exchange rates

Emerging economies' world share, 2010, %

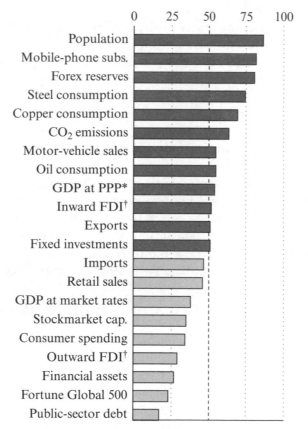

Sources: AT Kearney; Bloomberg: BP;   *Purchasing-power parity
dotMobi; Fortune; IMF; UBS; UN; World   †Foreign direct investment
Bank; World Steel Association; WTO.

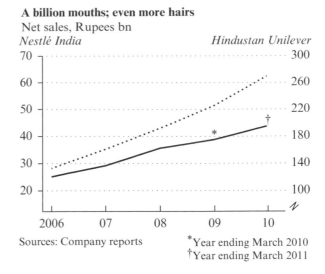

Source: *Economist* (2011b).

Figure 1.4 Nestlé's and Hindustan Unilever's net sales in India: 2006–2010

The relative dominance of the triad companies is also decreasing. Almost a quarter of the Fortune Global 500 firms in 2010 came from emerging markets; in 1995 it was 4 per cent (*Economist*, 2011b). In 2010, as many as 67 companies from BRIC countries were on Fortune's Global 500 list (*Financial Times*, 2011b). More broadly, while more than 90 per cent of all MNCs were headquartered in developed countries in the earlier 1990s, parent MNCs from developing and transition economies accounted for more than a quarter of the worldwide MNCs in 2008 (UNCTAD, 2010).

Despite these challenges to the thesis of regionalization, our view is that this perspective is a powerful antidote to naïve notions of the geographical scope of most MNCs. As Osegowitsch and Sammartino (2008) concede, it is clear that the world will remain in a state of 'semi-globalization' (Ghemawat, 2003) for the foreseeable future. In general the regionally integrated MNC remains more the rule than the exception (Oh and Rugman, 2012).

1.7 National identity and top management diversity

Despite the increase in globalization, most MNCs have home bases that give them resolutely national identities. General Electric and Microsoft are clearly American just as Honda and Toyota are Japanese. In 2008, shortly after he had become chief executive of Siemens, a German conglomerate with 70 business units and 430,000 workers in 190 countries, Peter Löscher, an Austrian by birth, concluded that Siemens was, 'Too German, too white and too male' (*Financial Times*, 2008a). However, the *Financial Times* argued that Peter Löscher's charge is 'one that could apply to most companies in continental Europe and the UK':

Too few are good at attracting not just women and ethnic minorities but also international talent. Fixing the imbalance is not just a matter of political correctness but something vitally important for the competitiveness of the Continent. It is also a topic that brings together nearly all of the factors that will affect the long-term success of business in the Continent from demographics to skills to immigration . . . The fact that most large European countries' boards contain primarily domestic directors (or those from culturally similar countries such as Germany, Switzerland and Austria) is a big issue. (*Financial Times*, 2008b)

When asked in the *Financial Times* interview if such diversity was critical to Germany's future, Peter Löscher replied '[a]bsolutely . . . If you are not representing your global customer base then you won't tap your full potential. If you are doing well you will have a massive advantage' (*Financial Times*, 2008a).

There are exceptions. Some companies, such as Nestlé, the Swiss foods group, resolutely pursue diversity at top management level. 'It has just one Swiss and another joint US–Swiss citizen on its 13-strong executive board (although no women), with the rest made up of three Spaniards, two Dutch, two Canadians, an American, a Swede and a German all led by a Belgian chief executive' (*Financial Times*, 2008b). Similarly Citigroup and Pepsico of the USA have both had Indian-born CEOs and Sony and Olympus of Japan have had British-born CEOs. However, there are few companies where the top management diversity genuinely reflects multinational identities. The most obvious exceptions tend to be located within professional services. However, these are often nationally owned partnerships that confer a degree of local independence. Outside professional services multinational identities are more elusive.

Organizational identities are not limited to the diversity of the top management teams. They are also shaped by identity claims projected by the organization as well as the perceptions of external stakeholders (Hatch and Schultz, 2002). Developing a shared organizational identity enables internal integration and can serve as 'glue' in geographically spread organizations. Because an increasing number of MNCs have more employees outside their home base country, external stakeholders may vary greatly across organizational units and constrain the development of a common organizational identity. Investing in the development of an inclusive organizational identity is therefore increasingly important to enhance knowledge flows for MNCs whose competitive advantages rely on integration across borders.

1.8 Liability of foreignness

MNCs have a number of advantages over local companies. In addition to the general location-specific advantages derived from their country of origin they carry with them the firm-specific advantages and strategic assets that enabled them to succeed in their home market. Furthermore their size provides them with the opportunity to achieve economies of scale in manufacturing and product development while their global presence exposes them to new ideas and opportunities regardless of where they occur. Additionally, their location in many countries can be used as a bargaining chip in obtaining favorable conditions from governments anxious to preserve inward investment and jobs.

However, despite all of their advantages MNCs are also exposed to a potential 'liability of foreignness' (LOF) (Zaheer, 1995). Foreign firms face a 'liability' that is derived from their lack of experience and knowledge about the culture and the 'rules of the game' of the host environment relative to local firms. They face further liabilities in lacking local business networks and being exposed to discriminatory hazards. None of these is necessarily always well understood or anticipated particularly in the initial entry phase. MNCs are therefore not necessarily successful when internationalizing. One classic investigation, the *Templeton Global Performance Index* (2000, 2001), revealed that in 1998 while the foreign activities of the world's largest MNCs accounted on average for 36 per cent of their assets and 39 per cent of revenues, these activities only generated 27 per cent of their profits. Over 60 per cent of these companies achieved lower profitability abroad than at home. Let us consider LOF in some detail.

An MNC will often have to compete head on with domestic companies that have a number of natural advantages. First domestic companies have a customer base they have cultivated and which is familiar with their brands. This loyalty to a local player has to be overcome in such a way that it does not evoke a nationalistic reaction. A French poll in 2006 indicated that 65 per cent of the French believe that it is the government's role to stop foreign bids (*Financial Times*, 2006). Second, local firms will also have developed supply chain relations that may involve long-term contractual relationships that effectively preclude newcomers. This has been a formidable barrier for companies entering the Japanese market. The two types of advantages described above are often referred to as non-transferrable, or location-bound, firm-specific advantages (LB FSAs), which MNCs need to develop or access to succeed in foreign markets. A third entry barrier is that national regulators will tend to discriminate against foreign subsidiaries. Except when they are so locally embedded that they are perceived as domestic, foreign firms will be significantly more investigated, audited, and prosecuted than their domestic counterparts (Vernon, 1998). Even in the United States, officially committed to applying the same 'national treatment' to the offspring of foreign companies that they give to their own companies, it has been empirically documented that 'foreign subsidiaries face more labor lawsuit judgments than their domestic counterparts' (Mezias, 2002: 239).

In regard to China there have been periods of outspoken criticism of its business environment from investors in numerous sectors and from a broad range of countries. These companies point to a wide range of discriminatory government practices and regulatory barriers to foreign investment, government procurement rules that favor domestic companies and the country's lack of a transparent and independent legal system (*Financial Times*, 2010). However, discrimination against foreign companies is by no means unique to China. In the USA in 1990 a group of foreign MNCs including Nestlé, Sony and Unilever banded together to form the Organization for International Investment (OFII), a body that monitors and responds to discrimination. Membership has expanded to 150 subsidiaries of foreign-based MNCs and OFII's primary task is to remain on alert for discrimination:

> Often legal and regulatory issues arise that uniquely or disproportionately target U.S. subsidiaries of companies headquartered abroad. (OFII, 2011)

Finally, a fourth entry barrier is the lack of institutional and cultural insight, where firms fail to identify and overcome the cultural and administrative distances discussed by Ghemawat. When Wal-Mart moved into Germany in 1998 it had little feel for German shoppers, who care more about price than having their bags packed, or German staff, who hid in the toilets to escape the morning Wal-Mart cheer. These cultural differences were further amplified by the inflexibility of local suppliers, the entrenched position of local discounters such as Aldi as well as the strength of trade unions. In the wake of losses of $300m a year, John Menzer, head of Wal-Mart International, admitted, 'We screwed up in Germany' (*Economist*, 2001a). Wal-Mart withdrew from Germany in 2006.

On the other hand, 'as the firm becomes more of an insider in a particular host society . . . developing linkages and aligning its values and actions to the institutional requirements of the host environment, its LOF should decline and perhaps even disappear' (Zaheer, 2002: 353). However, not all MNCs are necessarily able to learn and adjust. In particular many MNCs are not good at digesting foreign acquisitions. In a recent interview Michael Porter remarked:

And be especially careful when making and integrating acquisitions. You buy a Spanish company and all you're going to hear from them is how things are done in Spain. Economists have been studying mergers for twenty years and they find that the seller gets most of the value, not the buyer. Foreign acquisitions must be forcefully repositioned around your strategy, not allowed to continue theirs (unless, of course, theirs is better!). (Magretta, 2012)

But, 'forceful repositioning' also has its dangers. In August 2011 Hewlett-Packard (HP) acquired Autonomy of the UK. The $10.3bn deal was the biggest acquisition of a European IT company and was heralded by Leó Apotheker, HP's chief executive at the time, as a chance for HP to gain leadership in searching unstructured data. However, as HP began to exert control Autonomy employees found HP's internal procedures 'stifling' and as many as a quarter, including all senior management and many developers, left the company. In May 2012 the founder of Autonomy also departed (*Financial Times*, 2012a).

To outweigh and overcome LOF an MNC must possess some strategic capability that gives it a competitive advantage; whether it is advanced technological expertise, marketing competencies or scale economies. Organizational capabilities are equally important to succeed internationally. The ability to coordinate and leverage advantages from geographically spread organizational units enables MNCs to overcome LOF or barriers of 'outsidership'. These capabilities and the costs associated with developing them must not be taken for granted. Increasingly, managing the knowledge base of the MNC has become one of the most important organizational capabilities. This comprises not only the transfer of knowledge between the various parts of the MNC, but also the creation of new forms of knowledge by combining knowledge located transnationally both within and beyond the MNC.

The focus of this book is on the managerial and learning challenges that MNCs have to confront in order to create these organizational capabilities. Despite their strengths, globally dispersed companies can easily become bureaucratic and therefore non-entrepreneurial and insensitive to the many different environments in which they operate (Birkinshaw, 2000). Indeed some researchers claim that there is a non-linear inverted U-shaped relationship between international diversification and performance (for example Geringer et al., 1989 and Hitt et al., 1997). Beyond a threshold of international expansion, returns diminish due to the limits of the firm and its management. That is, at some point the transaction costs involved in co-coordinating and controlling geographically dispersed units outweigh the benefits of international diversification. Other researchers are less sure. In an extensive review of research articles measuring performance effects of international diversification, Hennart (2007) found no clear theoretical rationale to support performance effects. However, what is clear is that being an MNC does not guarantee success.

In short, successful MNCs must have the capacity to identify and respond to local conditions as well as the ability to benefit from their size through cross-border integration of resources, capabilities and activities. How much local responsiveness and how much global integration is needed may vary, but to a substantial extent they are the two most important issues MNCs face. Since the context within which MNCs operate involves national cultural differences, distance and regulations that vary by national setting, many MNCs choose a differentiated approach to its foreign operations. This creates particular challenges that most domestic firms do not face in terms of developing structures that match the strategic thrust of the company by defining the basic lines of reporting and responsibility. Developing a corporate culture that stimulates commitment to the company, entrepreneurial attitudes and a non-parochial mind-set, supported by appropriate reward and career systems, further strengthens the ability of MNCs to succeed internationally. We will address these challenges in the remaining chapters.

1.9   Summary

In this chapter we have defined what we mean by an MNC, that is actively managed substantial foreign direct investment made by firms that have a long-term commitment to operating internationally. We have thereby narrowed our scope from several prevalent forms of internationalization such as licensing and contract manufacturing. MNCs are a historically recent phenomenon whose presence is particularly evident in certain sectors. Despite local resistance, sometimes explicit and sometimes tacit, the MNC has proved itself to be a highly robust organizational form: the dramatic growth in numbers and proportions of MNCs, at least within the context of their own triads, is testimony to this. Nevertheless, the individual positions of MNCs are always under threat because of their size and geographical dispersion; factors that make communication and control problematic. Success for individual MNCs is far from guaranteed. They are 'playing away from home' and must therefore have the organizational capabilities that enable them to leverage whatever unique strategic capabilities they possess. Increasingly these capabilities are knowledge-based. This book is therefore about the managerial challenges involved in creating and sustaining the necessary organizational capabilities that in turn enable the MNC to harness its firm-specific advantages.

NOTE

1 FDI is defined as assets abroad where the MNC has both ownership and operational control. The criterion of operational control is key to differentiate FDI from portfolio investments. The OECD's definition of FDI uses a 10 per cent threshold to ensure that sufficient control can be exercised.

2
Foreign operating modes and ownership forms

2.1 Introduction

This chapter provides an overview of various operating modes and owner-ship structures that MNCs typically choose when entering and operating in foreign markets. After reading this chapter, students should be able to: (1) identify and compare the benefits and challenges of different operating modes and ownership forms, and (2) critically assess when certain operating modes and ownership forms may be more appropriate than others.

2.2 Operating modes

Once a firm has decided to enter the international arena it must make a choice regarding how to organize its foreign business activities. An MNC can choose from a range of operating modes that require different levels of commitment in the foreign markets. Operating modes are sometimes referred to as entry modes, reflecting that the operating mode was decided upon entry to a foreign market. The choice of operating mode when entering foreign markets was long considered discrete and static. More recent work in this area emphasizes that operating modes selected upon entry to a foreign market often evolve or change over time (Benito et al., 2009; Welch et al., 2007). We will therefore use the terminology operating mode rather than entry mode in this book to reflect ongoing dynamics. The operating modes are furthermore not mutually exclusive as MNCs often combine or 'package' different operating modes (Benito et al., 2011). In other words, although we introduce the operating modes and ownership structures separately, many MNCs combine multiple operating modes and ownership structures and/ or change these forms over time. The operating modes discussed in this chapter are often categorized according to equity commitment, as shown in Table 2.1.

Table 2.1 An overview of common operating modes

Non-equity (contractual) modes	Equity modes
Exporting (indirectly or through third party distributor)	Exporting with MNC-owned sales subsidiaries
Licensing	International joint ventures (equity-based alliances)
Franchising	
Contract manufacturing and service provision	Wholly owned subsidiaries (WOS)
Non-equity alliances	

Operating modes vary in terms of the risk they involve; they require diverse organizational, management and resource demands; and differ in the amount of control that can be exercised over foreign operations. We will now briefly describe the most common operating modes.

Exporting

Exporting is often viewed as a good starting point and relatively low-risk entry strategy as it involves little capital investment and lower exit barriers. As such it is an obvious alternative for firms lacking in capital resources. However, the attractiveness of exporting is directly affected by the presence of tariffs, quotas or various conditions of trade agreements. Geographical distances, as discussed in Chapter 1, can also generate higher transportation costs and reduce the feasibility of sending end products to a foreign market.

There are different forms of export. MNCs can choose to export indirectly (for example through other firms that are present in the domestic market), through third party distributors in the foreign market or by establishing foreign sales subsidiaries (Welch et al., 2007). Each alternative has both advantages and disadvantages. Exporting indirectly through a trading company can speed up the process and eliminate barriers associated with a lack of knowledge about the foreign markets. In the long term, however, such indirect relationships with markets may stunt growth opportunities and reduce the MNCs ability to respond to specific market needs. Exporting through third party distributors in foreign markets brings the MNC closer to the foreign market while tapping into existing local expertise. Foreign distributors often have well-established distribution channels and thus complement the MNCs transferrable FSAs with location-specific advantages.

However, even if MNCs choose to contract the distribution in a foreign market to a local firm that is deemed efficient and reliable, its continued involvement and cooperation is often necessary to ensure that local marketing and sales activities are aligned with the MNC strategy.

In his study of distributor agreements, Arnold (2000) found that relationships with third party distributors often failed because MNCs overestimated the abilities of local partners to identify and meet the MNCs' needs in terms of growth and market development. Arnold suggests that MNCs need to work more closely with the local distributors to combine their experience and skills with the complementary local market knowledge. Some MNCs instead choose to set up a wholly-owned sales subsidiary. This option relies on the MNCs' ability to establish or tap into local distribution channels, which may be both costly and time consuming. To address these trade-offs, Arnold (2000) proposes that MNCs invest in long-term relationships with third party distributors where the MNC maintains control over the marketing strategy while providing substantial continued investments in terms of resources and support, which may in some cases even result in equity stakes. As this discussion illustrates, exporting modes are often more complex than initially perceived.

Licensing

Licensing is another operating mode often perceived as low commitment and low risk. It is particularly useful in countries where regulations limit market entry or where tariffs and quotas make exporting a non-viable strategy. It is also often preferred when the target country is culturally distant from the home country or there is little prior experience of the host country. A licensing agreement gives a firm in a host country the right to produce and sell a product for a specified period in return for a fee. The main weakness with licensing is the licensor's lack of control over the licensee. This applies to quality standards that, if disregarded, can be detrimental to the brand's image. It also applies to the monitoring of sales that form the basis for royalty payments. That is why licensing is primarily suitable for the mature phase of a product's life cycle in which the technology that is transferred to the licensee is older and standardized. In other phases of a product's life cycle, direct ownership is more viable to avoid the risk that the licensee appropriates the competence underlying the product, thereby becoming a direct competitor. Markets with weak appropriability regimes (for example legal systems to protect patents and settle contractual disputes) are therefore less attractive for licensing as it increases the risk for unwanted knowledge dissemination (Hennart, 2009).

Franchising

Franchising is similar to licensing but more comprehensive. For a fee and royalty payments the franchisee receives a complete package comprising the franchiser's trademark, products and services, and a complete set of operating principles thereby creating the illusion of a worldwide company. The franchising agreement thus typically details the business concept and restrains the franchisee to specific marketing strategies and promotions (Welch et al., 2007). Holiday Inn hotels and, not least, McDonald's with its 31,000 restaurants in 119 countries are two familiar examples. Both of these franchisers place great emphasis on ensuring consistent quality. Despite the detailed contractual agreements, which in McDonald's case even includes a strict training program, McDonald's chief executive Jack Greenberg characterized McDonald's as in reality being 'an amalgamation of local businesses run by local entrepreneurs from Indonesia to France' (*Economist*, 2001b).

Contract manufacturing and service provision

Nike distinguishes between design, product development and marketing on the one hand, and shoe and clothing manufacturing on the other. The latter is not integrated in Nike but is contracted out to independent plants in developing economies such as China, Indonesia, Thailand and Vietnam, primarily for cost reasons. The main benefits to Nike are that it has none of the problems of local ownership, nor does it invest its own capital in manufacturing. Nonetheless, various pressure groups have ensured that Nike has become a focus for international scrutiny because of allegations of sexual harassment and physical and verbal abuse of workers at its contract factories. Increasingly Nike has recognized that it cannot relinquish moral responsibility for conditions at contractor manufacturers. It has even commissioned outside groups such as the Global Alliance for Workers and Communities to examine conditions in its contractor plants as a means to improving conditions.

Mobile phone vendors, including Ericsson, Apple and Motorola, have applied the same model to handset manufacturing. They outsource the production of handsets to Asian companies, such as the Singapore-based Flextronics, on a contractual basis while retaining control of research, design, branding and marketing. The key advantage to mobile phone vendors in not owning their own factories is that they have the flexibility to ramp production up or down in accordance with extreme fluctuations in demand without long-term capital investments or an increase in their labor forces. The disadvantage lies in that they are handing over control of a vital part of their supply chain. Not only is quality control more problematic, there is also a dependency on the contract equipment manufacturer (CEM) possessing or having access to the necessary parts.

Basically the task of the CEM is to manufacture products according to well-specified designs provided by their clients. Their use is appropriate when technology is less important as a differentiator and value is derived from competing on brand, distribution and style. Contracting out therefore involves no loss of critical learning opportunities. In the personal computer industry, the commodity model has been taken a step further. Vendors not only contract out manufacturing but also a large proportion of the work design is allocated to companies that offer original design manufacturing. Finally it should be noted that contract arrangements are by no means confined to manufacturing. Nearly half of the 500 largest MNCs regularly use Indian IT service providers on a contractual basis, attracted by the combination of low costs and advanced processing skills. The contracts involve a spread of IT services from low value work, such as systems maintenance, to the more lucrative development of new applications such as internet-based portals. Distribution may also be outsourced. Contracting taken to this extreme means that the MNC is not a firm in the traditional sense, that is a vertically integrated organization, so much as a network of contractually determined market-based obligations that together constitute a complete supply chain. This emerging organizational form makes for a new set of managerial challenges – the management of contracts and relationships across borders.

Non-equity alliances

An alliance is a term broadly used to cover many of the contractual and equity modes discussed in this chapter. The diversity of alliances and variations in the use of terminology make it a less clear choice for many managers. Welch et al. define alliances as 'arrangements where two or more companies engage in collaborative activity, while remaining as independent organizations, and result in foreign market operations' (2007: 277). They further specify that 'companies may pool, exchange and/or integrate resources in the process of setting up and operating an alliance' (ibid.).

The choice to enter into a strategic alliance is often driven both by the MNCs' ambitions and internal limitations. In some instances, however, foreign governments may exert pressure on the development of alliances. Obtaining licenses, for instance, related to large complex oil and gas fields or telecom licenses in deregulating markets, sometimes requires groups of MNCs to form alliances with other MNCs and/or local firms.

Some alliances are formed as non-equity partnerships such as the Oil Sands Leadership Initiative (OSLI) in Canada. OSLI was established by six MNCs (ConocoPhillips, Nexen, Shell, Statoil, Suncor and Total) to cooperate in order to achieve technological advances necessary to extract heavy oil from the Canadian oil sands in an economically and environmentally sound manner. While each member contributes financially to R&D projects, the alliance remains a relationship-based network rather than joint equity venture. Other alliances develop into equity-based joint ventures, such as Telenor's (the Norwegian telecomm giant) activities in Russia and other foreign markets (Telenor, 2011).

Foreign direct investments (FDI)

As discussed in Chapter 1, firms engage in FDI when three criteria are met: (1) the firm has strong transferable FSAs (firm-specific advantages), (2) there are benefits of localizing activities in a foreign market (localization advantages) and (3) the benefits of internalizing assets and activities outweigh their governance costs (internalization advantages). FDI enables the firm to own and control assets in a foreign market, which allows it to overcome some of the challenges with non-equity operating modes. Ownership and control is particularly attractive when FSAs are difficult and costly to transfer or institutions (or the lack thereof) in host markets make contracts difficult to enforce.

FDI can be established in different ways and take different forms. Some MNCs prefer to build an organization 'from scratch', that is engage in greenfield investment. Others choose to acquire or merge with an existing organization to benefit from the advantages of the existing local firm. The choice of an equity-based operating mode is furthermore not equivalent to a specific ownership form and can take the form of wholly-owned subsidiaries or international joint ventures where equity levels can vary.

According to internalization theory, MNCs are more likely to seek equity-based strategic alliances with local partners where distances are perceived high, when diversifying into a less related sector, or when the scale of foreign operations is large compared to the size of the MNC (Grøgaard and Verbeke, 2012). In all of these cases, relying on the MNCs' firm-specific advantages alone will likely be insufficient and the experience and expertise of the strategic partner becomes critical for success. The next section discusses these different forms of FDI in greater detail.

2.3   Ownership forms: full versus partial ownership

Equity levels in foreign direct investment should be determined by the relative ease of transacting each partner's assets and capabilities (Hennart, 2009). In other words, MNCs that incur high costs when transferring their FSAs to a foreign market, but are able to access local complementary assets easily, often prefer wholly-owned subsidiaries. Similarly, when FSAs from the MNC are easily transacted but local complementary assets are difficult to transact, the local owner should have ownership. If the MNCs and local complementary assets are both difficult to transact, joint ownership is preferred.

Collaboration or full ownership?

Collaboration allows the firm to extend its competitive advantages into more locations faster and with reduced cost and market uncertainty. This enables it to focus its resources on further developing its core competencies. Another advantage is that a local partner can provide necessary complementary assets such as knowledge of the local economy or product-specific knowledge. Transaction cost operation mode theory emphasizes two factors that will potentially influence the decision as to whether to collaborate or to internalize. The first of these concerns the level of firm-specific technology (asset specificity).

From a transaction cost perspective, the driver behind collaboration or full ownership is anchored in the efficiency of markets. In other words, MNCs would in general prefer full ownership when their firm-specific advantages are difficult or not desirable to transact in the market while the necessary complementary resources and capabilities are easily transacted. Full ownership may therefore be preferred whenever there is a significant proprietary content to the MNC's intangible assets, whether they be technology or brand loyalty. Indeed, empirical research has shown that entry by full ownership is positively related to intangible assets such as R&D intensity and advertising intensity (Anderson and Gatignon, 1986; Gatignon and Anderson, 1988). Similarly, knowledge that is tacit or poorly codified is difficult and costly to transmit across organizational boundaries. In other words, MNCs should avoid collaboration if the international exploitation of MNC-specific tacit knowledge is involved (Shrader, 2001). On the other hand, if the necessary complementary resources and capabilities are difficult to transact in the foreign market, collaboration is attractive where the MNC secures access to these assets through the collaborative agreement.

The second factor that transaction cost theory emphasizes is concerned with the costs of negotiating and monitoring the actions of potential partners. These particular transaction costs are more significant than the costs associated with training partners and providing technology and management assistance. Firms that perceive higher levels of transaction costs generally prefer to internalize operations by using wholly-owned modes of operation (Brouthers, 2002).

Negotiating and monitoring contracts are a particular problem in dealing with firms in countries with low transparency; that is unclear legal systems and regulations, macroeconomic and tax policies, accounting standards and practices, and corruption in the capital markets. The opacity index in Figure 2.1 measures these risks across 48 countries. Not least the index reflects cross-national institutional and cultural differences.

By itself the logic of transaction cost theory would predict that in settings with low levels of transparency, where enacting and monitoring contracts are high, internalization would be preferred. However, Brouthers (2002) has argued that transaction cost theory needs to be extended by including the influence of both the institutional context and the cultural context. He argues that these factors also influence managerial costs and uncertainty evaluations. Thus, as well as the costs of additional payrolls and overheads, investments in plant, property and equipment and added administrative costs, even more importantly internalization means the loss of relevant local institutional and cultural knowledge that a local partner might supply. The value of this knowledge increases with opacity. This explains why partial modes of ownership are preferred in settings that are regarded as very foreign and high risk (Gatignon and Anderson, 1988; Brouthers, 2002). In other words, when MNEs take the chance of entering high-risk countries, some form of IJV is often preferable to full ownership despite the difficulty in enforcing contracts

In Chapter 1 we defined MNCs as firms that not only have substantial direct investments in foreign countries, but which also actively manage these in an integrated way. It is these firms that we primarily focus on in this book, with less detailed attention to non-equity modes of entry, export, licensing, franchising, contract manufacturing and non-equity alliances. We also do not go in depth into the many specific challenges of IJVs. However, as many full-fledged MNCs also engage in other modes of entry, we need to examine the management challenges these pose. The case that follows, for instance, provides an opportunity to examine and consider IJVs in detail.

Source: *Economist* (2004).

Figure 2.1 The opacity index

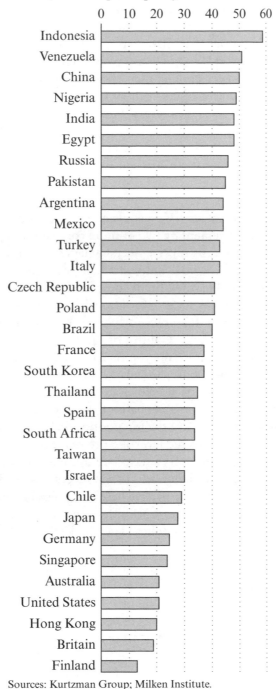

The opacity index

2004, 100–complete opacity

Sources: Kurtzman Group; Milken Institute.

International joint ventures (IJVs)

International joint ventures (IJVs) are defined by Chen et al. (2009: 1133) as 'legally independent entities formed by two or more parent firms from different countries that share equity investments and consequent returns'. The basis of most IJV structures involves a multinational enterprise (MNC) and a local partner pooling their respective competitive advantages. In the case of emerging markets such as China, the MNC typically contributes product and process technology, brand name/trade mark, and international marketing support; while the local partner contributes local knowledge-related expertise such as local marketing, local personnel management, and management of local government relations (Hitt et al., 2000; Inkpen and Beamish, 1997).

The establishment of IJVs has been an increasing trend since the 1970s. An IJV is an agreement by two or more companies to produce a product or service together. It involves a much higher level of investment and therefore of risk than the previous entry strategies. Generally an IJV consists of an MNC and a local partner. Equity proportions vary but usually relative ownership approximates to 50–50, although there are many variations including IJVs with more than two partners including relatively passive partners with minority holdings. Control of the five to ten management positions that typically constitute the top management group of an IJV is a central issue in IJV negotiations, particularly in regard to the top position of general manager. This position usually goes to the partner that has the dominant equity position or some other basis of power such as critical technology. The partner that does not win the top position will argue strongly for other slots that guarantee the desired level of representation. Typically members of the management group of IJVs have two agendas: on the one hand they are expected to commit themselves to the success of the IJV, on the other they are 'delegates' of their respective parents. As legal entities, IJVs have boards of directors who set strategic priorities and make decisions regarding the use of profits and investment policy (Hambrick et al., 2001).

Until recently, an IJV was the only means of entry in India because local participation was mandatory. In China, foreign retailers have been barred from having full control of mainland operations thus compelling retailers such as Carréfour of France, Wal-Mart of the USA and Tesco of the UK to look for local partners. Although China has eased its restrictions on full foreign ownership, some industries are still considered 'restricted areas'. However, even when local participation is not obligatory an IJV may be appropriate because a local partner can provide intermediate inputs, such as local market knowledge, access to distribution networks and natural resources, as well as making the MNC an insider in the host country. When Tesco entered the South Korean market in 1999 it chose to do so with Samsung, Korea's biggest conglomerate and most powerful brand. By choosing to put Samsung's name in the joint-venture title first, and by appointing a Samsung executive as chief executive, Tesco went a long way to diffuse potential criticism in a country dominated by small, traditional shops. In addition it was helped by Samsung to develop a hypermarket adapted to Korean tastes including assistants in traditional Korean dress who bow to each arriving customer, and octopus, squid and lobster that are plucked from tanks and chopped up alive, sushi-style.

The benefits of IJVs are that they provide a combination of rapid entry into new markets, risk-sharing and increased economies of scale. The problem they face relates to diverging expectations and objectives. Rarely are the two partners equally matched with the MNC usually the stronger partner in terms of technology and management skills. The result is that the local partner may come to view the MNC as overzealous in protecting its core technology and on imposing its control on the joint venture, while the MNC finds it difficult to trust its local partner. The friction that this generates is a major explanation of why many IJVs result in partner dissatisfaction or outright failure. Indeed some surveys have suggested such outcomes for about half of MNCs with IJVs (Bamford et al., 2004). Thus although IJVs are widespread, their success rate has been estimated to be no more than about 50 per cent (ibid.) and there is evidence of particular difficulties for IJVs involving Chinese partners (Child and Yan, 2003).

Endemic to the IJV literature is that congruent underlying motivations for forming the IJV should not be assumed (see, for example, Parkhe, 1991). Indeed it is not to be supposed that either parent is primarily committed to the long-term overall success of the IJV, not least in emerging economies such as China. Thus it may be the case that a Western partner seeks market experience, whereas technology acquisition may be the principal motive for Chinese partners (Luo et al., 2001). This latter motive may trigger anxiety on the part of the Western partner that its know-how may be appropriated by its partner. Thus Chen et al. (2009: 1142) characterize the IJV 'as a mixed motive game between parents who cooperate and compete at the same time'.

Because of its multiparty nature – foreign partner, local partner and management – the IJV control system can be 'particularly troublesome' (Chen et al., 2009: 1151). While the literature on IJVs acknowledges the importance of legally enforceable contracts in resolving opportunism (for example Chen, 2010), it also stresses that the effectiveness of contractually based control is questionable in emerging economies such as China due to the relatively lower legislative quality and effectiveness in law enforcement (Pistor and Xu, 2005). The significance of formal or legitimate ownership as a means of ensuring satisfactory control over IJV operations thus cannot be overstated, but having to resort to the courts is hardly conducive to maintaining trust and cooperation between partners. This institutional deficiency in emerging economies accentuates the distinction between ownership control and management control. Some argue that it is particularly the latter that is critical for exercising influence over IJV operations in the context of emerging economies such as China (cf. Steensma and Lyles, 2000).

Choi and Beamish (2004) delineate four broad management options available to MNC and local partners: (1) each partner controls its own firm-specific advantages (split control management); (2) both partners share control over all firm-specific advantages (shared management or shared control); (3) the MNC partner assumes a dominant control over all firm-specific advantages (MNC-partner-dominant management); and (4) the local emerging market partner assumes a dominant control over all firm-specific advantages (local-partner-dominant management). Choi and Beamish's review of previous research indicates an exclusive focus on the latter three options and, in regard to these three options, no consensus about their effect on IJV performance. Their own research includes all four options and suggests that split control management can have a positive effect on IJV performance in contrast to the other three alternatives which did not show any significant performance effects.

Split control is at the core of Madhok's (2006b) concept of structural trust. The structural aspect of trust comprises synergistic complementarities that constitute 'a reservoir of potential value' (Madhok, 2006a: 7). As such there is an inducement for both partners to contribute towards the relationship. To discontinue the relationship by acting in a self-interested manner would incur costs. Madhok (2006b) argues that while the structural dimension of trust is not of itself a sufficient reason for the 'sustained continuation' of the IJV relationship it is a necessary condition. 'It is necessary since, unless both parties are benefiting from the relationship, it is inherently unstable' (Madhok, 2006b: 33).

Madhok distinguishes two reasons why the structural dimension is not sufficient by itself. First:

> a weak social foundation undermines the potential value of the synergy that can be gained by two firms pooling their assets together, since contributions become

much more tentative . . . Furthermore, the cost of the operation increases since the greater expectation of opportunism by a partner causes the other to bear higher costs of installing safeguards against opportunism. (2006b: 33)

Second, because contributions to the IJV cannot be continuously evenly matched, the social dimension 'provides the tolerance through the social "glue"' to preserve the relationship during periods of disequilibrium and inequity. In other words deeply embedded social relations mitigate the breakdown of the relationship in periods of flux and inequity. However, social trust is not 'super glue' (2006b: 33): if 'complementary assets' disappear for an extended period then no amount of social trust can save the IJV.

Wholly-owned subsidiaries

Disregarding any local ownership restrictions imposed by host country governments, MNCs prefer fully owned subsidiaries to IJVs when this is considered more efficient in terms of governance costs and access to intermediate inputs. This calculation may well stem from problems in locating a reliable partner but is also to some extent influenced by the MNCs' national culture. It has, for example, been shown that all things being equal the propensity for US firms investing in Japan to choose joint ventures over wholly-owned subsidiaries is substantially higher than for Japanese firms investing in the USA (Makino and Neupert, 2001).

Wholly-owned subsidiaries can be established through mergers and acquisitions (M&As) on the one hand and start-ups (for example greenfield investments) on the other. Although it is often difficult to distinguish between mergers and acquisitions in precise terms, mergers are usually the result of a friendly arrangement between companies of roughly equal size, whereas acquisitions are unequal partnerships that can also be the product of a hard-fought battle between acquiring and target companies. The scale of M&As as a vehicle for FDI has increased rapidly since the beginning of the 1990s. By the end of the 1990s most new FDI was in the form of M&As and the preference for M&As over greenfield investments has continued over the past two decades (UNCTAD, 2010). The preference for M&As has partly been attributed asymmetric information, where '[f]inancial markets usually provide efficient mechanisms to set the value of M&A targets, while there is no such mechanism to assess the value of greenfield investments' (UNCTAD, 2010: 9). This also makes M&As more vulnerable to economic downturns as access to capital shrinks and the market evaluation mechanisms are more volatile.

M&As have the advantage of providing rapid entry into a market and there-fore economies of scale. Established product lines, distribution channels and insider status are all obtained. They can also be of great value as a means of capturing new expertise. On the other hand the difficulties encountered in integrating the acquisition into the culture and overall strategy of the MNC should not be underestimated, particularly in the case of acquisitions where there may be deep resentment amongst employees in the acquired unit. Frequently, despite due diligence, the acquirer also lacks a proper under-standing of what has been acquired. A new identity for the acquired firm has to be developed and as acquired businesses often involve a seat on the parent board there may be board-level disagreement as to precisely what that identity is. The difficulties are such that as many as 50 per cent of M&As fail (Child et al., 2001). While MNCs traditionally do 'not seem to be deterred by the relatively poor results that have been observed with respect to M&As' (UNCTAD, 1999: xxii), recent economic downturns have significantly reduced the level of cross-border M&As where the value of M&A transac-tions in 2008–2009 dropped by as much as 65 per cent (UNCTAD, 2010).

Greenfield investments do not involve having to grapple with the problem of integrating existing organizational cultures and creating a unified purpose. Such foreign investments can thus develop more gradually and in a more controlled way. Nevertheless, as an operating mode when entering a foreign market, they generally carry the highest risk, particularly in countries with nationalistic attitudes toward foreign ownership. Greenfield investments also require the longest time to establish, the greatest contribution of know-how, and the ability of the MNC to overcome elements of distance by developing necessary location-bound FSAs.

The choice of greenfield versus acquisition tends to be affected by the indus-try in which the MNC is operating. MNCs operating in industries that are driven by unique or superior technical expertise are characterized by a prefer-ence for greenfield investments since they can build their operations in a way that minimizes the costs in transferring their knowledge. This is particularly attractive when necessary complementary assets are easily transacted in the foreign market. An acquisition will often involve dealing with incompatible methods for absorbing and processing knowledge and even a low motivation for new knowledge. For example, Nokia, since it began to focus on mobile phones, has expanded mainly through greenfields, whereas ABB, operating in established technology sectors, has grown mainly through acquisitions.

Harzing (2002) has shown that differences in firms' international strate-gies also have an influence on the choice of entry mode. MNCs that are particularly focused on adapting their products and policies to the local market tend to prefer acquisitions because the acquired subsidiary will at the outset be aligned with host country conditions, while MNCs that regard their subsidiaries as pipelines for standardized, cost-efficient products will prefer greenfields where higher levels of control and coordination can be achieved. Finally, there is the impact of prior experience. MNCs that have successfully employed acquisitions will be more likely to choose acquisitions in subsequent entries (Chang and Rosenzweig, 2001).

2.4   Summary

As this chapter illustrates, MNCs must decide on both operating modes and ownership structures when expanding to foreign markets. Although the choices are far from static, changes in operating modes over time may involve a considerable loss of time and money, making the selection a very important strategic decision for MNCs. In essence, the decision is whether to collaborate in some way with local partners in the host markets or whether to internalize operations.

In the context of this book, we will focus more on equity modes, particularly wholly-owned subsidiaries or joint ventures with majority ownership as these enable greater control. However, as discussed in this chapter, MNCs often combine multiple operating modes and ownership structures and the issues discussed in the book are not limited to wholly-owned subsidiaries and joint venture. The case following this chapter featuring a Swedish MNC illustrates the frequent mixing of different operating modes generates managerial challenges to ensure that the modes interact successfully.

Case A

Durable and unstable IJVs: the case of BKT

Paul N. Gooderham, Michael Zhang and Atle Jordahl

A.1 Introduction

North American and European MNCs are increasingly investing in emerging economies. As the *Economist* (2011a: 59) stated: 'Foreign firms are increasingly lured by these countries' fast growing domestic markets as much as by lower wages.' In 2010 emerging economies accounted for 46 per cent of world retail sales. In terms of world motor vehicle sales they accounted for 52 per cent, up from 22 per cent in 2000. Of the emerging economies China is by far the single most important destination for FDI. Indeed China is now the second largest recipient of FDI after the USA (UNCTAD: 2010).

Many foreign firms have entered China via international joint ventures (IJVs). Typically the MNC provides capital and technology and the Chinese partner provides local production facilities that use cheap labor and access to local business networks. One such company MNC is BKT, a Swedish manufacturer of motor vehicle parts. In addition to its wholly-owned subsidiaries (WOS) in China, it has entered into two IJVs in order to supply European car manufacturers based in China with locally produced parts.

In general IJVs are often not durable. Madhok (1995) distinguishes between structural and social trust. Structural trust involves mutual satisfaction between IJV partners in regard what each partner is contributing. However, markets change and structural trust can easily unravel. Madhok argues that the durability of IJVs depend on the development of social trust between partners. Social trust provides the basis not just for weathering the inevitable down-turns in the market but also a mutual willingness to consider new opportunities. However, what is less clear is why some IJVs develop social trust while many do not.

This case study was conducted in 2009–10 and has as its focus BKT's two IJVs in China. In essence each of these IJVs comprises one of BKT's German subsidiaries and a Chinese state-owned enterprise (SOE). In other words national cultural and institutional distance between the two sets of IJV partners is identical. They are further matched in that both IJVs employ the same formal control and ownership mechanisms with both having balanced ownership structures (50/50) thereby maximizing the involvement of both partners. Finally, both IJVs are not only engaged in the same industry, delivering parts to European vehicle manufacturers operating in China, but both are experiencing significant contractions to their markets. Despite these commonalities the one IJV appears to be durable while the other is in danger of unraveling.

A.2 BKT

Founded in 1962, BKT of Sweden remained a domestic company until 2001 when it rapidly expanded its foreign activities both in Western Europe, Canada and in the Far East through a mix of entry strategies that included acquisitions, greenfields and joint ventures. In 2009 BKT directly employed 1,550 personnel worldwide, of whom 450 were located in Sweden and 640 in China. Only 8 persons were employed at corporate headquarters in Sweden. In all BKT comprised 27 business units in 14 countries, meaning that in a number of the countries in which it operated it had multiple business units. This was not least the case in China, where BKT had both IJVs and WOS in Dalian and Shanghai.

Two of BKT's most important Western European operations are located in Germany, BKT-Bremen (Bremen) and BKT-Lübeck (Lübeck). A third is located in Norway, BKT-Stavanger (Stavanger). All three are wholly-owned acquisitions. In simple terms these Western European operations contain the bulk of BKT's advanced competencies in various vehicle parts. In contrast, its Chinese operations are geared to low-cost production on the basis of standardized competencies. However, the view of BKT corporate headquarters is that its Chinese joint venture operations are critical for BKT not only because they reduce factor costs, but also because of the geographical access they provide to European vehicle manufacturers located in China.

BKT's two main operations in China, BKT–Shanghai-JV (Shanghai-JV) and BKT–Dalian-JV (Dalian-JV), are 50/50 joint ventures. The Chinese partners are both SOEs. The immediate BKT partner is not BKT corporate headquarters in Sweden. In the case of the Shanghai-JV the formal partner is Stavanger, but as Bremen is far more actively involved with it, it may be regarded as its de facto partner. The BKT partner of the Dalian-JV is Lübeck. Apart from the chairmen of their boards, neither Shanghai-JV nor Dalian-JV employs any BKT expatriates. BKT employees from the European operations are only at these operations when there are well-defined tasks to carry out.

In addition to its joint ventures in Shanghai and Dalian, BKT also has two WOS in these cities, BKT Auto Shanghai (Auto Shanghai) and BKT Auto Dalian (Auto Dalian). The former was set up to produce purely for export with local networks viewed as not particularly significant. As we shall see the latter was set up as a result of strained relations between the Dalian-JV and a division of Bremen that was acquired in 2005.

BKT's structure of global operations including the Dalian-JV and the Shanghai-JV is shown in Figure A.1 below (for further details see Table A.1 in the Appendix).

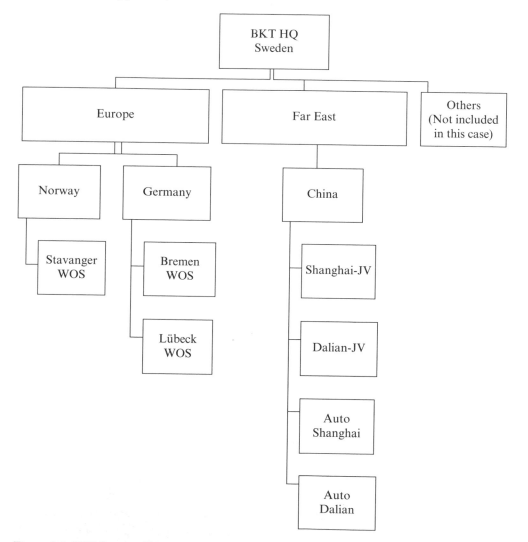

Figure A.1 BKT Europe–China operations and its global matrix structure

A.3 BKT's Western European joint venture partners in China

Neither BKT corporate headquarters nor any of its Swedish operations are directly involved in any of the joint ventures in China. Instead, as we have observed, the primary BKT interface with its two main Chinese joint ventures comprises WOS in Germany: Bremen and Lübeck. In essence the production in China is based on blueprints developed in Germany: thus close cooperation between German engineers and the Chinese partners is required.

Bremen has approximately 110 employees and consists of two main divisions. The older division is designated the fender 'Centre of Excellence' of BKT. Its first fender was designed and manufactured in 1963 for Swed-Auto. It was eventually acquired by Swed-Auto in 1983 before being acquired by UK-Auto in 1999 and then BKT in 2001. More recently, in 2005, Bremen acquired another Bremen company. This division of the Bremen operation is designated the alternators 'Centre of Excellence' and it was this division that had substantial, fractious and short-lived dealings with the Dalian-JV.

BKT's other German operation, BKT–Lübeck, focuses on wheels, both for autos and heavy machinery such as dumper trucks. BKT acquired Lübeck, an independent organization, as it went bankrupt in 2004. It has 60 employees. Lübeck is the immediate BKT partner of the Dalian-JV which entails that the production in Dalian is based on patents or engineering done at BKT-Lübeck.

One significant difference between Lübeck and the older division of Bremen is that while the latter has been part of various MNCs since 1983, the former was an entirely independent entity until 2004. Bremen and Stavanger have had a common ownership history since 1983 and both have had a substantial history of cooperation with the SOE partner of Shanghai-JV that predates their acquisition by BKT. As a consequence the Managing Director (MD) of Bremen, Mr Schmidt, regards Bremen as having developed a decidedly Scandinavian outlook on management whereas he regards Lübeck as 'entirely German in its approach to management'. Although he is not uncritical of Scandinavian leadership, which he characterizes as too discussion oriented, equally he is not uncritical of Lübeck's 'German approach' which he views as inflexible in relation to demanding clear guidelines and an unwillingness to engage in open discussion.

A.4   The joint ventures

Shanghai-JV

The BKT–Shanghai-JV has 80 employees. It specializes in the design, engineering and marketing of wheels and fenders primarily aimed at European vehicle manufacturers in China. The actual production of these parts is outsourced locally. Within its niche, the company has a market share in China of over 60 per cent. Although it has been a consistently profitable operation, as we conducted our research it was facing a serious downturn in its markets.

The Chinese SOE partner has had a long history of interacting with foreign companies. In the early 1990s it entered a licensing agreement with BKT's main competitor Fin-Auto. In 1997 it entered joint venture negotiations with Fin-Auto but these broke down because of a reluctance to concede Fin-Auto's demand for an 80 per cent equity ownership and the relationship ended. Instead in 1998 it established a 50/50 joint venture with what was to become BKT–Stavanger which at that point was owned by Swed-Auto. In 1999 Swed-Auto sold its share of the joint venture to the UK MNC, UK-Auto. In 2001 UK-Auto sold its share to BKT. Although Bremen is the Shanghai-JV's primary BKT partner, Stavanger continues to have occasional dealings with the Shanghai-JV mainly in the form of training and development. Furthermore, Stavanger remains the direct recipient of royalties from the Shanghai-JV.

Madam Tan, who joined the Shanghai SOE in 1992, has been the joint venture MD since its inception in 1998. After negotiations with Fin-Auto foundered she was charged with seeking out an alternative foreign partner. Consequently Madam Tan has been directly involved with joint venture foreign partners since 1998, first Swed-Auto, then UK-Auto and finally, since 2001, BKT. Madam Tan, who is now approaching retirement, spoke little English in 1998. However, she is now able to communicate in English effectively without the aid of an interpreter. While she is a member of the Communist Party, her son works for the global investment bank, Goldman Sachs. She is evidently proud of her son's career.

Madam Tan expressed general satisfaction with the performance of the Shanghai-JV and regards the cooperation with Bremen, as well as with Stavanger, as having been very positive. She observes that while every industry insider in China is well aware that Fin-Auto is globally stronger than BKT, BKT is actually somewhat larger in China because of its joint ventures. As such BKT is established as a leading brand within China. Madam Tan made it clear that she has a strong desire to maintain the IJV relationship because in her view 'BKT is exceptional at promoting the products of the IJV to European auto manufacturers'. Furthermore, she has confidence in BKT's capabilities regarding technology development. This optimism and desire to maintain the relationship existed despite a downturn in the market that she thought could last for the next three years – a downturn which she intended to use to train and develop her employees in order to be able to grow when the market revives.

Madam Tan's positive outlook on the IJV is not confined to the capabilities Bremen is contributing. On a more emotional level, Madam Tan comments that BKT has consistently taken a 'more kindly' approach to doing business than the former MNC partner, UK-Auto. Equally Madam Tan characterizes the workings of the Shanghai-JV as entirely transparent for both partners. Madam Tan explains that the relationship that has evolved between the partners has meant that there is increasingly less need for formal meetings. In 2001 there were eight board-meetings a year. This has been reduced to two. Her view of her role as the Shanghai-JV MD is that she is independent not only of BKT but also of the Shanghai SOE. However, she claims that, 'Sometimes I feel part of the BKT family' and regards it as critical that BKT keeps its joint ventures 'in the family'. As such she greatly appreciates that BKT has approached her to discuss setting up a new IJV specializing in after-sales service in China and beyond.

Mr Ericsson, a Norwegian, was appointed chairman of the Shanghai-JV board in 2005. He was engaged on the strength of more than 30 years' experience of industrial development in China and other Asian countries. He shares Madam Tan's generally positive analysis of the joint venture. As Chairman he leads board meetings and writes the minutes. He feels that not only has he a good insight into the finances of the Shanghai-JV, but that he is also able to request reports on all dealings with suppliers. As chairman of the board, Mr Ericsson has a casting vote but has never felt the need to use it. On a more personal note, not only has Mr Ericsson met Madam Tan's family, but also we observed Madam Tan and Mr Ericsson engaged in good-humored banter.

Mr Schmidt, the MD of Bremen, recounted that at the beginning there were problems relating to quality and 'a lot of fights' with Madam Tan as 'you have to be strong in China'. He reflected that in Germany one is used to perfect workshops containing employees who are so technically proficient that they are able to independently correct design problems. However, in China, because they lack experience, every aspect of a design has to be entirely correct. Nevertheless, he concludes, the partnership with the Shanghai-JV has worked well.

Mr Meyer, a management colleague of Mr Schmidt in Bremen, is of a similar opinion. Because of their 'brilliant local third-party manufacturing contacts' he views the Shanghai-JV as being an 'excellent' partner in China. In his view, had it not been because Fin-Auto had been 'unreasonable' in its equity demands, then it would have been Fin-Auto who would now have the market leadership in China that the Shanghai-JV enjoys. Mr Meyer is actually somewhat critical of what BKT has contributed to the Shanghai-JV. In his view for the most part all the Shanghai-JV has received from BKT is the use of its brand and support in order to be able to attract European customers who are skeptical of Chinese firms. The MD of Stavanger, Mr Selart, accepts this point of view as largely accurate. Beyond the brand name and marketing support in his opinion, 'the Shanghai-JV has received very little (technology) from us'. Indeed, he says, 'it is basically still using old technology that has been marginally developed'. As such he thinks that Bremen could probably start learning from the Shanghai-JV.

To summarize: all of our respondents regard the Shanghai-JV as having performed successfully. We have observed a history of inter-organizational synergistic complementarities; Bremen provides some technology, access to the BKT brand and marketing support supplemented by training supplied by Stavanger; the Shanghai-JV supplies locally-adapted design, local manufacturing contacts and additional marketing. However, Shanghai-JV is now experiencing a significant downturn in its market meaning that these complementarities are no longer of immediate value. Despite this the view is that the Shanghai-JV is a durable operation.

Dalian-JV

The Dalian-JV has about 80 employees. It is fully licensed to produce and sell BKT wheels. It was established at a new industrial site on the outskirts of Dalian in 2005 and is the outcome of an agreement between BKT and a second Chinese SOE for engineering, production and sale of wheels to European dumper truck makers in China. For BKT its decision to form a new 50/50 joint venture involving Lübeck and a second Chinese SOE was a product of its generally positive experience with the Shanghai-JV. Indeed the legal document that formed the contractual basis of the Shanghai-JV was used in establishing the Dalian-JV as a legal entity. In other words it was not a requirement that BKT ally itself with an SOE but a decision that reflected a positive experience with the Shanghai SOE.

In its first fully operational year, 2007, the Dalian-JV posted substantial profits and achieved a 40 per cent market share in China. It appeared that the assessment of complementary assets that would generate successful performance, underlying the setting up of the IJV, was confirmed. However, the market contracted in 2008, resulting in considerably more modest profits. Instead of the mutual forbearance observed at the Shanghai-JV, friction between the Dalian-JV partners quickly developed which threatened its continued survival. As we conducted our research at the Dalian-JV, we had a particular focus on why social trust had failed to emerge despite initial excellent performance.

The Dalian-JV's MD is Mr Wang, and the Chairman of its board is Mr Hansen. Mr Hansen speaks no Chinese and Mr Wang apparently speaks no English. While Mr Wang has been the MD of the Dalian-JV since it was established, Mr Hansen became Chairman late in 2008. Mr Hansen succeeded Mr Ericsson as Chairman because BKT's corporate headquarters concluded that his relationship with Mr Wang had become excessively acrimonious. Mr Wang characterizes the relationship with Mr Hansen as positive, but the latter is markedly less enthusiastic explaining that for the first six months no one came by his office, which is located in the company building. Although Mr Hansen considers that there are signs that he is beginning to be regarded as someone whose advice may have some value equally tensions are never far from the surface. This is exemplified by Mr Wang's refusal to consent to Mr Hansen to operate with his own interpreter rather than having to rely entirely on Mr Wang's. Mr Hansen also informed us that after a stand-off Mr Hansen had conceded the right to act as chair of the Dalian-JV board meetings proceedings, but continued in his position as formal chair of the board.

Both Mr Hansen and Mr Wang view the relationship with the primary BKT partner, Lübeck, as problematic. The standard parts of the Dalian-JV's wheels are manufactured by a network of local Chinese private firms and SOEs. This network of subcontractors has been developed by Mr Wang. Mr Hansen argues that this network could only have been developed by a local with the right connections. However, Mr Hansen points to problems with the quality of the work conducted by these subcontractors. This applies particularly to the privately owned sub-contractors and is, according to Mr Hansen, due to their tendency to employ the cheapest available labor. Much of this labor force is poorly trained. These quality problems usually only emerge when Lübeck employees are engaged in quality control initiated due to customer complaints. Because the costs of the added time involved in making repairs are borne by Lübeck, the Lübeck employees, according to Mr Hansen, react vociferously and very negatively to any and every deviation in quality.

Mr Hansen considers the Germans overly sensitive in their approach to quality issues and claims that many of the shortcomings they identify are no more than cosmetic. However, he also thought that BKT corporate management in Sweden had underestimated the time it takes to transfer quality-consciousness to a Chinese operation. Equally he feels that BKT corporate management has paid insufficient attention to the design of its contractual arrangements with its Chinese partner. Thus when Lübeck requested that their inspectors should be allowed to carry out quality checks at the subcontractors to pre-empt problems, Mr Wang not only refused to cooperate, but argued successfully that he was not contractually obliged to do so.

Mr Wang's interpretation of the contractual arrangements has also limited the degree of transparency Mr Hansen can request in regard to significant aspects of the Dalian-JV's operations. The financial accounts are prepared by appointees of Mr Wang and Mr Hansen has therefore no insight into their preparation. Similarly it is Mr Wang who single-handedly negotiates with the sub-contractors, all of whom belong to his own personal network.

Mr Wang's main concern with Lübeck is that it deliberately blocks core technical parameters so that the components it delivers to the Dalian-JV cannot be replicated locally. He remarks that if this issue cannot be resolved there will be a 'big problem'. He claims, though, that he has the full support of the BKT CEO in this matter. A secondary issue is that Lübeck has on occasion not made staff available in what Mr Wang considers a timely manner. On these occasions he has successfully demanded that BKT corporate management intervene on behalf of the Dalian-JV. Mr Wang is also exasperated that suggestions made by the Dalian-JV to Lübeck in regard to product improvements were rejected and that, again, it had been necessary to appeal to BKT corporate management. Mr Wang accepts that cultural differences are an issue in MNCs. For example he is shocked that 'Scandinavian managers are not prepared to work during their vacations and expect to be able to leave the office at 4 pm to pick up their children from daycare'. However, in regard to Lübeck he refuses to apply cultural explanations to the difficulties he has experienced.

Mr Wang finds the notion of belonging to a 'BKT family' problematic because he views the Dalian-JV as strictly a joint venture. Indeed his perception is that this is the view of BKT corporate management. For it to be more than a joint venture, BKT corporate management would have to play a significantly more active role as company-wide integrators. From the Lübeck perspective, the view of the difficulties besetting the Dalian-JV is very different. Ms Neuhaus, the Managing Director of Lübeck, finds dealing with the

Dalian-JV frustrating not least because of its 'continual reinterpretation of the joint venture contract' and the 'tremendous quality problem' in regard to its output. This poor quality of workmanship at the Dalian-JV 'hurts' Lübeck employees who have 'an obsession with quality'. Ms Neuhaus points out that when one uses independent suppliers, there are clear contracts and sanctions that can be deployed if those contracts are not met. However, 'joint ventures cannot be taken to court'. So 'the challenge is to find the right tone'. To date, though, Ms Neuhaus feels that in regard to quality and prices the 'Chinese do whatever they want' and they also win all of the arguments not least because 'when they do not get their way they threaten to stop production'. In regard to this threat she views BKT corporate headquarters as far too accommodating.

However, Ms Neuhaus is also conscious that immediately prior to its acquisition by BKT in 2004, Lübeck was bankrupt and that the relationship with the Dalian-JV has brought in significant orders – indeed 95 per cent of Lübeck's orders stem from the Dalian-JV. Effectively the Dalian-JV, under the 'well-connected Mr Wang has opened up a lot of doors for us in China'. Despite this positive aspect to the relationship between Lübeck and the Dalian-JV, and despite the fact that they were effectively out of work in 2004, Ms Neuhaus observes that 'the old Lübeck history is still there and that the "new spirit" has not been communicated'. Thus the basic attitude at Lübeck is that 'they [the Chinese] will take all our knowledge' accompanied by a bitterness that 'the Dalian-JV will have acquired everything in the space of a few years that has taken us sixty years of consistent effort to develop'.

This fear of what the future has to offer is accentuated by the contract with the Dalian-JV which stipulates that in 2011 all responsibility for the production of standard dumper wheels will rest with the Dalian-JV and that Lübeck will have to concentrate on more innovative products and after-sales service. If Lübeck cannot succeed in this, then it will have to lay-off employees.

Ms Neuhaus also believes that in addition to the reluctance to share knowledge with production engineers at the Dalian-JV, Lübeck has so many competing responsibilities within the areas of both design and training that there is also a 'capacity problem'. This capacity problem is compounded by high production staff turnover at the Dalian-JV meaning that there is a constant stream of new production employees who have to be trained. Additionally, the effect of poor knowledge sharing and poorly trained production employees is exacerbated by a second factor. Dalian-JV engineers, with Mr Wang's consent, choose to locally purchase steel structures of a cheaper and inferior quality than stipulated. Ms Neuhaus attributes Mr Wang's compliance with this practice to the contract that stipulates that quality problems are the responsibility, financial and technical, of Lübeck. Thus, when quality problems are observed Lübeck is obliged to carry out and finance the repairs.

Across BKT there is also criticism of Mr Wang's capabilities and outlook. For example, BKT's deputy CEO, Mr Nordstrom, while he acknowledges that Mr Wang played a useful role in getting the industrial site that Dalian-JV occupies built by local interests, points to a lack of 'a sales mentality that will make recovery from the current downturn difficult'. In regard to Mr Wang's selection and performance of steel structures, Mr Nordstrom states that BKT has never had any dialogue with the Dalian-JV's Chinese SOE owner.

The view that dialogue with Mr Wang is highly problematic formed the backdrop to the decision by BKT in 2008 to remove the responsibility for alternators from the Dalian-JV and to set up the wholly-owned Auto Dalian. Alternators are the specific responsibility of the department within Bremen that was acquired in 2005. Like Lübeck this unit of Bremen had been a local, independent company that was threatened with bankruptcy. In its dealings with Dalian-JV it rapidly became highly critical of the Dalian-JV's ability to meet its quality standards. The alternators the Dalian-JV assembled simply failed. The immediate reason for the failure appeared to be an inability to train production workers in the Dalian-JV because of high worker turnover. When Auto Dalian was set up it was located to the same industrial site as the Dalian-JV. However, despite this proximity the climate between the two Dalian operations may be summed up by a large clock that Mr Wang sent to Auto Dalian's Norwegian MD. Within Chinese culture such a gift symbolizes 'no future dealings'.

Madam Tan regards the Shanghai-JV as very different from the Dalian-JV. She is particularly critical of the Dalian-JV's capabilities which she views as being limited to manufacturing. As such she argues that the current downturn has exposed the Dalian-JV as overly dependent on BKT–Lübeck's capabilities. She further argues that the way forward for the Dalian-JV is that it needs to develop a design capability and to significantly improve its marketing capabilities. She is skeptical of Mr Wang's ability to develop these capabilities and characterizes him as a 'metal-bashing production boss' with, unlike herself, 'no feel for marketing'. As such she regards Mr Wang as unsuitable as MD. She is so disenchanted with Mr Wang that when Auto Dalian was established she defied him by offering her assistance.

Mr Ericsson, the chairman at the Shanghai-JV, echoes many of Madam Tan's views. He was Chairman of the Dalian-JV from 2005 to 2008. Above all he is critical of Mr Wang who he says will not accept any real responsibility for the situation. He is also critical of Mr Wang's inability to create customer relationships. Indeed he is so critical of Mr Wang that he regards the business model at the Dalian-JV as opaque and even implies that Mr Wang is not entirely trustworthy. However Mr Ericsson is also skeptical of the Dalian-JV chairman, Mr Hansen, who, he points out, unlike himself does not know the industry, and can therefore be more easily deceived and isolated.

Similar views are expressed by Mr Selart, the MD of Stavanger. Although Stavanger has no direct involvement with Dalian-JV he has strong views on behalf of BKT. He claims that 'Mr Wang has been a problem from day one'. He has no faith in Mr Hansen's ability to deal with Mr Wang, not only because the former does not understand the products but also because he is generally ineffective and weak in his dealings with Mr Wang. In terms of joint ventures in China, Mr Selart views them as generally challenging in that their success ultimately depends on personal chemistry.

Mr Schmidt, the MD of Bremen, acknowledges that when Bremen had dealings with the Dalian-JV it was much more problematic than working with the Shanghai-JV had ever been. He thinks that some of this difficulty may lie in Dalian itself which he views as much more provincial and much less business oriented than Shanghai, where 'the main religion is dollars'. However, the Dalian-JV has also been harder to fathom than the Shanghai-JV in that 'it seems more political in its workings'. Mr Wang in particular 'seemed to have a power focus rather than a business orientation'. Although Mr Schmidt believed Mr Wang understood English he assumed that his refusal to speak it was due to his fear of appearing weak. Further he observed that he viewed Mr Wang as a 'production guy' rather than a 'marketing guy'.

On the other hand, Mr Schmidt also points to Lübeck, which he regards as locked into an inflexible and 'typically German' mind-set. However, he thinks that the lack of cross-cultural understanding is only a partial explanation of the conflict between the two. The reality is that Lübeck does not want to give away its knowledge to the Chinese fearing that it will cost them their jobs. As a result of a lack of knowledge-sharing the Dalian-JV delivers wheels of such poor quality that there is a team of 16 Lübeck employees dedicated to repairing the wheels prior to their installation. Mr Schmidt characterizes this outcome as 'unacceptable'. Similar criticisms of Lübeck are leveled by the Chief Financial Officer at Stavanger, Mr Lindberg. While distrusting Mr Wang, he also views Lübeck as blinkered in its relationship with the Dalian-JV in that it fails to consider future possibilities such as developing new products for the Korean market.

A somewhat contrasting view of Mr Wang is expressed by Mr Larsen, the long-serving, locally married, Swedish MD of Auto Shanghai. He confides that he has been regularly asked by BKT corporate management to parley at the Dalian-JV. Mr Larsen knew Mr Wang before the Dalian-JV was established. He feels that Mr Wang trusts him and observes that Mr Wang is uniquely prepared to speak in English to him on the phone. Mr Larsen is disheartened with the Germans from Lübeck, regarding them as 'shrill and heavy-handed'. He points out that Mr Wang has no personal ownership interests in the Dalian-JV and that the Dalian-JV is dependent on the BKT brand so that it is unlikely that Mr Wang will initiate a break-up of the joint venture. Nevertheless he acknowledges that Mr Wang has an extremely hierarchical style of management that contrasts with what he regards as his own non-authoritarian Scandinavian style of management.

Another contrasting view of Mr Wang is expressed by Ms Dale, BKT's After-Sales Services manager. Although she characterizes him as insufficiently commercial in his outlook and is concerned about the long-term implications of the quality problem at the Dalian-JV, she also claims to have enjoyed a generally good relationship with him. However, she speculated that being a woman made her appear less of a threat to Mr Wang.

To summarize: after initially performing very successfully there is a consensus among our informants that the Dalian-JV has become unstable not just because of a fall-off in sales but, more importantly, because of the open tensions between it and Lübeck. Inter-organizational synergistic complementarities are problematic to identify with the Dalian-JV and Lübeck at loggerheads in regard to knowledge transfer. Lübeck fears that if it shares its competencies with the Dalian-JV it will no longer be of any value. Interpersonal relationships are also characterized by constant clashes. Neither partner appears to be capable of generating the social trust that could reduce the friction so that alternative, mutually beneficial, strategies could be considered.

 DISCUSSION QUESTIONS

1 Employing Madhok's (1995) distinction between the structural and social dimensions of trust, compare and contrast developments at BKT–Dalian-JV and BKT–Shanghai-JV.
2 What advice do you have for BKT in particular and MNCs in general?

Appendix

Table A.1 Overview of BKT's global operations beyond its headquarters in Sweden

Operation	Europe			Far East				Other
	Norway	Germany		China				
SBU	Stavanger	Bremen	Lübeck	Shanghai-JV	Dalian-JV	Auto Shanghai	Auto Dalian	Ni
Product/ technology	Electrical components	Fenders	Wheels	Design and marketing of fenders and wheels	Manufacturing and marketing of fenders	Axles	Alternators	
Year of entry	1983	2001	2004	2001	2005	2004	2008	
Entry mode	Acquisition	Acquisition	Acquisition	JV	JV	Turn JV to WOS	Greenfield	
Ownership	100% WOS	100% WOS	100% WOS	50:50	50:50	100% WOS	100% WOS	
Governance/ partnership				Stavanger as formal and Bremen as de facto partner : Shanghai SOE	Lübeck : Dalian SOE			
Management/ control	Local MD	Local MD	Local MD	BKT appointed foreign expatriate as Chairman : Chinese SOE appointed local manager as MD	BKT appointed foreign expatriate as Chairman : Chinese SOE appointed local manager as MD	Expat MD	Expat MD	
Size	110	60		80	80	120	40	

Notes: Headquartered in Sweden, BKT comprises 27 strategic business units (SBUs) in 14 countries across three continents. Ni = not included in this study.

Shanghai-JV

Notes: Solid lines represent direct working relationships between senior managers, whereas dotted lines represent indirect working relationships between senior managers.

Figure A.2 Relationships amongst managers in Shanghai-JV

Overview of methods

In this case study we draw on 12 one-hour semi-structured interviews with highly knowledgeable senior and mid-ranking executives from BKT corporate headquarters and four of its wholly-owned subsidiaries as well as from its two 50/50 joint ventures in China. For an overview of informants see Figures A.2 and A.3 and Table A.2.

All interviews were conducted on site between July 21 2009 and February 14 2010. Interviews were conducted either in Norwegian (with the

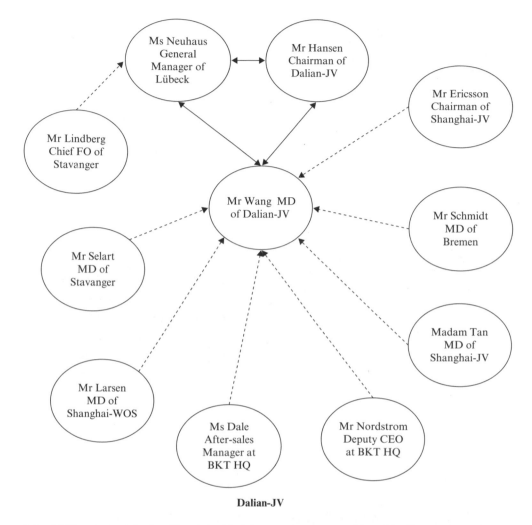

Dalian-JV

Notes: Solid lines represent direct working relationships between senior managers, whereas dotted lines represent indirect working relationships between senior managers.

Figure A.3 Relationships amongst managers in Dalian-JV

Scandinavian respondents) or English. An interpreter was used in our interview with the Chinese MD of the Dalian-JV. Interviews involved two of the three authors one of whom had the responsibility for note taking. The notes were transformed into text by the note-taking researcher and then discussed with the other author. We also collected secondary data by accessing company annual reports. The third author carried out desktop search of material and data by accessing online databases and websites of the companies under investigation. This was followed by a triangulation procedure (Denzin and Lincoln, 2008). Within-case analysis was conducted

Table A.2 Overview of key views of informants

	Shanghai-JV and Madam Tan	Lübeck and Ms Neuhaus	Dalian-JV and Mr Wang
Ms Dale After-sales Manager at BKT HQ			[Mr Wang] is insufficiently commercial in his outlook . . . but [I] have enjoyed a generally good relationship with him . . . being a woman may have made me appear less of a threat to Mr Wang.
Mr Nordstrom Deputy CEO at BKT HQ			[Mr Wang] lack of 'sales mentality that will make recovery from the current down-turn difficult'.
Mr Selart MD of Stavanger	Beyond the brand name and marketing support 'Shanghai-JV has received very little technology from us.'		'Mr Wang has been a problem from day one'. . . Mr Hansen is not able to deal with Mr Wang not only because the former does not understand the products but also because he is generally ineffective and weak in his dealings with Mr Wang.
Mr Lindberg Chief FO of Stavanger		Lübeck is blinkered in its relationship with Dalian-JV in that it fails to consider future possibilities such as developing new products for the Korean market.	
Mr Schmidt MD of Bremen	At the beginning there were problems relating to quality and 'a lot of fights' with Madam Tan as 'you have to be strong in China'.	Entirely German in its approach to management as being inflexible in relation to demanding clear guidelines and an unwillingness to engage in open discussion . . . Lübeck does not want to give away its knowledge to the Chinese fearing that it will cost them their jobs.	It was very much more problematic [to deal with Dalian-JV] than working with Shanghai-JV had ever been. . . [Dalian-JV] was much more provincial and much less business oriented than [Shanghai-JV] where 'the main religion is dollars' . . . 'it [Dalian-JV] seems more political in its workings'. Mr Wang in particular seemed to have a power focus rather than a business orientation.

Mr Meyer Operations Manager of Bremen	Because of the 'brilliant local third-party manufacturing contacts' Shanghai-JV is an 'excellent' partner in China . . . but for the most part all Shanghai-JV has received from BKT is the use of its brand and support in order to be able to attract European customers who are sceptical of Chinese firms.
Madam Tan MD of Shanghai-JV	Every industry insider in China is well aware that Fin-Auto is globally stronger than BKT, but because of its joint ventures BKT is actually the larger in China. 'Sometimes I feel part of the BKT family'
Mr Ericsson Chairman of Shanghai-JV	[I] lead board meetings and write the minutes . . . feel that not only have a good insight into the finances of Shanghai-JV, but also able to request reports on all dealings with suppliers.
Mr Larsen MD of Auto Shanghai WOS	The Germans from Lübeck are 'shrill and heavy-handed'.
Ms Neuhaus General Manager of Lübeck	'Dalian-JV will have acquired everything in the space of a few years that has taken us [Lübeck] sixty years of consistent effort to develop.'
Mr Wang MD of Dalian-JV	It [Lübeck] deliberately blocks core technical parameters so that the components it delivers to Dalian-JV cannot be replicated locally. . . The Germans [Lübeck] are overly sensitive in their approach to quality issues and many of the shortcomings they identify are no more than cosmetic.
Mr Hansen Chairman of Dalain-JV	Dalian-JV is overly dependent on Lübeck's capabilities and [Mr Wang] is a 'metal-bashing production boss' with 'no feel for marketing'. The business model at Dalian-JV is opaque and Mr Wang is not entirely trustworthy . . . Mr Hansen does not know the industry, and can therefore be more easily deceived and isolated. Mr Wang trusts [me] and he is uniquely prepared to speak in English [to me] on the phone . . . Mr Wang has an extremely hierarchical style of management. This poor quality of workmanship at Dalian-JV 'hurts' Lübeck employees who have 'an obsession with quality'. . . Dalian-JV, under the 'well-connected Mr Wang has opened up a lot of doors for us in China'.

by all three authors (Eisenhardt, 1989). In order to verify the accuracy of the factual substance underpinning our analysis we cross-checked the information we had collected with BKT's deputy CEO, Mr Nordstrom, shortly before embarking on our analysis. This final meeting resulted in only relatively minor changes.

3

Strategies, structures and learning networks

3.1 Introduction

The purpose of this chapter is to review the overarching international strategies and corresponding organizational capabilities required to meet these strategic needs. In the initial part of the chapter, our focus is on the motivations of establishing FDI. We then introduce four generic international strategies: simple international, multidomestic, global, and transnational. We complement the discussion of the four generic international strategies with Ghemawat's (2008) more recent international strategy classification: aggregation, adaptation and arbitrage (AAA). The next section discusses the corresponding structural characteristics in MNCs and related subsidiary roles. Finally, we discuss the increasing focus on MNCs as learning networks impact on how the MNC operates across borders.

3.2 Traditional motivations

Firms' motivations to internalize their transactions in international markets through the establishment of foreign operations are typically grouped into four categories: resource seeking, market seeking, efficiency seeking, and strategic asset seeking (Dunning, 2009). Resource-seeking motives are common among firms that are dependent on having a reliable supply of raw materials that can only be accessed in foreign locations. For example, European tire companies established rubber plantations in Malaysia and South America while aluminum companies established smelters where cheap energy was available. Internalizing transactions provide firms with a supply that may be less vulnerable and therefore, in the long run, cheaper than market solutions.

Firms with market-seeking motives have identified a need to expand the market for the company's products or services by capitalizing on its idiosyncratic strategic assets through their application in foreign markets. This has been particularly important for firms with small home markets such as Nestlé of Switzerland and Nokia of Finland.

Efficiency-seeking motives became more common from the 1960s onwards. As tariffs declined, firms located in the USA and Europe found themselves at a competitive disadvantage because of their relatively high labor costs. As a result a third motive for establishing foreign operations emerged, accessing low-cost labor. An added incentive to relocate production has been the willingness of some host governments to provide direct or indirect subsidies in the form of low levels of corporate taxation. MNCs are then able to spread their production processes across multiple countries thereby taking advantage of the different factor endowments located in their manufacturing chains. Each link in the production process is located in a country where the associated costs are the lowest. Production is moved to more favorable locations in accordance with changing wage rates, interest rates and factor prices.

The strategic-asset-seeking motive is driven by an increasing dependence among MNCs on knowledge-related assets. Many MNCs choose to acquire a local firm that either has valuable knowledge internally or is embedded in a local cluster of knowledge. By acquiring a foreign firm, the MNC immediately gains access to the desired knowledge and becomes an 'insider' of a knowledge cluster that may otherwise be difficult to tap into. Market entry through mergers and acquisitions (M&As) are often preferred to greenfield investments for MNCs with strategic-asset-seeking motives to ensure that the MNC actually does gain access to the desired knowledge in a timely manner. Successful MNCs with strategic-asset-seeking motives typically engage actively in the local market.

The product cycle theory, initially developed by Raymond Vernon (1966), makes particular use of efficiency- and market-seeking motives. With a focus on US firms he portrayed their internationalization as a gradual, incremental three-phase process. A firm located in phase one has all of its production within the US with some incidental export to developed markets in Europe. When export reaches significant proportions the firm, almost reactively, moves into phase two in which production facilities are established to serve its major foreign markets. As the product becomes highly standardized and competitors are able to produce similar products and make their presence felt by competing on price, the firm enters a third phase: production is transferred to nations where labor costs are low and, if necessary, new low-cost locations are sought.

In line with Vernon's view, internationalization was traditionally seen as primarily being motivated by access to low-cost factors of production particularly labor. This motive leads to offshore production of specific items, which are then exported either for further work or for sale. Any exceptions to this trend would be the product of markets protected by politically created barriers such as tariffs. To circumvent these barriers, the common response was to establish factories whose task would be to assemble the home product locally. These server plants might make some minor adaptations to suit local needs and engage in some localization of components, in order to overcome political barriers, but product design and development would remain centralized.

In terms of Vernon's product cycle theory we can distinguish two generic multinational strategies. Phase two of the product cycle may be labeled as representative of 'simple international' strategies, whereas phase three requires cross-border integration often referred to as a 'global' strategy. Not all firms follow the product life cycle, as proposed by Vernon. Some find that their products or services require greater adaptation to each market, necessitating a multidomestic strategy. Bartlett and Ghoshal (1989) also introduced a fourth strategy, the transnational, for MNCs that compete based on greater levels of internal differentiation. The next section will describe these international strategies in greater detail.

3.3   International strategies

The categorization of the four international strategies are largely a reflection of the degree of global integration the MNC chooses to exercise over its subsidiaries and the degree to which its subsidiaries are mandated to be flexible and responsive in regard to their local environments, as illustrated in Figure 3.1. Each of the four international strategies is discussed in greater detail below.

Figure 3.1 Four international strategies

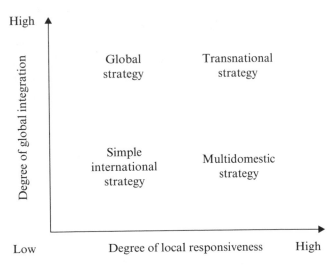

High

Degree of global integration

Global strategy

Transnational strategy

Simple international strategy

Multidomestic strategy

Low   Degree of local responsiveness   High

The simple international strategy

Foreign operations in MNCs with simple international strategies are characterized by having an adjunct or peripheral function. Despite being usually headed by parent company staff, that is expatriates, foreign subsidiaries are not integrated in any of the company's business units. This suggests that decisions relating to foreign operations are typically made in an opportunistic or ad hoc manner.

Another trait is that foreign subsidiaries of MNCs with simple international strategies lack the resources and mandate to adapt, let alone develop, the product to any significant extent. There is a one-way transference of technology and knowledge from the parent company to its foreign subsidiaries resulting in a low degree of local responsiveness. The approach is to exploit home-country innovations in order to achieve incremental sales rather than to develop flexible or high-scale operations. In their early days this was how Colgate Palmolive and many other American companies, such as Kraft and Procter & Gamble, operated in Europe. Firms pursuing simple international strategies are often in very early stages of internationalization. As Vernon suggests, this type of international organization is essentially a transitory phase that precedes a more globally integrated form of organization.

The multidomestic strategy

This strategy has historically been a particular feature of European firms operating subsidiaries in other European countries. Large national differences in consumer preferences between European countries, logistical barriers and, at one point, high tariff barriers all contributed to favoring a strategy involving high national responsiveness.

Nestlé's international expansion illustrates the multidomestic strategy. Its motive for expansion outside of Switzerland was entirely different from that underlying the simple international strategy. With a small domestic market, expansion could only come from establishing operations abroad. In other words, foreign activities were never viewed as purely incremental and this has influenced the way it has traditionally structured its operations. By 2011, Nestlé's products were sold in over 140 countries, accounting for 98 per cent of Nestlé's sales of EUR 67,840 million. It had also located factories in over 80 countries (Nestlé, 2011). Founded in 1866, by the early 1900s it had operations in Britain, Germany, Spain and the United States. This expansion was accompanied by a profound recognition that as tastes in human foodstuffs vary enormously from country to country, centralization was to be kept to a minimum. From its earliest days Nestlé delegated brand management authority to country managers who independently adjusted the marketing and manufacturing strategies in accordance with local tastes and preferences. In 1994, only 750 of its 8,000 brands were registered in more than one country. As such Nestlé was for many years a multidomestic company characterized by relatively weak global integration and pronounced local responsiveness.

When Peter Brabeck became CEO in 1997 there were two 'unique' Nestlé features he wanted to preserve. The first was that information technology (IT) would not play much of a role in the day-to-day running of the firm: Nestlé's focus on its people, products and brands would continue to be far more influential. Second, the group would keep its commitment to decentralization, seen as the best way to cater to local taste and to establish emotional links with clients in far-flung places. However, after a couple of years in the job Mr Brabeck abruptly switched tack. By the end of his tenure as CEO in 2008 Nestlé had become significantly less of a collection of fiefdoms. First Mr Brabeck made production more regional. For example Nestlé's operations in New Zealand had been run as a local company with four factories and very few imports and exports. Nestlé's operations in New Zealand were pooled with those of Australia and the Pacific Islands by consolidating accounting, administration, sales and payroll. It was not a popular decision with the Australians (*Economist*, 2004a). Overall between 1998 and 2002 Nestlé was able to close or sell about half of its factories.

Purchasing is another area Nestlé has attempted to integrate. Yet making the most of purchasing data is not easy. The first step was to improve the accuracy of the information. Nestlé, for example, was selling more than 100,000 products in 200 countries, using 550,000 suppliers, but the company was not using its huge buying power effectively because its databases were a mess. On examination, it found that of its 9 million records of vendors, customers and materials around half were obsolete or duplicated, and of the remainder about one-third was inaccurate or incomplete. The name of a vendor might be abbreviated in one record but spelled out in another, leading to double counting.

Since Brabeck changed strategic direction, Nestlé has been overhauling its IT system, using SAP software, and improving the quality of its data. This has enabled Nestlé to become more efficient. For just one ingredient, vanilla, its American operation was able to reduce the number of specifications and use fewer suppliers, saving $30 million a year. Overall, such operational improvements have saved more than $1 billion annually (*Economist*, 2010).

However, there are limits to how globally integrated Nestlé can become without losing the ability to adapt its products to local tastes and traditions. As CEO, Mr Brabeck was always conscious that there is no global consumer. For instance, Nestlé produces 200 different varieties of Nescafé, its instant-coffee brand, to cater to local palates. Russians prefer their coffee thick, strong and sweet mixed with milk powder. This would not go down well with western Europeans. KitKat in Japan comes in flavors such as lemon cheesecake, utterly different from the KitKat sold in Britain. As a rule, the simpler the wares, the more they need to be adapted to local preferences. Sophisticated products such as milk powder for premature babies, on the other hand, are the same everywhere (*Economist*, 2004a).

The lesson is that integrating multidomestic MNCs involves considerable effort and is time-consuming. Over time local subsidiary managers develop a fiefdom mentality that does not incline them to favor any form of MNC-wide integration that may involve a loss of strategic or operational discretion. Furthermore, a substantial proportion of the knowledge that is developed in multidomestic MNCs is locally developed and locally embedded. Typically these MNCs have little in the way of MNC-wide social networks that enable the pooling and integration of such knowledge. The lack of social networks also means that there is no common vision across the MNC and trust is underdeveloped. Finally, there are often limitations to how integrated a multidomestic MNC should become. The challenges involved the integration of multidomestic MNCs is the theme of this chapter's accompanying case.

The global strategy

In the early 1980s, the emphasis on global strategy increased dramatically and by some it was almost regarded as mandatory for competitive advantage. With increasing competition as a consequence of decreased tariff barriers, product life cycles had shortened dramatically, thereby escalating research and development costs. The ability to operate under such a cost burden entailed an expanded scale of production over and above what a firm's domestic market was capable of absorbing. As such foreign markets had to be sought out just in order to 'enter the game'. A further reason to seek out foreign markets was that without a presence in every market competitors could achieve dominant positions that granted high profit margins. Dominance and strong profitability in one or more markets could then be surreptitiously used to subsidize loss-making entries into other markets.

The influential scholar Theodore Levitt (1983) envisioned a world increasingly dominated by MNCs of the global organization type.

> Everywhere everything gets more and more like everything else as the world's preference structure is relentlessly homogenized . . . Ancient differences in national tastes or modes of doing business disappear. The commonality of preference leads inescapably to the standardization of products, manufacturing and the institutions of trade and commerce . . . (The global corporation) treats the world as composed of few standardized markets rather than many customized markets. It actively seeks and vigorously works toward global convergence. (It seeks) to force suitably standardized products and practices on the entire globe . . . Companies that do not adapt to the new global realities will become victims of those that do. (Levitt, 1983: 92–102)

Companies such as Sony epitomize MNCs with global strategies. Sony makes most of its value-added high-tech products, such as chips and personal computers, in Japan, where it can monitor quality and where it has location-bound advantages not least in terms of research and development. When products have become highly standardized, their production is transferred to other locations, either to lower costs or to improve market entry. In relation to Europe, Sony has transferred production of audio-visual products, such as televisions and computer displays to purpose-built greenfield sites that have been managed largely according to Sony's management principles. The standardized capabilities involved are easily transferred through training programs.

Firms that are pursuing the global strategy have to develop and deploy three distinct organizational capabilities (Bartlett and Ghoshal, 1995: 581). They must succeed in:

- gaining the input of subsidiaries into centralized activities,
- ensuring that all functional tasks are linked to market needs,
- integrating diverse functions such as development, production and marketing by managing the transfer of responsibilities among them.

The mentality underlying the global strategy is of course far from exclusively Japanese. IKEA's history is one of having ignored local taste and bucking fragmented furniture markets by producing scale-intensive globally standardized furniture. Despite serving a range of markets from Russia to North America, purchasing, distribution and design functions remain centrally controlled and served by Swedes. IKEA has indeed gradually allowed for minor market adaptations such as adjusting specific products like bed sizes to North American standards, but these adaptations are limited to their downstream activities. Similarly General Electric functions on the basis of a distinctly uniform corporate mentality although this does not preclude non-Americans. Its ten businesses are global businesses each with its own president who co-ordinates and integrates activities worldwide.

The transnational strategy

At the end of the 1980s, it was argued by, for example, Bartlett and Ghoshal (1989) that important as the global integration dimension is, there is also an increasing need to achieve close proximity to local markets or customers to be able to adapt products to local tastes. The ability to balance the two strategic challenges requires a focus on worldwide learning in MNCs. Customers are no longer prepared to accept a 'one-size-fits-all' product strategy. Furthermore, not only do customers have their idiosyncratic national preferences, host governments increasingly expect both local content and transference of technology. In terms of this perspective, global offshore plants based on cheap labor or global server plants making minor adjustments are no longer the critical modes of internationalization. Instead subsidiaries increasingly involve an ability to balance integration with the ability to adapt and enhance products in line with local market demands.

According to Bartlett and Ghoshal the requirements for global integration, local responsiveness and worldwide learning meant that a new MNC strategy, the transnational, was emerging:

> While some products and processes must still be developed centrally for worldwide use and others must be created locally in each environment to meet purely local demands, MNCs must increasingly use their access to multiple centers of technologies and familiarity with diverse customer preferences in different countries to create truly transnational innovations. (1995: 127)

Bartlett and Ghoshal took ABB as their core example of this new MNC strategy. ABB was a heavy engineering firm that was formed in 1988 as the result of a cross-border merger between Asea AB of Sweden and BBC Brown Boveri Ltd of Switzerland. Its first chief executive officer, Percy Barnevik, expounded a strategic vision that, with its focus on reaping global efficiencies, while being locally responsive and ensuring worldwide learning, constituted an 'almost a perfect description of the transnational' (Bartlett and Ghoshal, 1995: 788). In Barnevik's words:

We want to be global and local, big and small, radically decentralized with centralized reporting and control . . . You want to be able to optimize a business globally – to specialize in the production of components, to drive economies of scale as far as you can, to rotate managers and technologists around the world to share expertise and solve problems. But you also want to have deep local roots everywhere you operate – building products in the countries where you sell them, recruiting the best local talent from the universities, working with the local government to increase exports. If you build such an organization, you create a business advantage that's damn difficult to copy. (quoted in Taylor, 1991)

Arbitrage – the 'forgotten strategy'

While the four international strategies discussed above have persisted over time as the key international strategies, they have recently been criticized for not incorporating one of the most common international strategies through-out history, namely taking advantage of arbitrage opportunities (Ghemawat, 2003).

In an effort to incorporate this 'forgotten strategy', Ghemawat (2003, 2008) suggests that international strategies are more effectively categorized into aggregation, adaptation and arbitrage (the AAA framework). Aggregation extends the focus on global integration, where MNCs seek to overcome dif-ferences in foreign markets. Adaptation reflects local responsiveness where MNCs embrace local differences and build their competitive advantage on the ability to cater to differences across foreign markets. Finally, arbitrage strategies are developed when MNCs seek to benefit from location advan-tages limited to specific geographic areas, effectively exploiting differences across national borders. Ghemawat emphasizes that arbitrage opportunities are not limited to low-cost input or access to raw materials but span across much broader opportunities such as knowledge or the reputation of a host market.

Through the AAA framework, Ghemawat also challenges the dichotomous focus on integration and responsiveness. He argues that most MNCs will exhibit elements of all three AAA strategies. Categorizing a firm as either globally integrated or locally responsive can thus be an oversimplification. In practice, firms may have a dominant strategy while still recognizing the need to pursue the other two strategies when and where appropriate. Although this approach to strategy bears some resemblance to the arguments for adopting a transnational strategy, Ghemawat (2008) criticizes the transnational strat-egy for being insufficiently explicit and for overlooking the importance of arbitrage.

3.4   Basic MNC structures

To enable strategy implementation, organizational structures need to be aligned with the overarching international strategy. We will briefly discuss some of the most common organizational structures in MNCs and address how these support international strategies.

International division

The simplest form of MNC structure involves the establishment of a dedicated international division charged with the responsibility of overseeing and managing the international activities of the firm. These activities are not considered as integral to the company in that it is overwhelmingly focused on its home market, typical of firms pursuing simple international strategies. Initially the responsibilities of the international division may involve no more than overseeing the export of the company's products. That is, it is charged with attending to tariff and trade issues and securing and monitoring foreign agents. However, in succeeding phases sales offices are opened and manufacturing capacity established in order to serve better the company's most important markets. Figure 3.2 illustrates this structure in the context of the single product company.[1]

Source: Leontiades (1985).

Figure 3.2 The international division

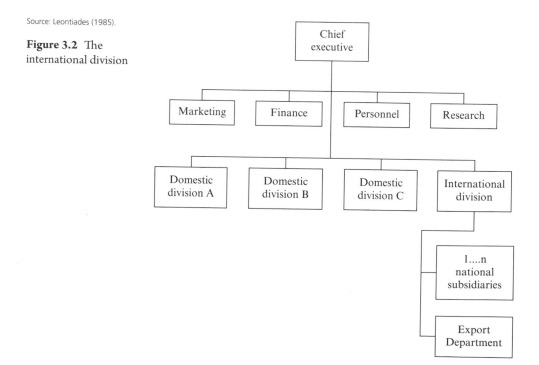

Multidomestic structure

MNCs with highly responsive foreign subsidiaries are typically structured as loose federations of relatively small, decentralized subsidiaries where most value activities are localized in the foreign markets and the subsidiaries are allowed significant freedom to adapt products in accordance with local preferences. The foreign subsidiaries are organized as separate units, often lacking focus on the transfer of resources across subsidiaries. Figure 3.3 illustrates this structure.

Global product division

By a global product division organization type we mean that the major line of authority lies with product managers who have a global responsibility for their product line. Japanese MNCs, particularly in the electronics, computer and automobile industries, have invariably adopted the global product division structure from the outset. Highly centralized scale-intensive manufacturing and R&D operations are leveraged through worldwide exports of standardized global products. When foreign subsidiaries are established there is no intention that they should respond actively to local market

Source: Leontiades (1985).

Figure 3.3 The multidomestic structure

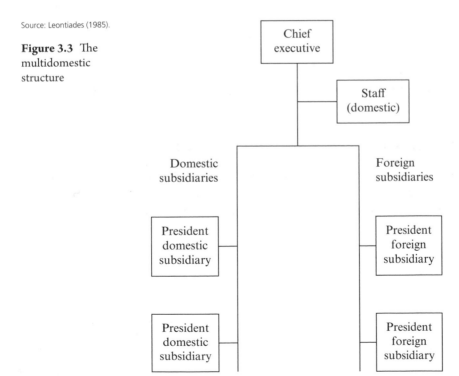

Source: Leontiades (1985).

Figure 3.4 The global product division

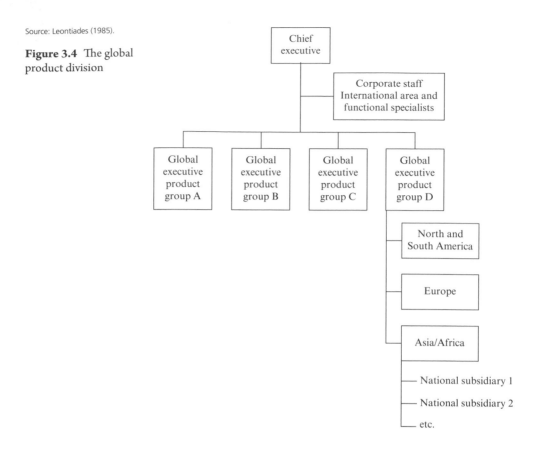

demands over and above that which is strictly necessary. The main structural features of the global-product division are shown in Figure 3.4.

The matrix organization as learning networks

The focus on worldwide learning and internal differentiation as discussed under the transnational strategy gained increasing attention in the 1990s. But how does one build such an advantage, which not least rests upon the ability to disseminate learning throughout the company? ABB's primary structural response, under Barnevik, was the implementation of the balanced global matrix for its 1,300 separate operating companies. Each operating manager was responsible for creating and pursuing entrepreneurial opportunities. Each of these front-line managers reported to a country manager, who was typically responsible for all the operating companies within a specific country, and to a Business Area manager who was responsible for developing worldwide product and technology strategies. Figure 3.5 illustrates the general principle.

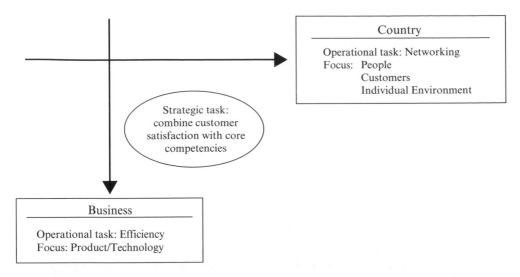

Figure 3.5 The initial balanced global matrix structure at ABB

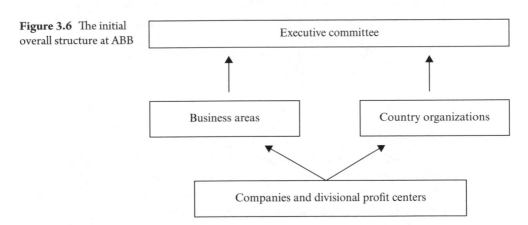

Figure 3.6 The initial overall structure at ABB

In turn each Business Area manager reported to one of 11 executive vice presidents. These vice presidents were the lynchpins of the matrix system in that they not only were responsible for an interrelated set of Business Areas but also for several regions. They constituted the Executive Committee that defined overall global strategy and broad performance targets (see Figure 3.6). Significantly, of ABB's 215,000 employees only 100 were located at corporate headquarters in Zurich.

A final feature at ABB was its deployment of a centralized reporting system, ABACUS, which collected performance data and compared it with budgets and forecasts. The system also allowed the data to be consolidated or broken down by business segments and worldwide product lines, countries and companies within countries. In that way the Executive Committee had not only a clear view of the usual measurements such as orders, cash flow and margins, but also emerging trends in performance, both globally and by country.

Bartlett and Ghoshal observed local responsiveness at ABB in its radical decentralization of assets and responsibilities to local operating units. Managers of the local operating units had a mandate to build their businesses as if they owned them with managers being allowed to inherit results. They also observed global integration in that the mandate of the Business Area manager was designed so as to facilitate horizontal integration between units in respect to knowledge, export markets and production facilities. 'He decides which factories are going to make what products, what export markets each factory will serve, how the factories should pool their expertise and research funds for the benefit of the business worldwide' (Bartlett and Ghoshal, 1995: 853). That is, any local unit may be upgraded by a Business Area manager to take on a central task or requested to contribute its expertise to the realization of a task at another unit. In structural terms the essence of ABB is thus the balancing and integrating of global business managers and geographic management groups.

In addition to the objective structural features, Bartlett and Ghoshal regarded the development of a structure of shared values at ABB, a 'common organizational psychology', as being of even greater significance. The essence of such a psychology is a shared understanding of and respect for the company's mission and objectives combined with non-parochial, collaborative attitudes. It is, they argue, achieved by selecting and promoting individuals whose personal characteristics predispose them towards non-opportunistic behavior and by creating an internal context that encourages people to act in the way they would as a member of a functional family or a disciplined sporting team.

Subsidiary roles

Figure 3.7 distinguishes different types of subsidiaries according to the degree of knowledge resources they possess. The framework distinguishes the two types of subsidiary common to the global product division type of MNC: offshores and servers. Additionally it includes a second type of server subsidiary. This is associated with multidomestics and is different from the global server in that it has the latitude to develop resources that enable it to significantly adapt products for its local markets. Subsidiaries of the more

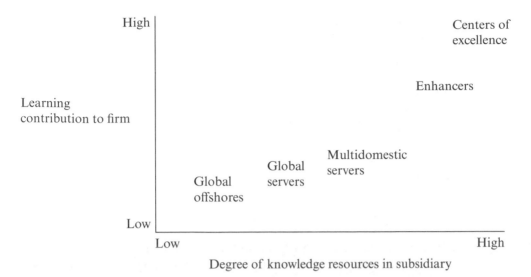

Figure 3.7 A categorization of foreign subsidiaries by degree of knowledge resources they possess and their learning contribution to the MNC

transitory international organization type do not feature, but in principle they will fall into one of the figure's three categories.

The framework includes a second dimension, the learning contribution of the subsidiary to the MNC. For all three subsidiary types this is low, indicating that even multidomestics have rarely systematically attempted to leverage learning from their various subsidiaries.

3.5 Emerging motivations

MNCs recognized that in acquiring or creating subsidiaries with a developmental capability, these subsidiaries could not only be used to adapt products, but also to enhance them (Kuemmerle, 1997). Coupled to this was the understanding that there were competitive advantages to be derived from integrating product developments stemming from 'enhancers' into the MNC as a whole, which meant that worldwide learning became a motivation for internationalization in itself. Firms increasingly recognized that that there were competitive advantages in being able to tap into and integrate critical knowledge resources wherever they might be located. As a result MNCs began to seek out regional centers of excellence in order to tap into world-class specialist knowledge from the local scientific community, including competitors as well as universities, from where it flows back to the companies' central R&D site and beyond to other sites in the firms' global network (Kuemmerle, 1997). For example, nearly all of the big European pharmaceutical companies have established an R&D presence in America, particularly in high-technology clusters such as Boston and San Diego. Likewise American pharmaceutical companies, such as Pfizer, have European research facilities. The result is that it is the subsidiary that is the center of excellence for the whole of the MNC for particular products and technologies (Birkinshaw, 1997).

The notion that what is increasingly driving the internationalization of firms' activities is their need to obtain and create new competencies in order to support and improve overall innovativeness, is viewed by Cantwell (1996) as representing a 'new evolutionary approach' for understanding the strategic intent of MNCs. No longer are MNCs to be exclusively viewed as agents of unidirectional international technology transfer. Instead they should be viewed as being driven by a need to develop technology and knowledge that is met by leveraging their presence in foreign locations to generate internationally coordinated learning processes. This is particularly the case in regard to technologically intensive industries such as pharmaceuticals and electronics, where levels of sophistication make labor costs increasingly less of an issue than skills and creativity. We return to this theme of the MNC as a knowledge network in Chapter 7.

3.6 Validation of the international strategies

Employing data from 166 subsidiaries of 37 MNCs headquartered in nine different countries, Harzing (2000) has substantially confirmed the validity of the typology of MNC organizational structures we have presented. Her analysis excludes the transitory international, focusing instead on the issue of the existence of MNCs with multidomestic, global and transnational strategies. In the first stage of her analysis, Harzing divided her sample into three according to the type of international strategy being deployed. Those firms with a focus on global competition and economies of scale were categorized as globals, firms emphasizing domestic competition and national responsiveness were classified as multidomestics, and firms combining these features were labeled transnationals. In the second stage of her analysis Harzing examined the association between the three MNC types and a number of core organizational characteristics. Overall Harzing's findings are in line with our theoretical discussion above. Table 3.1 features Harzing's main findings.

Harzing's research also features an analysis of the main control mechanisms associated with the three MNC strategies. An expected characteristic of subsidiaries in MNCs with a multidomestic strategy is that there is little in the

Table 3.1 Harzing's validation of the international strategies

MNC type	Characteristics
Multidomestic	Decentralized federation
	Low level of HQ dependence
	Low level of interdependence
	High level of product modification, adaptation of marketing
Global	Subsidiaries have a 'pipeline' role
	High level of HQ dependence
	High level of HQ interdependence
	Low level of product modification and adaptation of marketing
Transnational	Network structure, centers of excellence, inter-subsidiary flows
	Medium level of HQ dependence
	High level of interdependence
	High level of product modification and adaptation of marketing

Source: adapted from Harzing (2000).

way of centralized control over and above an evaluation of their financial results. However, in MNCs with global strategies, decision making is much more than simply output control. Control is highly centralized and at the subsidiary level there are surveillance mechanisms in addition to written rules and procedures that have to be adhered to. Transnational MNCs are harder to distinguish from global than multidomestic MNCs. However, they do appear to be more inclined to use what we referred to above as a 'common organizational psychology' than is the case for MNCs pursuing multidomestic or global strategies.

3.7   The evolution of the MNC

For a substantial part of the 1990s it was speculated that MNCs were evolving into transnational organizations. However, Harzing's research (1999) undermined this thesis because she found that a significant proportion of transnational firms did not grow out of multidomestic or global companies. That is, they started out as transnationals. Another problem for the transnational thesis was that during the 1990s ABB changed its structures to such a degree that it no longer could be classified as a transnational. In addition to a downturn in its industry, ABB had been unable to develop an organizational psychology that was capable of offsetting internal rivalries between the various profit centers, between the business segments and between the business area dimension and the regional dimension. In August 1998 the balanced matrix structure in which an operating manager is equally accountable to regional and Business Area managers was scrapped by Barnevik's successors and the balancing act between global integration and local responsiveness, which had been a core feature of ABB's mission since its inception, was significantly tilted towards global integration. As one ABB executive remarked, 'Now Zurich is ruling the world [of ABB]'.

The reality is that there is no one satisfactory way of organizing an MNC. Moreover, internal structures are becoming increasingly complex and differentiated. As a consequence: 'For most global companies it is a question of choosing the least-bad structure and then figuring out how to mitigate its greatest weaknesses' (Birkinshaw, 2000: 3). A feature of the case accompanying this chapter is the difficulty in achieving and maintaining both local responsiveness and global integration at the same time.

3.8   Global learning and knowledge networks

The degree of formal balance that is struck between global integration and local responsiveness is, however, only one aspect to the transnational thesis. There is also the need to develop organizational capabilities that ensure that ideas and information flow across the MNC in order to stimulate cross-national learning. The nature of this flow varies according to the resources located in the subsidiaries. As we have observed, in some cases subsidiaries are centers of excellence with global mandates, whereas in others subsidiaries are no more than low-cost, low-skilled, production units or local marketing channels. Involving the latter in a knowledge exchange network is obviously less important than involving the former. Regardless of the precise balance between global integration and local responsiveness, MNCs are increasingly becoming knowledge network organizations. The knowledge network organization is not an alternative to structures but an informal overlay that makes use of computer systems, employee transfer policies and organizational culture. This issue will be more fully addressed in Chapter 7.

3.9   Summary

Developing strategies and structures that reflect the need to find a strategically appropriate balance between local responsiveness and global integration is a task that calls for continuous adjustments and fine-tuning. There is no end state and within one and the same MNC there may be a mix of centralized and decentralized operations making for structural diversity. Regardless of strategy there has to be an overlay of relatively informal systems that ensure the flow and combination of knowledge between constituent parts of the MNC. Developing these systems has evolved into an organizational challenge of major significance. An MNC needs to know what it knows, learn what it needs to learn and apply that knowledge as quickly as possible for sustainable competitive advantage. The network MNC is the ideal, but it is a mental construct rather than an objective structure. Obviously a variety of paths have to be constructed in order that knowledge may flow, but the degree to which these paths are actually used is dependent on the application of various incentives, the sensitive use of authority and the development of a sense of community across the MNC.

The case following this chapter addresses the issue of what challenges an MNC faces when its strategy dictates a new structure. Scandinavian Food Corporation (SCF), a multidomestic MNC, has come to recognize that it must integrate its purchasing if it is to survive. Its first attempt to achieve purchasing integration is not successful. Its second attempt is much more successful. The case presents theory about the role social capital plays in achieving the knowledge sharing needed for successful purchasing integration. This theory will be more extensively presented in Chapter 7.

NOTE

1 Figures 3.2, 3.3 and 3.4 are reproduced from Leontiades (1985) with permission of Rowman & Littlefield Publishing Group.

Case B

From multidomestic to globally integrated: when local taste matters[1]

Paul N. Gooderham

B.1 Introduction

Multidomestic MNCs with structures that resemble federative rather than unitary organizations have been common particularly among European MNCs and above all in industries such as foodstuffs, where local taste matters (Bartlett and Ghoshal, 1989; Porter, 1986). Characteristic features of such MNCs are that their subsidiaries have a national focus and substantial latitude to forge locally oriented strategies. The essence of the multidomestic strategy is its emphasis on the need to be responsive to each local environment in order to achieve local competitive advantage (Yip, 1989). In contrast, a global strategy views competitive advantage as being based on capturing global scale or scope economies through the integration of the activities of the business and focusing on customer demands that are standardized across markets (Roth, 1992). Thus, in terms of the degree of integration of activities across locations, whereas MNCs pursuing a global strategy seek to exploit cross-national sources of advantage through a high level of intra-firm integration of resources, those pursuing a multidomestic strategy allow subsidiaries to be largely autonomous and to depend more on locally-sourced resources as opposed to centralized procurement. Thus not only is there local production, but also local purchasing responsibility.

Among others, Yamin and Sinkovics (2007) have argued that globalization and environmental drivers, including increasing market liberalization and advances in information and communication technologies, are causing multidomestic or federative MNCs to seek global integration of operational and functional activities (see also Buckley and Ghauri, 2004). Indeed Birkinshaw (2001: 281) has claimed that:

Most MNCs have now moved towards some variant of the global subsidiary structure in their international operations and a corresponding dilution in the power and responsibilities of the country manager.

Present theory suggests that when multidomestic MNCs engage in making the transition to the global state they are confronted by the very conditions that enable them to maintain local taste: that is the decentralization of decision making and the concomitant loose-coupling of the organization. Consequently extant theory points to a political and a social network challenge. What is lacking is a process theory of how multidomestic MNCs overcome these challenges when greater integration is viable.

To address this challenge this case features a Scandinavian multidomestic MNC, Scandinavian Food Company (SCF), which has been engaged in the transition to a more integrated state for nearly a decade. More specifically we focus on the attempts by the corporate center to integrate the purchasing activities of its group of subsidiaries. We compare its early, and largely unsuccessful, initiative to achieve purchasing integration with its more recent, largely successful, initiative.

The case is structured as follows. First, we draw on extant theory that identifies two significant barriers to moving from the multidomestic to the global state. The first of these is political and the second concerns the lack of social networks across subsidiaries and the concomitant difficulty of facilitating knowledge transfer. We then present the case of the SCF and its main subsidiaries, Voso (Norway), Pelecta (Czech Republic) and Pitana (Poland) (all names anonymized at the request of the company). We compare SCF's two contrasting efforts at integrating the purchasing activities of its subsidiaries. This polar sample, an unsuccessful and a successful effort, makes it possible to observe emergent constructs and theoretical relationships (Martin and Eisenhardt, 2010). In so doing we develop two sets of propositions.

B.2 Extant theory

For multidomestic MNCs, particularly those operating in industries where local adaptation continues to matter, product standardization is clearly problematic. Thus, for example, MNCs located within the food industry, where meeting local taste sensibilities is of critical importance, cannot disregard the issue of local responsiveness in regard to their end products. To a significant extent they must retain their ability to be experienced by local consumers as, to employ SCF's concept, 'local-taste champions'. However, the integration and centralization of underlying activities such as purchasing and production is in principle viable. In practice, though, the integration of such activities by multidomestic MNCs will involve having to confront two particular barriers that to a significant extent are products of their multidomestic heritage. The first derives from the polity of multidomestic MNCs and the second from the lack of social networks between subsidiaries. Either of these has the potential to block the transition from the multidomestic to the global state.

The political challenge

'Power (in MNCs) is far from being just a question of ownership' (Vahlne et al., 2011: 3). Indeed it has been argued that MNCs may be conceived of as 'resembling highly political arenas in which power games continuously take place' (Bouquet and Birkinshaw, 2008: 492). As such 'micro-politics and conflicts (are) an unavoidable social reality and a natural mechanism of social interactions in MNCs' (Dörrenbächer and Geppert, 2006: 261). In other words actors within MNCs are intentionally and strategically attempting to advance their own interests, strengthen their influence and avoid conceding previous mandates. Mudambi and Pedersen (2007) distinguish two political theory pillars upon which to understand decision making by managers in MNC subsidiaries: agency theory and resource dependency theory. Both theories suggest that the political character of the MNC will be particularly discernible when corporate headquarters seeks to move the MNC from a multidomestic to a global stance.

Agency theory assumes that the headquarters–subsidiary relationship in MNCs is founded on self-interest and opportunism so that 'the local interests of the subsidiaries may not always be aligned with those of the headquarters or the MNC as a whole' (Nohria and Ghoshal, 1994: 492). According to O'Donnell (2000) in order to counter this agency problem the corporate center has two generic alternatives at its disposal. The first of these is that of bureaucratic monitoring mechanisms in the form of centrally determined rules, programs or procedures in order to obtain information about the behaviors and decisions of subsidiary management. However, in the case of subsidiaries of multidomestic MNCs, because they are perceived as being in a better position than headquarters to evaluate the needs and demands of the particular markets they serve, they have substantial strategic autonomy. Additionally, because they are also considered to be in a better position to identify the particular physical, technological, knowledge, financial and human resources that are needed to serve their particular markets, they also have operational decision making autonomy. As such subsidiary management has considerable discretion in dealing with the demands of the local market and task environment. Thus, as O'Donnell (2000) argues, and finds empirical support for, this degree of discretion reduces the feasibility of applying bureaucratic monitoring mechanisms to subsidiaries of multidomestic MNCs.

The second generic device for countering the agency problem is the use of financial incentives that align subsidiary management goals with those of corporate headquarters. Given that outcome measurability is unproblematic, and as monitoring devices are unviable, financial incentives that reflect subsidiary performance are the chosen governance device in the case of multidomestic MNCs (O'Donnell, 2000).

Thus typically an MNC that has pursued a multidomestic strategy over time has institutionalized a semi-autonomous mode of governance characterized by substantial local strategic and operational discretion at the subsidiary level (Roth and Ricks, 1994). Furthermore, it has established incentives that reward local subsidiary managements on the basis of their own outputs. In other words the multidomestic MNC customarily comprises 'fiefdoms' whose managers have developed a local view of their roles (Bartlett and Ghoshal, 1989). A transition from the multidomestic to the global state constitutes a profound challenge to this local view and it will be resisted if subsidiary managers are unconvinced that it will confer benefits.

Resource dependency theory posits that power is based on the control of resources that are considered strategic within the organization (Pfeffer and Salancik, 1977; Pfeffer, 1981) and suggests another source of political strain in any move from the multidomestic state. Because the various national subsidiaries units of a multidomestic MNC are confronted by different local markets, some of which will be larger and more munificent than others, over time subsidiaries will vary considerably in terms of their resource ownership and control. In other words some subsidiaries will be relatively resource-strong while others will be relatively resource-weak. From a resource dependency perspective, when a multidomestic MNC attempts to move to a global, integrated state its various subsidiaries will attempt to acquire control over those resources that minimize their dependence on other subsidiaries while maximizing the dependence of other subsidiaries on themselves. In practice this will mean that the most resource-powerful subsidiaries will seek to achieve the dominant role in the integrated MNC, while the weaker subsidiaries will resist possibly through alliance-seeking with other similar subsidiaries.

The social network challenge

Social networks can be broadly defined as a web of personal ties and connections that enable individuals to secure favors such as access to novel information (Granovetter, 1985; Burt, 1992). In organizational settings such as MNCs, social network theory emphasizes how social relationships among subsidiaries and their managers within MNCs are necessary conditions for effective cross-subsidiary collaborations (Martin and Eisenhardt, 2010). In short: 'Coordination (between subsidiaries) requires communication, and for that communication to be effective a network of contacts between units has to be developed' (Vahlne et al., 2011: 5).

Social capital theory (Nahapiet and Ghoshal, 1998; Tsai, 2000) extends social network theory by arguing that it is not ties as such that enable collaboration but ties characterized by common vision, common language, identification and mutual trust. It is these cognitive and relational aspects to social capital features that give rise to the exchange not only of basic information but also to the exchange and combination of locally embedded tacit knowledge.

Dimaggio and Powell (1983) emphasize the socially embedded nature of knowledge. Knowing is a social act, the tools we use for thinking and acting, the categories available to us to through which we know are the products of social action and negotiation. Thus the social institutions in which we partake frame the ways we know. In this view, expertise is a property of social groups (Hakkarainen et al., 2004). In his knowledge-based theory of the firm Spender (1996) proposed that in addition to distinguishing explicit and tacit knowledge one should distinguish individual from social knowledge (see also Chapter 7). Spender refers to knowledge that is both tacit and social as 'collective' knowledge. Spender (1996: 52) argues that in terms of organizational advantage 'it is collective knowledge (that) is the most secure and strategically significant kind of organizational knowledge'.

Collective knowledge is such that individuals can only be proficient once they are 'socialized' into the organization and 'have acquired much of the collective knowledge that underpins "the way things are done around here"' (Spender, 1996: 54). In other words knowledge acquisition and its transfer within an organization are dependent on sustained exposure to that organization's collective knowledge.

Because multidomestic MNCs comprise units that are locally responsive, a considerable proportion of knowledge development takes place locally. To the degree this knowledge is 'collective' it is not readily transferable across the MNC. In the case of a multidomestic MNC that is, for example, seeking to integrate its devolved, local approach to purchasing, it needs to facilitate the exchange and combination of subsidiary-based collective knowledge in order to develop a purchasing approach that is relevant and viable across subsidiaries.

Social capital theorists (for example Burt, 1992; Adler and Kwon, 2002; Edelman et al., 2004) have emphasized the distinction between the bonding and bridging aspects of social capital. Bonding social capital concerns the internal ties within a group which gives that group cohesiveness and facilitates the development of collective knowledge. In network terms, bonding social capital will be a feature of 'closed' networks such as the subsidiaries of multidomestic MNCs. Bridging social capital refers to the 'external', between-group, social ties of focal actors which bridge social networks. Because of the semi-autonomous status of subsidiaries in multidomestic MNCs, bridging social capital will be largely absent in such MNCs.

Thus in the context of multidomestic MNCs one should expect to find bonding social capital within the geographically bounded subsidiaries, but little bridging social capital between these locations. Indeed subsidiaries are more likely to be connected to their external within-country social networks than to other units within the MNC (Forsgren et al., 2005). A transition from the multidomestic to the global state will have to address the lack of inter-subsidiary social networks if knowledge exchange is to occur.

To summarize, extant theory posits significant barriers in making the transition from the multidomestic to the global state. On the one hand there is a political barrier that stems from the self-interest subsidiaries have been rewarded for pursuing. On the other hand there is a lack of social networks and bridging social capital that undermines the exchange of collective knowledge between subsidiaries. As we will argue, these were clearly factors in the initial unsuccessful attempt SCF made to integrate its purchasing operations. However, they do not provide any substantial insight into the success of SCF's second and successful attempt at purchasing integration.

B.3   Methodology

As stated, the setting of this case is a Scandinavian headquartered multidomestic MNC, SCF, located in the dry foods industry. In other words it is an industry where responding to local taste preferences is critical. We analyse two temporally distinct attempts by SCF to integrate the direct purchasing of its main subsidiaries; one that resulted in little change and one that resulted in significant integration. These two contrasting attempts constitute polar cases within one and the same setting which lends itself to observing emergent constructs and theoretical relationships (Martin and Eisenhardt, 2010).

Sampling within firms is also advantageous because it controls firm-level factors such as firm size, industry, product range and type and production technology.

Data

SCF's roots go back some 150 years. For most of the previous century and through until 2000 it was the corporate center of a conglomerate spanning a number of unrelated industries including asphalt production and dry foods. At that point it divested itself of all of its businesses apart from those in the dry foods industry. In addition to its Norwegian subsidiary, Voso, this left SCF with a number of fully-owned foreign-based subsidiaries that it had acquired during the 1990s. The most important of these were Pelecta (Poland) and Pitana (Czech Republic). In addition it had smaller operations in five other European countries and sales and market offices in a further six countries. In 2007 SCF owned 28 brands in 12 countries. Its workforce comprised nearly 4,000 employees of whom 1,000 were located in Norway. Of its subsidiaries, while Voso (Norway) has for many years been highly profitable, its non-Scandinavian subsidiaries units are markedly less so. In other words, like a significant proportion of other MNCs, SCF is for the most part achieving lower profitability from its operations abroad than from those in its home country (Gooderham and Nordhaug, 2003). In the specific case of SCF, differences in profitability have a number of explanations. In relation to Pelecta and Pitana, whose development was curtailed under communism, Voso has been developing its capabilities continuously since its establishment in 1933. Furthermore, while the Norwegian market Voso operates in is relatively protected from competition that is not the case for either Pelecta or Pitana, both of which operate within EU member countries. In addition the spending power of Norwegian consumers is such that private labels as opposed to branded products are a less established alternative in Norway than in the Czech Republic or Poland.

When our research began in 2007 it would be reasonable to categorize SCF as the corporate center of a multidomestic MNC. Its approach to product development across its markets was summarized as that of being 'a local taste champion'. Despite the potential savings that could be realized by concentrating production to SCF's low-cost sites in the Czech Republic and Poland only 7 and 4 per cent of Pitana's and Pelecta's production volume respectively was for inter-subsidiary customers. Purchasing, the focus of this paper, was also largely uncoordinated. For Voso alone, raw materials were supplied by 268 different suppliers,

39 of which accounted for 70 per cent of raw materials by value. For packaging for Voso the figures were 132 suppliers of which 28 covered 95 per cent of packaging needs. The situation was repeated across Pelecta and Pitana with virtually no co-ordination of purchasing between any of the subsidiaries.

SCF has made two attempts to integrate its purchasing. The first, the Unification Project, spanned 2004–2007, and is acknowledged by corporate and subsidiary managers and board members as having been largely unsuccessful. The second, the significantly more successful Program Amalgamation, commenced September 2008 and was in the main completed by March 2010.

Our primary source of data on the Unification Project was a series of interviews with managers at SCF and the main subsidiaries, Voso, Pelecta and Pitana who had been closely involved in the project. These took place as the project was drawing to a close and in its immediate aftermath (October 2007–February 2008). In regard to Program Amalgamation we conducted interviews at three stages: prior to the actual start of Program Amalgamation in September 2008 (May–August 2008), during its early stage (September 2008–mid-March 2009) and in its final phase (March 2010). In addition to managers from SCF and the three main subsidiaries we also interviewed the chair of the board of directors in April 2008. Some key managers were interviewed at more than one point in time. In particular, at each stage, we interviewed the individual who during the Unification project became the Group Purchasing Director and who during Program Amalgamation was the Project Director. Table B.1 provides an overview of our informants for both projects.

In general interviews lasted about one hour and although they revolved around the issue of purchasing integration, and addressed both the political and social network challenges, the interview guides allowed for a semi-structured approach. Interviews with Norwegian personnel were conducted in Norwegian and all other interviews in English, the official company language. With the exception of one interview all of the interviews were conducted by two researchers. In addition to detailed note taking, nearly all of the interviews were tape-recorded. A second important source of data was documentation relating to the Unification project and Program Amalgamation supplied by SCF. Finally, one of the researchers was provided with the opportunity to attend a Program Amalgamation 'launch' seminar aimed at Voso managers in September 2008 and a meeting of the SCF General Management Team (GMT) in March 2009.

Table B.1 Overview of informants

	SCF	Voso	Pelecta	Pitana
Unification Project Interviews (October 2007–February 2008)	Acting CEO 2 senior managers	2 senior managers	MD 2 managers	MD Senior manager 3 managers Group Purchasing Director
Pre-Program Amalgamation Interviews (May 2008–August 2008)	Chair of the SCF Board 3 senior managers			2 senior managers Group Purchasing Director
Early Program Amalgamation Interviews (September 2008– mid-March 2009)	CEO 3 senior managers Project Director (3 interviews)	MD Head of Category Team for Traded Goods Head of Category Team for 'Foils'	MD	MD 2 senior managers Manager
Concluding Program Amalgamation Interviews (March 2010)	CEO 5 senior managers Project Director	MD Head of Category Team for Traded Goods Head of Category Team for 'Foils'	MD 2 managers	MD Senior manager Manager

Data analysis

The case study method that we have used is well suited to the exploration of complex ongoing processes with uncertain outcomes, that is processes that therefore do not lend themselves to being studied using more theoretically pre-structured approaches (Yin, 1994). Additionally we viewed the case study approach as being well suited to an exploration of the micro-processes involved over time in purchasing integration. The method also allows the use of multiple research methods and the use of different sources of information placed at the researchers' disposal by the organization (Eisenhardt, 1989; Miles and Huberman, 1994).

Following Eisenhardt (1989) we used cross-case analysis with no a priori hypotheses. However, underling our analysis was an assumption that mechanisms underlying failed commitments inside the MNC may be best inter-preted by employing Verbeke and Greidanus' (2009) envelope concept of 'bounded reliability'. 'Bounded reliability as a concept includes two main components within the context of MNC management: opportunism as intentional deceit, and benevolent preference reversal' (Verbeke and Greidanus, 2009: 471). Benevolent preference reversal as a bound on reli-ability as opposed to opportunism has its roots in an analysis conducted by Verbeke and Greidanus of failed commitments in global MNCs. They found that a substantial proportion involved managers having made *ex ante* commitments in good faith (with benevolent intent), but the importance of these had diminished over time (preferences were reordered).

The primary focus is to isolate those features that were present in the suc-cessful case of Program Amalgamation, but not present in the unsuccessful Unification project.

B.4 The unification project (2004–2007)

In addition to their own brands, and their own product development and marketing specialists, in 2004 Voso, Pitana and Pelecta all had their own pur-chasing specialists. Given strong price growth in agricultural commodities worldwide, SCF decided that the lack of inter-subsidiary synergies was an issue, particularly in regard to purchasing, that could no longer be ignored. Under the so-called 'Unification Project', during 2004–2007, a number of activities were implemented in order to take out purchasing synergies across subsidiaries. The approach was to harmonize raw material specifica-tion across subsidiaries and then for each category to allocate a central lead buyer with responsibility for sourcing across subsidiaries. For the most part these individuals were Norwegians located at Voso. In addition the posi-tion of Group Purchasing Director was established whose task was to coor-dinate between the purchasing departments in the respective subsidiaries. This position was allocated to a senior Pitana manager. To support these initiatives a number of supporting measures were undertaken: the enterprise resource planning (ERP) system, SAP, was introduced; inter-subsidiary networks for marketing and sales managers were formed; a common set of performance appraisal principles were introduced; annual two day strategy meetings for subsidiary heads were organized.

A feature of the Unification project was that no subsidiary was to be obliged to go against its business judgment and use the central lead-buyers. In other words each subsidiary had the latitude to decide the degree to which it was in their interest to employ the services of the central lead-buyers. At its launch at a gathering of subsidiary managers the project and its core idea of using central lead-buyers was generally greeted positively. However, despite this initial reaction by the end of the project the subsidiaries had on the whole opted to continue to use local buyers. As a manager with product development engineering responsibilities at Pitana observed, because product development continued to be done locally, it was generally the case that she and others at Pitana decided that it was more efficient to use the local buyer rather than the central lead-buyer. Not only were the communication opportunities significantly greater but mutual understanding was already established. According to another manager at Pitana with purchasing responsibilities an important aspect to this mutual understanding was that local purchasers were significantly more cost conscious than central lead-buyers based at Voso in affluent Norway.

This lack of confidence or trust on the part of Pitana managers in the central lead-buyers based at Voso was experienced in reverse by one of the few central lead-buyers located outside of Voso. Based at Pitana, his perception was that the view of managers at Voso was that 'anything that originated from the Czech Republic was by definition sub-standard'. As the Unification project concluded, his experience was that rather than consulting with him 'Voso managers would simply buy what they wanted behind my back'. However, as he himself recognized, this deficiency in trust was not just a matter of chauvinism. He acknowledged that one of the difficulties central lead-buyers experienced was their lack of deep understanding of the end-products of the other subsidiaries. He recalled that in regard to one relatively large order for an ingredient he had placed on behalf of several subsidiaries Voso rejected it for what he came to accept were substantially objective reasons. The particular ingredient would have resulted in a taste that Norwegian consumers would have rejected. As a senior manager at SCF with long-term experience of purchasing for Voso emphasized, 'the challenge for a purchaser is to get the precise quality needs of the subsidiary right. Otherwise the brand suffers.' Furthermore, getting the quality right depends not only on understanding the needs of the subsidiary but also on communicating these to suppliers. His experience was that getting the supplier relationship to work could take as much as two years of steady interaction (see, for example, Johanson and Vahlne, 2009).

The deficiency in trust across the group in the central lead-buyers evolved into skepticism of the Unification project. By the end of the project this was understood not least by the Group Purchasing Director. A Czech national and based at Pitana, he felt that the general attitude at Voso was that his position would eventually 'evaporate'. When it became clear that the position was actually going to be permanent his Voso colleagues simply 'pretended to cooperate'. He experienced that it was significantly easier for him to gain respect and a measure of cooperation from the other subsidiaries such as Pelecta.

As the Unification project came to an end, the view of managers at SCF was that the managing directors (MDs) of the various subsidiaries had failed to identify with its potential. One senior SCF manager stated that in the early phase of the project she and colleagues had calculated that savings from an integrated, group-wide approach to purchasing could have been in the order of NOK 280 million. However, in her view the subsidiary MDs failed to accord this group-level analysis any serious attention. She ascribed this in part to their lack of integration in the Unification project and in part to their remuneration being exclusively calculated on the basis of their local performance rather than on the basis of group-level performance. Like others she acknowledged that by the end of the project the old local purchasing mentality had reasserted itself and that the Unification project had achieved relatively little.

The view from the subsidiaries was similar. The Pitana-based Group Purchasing Director viewed the Unification Project as having been a 'great idea' but 'old habits had quickly largely reasserted themselves'. Likewise the MD of Pelecta concluded that a unified group mentality across SCF remained underdeveloped and that the process of integration had barely begun. In his view one significant barrier had been the lack of willingness on the part of Voso to concede any significant purchasing responsibilities to the non-Norwegian operations. However, as he somewhat lightheartedly remarked, had Pelecta been as profitable as Voso he 'would not have voluntarily sacrificed anything for the greater good of the whole group'.

In short, after a flurry of top-down initiated activities SCF's group of subsidiaries still constituted very much a multidomestic MNC with not only predominantly locally evolved products and local production but also mostly local purchasing. The view that the Unification project had been largely unsuccessful was one that was shared not least by the SCF board. As a consequence towards the end of 2007 it instructed SCF's CEO to leave the company.

In terms of the extant theory we have presented the inability of SCF to move its approach to purchasing from a multidomestic to a global state was arguably hardly unexpected. Indeed it would be reasonable to contend that SCF's experience with its Unification project constitutes an almost perfect illustration of the existing theory. In line with agency theory we observed that the corporate center, SCF, was confronted by a fiefdom mentality. Given the critical importance of meeting local taste, SCF's approach was to accept that the subsidiaries should continue to determine which aspects of purchasing could be viably integrated. Likewise it did not attempt to change the locally-focused remuneration system. In line with resource dependency theory Voso, the most powerful subsidiary, dominated the central lead-buyer functions and undermined initiatives fronted by non-Voso employees. To the extent there was inter-subsidiary cooperation this was between the non-Voso subsidiaries. Finally, in line with social network theory we observed the lack of inter-subsidiary social networks. Perceived as being too deeply embedded in their own respective subsidiaries and their particular notions of 'local taste', the central lead-buyers failed to develop the degree of bridging social capital that would have facilitated critical knowledge exchange.

It should be noted, though, that the outcome of the Unification project cannot readily be reduced to opportunism as intentional deceit (Williamson, 1985) from the outset. On the contrary our informants insisted that at the outset the subsidiaries had been encouraging about their willingness to engage with the project. Instead what we have observed is what Verbeke and Greidanus (2009: 1482) refer to as 'benevolent preference reversal associated with reprioritization'. That is subsidiary managers had made *ex ante* commitments to the Unification project in good faith. However, that commitment diminished over time in the face of pressure to focus on proximate events and as the costs of that commitment emerged. Thus subsidiary priorities were reinstated at the expense of corporate center priorities.

B.5   Post-unification project

The SCF board decided to engage in a second and, what it signaled, would be a final attempt at achieving group-wide purchasing integration. As a first step it initiated a purchasing and supply management (PSM) analysis conducted by external consultants from McKinsey. The PSM analysis benchmarked the group's overall PSM performance against other companies in the same industry. The McKinsey analysis concluded that purchasing represented an unexploited cost savings potential of NOK 300 million. Two thirds of this derived from direct purchasing (raw materials and packaging materials) and one third from indirect purchasing/operating (for example travel costs and office cleaning costs). This figure was almost identical to the calculation by corporate headquarters we referred to above.

On the basis of the McKinsey analysis the board and the interim CEO took the decision to launch Program Amalgamation starting early September 2008, some two weeks before the new CEO was due to start. The core aim of

Program Amalgamation was to integrate direct purchasing across the group. This would mean transforming the highly decentralized structure of the group. At the same time, the board reiterated the need for each subsidiary to be its respective country's 'local taste champion'.

Whereas the Unification project had been loosely structured the board was determined that Program Amalgamation should have a clear structure from the outset. A working group comprising the Group Purchasing Director, who moved from Pitana to SCF, a Voso manager and a SCF corporate manager was formed to prepare the ground for Program Amalgamation. Building on the work of the Unification project the working group divided purchasing into 50 categories. It was then determined that the purchasing project should comprise four waves with each wave accounting for 25 per cent of the total savings and roughly 25 per cent of the categories. The plan was that the project was to be completed by early 2010. Each purchasing category was to be assigned a team by the Program Amalgamation project organization which also had the responsibility for monitoring the progress of the category teams and reporting its findings to SCF corporate management. Each category team was to comprise about five category experts who would also have access to advice from an external purchasing consultancy. It was understood that the release of these experts by the subsidiaries would have to be based on cooperation between the Program Amalgamation project organization and the subsidiaries. In terms of the category teams, we collected our data within the Flexible Foils and the Traded Goods teams.

The category teams were charged with defining the group-wide needs within each category and signing new group-wide contracts with new suppliers. Even before Program Amalgamation commenced the Voso member of the working group was deeply concerned that the category teams might fail to acquire sufficient understanding of the products for which they would be purchasing. His particular concern was that the precise quality needs of the Voso brand might be compromised. As Program Amalgamation got under way in September 2008 under the leadership of the Project Director (formerly the Group Purchasing Director) our research was to indicate that this skepticism was widespread across the group.

B.6 Program amalgamation (2008–2010)

Initial reactions

One month after the launch of Program Amalgamation, the Project Director was concerned that the MDs of Voso, Pelecta and Pitana viewed

Program Amalgamation as a top-down operation driven by a McKinsey analysis that was insufficiently anchored in the realities of their businesses. His impression was that 'things are moving too fast' for the subsidiaries and that there was a lack of common vision and trust in the project. He speculated that this would explain why subsidiary MDs had, in his view, resisted releasing their most qualified personnel to serve in the category teams. Instead of being composed of the 'best people' for the job, the Project Director characterized their nominees as being no more than 'somewhat above average'. He referred to one subsidiary MD as having said that 'my best sales people should sell', and to another MD who had labeled the travel costs of his single employee thus far involved in Program Amalgamation as a 'punishment'.

The Project Director had also observed that the category team members themselves had their concerns. He thought that they were anxious that while they were involved in Program Amalgamation their stand-ins either might harm the day-to-day business or, alternatively, might replace them on a permanent basis. Finally, he had no illusions about his own standing remarking that: 'Some don't see me as a sufficiently strong guarantor. If he's fired – well, life goes on.'

At highly profitable Voso the view was that the McKinsey analysis was correct. However, skepticism was also voiced by its MD who commented that '[o]ur attitude to the issue of quality is a different to that of Eastern Europe'. He pointed out that nearly 70 per cent of the (Norwegian) customer complaints Voso receives involve products emanating from Pitana, although Pitana accounts for no more than 10 per cent of the products Voso delivers to the Norwegian market. Likewise, attempts to get Pelecta to produce cake mixes on behalf of Voso had always been undermined by quality problems whose causes were impossible to determine. 'Therefore' he commented, 'we are skeptical as to "their" ability to deliver quality over time' and (given Voso's long-term quality criticisms) '"they" are browned-off with "us"'.

At Pelecta the MD recalled that in the course of his six years tenure he had seen a number of company-wide projects aimed at greater integration. However, he remarked that 'few of these had been successful in the sense that they had delivered lasting, tangible, results'. They had been characterized by a lack of consistency and continuity. While he supported greater integration because it could ultimately lead to the greater use of Pelecta's production capacity, his immediate reaction to Program Amalgamation was that it might prove to be 'just another time consuming project'.

At Pitana the initial reaction of the MD to Program Amalgamation was even more skeptical. It was 'yet another so-called "improvement"' and one that could threaten Pitana's limited resources in a period of substantial improvement because of improved cost control and increased product focus. In short the Pitana MD was concerned that Program Amalgamation would distract critical personnel from their pressing Pitana responsibilities. He viewed the hazard posed by the demands inherent in Program Amalgamation as relatively much greater for Pitana than Voso because the latter had significantly more 'slack'. In other words potential sub-optimality was not evenly distributed across SCF.

At this point in time, in line with overall extant theory, Program Amalgamation appeared to be another unsuccessful attempt to move from the multidomestic to the global stance.

Concluding reactions

In March 2010 our findings indicated that the initial misgivings to Program Amalgamation had largely evaporated. The Project Director viewed Program Amalgamation as having delivered on its targets and as having been perceived as having done so by the subsidiary MDs. Not only had the category teams worked well together but they had 'created a lot of knowledge'. Furthermore, although Voso employees had constituted the largest contingent of category team members in his opinion they had not been perceived by the other subsidiaries as having dominated the work of the category teams. Our other interviews confirmed that the view of the Project Director was shared by of all of the senior management team at SCF, including the CEO, and the subsidiary MDs. In the words of a senior manager at SCF 'this good result had resulted in a good feeling around the whole of the company'. Furthermore, subsidiary MDs were actively discussing the development of products based on common platforms. A further measure of the success of Program Amalgamation was the assertion by another senior manager at SCF was that purchasing had moved from being a marginal function to 'being in the driving seat'.

One senior SCF manager had two caveats to the success of Program Amalgamation. First, he pointed out that there is a time lag before one would see all of the tangible profit and loss (P&L) effects. Not only does it take time to get contracts signed, but old stocks have to be disposed of, inattentive employees continue to order the old materials, and suppliers who are being phased out may renege on current contracts in terms of, for example, lower quality. Second, he had registered that SCF's competitors had in the meantime also improved their purchasing strategies. However, he also observed that Program Amalgamation had been so successful that McKinsey regarded it as an exemplar of 'how things should be done'. Indeed during the latter part of 2010 and early 2011, as the tangible P&L effects were fully realized and communicated to the markets, there was a substantial increase in the value of SCF stock.

B.7   The distinctive elements of program amalgamation

The contrast between the respective outcomes of Program Amalgamation and the Unification project is considerable. There also is a pronounced contrast between the initial reactions to Program Amalgamation and the concluding reactions to it. Our research question is how do managers create the conditions for a successful transition from the multidomestic to the global state? By identifying those elements that were introduced to Program Amalgamation and that were not features of the Unification project we develop an emergent theoretical framework.

Governance reconfiguration: the general management team

When SCF's CEO joined the company in late September 2008 he was acutely conscious that the implementation of Program Amalgamation was to be his key responsibility. Reflecting on the significance of Program Amalgamation at the start of his tenure his view was that it was a highly critical 'journey' for SCF's long-term success. For him the challenge was to get managers to develop a 'dualistic' view of their roles. On the one hand they were to have a focus on the needs of their local markets, while on the other hand they were to have an equally strong commitment to the need for the integration of purchasing.

His first action in this 'journey' was during early October 2008 to conduct one-to-one meetings with each of the MDs of the main subsidiaries. He explicitly requested that they act on behalf of the whole business rather than their own subsidiaries. Late October 2008 he presented a two-page memo to subsidiary MDs, 'From a food conglomerate to an integrated food company'. This outlined a radical shift in the structure of the company. In it the new CEO stated that 'the history of SCF has been that of a conglomerate in which the performance of subsidiaries had been discretely measured with cooperation between subsidiaries . . . relatively voluntary. In 2009 we must take the step from a food conglomerate to an integrated food company to improve performance and efficiency.'

However, a much more substantial action by the new CEO was his decision to form an entirely new GMT which, in addition to himself, the CFO, the head of human resources, the director of marketing and sales, and the new supply chain director included the MDs of the main subsidiaries. For the first time in the history of SCF subsidiary managers were now integrated in the corporate center. From December 2008 the GMT held monthly meetings in different locations supplemented by telephone conferences half way through each month. At each and every GMT meeting the Project Director of Program Amalgamation reported on the progress of the project including any personnel issues that had arisen in the wake of manning the category teams.

At its outset the new GMT was a brittle entity. One senior manager at SCF recounted that there was a lack of understanding on how to cooperate in order to function as an effective top management team. She described the CEO's use of a variety of informal methods to develop the way in which GMT members interacted. The policy of the CEO was that critical views could be expressed at GMT meetings but once decisions had been taken those decisions should command collective loyalty. Another senior manager at SCF had a somewhat different recollection of the initial GMT phase. He recalled 'innumerable meetings' with the CEO 'hammering home Program Amalgamation'. Unlike under the Unification project it was now no longer the case that subsidiaries could use their local needs as 'an excuse for inaction'. Such was the pressure from the CEO that those who opposed Program Amalgamation thought 'it wise to keep their skepticism to themselves'. Indeed as our 'Early Program Amalgamation Interviews' indicated that is precisely what the subsidiary MDs did. Nevertheless, according to this manager, the GMT, even in its initial phase, provided a powerful mandate for Program Amalgamation. He argued 'that none of the achievements of Program Amalgamation would have been possible without this powerful mandate coming not just from the CEO but also from the collective voice of the GMT'.

Overall what we observe at SCF is governance reconfiguration. The fiefdom mentality of the subsidiary MDs is not only challenged but the MDs are incorporated in a new group-wide governance mechanism. GMT meetings are an arena for exchanging views, for developing a common vision of the group and for reaching common binding decisions.

Realignment of rewards

Coupled to the new GMT was a fresh approach to MD compensation. Whereas the former system had been primarily local in its orientation, rewarding subsidiary MDs on the basis of their unit's performance, the new CEO introduced a new rewards system that to a significant extent rewarded the subsidiary MDs on the basis of overall group performance. Thus as the new GMT set to work on making Program Amalgamation operational, for the subsidiary MDs this coincided with the introduction of a rewards package whose primary element reflected overall group performance. There would still be an element that reflected subsidiary performance, but for the first time in SCF's history group performance as a metric was not just a metric, but the most significant metric.

Rolling measures of outcomes

A transition to a new centralized and integrated purchasing process challenges the local view of subsidiary MDs. As the 'Early Program Amalgamation Interviews' indicated, the adoption of an integrated approach to purchasing was initially viewed by MDs with some doubt. Part of the design of Program Amalgamation comprised the regular monitoring by a controller of each category team in order to objectively identify tangible savings. Thereafter these unambiguous outcomes were immediately communicated to the GMT by the Project Director.

The communication of 'early wins' (that is immediate substantial savings) to the GMT not only persuaded subsidiary MDs that Program Amalgamation was working but it even generated a conviction that further integration was both possible and desirable. Thus, by the end of Program Amalgamation, with profitability improving for the group as well as the subsidiaries as a consequence of the realized savings, the GMT had embarked on a discussion on how to develop 'common platforms' for products that could span several countries. The initial skepticism to Program Amalgamation was converted into a belief in it and a greater commitment to making it work. The issue of which nationality dominated the category teams was transformed into a discussion of which individuals were most competent to lead and serve in them.

Of course one may ask what the outcome would have been if 'early' tangible savings had not been achieved. However, that does not invalidate the importance of directly and almost instantly communicating credible results to the GMT and not least to its subsidiary MD members. Nor does it invalidate the significance of Program Amalgamation focusing on those aspects of purchasing integration that were readily measurable. In other words measurability precedes actual measuring.

Mandated category teams

In our analysis of those elements that were features of the successful Program Amalgamation, and not a feature of the unsuccessful Unification project, we have thus far focused on elements that directly impacted on the subsidiary MDs. We now turn to the core operational element of Program Amalgamation, the category teams.

In terms of the overall task of the category teams, this was very similar to the task assigned to the central lead-buyers of the Unification project. It was to define the group-wide needs within each purchasing category and then to sign new contracts with suppliers on behalf of the group. However, in operational terms there were profound differences. The SCF approach to the operational integration of purchasing in the Unification Project was to appoint central lead-buyers for the various purchasing categories and to provide them with authorization to invite cooperation from the purchasing managers based in the various subsidiaries. The approach of Program Amalgamation to developing category teams was not to devolve the responsibility for forming them but to centralize it. Category teams were formed at the outset of each phase of Program Amalgamation with designated team members covering a variety of relevant competencies including production, product development, logistics and marketing. Furthermore, unlike the Unification project where central lead-buyers remained in their regular purchasing roles, category team leaders were designated on a full-time basis while the team members were to spend an average of 60 percent of their working week on category team-related activities.

Initially both category team leaders and their members were appointed by the Project Director on the basis of nominations from the subsidiaries. The Project Director was not pleased with the outcome of this approach. As we have noted above, in his view cost-conscious subsidiary MDs were not only trying to limit the number of nominees they forwarded, but more significantly they were resisting nominating their most qualified personnel for category team service. However, after the formation of the new GMT which included subsidiary MDs, both the nomination process and the category team appointments became subject to GMT scrutiny and monitoring. This scrutiny and monitoring effectively constituted a mandating and therefore legitimatization of the category teams by the GMT. Furthermore, the scrutiny and monitoring was also immediately applied to the category teams that had been formed shortly prior to the formation of the new GMT. As Program Amalgamation concluded, the view of the Project Director was that the members of the category teams had been more than sufficiently qualified for their tasks. This was a view that was endorsed by a Pelecta manager who had herself participated in a category team. Finally, as the Voso MD pointed out, the boundaries of the category teams had in effect been buffered by the GMT against disruptive, competing tasks thereby 'enabling its members to work outside of their normal functions and to work across both functions and geographies'. Effectively the subsidiary MDs of the GMT had acted as 'sentries and guards' (Yan and Louis, 1999: 31).

Inter-subsidiary category teams

We have indicated that social network theory points to two salient features of multidomestic MNCs. First, because they comprise business units that have to be responsive to local taste, product, and therefore purchasing, knowledge is both geographically distributed and locally embedded. Particularly that proportion of knowledge that is 'collective' – that is knowledge that is both tacit and held by groups rather than individuals – is problematic to transfer across the MNC. Second, because of the lack of bridging ties there is little in the way of social capital between subsidiaries.

In terms of the first of these features, as we have observed, the Unification project was spearheaded by central lead-buyers who for the most part were Norwegians located at Voso. The view of non-Voso colleagues was that they failed to understand their idiosyncratic local needs. Equally in relation to colleagues at Voso the central lead-buyer located at Pitana fared no better. The approach to Program Amalgamation was very different to that of the Unification project in that it aimed to form inter-subsidiary category teams. In so doing Program Amalgamation created arenas for the exchange and sharing of locally embedded knowledge. On the whole, according to the Project Director, these arenas worked well and resulted in 'a lot of knowledge' being created. A Pelecta manager referred to the category team she had belonged to as having consisted of 'a great mix of people'. The Voso MD also commented on the inter-subsidiary character of the category teams observing that 'the Norwegians (at Voso) had their fixation with quality questioned by the Czechs (at Pitana) and the Czechs (at Pitana) their focus on costs'. He further remarked that this had led 'to a much greater understanding of one another's thinking'.

Bridging category teams

In relation to the second salient feature of multidomestic MNCs underscored by social network theory, the lack of bridging ties, the category teams of Program Amalgamation were specifically instructed to interact not just with suppliers but with local stakeholders across the group. Furthermore, their success in doing this was monitored by the Project Director and the GMT. By contrast bridging ties were not an explicit priority of the Unification project.

The Voso senior manager in charge of the Traded Goods category team recounted that her team had consistently involved local purchasers drawing on their knowledge particularly in regard to extant suppliers. This shared understanding created a 'buy-in' and also a sense of common achievement when improved contracts with suppliers were achieved. Networks across the subsidiaries were developed that could be drawn on in the future. One of the Pitana managers that had had extensive dealings with the Traded Goods team concurred with this analysis. She added that as a result of the interaction both her purchasing competence and her inter-subsidiary contacts had increased significantly.

The Flexible Foils category team told a similar story. The Voso senior manager who led this team observed that in developing its new purchasing competencies the team had not only developed a strong internal network, but also a network across the company. A Pelecta manager who was member of this team observed that when the team started its work 'not everybody was aware of what was going on and nobody really strongly believed in it'. The 'just-another-project syndrome' ruled. However, at the conclusion of Program Amalgamation she now observed a marked change of attitude and 'quite a high level of trust' in Program Amalgamation. She ascribed this change to the extensive use the category team made of stakeholders and specialists across the company. In all more than 20 people from product development, marketing, technical support, production and maintenance as well as controllers had been involved. It was not just a matter of consulting with these individuals but also 'lots of knowledge sharing'. She described the networking undertaken by the team as 'priceless', and emphasized the value of the interpersonal relations and the shared understanding that had been developed. She summed up her experience as '[i]f you know people you can fix it' and referred to several 'fantastic experiences where new knowledge and insight had been created because the right people were in the right place at the right time'.

On the whole her account was validated by a senior manager at SCF who was also a member of the GMT and therefore had monitored the progress of the Flexible Foils category team. He remarked that these 'success stories' had functioned as 'change ambassadors' across the company. More substantially he argued that by interacting with internal stakeholders across the subsidiaries, new purchasing knowledge was generated that enabled the category teams to favorably re-negotiate with suppliers. Indeed the savings were the double of the original aim. Likewise, he thought, the Traded Goods category team had also done 'an unbelievably good job'.

B.8 Discussion

We have argued that for multidomestic MNCs attempting to make the transition from the multidomestic to the global state, extant theories indicate two fundamental challenges: a political and a social network challenge. So significant are these two challenges that achieving transition is a case of 'easier said than done'. In industries where 'local taste' continues to matter, integration is subject to limitations. A significant degree of purchasing integration may be achieved, but the integration of product development is considerably more problematic. However, even in the case of purchasing integration, the experience of SCF in conjunction with its unsuccessful Unification project provides a potent illustration of the difficulty in surmounting the political and social network challenges. The aim of this case has been to add to extant theory by observing the design elements that featured in the contrastingly highly successful case of Program Amalgamation. Naturally only further research can determine the degree to which these have general validity or to which they have to be supplemented.

Our propositions involve necessary rather than sufficient conditions for a transition from the multidomestic to the global state, and as such they do not constitute a guarantee of successful transition. Indeed, given particular contingencies failure is entirely possible. These contingencies may include a lack of critical skills on the part of key managers or unfavorable market conditions. In particular one may wonder what would have happened to Program Amalgamation if the data from the early rolling measures had been negative. However, unlike extant theories, which in many regards are negative, this case is attempting to identify lessons that can shape and guide the deliberate actions of managers for the creation of a favorable context for transition.

Comparing and contrasting two initiatives to achieve purchasing integration within the same company at two different points in time is an approach that has its limitations in that both the company and its context are evolving. In the case of SCF, one obvious difference in 2008 when it launched Program Amalgamation was that the corporate center and the subsidiaries had significantly more knowledge of one another than they had had in 2004 at the launch of the Unification Project. Not all of this knowledge could be construed as constructive or positive. Indeed in the wake of the failure of the Unification Project there was considerable mutual skepticism across the subsidiaries borne out by the Pelecta MD's misgiving that Program Amalgamation appeared to be 'just another time consuming project'. In other words the likelihood of Program Amalgamation eliciting a response of 'benevolent preference' (Verbeke and Greidanus, 2009) was significantly lower than had been the case for the Unification project. Indeed, as we observed, as Program Amalgamation got under way the Project Director was concerned that the attitude of the subsidiary MDs to manning the category teams indicated resistance or what Williamson (1985: 47) refers to as 'calculated efforts to mislead'.

However, there were other differences. As we observed, in 2008 the SCF corporate board communicated a much greater sense of urgency to its subsidiaries than was the case in 2004. This had its roots in the benchmarking exercise conducted by McKinsey that revealed the extent of purchasing integration undertaken by competitors. Another difference was the amount of resources the board was prepared to commit to Program Amalgamation. By 2008 the board had understood how time consuming and costly purchasing integration in the context of a multidomestic is.

Finally we would add a footnote on how SCF might be categorized in the wake of Program Amalgamation and how it might develop. A narrow focus on the integration of direct purchasing would suggest that SCF has moved from the multidomestic to the global state. However, in other important regards such as production, marketing and product development, as well as indirect purchasing, SCF undeniably remains a multidomestic. Thus, as we completed our research, SCF was moving to a distinctly hybrid form. In terms of its future development it is worth bearing in mind Vahlne et al.'s (2011: 4) perspective on the globalization of internationalizing firms in general:

> we do not believe that (MNCs) can come up with the 'optimal solution' to issues of configuration and coordination rapidly. (They) must deal with an array of practical constraints, and inertia too . . . . All of this is exacerbated by the simple fact that human beings can only deal with a certain number of things at a time. For all these reasons we expect that the globalization process . . . is characterized by a series of incremental adjustments, with the most obvious and performance impacting changes handled early in the process.

We would argue that this is significantly more the case in regard to multidomestic MNCs which are operating under the constraint of having to satisfy local taste. In other words we should expect that SCF will retain a hybrid form for some extended period of time.

DISCUSSION QUESTIONS

1 What are the pitfalls in making a transition from the multidomestic to a more globally integrated state?

2 What steps need to be followed to ensure the successful transition from the multidomestic to a more globally integrated state?

NOTE

1 A version of this case has been published as: Gooderham, P.N. (2012). The transition from a multidomestic enterprise in an industry where local taste matters. *European Journal of International Management*, 6(2), 175–198.

4

Risk management

4.1   Introduction

The objective of this chapter is to discuss common internal and external risks that multinational companies are facing. Specific emphasis will be placed on how risk can impact strategic decisions. After reading this chapter, students should be able to (1) identify potential internal and external risks; (2) discuss how these risks impact the overall attractiveness of international opportunities; and (3) consider managerial complexities arising from the identified risks.

4.2   What do we mean by risk?

Most of us use the word risk in a variety of contexts without providing a clear definition. Since there are many different forms of risk, clarifying the specific types of risks to consider will improve strategic decision making. Kallman suggests that we build on the objective and simple definition from finance and statistics to ensure a common understanding of risk, which states that 'risk is the variation from the expected outcome over time' (2005: 57). In other words, the concept of risk incorporates both opportunities and costs. Although we often focus on the potential costs in terms of how to mitigate risk or reduce our risk exposure in management contexts, we also need to keep in mind that there are upsides related to risk that create business opportunities. Limiting a firm's exposure to risks thus consequently also limits its exposure to potential opportunities.

4.3   Why focus on risk in MNCs?

In an ideal world, managers would make rational decisions based on full information and certainty. Dominant MNC theory, however, relies on the fundamental assumptions that all decision makers are affected by an inherent bounded rationality. MNC managers can therefore never assume to have, or be able to process, all available information when making a decision. Internal and external dynamics also create uncertainty in strategic decision

Table 4.1 Levels of foreign direct investment (FDI)

In million USD	Inward FDI (stock)			Outward FDI (stock)		
Country:	1990	2000	2009	1990	2000	2009
Brazil	37,143	122,250	400,808	41,044	51,946	157,667
Canada	112,843	212,716	524,938	84,807	237,639	566,875
China (excl. Hong Kong)	20,691	193,348	473,083	4,455	27,768	229,600
France	97,814	390,953	1,132,961	112,441	925,925	1,719,696
Germany	111,231	271,613	701,643*	151,581	541,866	1,378,480*
India	1,657	16,339	163,959	124	1,733	77,207
Italy	59,998	121,170	393,990	60,184	180,275	578,123
Japan	9,850	50,322	200,141	201,441	278,442	740,930
Russia	–	32,204	252,456*	–	20,141	248,894*
UK	203,905	438,631	1,125,066	229,307	897,845	1,651,727
US	539,601	2,783,235	3,120,583	731,762	2,694,014	4,302,851
EU	761,851	2,322,127	7,447,904	810,472	3,492,879	9,006,575
Developing Economies	524,526	1,728,455	4,893,490	145,172	862,628	2,691,484
World	2,081,782	7,442,548	17,743,408	2,086,818	7,967,460	18,982,118

Note: * = estimates.

Source: UNCTAD *World Investment Report 2010*.

making. While all firms are exposed to some form of risk, cross-border activities generate 'new' and different risks such as exposure to fluctuating exchange rates or changes in regulations and economic conditions that are not aligned across borders. The salience of risk management in multinationals is amplified by the increasing levels of foreign direct investment (FDI). Table 4.1 shows the development of FDI for some of the world's largest economies (G8), the emerging BRIC economies as well as total figures for the EU, developing countries and world. As the figures suggest, both inward and outward FDI has grown significantly over the past decades.[1]

According to recent World Investment Reports (UNCTAD, 2010, 2011), global trends suggest further liberalization of policies that facilitate foreign investments. As markets deregulate and multinationals increasingly globalize their value chains, MNCs must improve their ability to effectively manage risks. Cross-border activities are not limited to FDI. The use of non-equity modes such as outsourcing to lower cost countries also expose MNCs to 'new' and different risks. In their widely recognized article on offshoring, Aron and Singh (2005) suggest that most MNCs focus on simple cost–

benefit analysis when deciding to offshore, while neglecting to take relevant risks into account.

As discussed in Chapter 1, firms engaging in international business must inherently address various forms of distances (categorized by Ghemawat (2001) into cultural, administrative, geographic and economic distances). These distances create both valuable opportunities for businesses but also expose MNCs to unwanted costs and challenges when engaging in cross-border business. Distances and the related risks may be reduced at a geo-political level through trade agreements that tie national governments together and regional integration schemes (such as the EU, NAFTA or ASEAN) that increase intra-regional trade. This creates both opportunities for firms operating across borders and reduces unexpected costs.

Most MNCs attempt to act on opportunities while trying to quantify poten-tial costs. Unfortunately, many concepts and frameworks in international management oversimplify risk or overemphasize one specific type of risk. Easily identified and quantifiable economic risks are frequently addressed such as exchange rates, inflation and growth, while there is a tendency to underestimate more subjective sources of risk that are difficult to assess and quantify, such as political instability.

Identifying and assessing relevant risks does not imply, however, that all risk should be avoided. MNCs may actually have internal advantages that may make them more capable of taking on certain risks than other market actors. MNCs should therefore continuously consider which risks are better dealt with internally, that is, determine their risk appetite. By ignoring active risk manage-ment, multinationals may either overexpose themselves to risk or become too risk averse. Becoming very risk averse will mitigate unwanted negative conse-quences of risk exposure, but it can also limit the firm's ability to realize full value creation and lead to unnecessary high costs of capital (Buehler et al., 2008).

The type, magnitude and impact of risks will vary across geographical loca-tions, industries and firms. Some multinationals, such as oil and gas compa-nies, have extensive experience from operating in high-risk environments and often establish separate organizational units with dedicated professionals assessing and managing risks with systematic analyses and top-management focus. Others find themselves in reactive crises management after failing to recognize and address their risk exposure.

In the remainder of this chapter, we will identify some of the most common risks facing multinationals and discuss why these are important to focus on and how they impact perceived opportunities and firm strategies. The chapter will not provide an exhaustive list of all potential risks, as this would warrant an entire book in itself. Rather, the overview is intended to provide an initial tool to identify potential risks and facilitate the discussion of the importance and impact of risk management in multinationals.

4.4   Types of risk that affect MNCs

In general, MNCs assess the overall attractiveness of a location by determining the risks involved in tapping into the location advantages in a particular geographical location. Risks are not mutually exclusive and often interrelate and influence each other. We have summarized a number of risks commonly faced by MNCs below.

Country risk

The term country risk encompasses several external risks such as political, institutional/legal, economic, and social factors associated with a specific location. While specific risks will be discussed separately in greater detail below, the benefits of assessing aggregate country risks warrant some attention. Risk factors in a particular location can directly influence and amplify other types of risk. Country-based risk analyses combine the various elements of risk into an aggregate assessment where their interdependencies are more clearly recognized. A thorough country analysis should not only identify the occurrence and impact of events, but also consider the antecedents (such as the interrelationship between various economic and political factors) and the country leaderships' ability to manage them.

Country risk assessments were initially developed for the financial sector to monitor the creditworthiness of nations, but its use has since expanded to MNCs comparing the attractiveness of business opportunities across geographical locations (Di Gregorio, 2005). Some MNCs have internal expertise to assess country risks. One of the main benefits of internal expertise is the ability to view risk factors from an enterprise specific perspective (Al Khattab, 2011). There are also numerous professional rating agencies that develop periodic detailed country reports such as the Economist Intelligence Unit (EIU) and the Political Risk Services (PRS) Group.

Country risk assessments are often central to MNCs' investment decisions, and are typically operationalized in the form of adjustment in the required rate of return (Di Gregorio, 2005). There is an ongoing debate, however, as to the applicability of using traditional country risk analyses. Drawing on entrepreneurial theory, Di Gregorio (2005) argues that firms may miss entrepreneurial opportunities by relying on established country risk analyses because the established methodologies fail to measure the predictability of the environment. Concern has also been voiced that traditional measures of country risk may fall short in emerging markets due to their rapid changes and significant institutional voids (Khanna et al., 2005; Witold and Bennet, 2010).

Economic risk

Economic risks arise when economic changes in the host country impact a firm's finances, competitiveness, or goals. Engaging in cross-border interactions often immediately expose firms to economic risks such as currency fluctuations. Most of us have experienced effects of exchange rates when travelling or comparing the price of the same products across countries. While most individuals are able to absorb the currency fluctuations affecting single events or purchases, the impact on firms with significant international activity can be critical. Firms that do not actively address exposure to currency fluctuations may experience unanticipated effects on sales, profits and their overall financial strength. Simply stated, when receivables and payables consist of different currencies, firms are exposed to exchange rate risks. Similarly, currency fluctuations may affect the attractiveness of goods that are produced in one location and sold in another location. Most firms are now quite skilled in assessing their exposure to currency fluctuations and have the option of externalizing such risks through financial hedging tools readily available in the market, or use product and geographical diversification to obtain natural hedging internally in the multinational. Currency fluctuations are one of the most quantifiable risks where MNC can access and utilize hedging tools that enable them to predict currency impacts by engaging in long-term contracts for receivables and payables.

Common economic distances between the home and host countries also include differences in the economic robustness and growth of foreign markets, income distribution, purchasing power, and the cost of access to resources (for example financial, human or natural resources). High inflation and reduced purchasing power can make products less attractive in a foreign market. Similarly, offshoring decisions can become less lucrative if labor costs increase in locations that were previously attractive due to lower cost labor.

While economic risks are often quantifiable, they can also directly influence and amplify other types of risk. Economic downturns or extreme differences in income distribution may cause social unrest and political instability, as exemplified by the mass demonstrations and social unrest in Greece during 2011 caused by fear and anger over the nation's economic crisis. Firms that tap into arbitrage opportunities such as low-cost input (labor or raw materials) in less democratic geographical areas may, for instance, increase their exposure to reputational risks.

Political risk

Political risk arises when political changes may affect the business environment in a foreign location. Cosset and Suret argue that for political factors to be considered a risk, they 'must have the potential for significantly affecting the profit or other goals of a particular enterprise' (1995: 303). It is often more subjective and less quantifiable compared to economic risks. Reassuring economic indicators thus sometimes overshadow political risks (Bremmer, 2005). History shows, however, that political volatility has significantly impacted markets and business opportunities. Political risk is of course not completely isolated from economic risk (Agarwal and Feils, 2007). Economic struggles can lead to social unrest and anti-business trends and political instability. While analysis of economic risks can show a country's potential, analyses of political risks may better capture the likelihood of certain actions (Bremmer, 2005).

Expropriation, or the nationalization, of assets has traditionally been considered the greatest political risk. Although this is still a risk, exemplified by the recent nationalization of petroleum assets held by oil majors in Venezuela, the characteristics and complexities of risk factors may be changing over time. Just looking at the world map over the past 25 years illustrates the enormous changes that have occurred on the political arena. The fall of the former Soviet Union in the early 1990s resulted in 15 countries declaring independence. Many of these markets now represent emerging economies that increasingly attract FDI despite the varying political stability and strength of institutions to support market activities. Similarly, the dissolution of the former Yugoslavia and Czechoslovakia led to new independent countries where FDI activity is increasing. These dynamics suggest that our perception of political risk just a few years ago will differ dramatically from our perceptions today.

Emerging economies in particular have focused on developing policies that induce inward FDI. In his study of political risks in the 21st century, Jakobsen (2010) warns that MNCs should not be fooled by investor friendly policies. Accordingly, the policies do not necessarily reflect the multitude and complexity of political risks that occur after entry into a market, and MNCs should continue to treat political risk analysis as a top priority after entering a foreign market.

Some argue that the impact of political risk is becoming even more important to focus on in regard to cross-border interactions. First, markets are becoming increasingly interconnected at multiple levels. This creates greater ripple effects of political instability in one area. Second, more firms are globalizing their value chains to tap into location advantages such as low-cost labor. Many of the lower-cost resources, however, are located in less democratic areas with greater social unrest and weaker protection of property rights. Finally, there is an increasing dependence on energy which forces firms to engage in business activities in politically unstable countries where the natural resources are located (Bremmer, 2005).

Low political risk does not mean that a country will not endure any turbulence. In other words, the occurrence of turbulence, or shocks, does not in itself determine whether a country is politically stable. Rather, political stability should be evaluated based on a country's openness and ability to implement policies during shocks as well as their ability to avoid creating new unwanted shocks (Bremmer, 2005).

Institutional/legal risk

Closely related to political risk is the issue of a country's appropriability regime, affecting the MNCs' ability to enforce contracts. Institutional and legal risks have long been central in internalization theory, suggesting that MNCs should prefer to internalize activities when entering host markets with weak appropriability regimes (Hennart, 2009). This is particularly relevant for emerging economies which often have weaker institutions and high levels of corruption (Hahn et al., 2011).

The institutional voids in emerging markets, as discussed under country risk, significantly increase the institutional/legal risks in these markets. Avoiding such host markets, however, may drastically limit the MNCs' growth potential and remove competitive advantages arising from strategically positioning the MNC in key global growth areas. MNCs can instead benefit from deviating from traditional approaches to risk management in such markets. Henisz et al. (2010) suggest that the MNCs' ability to manage the policy-making process may be the most important success factor rather than relying on risk mitigation through external parties. Accordingly, external hedging tools may become too costly and ineffective as pricing is difficult and firms willing to underwrite may be scarce. Instead, the MNCs' ability to build and manage long-term relationships may be more important to allow them to manage risk through goodwill investments. This is a constructive framing of the debate that contributes to the local development without locking into specific political parties and the ability to assemble coalitions of interest (Khanna et al., 2005; Henisz et al., 2010).

Reputational risk

The above-mentioned external risks can also lead to reputational risk where the MNC is exposed to changing perceptions among stakeholders. A positive reputation creates valuable opportunities such as the development of a strong brand and perceived value that can enable premium pricing. A good reputation further attracts investors and new talent, and enables the MNC to obtain social 'licenses to operate' which can be particularly important in industries with pressure on social and environmental sustainability. Reputational risks are often difficult to quantify, however, even though an estimated 70–80 per cent of a firm's market value has been attributed to intangible assets (Eccles et al., 2007).

External factors relating to social and economic inequalities or environmental issues can pose unexpected threats to the reputation of multinationals. Several MNCs that have relocated or outsourced manufacturing to low-cost areas have experienced negative reputational effects from undemocratic or unfair treatment of workers. The well-known footwear company Nike represents one of the most publicized cases of reputational risks related to the relocation of manufacturing to low-cost countries. After labor activists and media exposed poor labor conditions, low wage levels and the use of child labor among Nike's contractors in low-cost countries, the company image suffered tremendously which eventually led to a financial downturn. Nike gradually managed to rebuild its reputation through a significant investment in developing, communicating, and enforcing a code of conduct for all contractors (Spar, 2002). Still today, more than 20 years after the initial criticism of Nike's involvement in unfair treatment of workers, Nike's reputation remains under constant scrutiny and management of reputational risks continues to be a top strategic priority (Levenson, 2008).

Reputational risk can be particularly difficult to quantify as it is based on perceptions, which may or may not reflect reality. One of the main challenges with reputation risk is that many MNCs are too reactive in their approach and effectively engage in crises management rather than risk management (Eccles et al., 2007). As the Nike example illustrates, long-term effects of the initial reactive approach can linger even after the MNC has established and implemented sound codes of conduct and more proactive engagement in corporate social responsibility. Reputational risk is not limited, however, to situations where the firm's reputation is worse than its actual character and behavior. MNCs that explicitly communicate high standards may also experience difficulties living up to its positive reputation, potentially leading the firm to perceived 'failure'. The energy company BP exemplifies this, as their environmentally friendly campaign of 'Beyond Petroleum' in 2000 increased public expectations of superior qualities related to environmental sustainability. BP failed to live up to these expectations when the MNC experienced numerous environmental and safety-related incidents such as the Texas refinery explosions and leaking pipelines in Alaska (Eccles et al., 2007). BP's reputation later took an even harder hit after extensive environmental damage in the Gulf of Mexico.

The above-mentioned examples illustrate the complexities of reputational risks. On the one hand, approaching reputational risk too reactively may have long-term negative effects for the perceived ability of the MNC to address issues satisfactory. On the other hand, failing to live up to a strong reputation that has been built proactively creates an unwanted gap in perception and reality. In their *Harvard Business Review* article on reputational risks, Eccles et al. (2007) propose that managers actively identify and monitor how stakeholders perceive the firm's reputation. Gaps must continuously be addressed to ensure perception and reality is aligned. This requires the MNC to keep a focus on reputational risk as a prioritized strategic issue and actively engage in stakeholder management.

Strategic risk

Most strategic decisions involve elements of risk no matter how thoroughly the options are analyzed prior to decision making, as internal and external dynamics generate unexpected changes. Distance, as discussed by Ghemawat (2011) can amplify these risks due to increasing interdependencies and key variations in for instance regulatory environments.

Projects might fail despite extensive planning, technology shifts may make products and processes obsolete, social or environmental events might rapidly erode brands, and aggressive competitor moves may weaken a firm's competitive position. It will be impossible, and undesirable, to attempt to fully avoid such risks. Managers should instead try to anticipate them and build on potential opportunities that may arise (Slywotzky and Drzik, 2005).

The increasing reliance on information technology (IT) represents one of the greatest strategic business risks for firms. It is estimated that approximately two thirds of all capital spending relates to information technology, while company boards typically only approve a fraction of this amount (Parent and Reich, 2009). Failures of information systems or technology may lead to supply chain disruptions and communication difficulties, and ultimately loss of reputation and shareholder value.

Other strategic business risks may threaten the fundamental logic of a firm's value proposition and business model (Slywotzky, 2008). MNCs that rely on offshoring² exemplify such risks where the strategic decision to externalize activities in a lower-cost country expose the organization to both the upside potential of increased competitiveness but also downside risks that threaten the long-term sustainability of the MNC. In their influential *Harvard Business Review* article, Aron and Singh (2005) identify operational and structural risks as particularly important to consider when offshoring. The importance and characteristics of these risks are discussed below.

Operational risk

Many MNCs seek offshoring to tap into specific location advantages in a host market such as the lower cost of labor, often combined with access to a highly skilled and educated workforce (Kedia and Mukherjee, 2009). Extensive focus on bottom-line benefits, however, may lead managers to overlook implementation complexities and long-term impacts on the MNC's competitive advantage. Aron and Singh (2005) suggest that MNC managers must not only carefully assess whether the activities are strategically desirable to offshore (where core value-creating activities should remain inside the MNC), but also determine how codifiable and measurable the activities are. Too often, managers overestimate the ability to transfer activities to an external partner and underestimate the difficulties of codifying and accurately measuring the quality of the activities performed by the contractual partner. At best, it requires additional investment and time before the expected cost benefits are obtained. A worse scenario involves a failure of the offshoring agreement and a strategic loss of valuable knowledge in the MNC that may affect its future competitiveness.

The Danish toy manufacturer, the LEGO Group, experienced such operational risks when it decided to offshore over 70 per cent of its manufacturing of LEGO bricks to lower-cost countries. The experience resulted in a painful but valuable learning process for the MNC where it had not only underestimated the numerous tacit aspects of the manufacturing process, which made the activities difficult to codify and measure, but also failed to recognize the strategic importance of ensuring that this knowledge was internalized to best create value for its customers. As a result, the LEGO group terminated the offshore agreement and refocused on how to build on this experience and best optimize its internal value chain to create value (Larsen et al., 2010).

Structural risk

MNCs must also consider the possibility that contractual relationships will not work as expected, referred to as structural risk (Aron and Singh, 2005). Offshoring partners may for instance fail to fulfill contractual expectations, reduce investments in their employees or unexpectedly increase prices over time. Such outcomes can quickly overshadow any expected cost benefits that may have triggered the initial offshoring decision. According to Aron and Singh, MNCs must therefore ensure that they are able to monitor the work and that metrics to measure the process quality are precise.

The external factors that influence structural risks vary across geographical locations. As discussed under legal and administrative risks, emerging markets may have weaker institutions to strengthen contract enforcement and reduce elements of corruption. These factors will heighten the risk that contractual relationships will not work as expected, and has led several MNCs to prefer 'nearshoring', defined as offshoring to neighboring countries, where such distances are lower (Hahn et al., 2011). An MNC from an EU country would then prefer to 'nearshore' to another EU country, despite potential cost benefits of locating in higher distance countries in order to minimize the downsides of structural risk.

Structural risk is also expected to increase when offshoring activities represent higher value-creating activities that require closer integration with the MNC's activity set (Lampel and Bhalla, 2011). Although we have primarily focused on structural risk in relation to offshoring decisions, it is also an issue for other ownership and operating modes such as joint ventures, licensing or franchising agreements.

4.5   Managing risk

The above discussion of different types of risk, although not exhaustive, illustrates many of the complexities facing today's MNCs. Most of them have a range of approaches available to address these risks; ranging from avoiding the risk altogether, to reducing risk through, for instance, hedging tools (which also often limits the upside potential), to actively seeking to increase risk in order to act on arbitrage opportunities that arise. Most importantly, an increasing number of multinationals are recognizing the strategic importance of risk management (Slywotzky and Drzik, 2005).

Extant MNC theories generally do not elaborate on risk management. While some argue that internalization theory implicitly assumes that MNCs are risk neutral (Buckley and Strange, 2011), many of the risk elements mentioned in this chapter are identified as key external factors influencing entry mode and ownership decisions that reduce anticipated costs (Hennart, 2009). The internationalization process perspective (also referred to as the Uppsala model) also incorporates elements of risk in the discussion of commitment and uncertainty (Figueira-de-Lemos et al., 2011). While risk factors are identified, particularly related to investment decisions, scarce attention is given to *how* managers should actively manage risk.

Nassim Taleb, the author of well-known risk management book *The Black Swan*, and associates elegantly summarize the main challenge of managing risk in this way: 'Remember that the biggest risk lies within us: We overestimate our abilities and underestimate what can go wrong' (Taleb et al., 2009: 81). As mentioned throughout this chapter, one of the first steps in managing risks is to identify the major risks that can affect the organization (Buehler et al., 2008). Many managers focus too much on extreme events, often referred to as Black Swans, that are difficult, if not impossible, to predict (Taleb et al., 2009). Focusing too much on extreme risks that are highly unlikely and difficult to comprehend diverts management attention from other risks that are more probable and possible to manage. Although many risks are easily identified and possible to manage, MNCs should avoid relying too heavily on historical data. Increasing interdependencies, fast-growing emerging markets, and elements of randomness all create dynamics that differ from the past (Stulz, 2009; Taleb et al., 2009).

Many MNCs seek to avoid particular risk all together, such as choosing not to enter a country due to high levels of corruption or political instability. This can be particularly appropriate if downside effects are likely and have detrimental effects for the business. Avoiding all risk, however, is neither feasible nor desirable. Many multinationals thus try to reduce the downside potential through mitigating action and hedging tools. Before engaging in risk-reducing activities, however, managers should develop a clear understanding of the MNC's risk profile or risk appetite. Certain risk may be natural for the MNC to 'own' because of the overall portfolio of asses or internal capabilities (Buehler et al., 2008). The MNC may thus do a better job of managing these risks, or it may make more economical sense to try to offset the risks naturally within the company. It is insufficient to look at risk as something that always needs to be avoided or reduced, as some firms can create value by managing risk better than their competitors, hence effectively increasing risk (Girotra and Netessine, 2011).

Ensuring that risk is continuously on the strategic agenda is central for good decision making. Ideally, risk management that enable avoidance, reduction and increasing risks should be built into the business model of any organization (Girotra and Netessine, 2011). This requires a strategic focus on risk management throughout the organization. It also necessitates a certain degree of flexibility in organizations to reprioritize or delay commitments, rewrite contracts, double bet on investments and gather more data (Slywotzky, 2004; Buehler et al., 2008; Girotra and Netessine, 2011). All too often, the emphasis on operational efficiency and specialization increases the MNCs' exposure to risks and leaves little room for flexibility to effectively manage them (Taleb et al., 2009).

4.6 Summary

In this chapter, we have discussed the importance of identifying and assessing a range of risks. Since the relevance and impact of risks will vary across firms, industries and locations, MNCs must take an active role in determining their abilities to manage the risks. The goal should not necessarily be to avoid all risk as MNCs often have different risk appetites. Some firms may actually gain competitive advantages by taking on specific risks if they are better at managing them than their competitors. The McDonald's case adjoining this chapter illustrates some of the discussed risks and complexities.

NOTES

1 The FDI flows peaked in 2007 and then contracted due to the global economic crises. The numbers have since risen, although the 2011 World Investment Report (UNCTAD 2011) suggests that figures for FDI flows are still 15 percent below their pre-crises average.

2 We use the term 'offshoring' for activities that are outsourced to firms located in a foreign country (see Tadelis, 2007).

Case C
McDonald's thrives and dives in Russia and Iceland

Jill Thorlacius and Birgitte Grøgaard

C.1 Introduction

McDonald's, an icon of American culture, started as a humble San Bernardino, California drive-thru back in 1940. Founders Maurice and Richard McDonald found success by implementing an assembly line technique to deliver fast, quality products to their customers. In 1954, McDonald's caught the eye of Ray Kroc, a milkshake mixer salesman, who was impressed by the effectiveness and quality of the operation. Despite having had little experience operating franchises, Kroc became determined to turn it into a nationwide success. McDonald's Corporation was founded in 1955 and Kroc later bought exclusive rights to the name (McDonald's Corporation, 2012a). By 1969 McDonald's operated over 1000 locations across the United States (Chung, 2009). McDonald's strategy emphasized growth through franchising (Arndt, 2007), allowing the company to expand rapidly while still maintaining tight control of its brand. Once McDonald's started to reach saturation in the United States, it looked to internationalization to sustain its growth.

In 1967, McDonald's identified Canada as a promising market for its first experience in international expansion, due to the similarities in tastes and eating habits with Americans. Market conditions such as political stability and proximity to the United States were additional factors that increased the attractiveness of the market (Curtis, 1982). George Cohon established franchises in eastern Canada, and spearheaded the company's strong growth throughout the country (McDonald's Corporation, 2012a). International expansion in other markets soon followed (Curtis, 1982), as illustrated in Table C.1.

Today, McDonald's is the leading global foodservice retailer with over 33,000 locations and 1.7 million employees found across the globe (McDonald's

Table C.1 McDonald's international expansion

Year	Country
1967	Canada, Puerto Rico
1970	Virgin Isles, Costa Rica
1971	Guam, Japan, Netherlands, Panama, Germany, Australia
1972	France, El Salvador
1973	Sweden
1974	Guatemala, England
1975	Hong Kong, Bahamas
1976	New Zealand, Switzerland
1977	Ireland, Austria
1978	Belgium
1979	Brazil, Singapore
1981	Spain, Denmark, Philippines
1982	Malaysia
1983	Norway
1984	Andorra, Wales, Finland
1985	Thailand, Aruba, Luxembourg, Venezuela, Italy, Mexico
1986	Cuba, Turkey, Argentina
1987	Macau, Scotland
1988	Serbia, South Korea, Hungry
1990	Soviet Union, China, Chile
1991	Indonesia
1992	Czechoslovakia, Guadeloupe, Poland, Monaco, Brunei, Morocco
1993	Marianas, Iceland, Slovenia, Saudi Arabia
1994	Botswana, Kuwait, New Caledonia, Oman, Egypt, Bulgaria, Bahrain, Latvia, United Arab Emirates
1995	Estonia, Romania, Malta, Columbia, Slovakia, South Africa, Qatar, Honduras, Saint Martin
1996	Croatia, Samoa, Fiji Islands, Liechtenstein, Lithuania, Cyprus, India, Peru, Jordan, Paraguay, Dominican Republic, French Polynesia, Belarus
1997	Ukraine, Yemen, Republic of Macedonia, Ecuador, Reunion, Isle of Man, Suriname
1998	Moldova, Nicaragua, Lebanon, Pakistan, Sri Lanka
1999	Georgia, San Marino, Gibraltar, Azerbaijan
2000	French Guiana
2001	Mauritius
2003	Kazakhstan, Mayotte
2004	Montenegro
2006	Algeria, Kenya, Iraq

Source: Hitt et al. (2012).

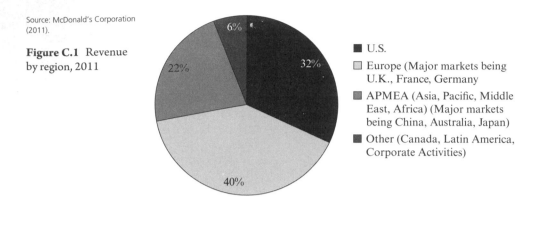

Source: McDonald's Corporation (2011).

Figure C.1 Revenue by region, 2011

- ■ U.S.
- ☐ Europe (Major markets being U.K., France, Germany
- ▨ APMEA (Asia, Pacific, Middle East, Africa) (Major markets being China, Australia, Japan)
- ■ Other (Canada, Latin America, Corporate Activities)

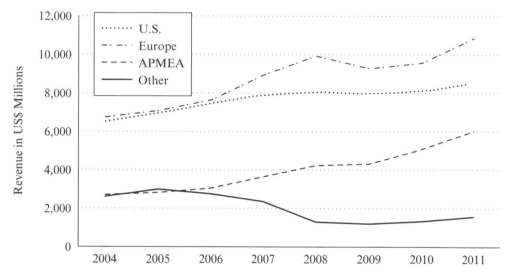

Source: McDonald's Corporation (2011).

Figure C.2 Region growth

Corporation, 2012b). Its global operations, which are divided into four geographical segments, generated over $27 million in revenues in 2011, as illustrated in Figures C.1 and C.2. The company has succeeded in international markets by emulating its American brand culture through its use of franchising (Vignali, 2001). By 2012, approximately 80 per cent per cent of the restaurants found worldwide were franchised (McDonald's Corporation, 2012c).

However, due to the complexity of operating a business in 119 different countries, McDonald's adapts its strategy to best work within its local markets, given their constraints and challenges (McDonald's Corporation, 2012b). The company's experiences in Russia and Iceland have taught the company the importance of responding to both country conditions and risks in order to ensure long-term operational success.

C.2 The push for Russia

During the 1976 Summer Olympic Games in Montreal, George Cohon, the founder of McDonald's Canada, saw an opportunity to introduce delegates from the Soviet Union (USSR) to McDonald's cuisine. The USSR was then in the midst of the Cold War, which saw extreme tension between the primarily capitalist West and the communist East. Cohon took a keen interest in the Soviet market. He saw the USSR as a country on the brink of change and knew that for international players this was an exciting business opportunity. It was an untapped market with the potential to become a thriving economy. Natural resources remained unexploited and a booming population of approximately 260 million meant potential consumers with increasing purchasing power. Cohon believed that a Soviet McDonald's '[would] be the highest-volume McDonald's in the world' (Barringer, 1988).

Well aware of the restrictions on communicating with Olympic delegates, Cohon sidestepped the red tape and began building a relationship by lending a company bus to the Soviet delegates and guiding them to a McDonald's restaurant (Adamy, 2007). After receiving a positive reaction from the delegates, Cohon knew the USSR was worth pursuing. He spent the next several years attempting to persuade the Soviet government to allow McDonald's to establish its very first restaurant in the country. Despite the arduous effort, McDonald's consistently hit roadblocks due to differing government ideologies and bureaucratic processes. Perestroika, implemented by former Soviet Head of State Mikhail Gorbachev in the late 1980s, reformed the economic and political system and opened the door for McDonald's to finally enter the country. In 1988, after 12 years of effort, McDonald's was granted the right to open its first location in Moscow's Pushkin Square.

However, McDonald's was well aware that gaining approval from the government was only a small step in establishing a presence in the Soviet market. Cohon questioned, 'where do you start when you decide to introduce one of the most potent symbols of Western capitalism into a system dedicated to the very opposite? No one knew' (Ivanov, 2000).

Market Challenges in the Soviet Era

McDonald's was not alone in its foray into the USSR. Burger King was also keen to enter into the Soviet market in the late 1980s; however, it held off expansion plans after finding shortcomings in the country's supply chain capabilities and foreign currency policies (Adamy, 2007). Supply chain issues were common in the Soviet food industry due to heavy regulations and the infancy of the Soviet Union's infrastructure. The socialist reform reduced the number of private suppliers that were available in the market place, creating barriers to access resources. Additionally, the country was known for having food shortages, which made the availability of ingredients unreliable.

McDonald's was aware that the lack of available resources would be substantial, and that it would have to produce or import over 80 per cent of its ingredients (Kramer, 2010). This forced the company to invest $45 million to build its own facility, called the McComplex, which produced everything from hamburger buns to pie filling (Kramer, 2010). In no other markets has McDonald's had to produce ingredients on the same level that was required in the Soviet Union. The company's intention was to eventually source all ingredients from local suppliers once these businesses could produce on larger scales. This goal was common to all of McDonald's international operations, which aim to be fully integrated into the community they serve (McDonald's Corporation, 2012b).

McDonald's entrance into the Soviet Union during the later years of the Cold War raised concerns as east versus west tensions still lingered. The uncertainty in how McDonald's would be perceived in the Soviet Union, as well as back in the United States, was a significant concern for the company's reputation. As McDonald's continued its mission, it was met with pessimism from the Soviet media, which forewarned of the challenges ahead. Some believed that the communist Soviet state was just not ready for the American capitalist icon to move in (Zuber, 2000). However, apprehensions were partially eased when a job posting in a Soviet newspaper received over 27,000 responses from applicants (Adamy, 2007).

On opening day in 1990, swarms of people lined up for their first taste of McDonald's, and by the end of the day the store had served an estimated 30,000 customers (Osborn, 2011). Russian restaurant tycoon, Rostislav Ordovsky, believed the perception of McDonald's was successful because '[i]n a country where there was nothing available, McDonald's was everything' (Adamy, 2007). It was even debated by some that the successful opening of a McDonald's restaurant signified the public's keen support of glasnost and perestroika (Arvedlund, 2005). For some, it signified the 'first taste of freedom, in a closed country' (VOA, 2010). Cohon attributed the initial success to the company delivering what they promised to citizens, a quality that the communist government had often failed to uphold (VOA, 2010).

Political changes

By 1990, the USSR was facing severe political and economic turmoil. The country transitioned from a command economy to a market economy, Soviet Republics began pushing for independent statehood, and the fall of the Soviet Union became imminent. Uncertainty in the political and economic situation made it difficult to predict the future operating environment of McDonald's in the USSR (VOA, 2010).

Additional political and institutional barriers created lengthy processes and further uncertainty in McDonald's expansion within the country. Opening up a restaurant required McDonald's to follow several bureaucratic processes. Western organizations were required to manage all contracts in Moscow with government approval, and obtaining retail locations required purchasing licenses from the municipal government (Bayer, 1995). An estimated 200 signatures were needed to be able to open up one McDonald's store in the Soviet Union (Adamy, 2007). It was even rumored that McDonald's needed the direct influence of Mikhail Gorbachev to push the approvals forward. Sustaining healthy political ties was therefore imperative in the company's expansion in the Soviet Union (Bayer, 1995).

The government also enforced restrictions on the exchange of the Soviet currency, the Ruble, into any developed country currency. With the struggling economy facing the possibility of high inflation rates, and subsequent devaluation of the Ruble, this created an extreme risk for foreign companies operating in the country.

The fall of the Soviet Union in 1991 brought volatility to the Russian economy, and McDonald's operations. During periods of economic strength, real estate prices surged and low unemployment rates made it challenging to find suitable staff. During economic downturns, sales decreased due to lower disposable income among consumers. Although the Russian economy entered a recession in the late 1990s, McDonald's managed to weather the downturn by altering its menu to better meet customer demands. Putting local dishes on the menu allowed for lower priced options, while price increases were rarely used due to the price sensitivity of the Russian consumers (Zuber, 2000).

Future challenges in Russia

In April of 2012, McDonald's announced its plan to open the first franchised store in Russia. McDonald's has paired with Rostik, an established and prominent fast food chain to initiate the franchise move. Although the majority of McDonald's international operations are franchised, Russian regulations have long made franchising an unviable option in the country (Kramer, 2010). Processes to apply for franchising rights were tedious and left little protection for the company's intellectual property. Additionally, logistical issues and inexperienced managers have made it difficult for franchises to operate effectively in Russia (Romriell, 2002). However, McDonald's believes that franchising is 'important to delivering great, locally-relevant customer experiences, and driving profitability' (McDonald's Corporation, 2011: 10).

Twenty-two years after entering the Soviet Union, McDonald's Russian operations produce and import only 20 per cent of their ingredients, a substantial turnaround from their initial numbers (Kramer, 2010). McDonald's Russian operations have become an integral part of its international sales, with traffic in most Russian stores doubling the average number of customers served in other international stores (Adamy, 2007). The company has developed a strong reputation in Russia. This success has allowed the company to expand to having 314 stores in Russia by the end of 2011 (Companies & Markets, 2012).

In 2012, McDonald's continues to expand across Russia but takes significant time to ensure each location is a qualified investment (Adamy, 2007). Managing risk is a constant process as the business environment changes in the emerging Russian economy. Corruption has continued to be a considerable concern for companies operating in Russia. Despite the risks and efforts required to enter the Russian market, however, the move has paid off for McDonald's and illustrates the benefits of proactively managing risks.

C.3   McDonald's in Iceland

The early 1990s was a period of aggressive growth for McDonald's, and in 1993 the company was ready to take on its next market: Iceland. McDonald's entry into Iceland coincided with the franchise giant's expansion into diverse markets such as Northern Africa, Asia, and the Middle East.

The country of Iceland is located at the periphery of Europe in the North Atlantic Ocean and has a small population of around 300,000. It is a member of the European Economic Area, which enables it to trade freely with countries in the European Union. With success in many other European countries by the early 1990s, McDonald's saw Iceland as a natural target.

However, McDonald's struggled to replicate the success in Iceland that it had recently achieved in other international markets, such as Russia. By 2009, McDonald's was operating only three locations in the relatively small country, yet it continued to face economic difficulties.

Market challenges on the periphery of Europe

When McDonald's initially expanded into Iceland, the company was able to source several ingredients, such as beef, from local suppliers. However, the attempt to source locally and integrate into the local community proved difficult in the remote country. The cool climate and short farming season restricted local sourcing opportunities. Sourcing was disrupted due to shortages, which forced McDonald's to import all ingredients from Germany. Strict franchise specifications on product quality also made it difficult for McDonald's to use local suppliers, and forced the company to rely more on imports than local competitors did. For example, McDonald's needed to ship in ingredients from Germany twice a week to keep perishable items fresh, and replenish stock for their stores (Raz, 2009). This allowed the company's local competitors to better manage costs and reduce foreign exchange risk exposure compared to McDonald's.

The Icelandic government implemented a high import tariff on agricultural goods, which further increased McDonald's input costs (CNN, 2009). The company could not mitigate these costs by developing its own production complex, as it had done in Russia, as this was not feasible in Iceland, given the difficult climate and small size of its operations.

Economic crisis

Between 2003 and 2008 the country faced a growth period following the increased privatization of the banking industry by the government (Halpern, 2011). Bank assets grew substantially and the amount of foreign money invested in Iceland swelled. Growth in the booming economy halted abruptly when the global financial crisis materialized, and several major Icelandic commercial banks collapsed, sending the country into a recession. Three of these major banks, which carried an aggregated debt ten times larger than the entire

Icelandic economy, failed within a matter of days of each other (Valdimarsson, 2009). Additionally, an estimated 40 per cent of citizens had reached the 'danger limit' of personal debt (Olson, 2009). With the country on the brink of collapse at the end of 2008, the IMF intervened and injected $2.1 billion into Iceland to keep the country afloat. However the impact of the recession had an inevitable effect on the stability of the Icelandic currency, the Krona.

In 2009, after a year of economic shock, the Krona depreciated 80 per cent against the Euro (Valdimarsson, 2009). This significant change in value more than doubled the cost for resources purchased in Euros. Iceland's McDonald's franchise owner, Jon Gardar Ogmundsson, stressed: 'It just makes no sense. For a kilo of onion, imported from Germany, I'm paying the equivalent of a bottle of good whisky' (BBC, 2009). As costs soared above targets, the company's margins in Iceland dwindled, and there was little it could do to turn around its business. The company estimated that it would need to increase prices by 20 per cent to keep up with rising costs; however, Icelandic consumers were already paying prices higher than the global average (Valdimarsson, 2009). According to the 2009 Economist Big Mac Index, where a cost of the famous hamburger is compared globally to formulate purchasing power of parity, the price of a Big Mac in Iceland totaled $5.29 USD compared to $3.54 USD in the United States (CNN, 2009). This amount is one of the highest in the world, illustrating key economic challenges facing McDonald's.

The fall of Iceland

The collapse of the Icelandic economy inevitably ended McDonald's venture in the country. McDonald's corporation made efforts to develop a suitable resolution with Icelandic franchise owners, but after long consideration the company decided to pull out of Iceland. On October 31, 2009, McDonald's closed all three restaurants in the country.

McDonald's attributes its failure to the 'unique operational complexity' of Iceland (BBC, 2009). The market's size and agricultural capabilities reduced the ability for McDonald's to fully integrate its operations into Iceland. This forced the company to become dependent on foreign suppliers, which heavily exposed it to the foreign exchange rate volatility faced by the small country. This unforeseen economic risk was enough to end McDonald's days in Iceland.

Although McDonald's operations in Russia and Iceland vary substantially, important lessons have emerged in regards to managing new markets. The ability to utilize local suppliers and integrate with the community can be a major deciding factor in the eventual success of the operation. Finding local suppliers and producing locally allows for greater flexibility to manage unforeseen risks. McDonald's head of supply lines and chain-expansion strategies, Al Bryant, states 'When you make an investment in a new market, stick with it . . . Doing business on an international scale means that you will always have a wide range of business and economic conditions in different parts of the world at any point in time'(Prewitt, 2002). The company has taken its successes and failures in its stride as it continues to serve its famous food under golden arches worldwide.

? DISCUSSION QUESTIONS

1 What external and internal risks did McDonald's face entering the Soviet Union?
2 Based on the information presented in the case, can you prioritize the risks that were of most concern for McDonald's operations in the Soviet Union?
3 Can you determine other risks that McDonald's may have faced in the Soviet Union that were not discussed in the case?
4 What additional risks might McDonald's experience when franchising in Russia in 2012?
5 What external and internal risks did McDonald's face in Iceland?
6 Can parallels be drawn between McDonald's operations in Russia and Iceland? Were risks managed similarly or differently?

5

Cultural distance

5.1 Introduction

The main purpose of this chapter is to generate an awareness of how culture affects our assumptions of how to manage and organize. Our starting point is the concept of national culture. Cultures differ from each other and these differences are commonly referred to as cultural distance. We refer to research that shows that cultural distance is important to address because it has significant performance implications for MNCs. However, agreeing on how to measure cultural distance has proved challenging. We present and compare cultural distance measures from two influential studies, that of Geert Hofstede and Fons Trompenaars. Thereafter we review a more recent approach to measuring cultural distance, that of the GLOBE project. As we indicate, all three measures have been subject to criticism. Finally we introduce the concept of cultural intelligence.

5.2 The concept of culture

Stahl et al. (2010) refer to culture as the commonly held body of beliefs and values that define the 'shoulds' and the 'oughts' of life, and guide the meaning that people attach to aspects of the world around them. It is shared by members of a particular group of people and it distinguishes them from members of other groups. Hosftede (1991) states that culture is a product of 'the collective programming of the mind': that is it is acquired through regular interaction with other members of the group. Cultural differences can be found at many different levels – professional, class and regional – but it is particularly potent at the national level because of generations of socialization into the national community. As individuals we generally only become aware of our own culture when confronted by another. However, what we usually observe are the artifacts of cultural dissimilarity – the numerous and often pronounced differences in greeting rituals, dress codes, forms of address and taste. The underlying system of values is, though, neither readily observable nor readily comprehensible. The core differences in values between cultures go back to questions of what works for ensuring survival in relation to the natural environment. The Dutch have had to cope with flooding, the Swiss with avalanches, the Russians and the Finns with long cold winters. Trying to understand the origins of various cultural differences is an immense task that lies outside the remit of this book. What is achievable, though, is to equip MNC managers with sufficient insight to be able to determine what values are of particular importance to take into account when designing management systems. However, before we examine how cultural distance is measured we address the issue of how cultural distance affects MNC performance.

5.3   Cultural distance and MNC performance

MNCs are radically different from export-based firms not least because of their foreign subsidiaries. Not only does physical distance pose a challenge for effective communication, but MNCs have also got to learn to cope with cultural distance: that is the underlying differences in national cultural values for managers between their MNC's home and foreign operations.

Hutzschenreuter and Voll (2008) argue that cultural distance adds complexity in a number of ways. Individuals have to learn to deal with work team members, customers, suppliers, and others who act differently than they do themselves and who have different belief systems and values. This can lead to interpersonal barriers and friction which interferes with knowledge sharing across the MNC. Learning to adapt to a new culture is both demanding and time-consuming. Cultural distance also necessitates adaptation of structures, systems and processes. Some MNCs regard cultural differences as so complex that they prefer to operate as multidomestics with subsidiaries given considerable latitude not just in product development but also in management style. The attitude is that people in the subsidiaries know best and should be allowed to go their own ways. However, taken to an extreme there is little in the way of synergies and MNCs are reduced to holding companies. The management challenge for many MNCs is to be able to adapt their organizations to culturally distinct environments without losing organizational consistency.

When examining the role of cultural distance, most studies theorize that, as the cultural differences between an MNE's home country and a host market increase, the underlying ability of the MNE to operate effectively in the host market decreases and that this has a negative effect on performance. Nevertheless, when Tihanyi et al. (2005) undertook an empirical synthesis of prior research on the relationship between cultural distance and MNC performance they found no evidence of a negative relationship. Indeed they even found an indication that high cultural distance may provide performance benefits in those cases when MNCs are operating in other developed countries. They speculate that when markets and institutions are well developed, cultural distance may actually stimulate innovation and creativity that in turn leads to enhanced MNC performance.

However, Hutzschenreuter and Voll (2008) argue that the problem with the prior research is that it failed to distinguish among different types of expansion steps by MNCs. They argue that if too much cultural distance is added over a short period of time, the MNC will be overwhelmed and performance will be negatively affected. This is because without sufficient time, individuals within the MNC are unable to adapt their behavior, and structures, systems and processes will not be correctly implemented so that the new subsidiaries will not be adequately integrated. Using German MNC panel data they find strong support for this prediction. MNCs are limited in their ability to handle the complexity that arises from entering culturally distant markets. In other words MNCs must give themselves sufficient time to learn before they add yet more complexity. Indeed, given time then it is possible that, as Tihanyi et al. (2005) suggest, cultural distance may actually stimulate innovation.

5.4 Measuring cultural distance

Dissecting and explaining any foreign culture is potentially an endless exercise. As an alternative to in-depth single-country studies, scholars have attempted to classify cultures in relation to one another by using a few, relatively broad, fundamental dimensions that are particularly relevant to management practice. National cultures are plotted along these dimensions and their measures express the degree of cultural distance between them. Cultures can then be clustered, thereby pinpointing which cultures are similar enough to make a standardized management approach viable. However, although national culture is a well-established concept, its more precise conceptualization and measurement is 'still hotly debated' (Stephan and Uhlaner, 2010: 1348). We now present Hofstede's approach to measuring cultural distance.

5.5 Hofstede's four dimensions

Between 1967 and 1973 Hofstede surveyed 116,000 IBM employees in 40 different nations using a questionnaire containing about 150 questions enquiring about their preferences in terms of management style and work environment (see Hofstede, 1980a, 1983). Among these 150 items were 32, which Hofstede labeled as work-related values. For each of the 40 nations he computed an average score in relation to each of the 32 work-related values. Taking the 32 'average-nation' values he generated a correlation matrix, which was then factor analysed. The initial analysis revealed three factors, the largest of which Hofstede sub-divided thereby creating four value dimensions: Power Distance, Uncertainty Avoidance, Individualism–Collectivism, and Masculinity–Femininity. Thereafter he compared each of the 40 national cultures in his sample. It should be noted that these dimensions are not intended to describe individuals but are descriptions of national norms.

Power distance

This dimension indicates the extent to which a society expects and accepts a high degree of inequality in institutions and organizations. In a country with a large power distance organizations are characterized by formal hierarchies and by subordinates who are reluctant to challenge their superiors. The boss is very much the boss. In a country with a small power distance subordinates expect to be consulted, and the ideal boss is a resourceful democrat rather than a benevolent autocrat. Table 5.1 shows differences in values associated with small and large power distance.

Uncertainty avoidance

This refers to the degree to which a society prefers predictability, security and stability. In societies with high scores on this index there is an emotional need for rules, written and unwritten. Thus organizations in these societies will deploy formal rules in order to ensure that work situations are highly structured with clearly defined task roles and responsibilities. Deviant ideas and behaviors are not tolerated. Societies in which uncertainty avoidance is strong are also characterized by higher levels of anxiety that in turns results in a pronounced need to work hard. Table 5.2 shows differences in values associated with weak and strong uncertainty avoidance.

Table 5.1 Small versus large power distance

Small Power Distance	Large Power Distance
Those in power should try to appear less powerful than they are.	Those in power should try to look as powerful as possible.
People at various power levels feel less threatened and more prepared to trust people.	Other people are a potential threat to one's power and can rarely be trusted.

Table 5.2 Weak versus strong uncertainty avoidance

Weak Uncertainty Avoidance	Strong Uncertainty Avoidance
There is more willingness to take risks. Uncertain situations are acceptable.	There is great concern with security in life. Career stability is needed.

Table 5.3 Collectivist versus individualist

Collectivist	Individualist
Identity is based in the social system. Order is provided by the organization.	Identity is based in the individual. Autonomy, variety and pleasure are sought in the system.

Individualism–collectivism

This dimension relates to the extent to which people prefer to take care of themselves and their immediate families rather than being bound to some wider collectivity such as the extended family or clan. In terms of organizational life, in highly individualistic societies there will be a sharp distinction between work and personal life. Tasks will prevail over relationships. Also individuals will prefer work settings in which they can make their own decisions. Table 5.3 shows differences between collectivist and individualist values.

Masculinity–femininity

Masculine societies value assertiveness, competitiveness and materialism as opposed to the 'feminine' values of relationships and the quality of life. In terms of the workplace, organizations in feminine societies will aim for harmonious relations with a strong emphasis on social partnership. In masculine societies, organizations will be more task-oriented and motivation more materialistic. Individual assertiveness is acceptable and appreciated. Not surprisingly, within nearly all societies men score higher in terms of masculinity. Table 5.4 shows differences between feminine and masculine values.

Table 5.5 contains a small selection of Hofstede's country index scores for each of the four dimensions. The first two rows indicate the range of the scores for each of the four dimensions for all of the countries included in Hofstede's original research. Thus for Power Distance the largest score

Table 5.4 Femininity versus masculinity

Feminine	Masculine
People and the environment are important.	Money and things are important.
Quality of life is what counts.	Performance is what counts.
Service provides the drive.	Ambition provides the drive.
One sympathizes with the unfortunate.	One admires the successful achiever.

Table 5.5 Selected country index scores

Range/country	Power Distance	Individualism	Masculinity	Uncertainty Avoidance
Largest score	104	91	95	112
Smallest score	11	6	5	8
United Kingdom	35	89	66	35
United States	38	91	62	46
France	68	71	43	86
Italy	50	76	70	75
Greece	60	35	57	112
Austria	11	55	79	70
Germany (F.R.)	35	67	66	65
Norway	31	69	8	50
Sweden	31	71	5	29
Brazil	69	38	49	76
Guatemala	95	6	37	101
India	77	48	56	40
Japan	54	46	95	92
Malaysia	104	26	50	36
Singapore	74	20	48	8

Source: Hofstede (1991).

Hofstede recorded was 104 and the smallest score was 11, whereas for Uncertainty Avoidance it was 112 and 8 respectively.

Anne-Wil Harzing, a prominent international management scholar, provides an Excel spreadsheet which contains an expanded number of country scores for the Hofstede dimensions. Go to: http://www.harzing.com and then click on to 'Resources'.

Hofstede identified various country clusters arguing that the scores enable us to draw some broad distinctions between the Nordic, Anglo, Latin, and

Asian countries. For example while the Scandinavian and Anglo-Saxon countries are similar in terms of the Uncertainty Avoidance, Power Distance, and Individualism–Collectivism dimensions, they are markedly different in relation to the Masculinity–Femininity dimension. Latin countries coalesce markedly in terms of uncertainty avoidance and power distance, whereas Asian countries such as India and Malaysia are distinguished by their combination of large power distance and weak uncertainty avoidance.

5.6 Hofstede and US management theories

Many MNCs apply organizational designs, systems and procedures in foreign subsidiaries that are derived from, and are successful in, their own culture. Pay-for-performance can, for example, be successful in the USA or the UK but has often been experienced as difficult to apply in Scandinavia, Germany or large parts of Asia. The assumption behind transplantation of management practices is that management theories are universal and that what works well in one context will work well in another. Hofstede (1980b) was one of the first to not only question this assumption but to do so on the basis of a theoretical analysis. In particular he focused on American theories of motivation, leadership and organization and their applicability in other cultural contexts. His analysis has important implications for the management of subsidiaries.

David McClelland, Abraham Maslow and Frederick Herzberg developed motivation theories that are, in Hofstede's view, peculiarly American. They all assume a universal achievement motive. For example, Maslow's (1954) hierarchy of human needs postulates that when the more basic needs such as physiological needs, security and social needs are met there is a need for esteem and thereafter for 'self-actualization'. Once our lower needs are satisfied we attempt to satisfy our higher needs.

Hofstede argues that the concept of the achievement motive presupposes (1) a willingness to accept risk (equivalent to weak Uncertainty Avoidance) and (2) a concern with performance (equivalent to strong Masculinity). This combination is a feature peculiar to the US and other Anglo-Saxon cultures. In the case of Germany or Austria while the Masculinity index is strong, Uncertainty Avoidance is also relatively strong. Thus the fundamental motivation in these societies is directed towards meeting security needs rather than self-actualization. While Sweden and Norway share the weak Uncertainty Avoidance of the USA, on the other hand they have much lower scores on the Masculinity index. Thus for these countries, while security needs are not fundamentally important, nor is self-actualization. Instead there is an emphasis on the social aspects to the work environment resulting in a de-emphasis on inter-individual competition.

Hofstede's overview of American leadership theories takes in the work of Douglas McGregor (Theory X versus Theory Y), Renis Likert (System 4 management), and Robert R. Blake with Jane S. Mouton (the Managerial Grid). All of these advocate participation in the manager's decisions by subordinates. However, these theories take it for granted that it is the manager's responsibility to initiate the participation. Manager-initiated participative management is, argues Hofstede, a product of the middle position of the USA on the Power Distance dimension. In countries with smaller power distances such as Sweden, Norway and Germany, the assumption that it is the manager who unilaterally initiates participation is unacceptable. Industrial democracy is a pronounced feature of work-life in these countries. Interestingly, though, Scandinavian and German industrial democracies are very different. In Germany, with its strong uncertainty avoidance, industrial democracy was first established through legislation prior to being put into practice in work life ('Mitbestimmung'). In Norway and Sweden, weak in terms of uncertainty avoidance, the origins of industrial democracy lie in local experiments. The legislative framework followed an established practice. One implication is that Scandinavian and German managers who move to the USA must learn to manage more autocratically in order to be effective.

Hofstede's analysis of US thinking on the nature of the organization focuses on the 'hire and fire' assumption. In the extremely individualistic USA, with only weak mutual loyalty between company and employees, this is tenable. However, warns Hofstede, US organizations may get themselves into considerable trouble in more collectivistic environments if they attempt to operate in this manner.

The core implication of Hofstede's analysis for MNCs is that identical personnel policies may have very different effects in different countries. The dilemma for the MNC is whether to adapt to the local culture or to try and change it. Particularly in the case of acquisitions the latter may prove to be a difficult route to follow. However, whichever route is taken it must be based on a thorough familiarization with the other culture.

5.7 Criticism of Hofstede

Hofstede's research has been criticized on a number of counts. The first area of criticism concerns the methodology Hofstede employed. Tayeb (1988; 1996) objects to the fact that Hofstede's research is entirely based on an attitude-survey questionnaire, which he contends is the least appropriate way of studying culture. However, for comparative purposes it is efficient. Another, and particularly significant, methodological criticism concerns the deliberate choices Hofstede made in defining his four factors particularly in regard to Individualism–Collectivism. Bond (2002) reminds us that this dimension was a product of a decision by Hofstede to sub-divide a large factor that emerged through the original three-factor solution. Hofstede labeled the other factor Power Distance. Had Hofstede remained true to his original three-factor solution his findings would have been very different. Bond concludes that it is unlikely that the USA would have been located at an extreme, as it is terms of the Individualism–Collectivism dimension. Without this finding much of Hofstede's critique of the applicability of US management theories falls by the wayside. Bond also questions the validity of this dimension, which comprises six work goals. Personal time, freedom, and challenge were added together to constitute the individualism end of the dimension; use of skills, physical conditions, and training were added together to define the collectivism end of the bi-polar factor. As Bond (2002: 74) remarks: 'The first three work goals bear obvious relations to individualism . . . How the last three work goals described anything resembling collectivism was, however, a mystery to many.'

A second and the most common criticism is that the sample is not representative, because it is drawn from a single company comprising middle-class employees. Hofstede's response has been to argue that IBM employees in different countries constitute suitably matched samples so that the work-value distance between an average IBM employee in Germany and one in the UK is equivalent to that between an average German adult and an average UK adult. The question is, though, whether IBM, which has a powerful US-derived organization culture, may have socialized its employees so powerfully that their values do not reflect aspects of local national cultures or, equally, that this socialization may have varied from country to country (McSweeney, 2002). Hofstede's (1994: 10) riposte is to argue that work organizations are not 'total institutions' and 'that the values of employees cannot be changed by an employer because they were acquired when the employees were children'. This means that the matching of his different samples is based on occupational equivalency. However, even this assumption has been questioned. McSweeney (2002) observes that similar occupations have very different entry requirements and social status from country to country.

A third criticism is that four dimensions are simply inadequate to convey cultural differences. Subsequently, Hofstede (1986, 1991, 1994) identified a fifth dimension, which he refers to as Long-term versus Short-term

Orientation. Long-term refers to such values as perseverance and thrift, while short-term values include respect for 'saving face', tradition and social obligations in the sense of reciprocation of greetings, favors and gifts. Asian societies are strongly short-term in their orientation, while Anglo-Saxon and West European societies have a long-term orientation. However, Hofstede (1994) acknowledges that his research on the implications of differences along this dimension is as yet not sufficient to allow the composition of a table of differences similar to those for the other four dimensions. Moreover, simply adding a fifth dimension does not counter the criticism of over-simplification.

(A fourth objection is that Hofstede's four dimensions may not be the most important. It is not improbable that Hofstede would have 'found' different national cultures had he used additional, amended, or alternative questions) (McSweeney, 2002).

Finally, his research has been criticized as dated. It is argued that because of globalization, younger people in particular are converging around a common set of values. Hofstede (1980b) has been skeptical of this viewpoint arguing from the outset that culture changes slowly.

5.8 Trompenaars' cultural dimensions

Trompenaars' research, published in 1993 and extended in 1997, is similar to that of Hofstede's not least in its use of a series of bipolar dimensions. However, while Hofstede's dimensions were primarily empirically derived, Trompenaars' are theoretically derived largely from the work of sociologist Talcott Parsons. In the 1980s he administered questionnaires to 15,000 managers and administrative staff in a number of companies across 28 countries, expanding this by a further 15,000 during the 1990s. As well as looking at attitudes toward both time and the environment Trompenaars employed five cultural dimensions that relate to the question of inter-personal relationships and work-related values. These are:

- *Universalism versus Particularism*. In cultures with high universalism there is an emphasis on formal rules and contracts and to their application regardless of individual circumstances. In high particularism cultures the emphasis is on relationships and trust: rules may be bent to help a friend.
- *Communitarism versus Individualism*. In strongly communitarian cultures people regard themselves as belonging to a group, whereas in cultures with strong individualism people regard themselves as individuals.
- *Neutral versus Emotional*. A high neutral culture is one in which emotions are not readily expressed in interpersonal communication. In contrast a

high emotional culture is characterized by the free expression of emotions even in a business situation.

- *Specific versus Diffuse.* A specific culture is one in which a distinction is made between work and private life. That is, individuals tend to compartmentalize their work and private lives. For example a manager in a specific culture segregates out the task relationship she has with a subordinate and insulates this from other dealings. Almost none of the authority in the work situation diffuses itself into non-work arenas. In diffuse cultures work and private life are closely linked and a great deal of formality is maintained across a wide range of social situations.
- *Achievement versus Ascription.* All societies accord some of their members more status than others, but the principle for doing so varies. An achievement-oriented culture is one in which status is given to people on the basis of how well they have performed their tasks recently, their level of education and experience. In an ascription-oriented culture status is conferred on the basis of durable characteristics such as age, kinship and gender, and status differences are thereby more pronounced. Power in such cultures does not require legitimizing in the same way as in achievement-oriented cultures.

According to Trompenaars (1993 Trompenaars and Hampden-Turner, 1997) these five value orientations greatly influence our ways of doing business and managing as well as our responses in the face of moral dilemmas. We will illustrate each of Trompenaars' cultural dimensions and point to some of the many lessons that MNCs can draw from his findings.

One example of the latter that illustrates the Universalism versus Particularism dimension is the dilemma of how you would respond if you are riding in a car driven by a close friend who is driving at least 25 km per hour over the speed limit in a built-up area and who hits a pedestrian. There are no witnesses. The question is whether you would feel obliged as a sworn witness to testify that your friend was keeping to the speed limit.

Trompenaars observes, as illustrated in Table 5.6, that the response to the question varies according to how seriously the pedestrian is injured. For North Americans and most North Europeans the reluctance to not testify on behalf on the friend increases with the seriousness of the accident. However, for Asians and Russians the response is the opposite. In short: in these cultures relationships matter. Companies from universalist cultures negotiating with a potential joint venture partner in China must recognize that relationships matter and take time to develop. They form the basis of the trust that is

Table 5.6 Selected examples of percentage of respondents who would testify against their friend

Russia	44
China	47
India	54
Japan	68
France	73
Spain	75
Germany	87
UK	91
Sweden	92
USA	93

necessary in order to do business. In a particularist culture, contracts are only a rough guideline or approximation.

In regard to Communitarism versus Individualism, one of Trompenaars' illustrations is the issue of responsibility in the case of defects being detected that stem from the negligence of a team member. The question is whether the team usually shoulders the responsibility, or whether it is the person who caused the defect who shoulders it. Asians and Germans tend to opt for the communitarian solution, while North Americans, the British and Eastern Europeans such as Russians prefer the individualistic solution, as illustrated in Table 5.7.

Companies from individualistic cultures such as the US will face difficulties in introducing methods of individual incentives such as pay-for-performance and individual assessment in subsidiaries in communitarian cultures such as Germany or Japan.

Table 5.7 Selected examples of percentage of respondents opting for individual responsibility

Japan	32
Germany	36
India	36
China	37
Spain	46
UK	48
Denmark	53
USA	54
Russia	69

Table 5.8 Selected examples of percentage of respondents who would not show emotions openly

Spain	19
Russia	24
France	30
Denmark	34
Germany	35
USA	43
UK	45
India	51
China	55
Japan	74

Trompenaars exemplifies the Neutral versus Emotional dimension through the question of the acceptability of exhibiting emotion if you are upset about something at work. Whereas the Spanish, Russians and the French largely find it acceptable to show emotions openly, the Chinese and Japanese do not. Table 5.8 illustrates selected examples of such cultural differences.

Multinational teams consisting of individuals from highly neutral and highly affective cultures need careful management and considerable inter-cultural understanding. Otherwise, the affective persons will view the neutral persons as ice-cold, and the affective persons will be viewed as out of control by the neutrals.

The Specific versus Diffuse dimension is illustrated by the question of whether the company is responsible for providing housing for its employees. The proportions that disagree with this are much smaller for China, Russia, Japan and India than for North European countries and North America, as exemplified in Table 5.9.

Managers from specific cultures such as Denmark are much more prone to criticize subordinates directly and openly without regarding their criticism as a personal matter. In the context of a subsidiary in a diffuse culture such as Russia this may constitute an unacceptable loss of face.

The issue of whether the respect a person gets is highly dependent on their family is one of the ways Trompenaars exemplifies the Achievement versus Ascription dimension. Trompenaars observes that Protestants in particular, such as Scandinavians, North Americans and the British generally disagree

Table 5.9 Selected examples of percentage of respondents who think that the company should not be responsible for providing housing for employees

China	18
Spain	19
Russia	22
Japan	45
India	46
Germany	75
France	81
UK	82
Denmark	84
USA	85

Table 5.10 Selected examples of percentage of respondents who disagree that respect depends on family background

India	57
Russia	74
Germany	74
Japan	79
China	81
Spain	82
France	83
USA	87
UK	89
Denmark	92

with this. Other cultures tend to be more ascriptive. Table 5.10 compares this question across select countries.

Sending a young manager to run a subsidiary in an ascriptive culture such as India will involve difficulty. Likewise, promoting younger people within the subsidiary on the basis of their performance is challenging in an ascriptive culture.

5.9 Hofstede and Trompenaars compared

Making comparisons between Hofstede's research and that of Trompenaars is problematical because they are for the most part exploring very different cultural dimensions. As such their research efforts should be regarded as supplementing one another rather than duplicating one another. However, their research is analogous in regard to one dimension: Trompenaars' Communitarianism versus Individualism dimension is similar to Hofstede's Individualism–Collectivism dimension. An examination reveals broad consistency in the respective classifications of countries. For example Japan and India are both relatively weak in terms of individualism according to both Hofstede and Trompenaars, while Denmark, the UK and the USA are relatively individualistic. However, many countries appear to be more individualistic according to Trompenaars than Hofstede's research indicates. This is particularly the case for countries such as Mexico, Greece and Spain. Differences of this kind cannot be entirely explained away by pointing to the differences in the items employed by Hofstede and Trompenaars. Hodgetts and Luthans (2000) have suggested that what is possible is that the differences may be due to the different time frames of the two studies, indicating that cultural change has taken place. In turn this implies that Hofstede's findings are becoming out of date. For example Mexico's integration into the global economy may be generating a move away from communitarian values. In other words, '[c]ultures do not stand still; they evolve over time, albeit slowly. What was a reasonable characterization in the 1960s and 1970s may not be so today' (Hill, 2000: 100). It is also interesting to note that Trompenaars' findings indicate that former communist countries such as Russia, Hungary and the Czech Republic are relatively individualistic despite their communist past.

Trompenaars has also extended his research by examining corporate cultures by nationality. In order to do so he introduced yet another dimension: Equality versus Hierarchy. The hierarchical corporate culture is one that is power-oriented in which the leader has considerable authority and knows best. This dimension is akin to Hofstede's Power Distance dimension. Furthermore, there are a number of similarities in their findings: the Scandinavian countries, North America and the UK have relatively egalitarian cultures according to Trompenaars, and are low in terms of power distance according to Hofstede. France and Spain figure as hierarchical according to Trompenaars and relatively high in terms of power distance in Hofstede's research. There are, however, pronounced disagreements not least in regard to Germany. Trompenaars' findings suggest that German corporate culture is decidedly hierarchical, whereas Hofstede identifies Germany as relatively low in terms of power distance.

5.10 The GLOBE study

The most recent major approach to operationalizing cultural distance is that of the GLOBE study (House et al., 2004) which was conducted in the mid

Table 5.11 Power distance: the degree to which a community maintains inequality among its members by stratification of individuals and groups with respect to power, authority, prestige, status, wealth, and material possessions

High Power Distance	Low Power Distance
Society is differentiated into classes.	Society has a large middle class.
Power seen as providing social order.	Power is seen as a source of corruption and coercion.
Upward social mobility is limited.	Upward social mobility is common.
Resources and skills available to only a few.	Resources and skills are available to almost all.
Civil liberties are weak.	Civil liberties are strong.

Source: Based on House et al. (2004), Table 17.2, p.536.

1990s and involved 127 investigators in 62 countries or regions. The study was designed to replicate and expand on Hofstede's (1980a) work and to test various hypotheses that had been developed in particular on leadership topics. Survey questionnaires were developed and collected from more than 17,000 middle managers in 951 organizations across three specific industries.

GLOBE empirically established nine cultural dimensions that make it possible to capture the similarities and/or differences in norms and values among societies. They are: power distance, uncertainty avoidance, humane orientation, institutional collectivism, in-group collectivism, assertiveness, gender egalitarianism, future orientation, and performance orientation. Tables 5.11 to 5.19 elaborate on the dimensions in more detail.

Table 5.12 Uncertainty avoidance: the extent to which a society, organization, or group relies on social norms, rules, and procedures to alleviate unpredictability of future event

High Uncertainty Avoidance Societies tend to. . .	Low Uncertainty Avoidance Societies tend to. . .
Formalize their interactions with others.	Use informality in interactions with others.
Document their agreements in legal contracts.	Rely on the word of others they trust rather than contractual arrangements.
Rely on formalized policies and procedures.	Rely on informal norms rather than formalized rules.
Take moderate calculated risks.	Are less calculating when taking risks.
Show stronger resistance to change.	Show only moderate resistance to change.

Source: Based on House et al. (2004), Table 19.1, p.618.

Table 5.13 Humane orientation: the degree to which an organization or society encourages and rewards individuals for being fair, altruistic, generous, caring, and kind to others

High Humane Orientation Societies	Low Humane Orientation Societies
Others are important.	One's own self-interest is important.
People are motivated by a need for belonging and affiliation.	People are motivated by a need for power and material possessions.
Members of society are responsible for promoting the well-being of others. The state is not actively involved.	The state provides social and economic support for individuals' well-being.
Children should be obedient.	Children should be autonomous.
People are urged to be sensitive to all forms of racial discrimination.	People are not sensitive to all forms of racial discrimination.

Source: Based on House et al. (2004), Table 18.1, p. 570.

Table 5.14 Collectivism I (institutional): the degree to which institutional practices encourage collective action

Organizations that score high on collectivism	Organizations that score low on collectivism
Employees tend to develop long-term relationship with employers from recruitment to retirement.	Employees develop short-term relationships, and change companies at their own discretion.
Organizational commitment is based on expectation of loyalty and in-group attitudes.	Organizational commitment is based on individuals' rational calculations of costs and benefits.
Compensation and promotions are based on what is equitable for the group and on considerations of seniority and personal needs.	Compensation and promotions are based on an equity model: rewards reflect an individual's contribution to task success.
Organizational citizenship behaviors are more common.	Organizational citizenship behaviors are less common.

Source: Based on House et al. (2004), Table 16.2, p. 459.

GLOBE provides two measures for each of these nine dimensions: one for norms and one for values. Norms encompass actual society practices ('As Is') while values encompass preferred states of affairs ('As Should Be'). For the most part, the norm-based practices and value dimensions measured by the GLOBE study are negatively correlated meaning that standard practices may differ from either what may be generally desired or considered desirable.

Table 5.15 Collectivism II (in-group): the degree to which individuals express pride, loyalty, and cohesiveness in their organizations or families

High In-Group Collectivism Societies have features such as. . .	Low In-Group Collectivism Societies have features such as. . .
Individuals are integrated into strong cohesive groups.	Individuals look after themselves or their immediate families.
Duties and obligations are important determinants of social behavior.	Personal needs are important determinants of social behavior.
A strong distinction is made between in-groups and out-groups.	Little distinction is made between in-groups and out-groups.
People emphasize relatedness with groups.	People emphasize rationality in behavior.
The pace of life is slower.	The pace of life is faster.
Love is assigned little weight in marriage.	Love is assigned great weight in marriage.

Source: Based on House et al. (2004), Table 16.1, p. 454.

Table 5.16 Assertiveness: the degree to which individuals are assertive, confrontational, and aggressive in their relationships with others

High Assertiveness Societies tend to. . .	Low Assertiveness Societies tend to. . .
Value assertive behaviour.	Value modesty.
Value success and progress.	Value people and warm relationships.
Try to have control over the environment.	Try to be in harmony with the environment.
Emphasize results over relationships.	Emphasize tradition, seniority and experience.
Act and think of others as opportunistic.	Think of others as inherently worthy of trust.

Source: Based on House et al. (2004), Table 15.1, p. 405.

Table 5.17 Gender egalitarianism: the degree to which a collective minimizes gender inequality

High Gender Egalitarianism Societies tend to. . .	Low Gender Egalitarianism Societies have characteristics such as. . .
Have more women in positions of authority.	Have fewer women in positions of authority.
Have less occupational sex segregation.	Have more occupational sex segregation.
Have similar levels of educational attainment for males and females.	Have a lower level of female educational attainment, compared to that of males.
Afford women a greater decision-making role in community affairs.	Afford women little or no decision-making role in community affairs.

Source: Based on House et al. (2004), Table 14.2, p. 359.

Table 5.18 Future orientation: the degree to which a collectivity encourages and rewards future-oriented behaviors such as planning and delaying gratification

High Future Orientation Societies tend to. . .	Low Future Orientation Societies tend to. . .
Have a propensity to save for the future.	Have a propensity to spend now, rather than save.
Value working for long-term success.	Prefer gratification as soon as possible.
Have organizations that are flexible and adaptive.	Have organizations that are inflexible and maladaptive.
View material success and spiritual fulfillment as an integrated whole.	View material success and spiritual fulfillment as separate, requiring trade-offs.

Source: Based on House et al. (2004), Table 13.1, p. 302.

Table 5.19 Performance orientation: the degree to which a collective encourages and rewards group members for performance improvement and excellence

High Performance Orientation Societies tend to. . .	Low Performance Orientation Societies tend to. . .
Reward performance.	Have high respect for quality of life.
Expect demanding targets.	Value harmony with the environment.
Value bonuses and financial rewards.	View merit pay as potentially destructive to harmony.
View formal feedback as necessary for performance improvement.	View formal feedback as judgmental and discomforting.
Value 'what one does' more than 'who one is'.	Value 'who one is' more than 'what one does'.
Expect direct, explicit communication.	Expect subtle communication.

Source: Based on House et al. (2004), Table 12.1, p. 245.

One observation of GLOBE is that for the most part, the normative and value dimensions are negatively correlated; meaning that what may be either generally desired or considered desirable cannot be assumed as providing any guide to actual management practice. A second criticism is that nine dimensions for each set of values and norms are unwieldy for research purposes. Thus Tung and Verbeke (2010: 1264) recommend that 'any empirical design should include only those cultural distance dimensions, and the measures associated with them that can really be expected to affect *ex ante* managerial choice . . . and/or *ex post* behavior and performance'. In other words one should carefully consider which of the 18 alternative values and norms one should select.

5.11 Hofstede and GLOBE compared

Hosftede (2010) is highly critical of GLOBE, questioning whether GLOBE actually measures culture at all. Others such Venaik and Brewer (2010; Brewer and Venaik, 2011) have pointed out that while there are a number of similarities between GLOBE and Hofstede's study in the way in which the concept of national culture is measured, there are also significant differences that should give rise to concern. For example, while both studies include the dimensions of uncertainty avoidance and power distance, the GLOBE dimensions of performance orientation and humane orientation are not measured by Hofstede. Hofstede's masculinity dimension is measured with the two dimensions of gender egalitarianism and assertiveness in the GLOBE study. Similarly, Hofstede's collectivism is measured with two constructs: institutional collectivism (collectivism I) and in-group collectivism (collectivism II).

However, what concerns Venaik and Brewer in particular is the lack of congruence between Hofstede's dimensions and those of GLOBE. In contrast, Hofstede's uncertainty avoidance has significant positive correlation with GLOBE uncertainty values, but significant negative correlation with GLOBE uncertainty avoidance practices. In other words, the same label of 'uncertainty avoidance' seems to be used to represent polar opposite national culture concepts.

Venaik and Brewer (2010) conclude that both Hofstede and GLOBE are highly valuable studies on cross-cultural management, with GLOBE being a recent extension of the Hofstede study. They further view both culture models as supported by powerful arguments as to their validity. However, they observe that there is no consensus in the research community on which model should be preferred with both sources of cultural dimension scores being applied often producing contrary results.

5.12 Which measure of cultural distance?

Early in this chapter we indicated that the precise conceptualization and measurement of culture is 'still hotly debated'. Given this level of debate which of the three approaches to measuring culture should one adopt? At this point in time we argue that one should be aware that Hofstede is the most widely cited author in the field. His pioneering role has been accepted by Trompenaars (1993: iii), who credits Hofstede 'for opening management's eyes to the importance of the (cross-cultural management) subject'. In empirical research by far the most used measure of cultural distance is Kogut and Singh's (1988) index which is a composite measure of cultural distance from the USA. This index employs Hofstede's four dimensions of national culture: power distance, uncertainty avoidance, masculinity–femininity and individualism–collectivism. However, equally one should be aware that the data Hofstede's measures build on are relatively old and that change may have occurred (Gooderham and Nordhaug, 2003).

We view supplementing Hofstede's dimensions with those of Trompenaars as relatively unproblematic. However, in line with Venaik and Brewer we acknowledge a challenge in applying the GLOBE measures. First, one should be aware that although a number of its dimensions have labels that are identical to Hofstede's dimensions the GLOBE measures are not measuring the same phenomena. Second, one should be clear that GLOBE contains measures of both aspirations and practices. In other words on the basis of what one is studying one should select carefully among the GLOBE measures.

5.13 Cultural intelligence

Hofstede has consistently refused to apply his concepts to levels of analysis other than the national. However, Kirkman et al. (2006) argue that one might reasonably infer that it also applies to smaller groups within nationalities, such as organizations and teams. But what one cannot do is to apply Hofstede's concepts to individuals. In other words, at the level of actual managers and employees within nations there are many variations in terms of values.

One challenge for international managers is to resist stereotyping foreign colleagues. Hambrick et al. (2001: 1034) describe IJVs as inherently prone to conflict because:

> The managers are almost always of differing nationalities – often (but not necessarily) the nationalities of the parent firms' headquarters. And, because of systemic differences in the social and economic institutions of their home countries . . . there are likely to be schismatic, factionalized perceptions and behaviors among top managers.

IJVs are characterized by nationally based fault-lines with trust across these being highly problematic to develop. MNCs that comprise wholly-owned subsidiaries have the opportunity to counteract the tendency for national factions to develop by developing a common organizational culture. This can be developed in a number of ways including management training, exchanges of personnel, in-house seminars and joint projects. However, it has been argued that MNCs need to recruit individuals with high levels of 'cultural intelligence' (CQ). Earley and Ang (2003) have applied the concept of CQ to capture variations in the ability of individual managers to function in culturally diverse settings. It is distinct from social intelligence in that individuals who are highly proficient in interacting with individuals from their own national communities may be very much less successful when they operate abroad or have to interact with groups who do not share their national context. More specifically it refers to an outsider's natural ability to interpret and respond to unfamiliar cultural signals in an appropriate manner. In defining CQ, Earley and Ang distinguish three interrelated components of CQ:

1. *Cognitive intelligence*, which refers to the knowledge an individual can acquire about a new culture on the basis of processing and reasoning from the available information.
2. *Motivational intelligence*, which refers to the propensity to act on the cognitive facet and to persevere in acquiring knowledge and to overcome stumbling blocks and failure. Individuals with a high level of motivational cultural intelligence have the ability to adapt and learn within new cultural settings due to their innate desire to do so.
3. *Behavioral intelligence*, which refers to the capability of a person to enact his or her desired and intended actions in a given cultural situation. Individuals with a high level of behavioral CQ are able to act in an appropriate manner in diverse cultural settings in regard to such behaviors as tone of voice, language, greetings, and social gestures. Individuals with no regard for other's impressions of them will be disparaged and even ostracized.

Individuals with high CQ are more readily able to distinguish behaviors driven by culture from those specific to an individual. As such they are more willing to suspend judgment until enough information about the other person becomes available and are therefore more able to respond appropriately to the situation. Earley and Ang argue that an individual should possess a certain level of all three of the intelligences in order to be capable of a successful cross-national interaction. Individual managers should be assessed against all three types of intelligence and where there are gaps training should be initiated. Although CQ has primarily been applied to expatriates it clearly has relevance for all managers in MNCs engaged in cross-national interaction.

5.14 Summary

It has not been the ambition of this chapter to try to understand the origins of various national cultures. Nor have we attempted to provide in-depth analyses of particular national cultures. Instead we have presented the concept of cultural distance and thereafter considered three different approaches to measuring it. If used critically these measures of cultural distance provide a valuable starting point for a discussion of the cultural challenge faced by MNCs in achieving high performance across its operations. However, awareness of cultural distance is only the first stage to becoming an effective international manager. Cultural intelligence involves considerably more than acquiring explicit knowledge of cultural distance. As we will see in the accompanying case, even in MNCs that are committed to the notion that cultural diversity is beneficial, developing cultural intelligence is of critical importance if alienation from the MNC is to be avoided.

Case D

Cultural diversity in a Danish MNC

Vasilisa Sayapina and Katya Christensen

D.1 Introduction

Workforce diversity is a complex phenomenon and a major challenge for HR managers in MNCs. The case presents a Danish MNC, Danvita (not its real name), that has committed to pursuing a diversity strategy. The essence of a diversity strategy is a commitment to providing equal opportunities for employees regardless of their gender, age, nationality, disability and political or sexual orientation. In this case our focus is on cultural diversity. Drawing on individual perceptions of Danvita employees this case explores how these employees experience diversity.

Diversity as a strategic resource

Scholars have different opinions about how diversity impacts organizational performance. On one hand it has been argued that MNCs that are able to draw on a diverse mix of employees can develop a strategic advantage (Richard, 2000). This is because workforce diversity establishes the potential for diverse perspectives that in turn facilitate creative thinking and effective problem solving (Cox, 1991; Cox and Blake, 1991). Understanding and valuing diversity can enable constructive conflict resolution, reduce miscommunication and lead to lower employee turnover and result in cost savings (Robinson and Dechant, 1997). A diverse workforce that can draw on a variety of cultural insights can also have a positive impact on international marketing and sales (Blake-Beard et al., 2008; Robinson and Dechant, 1997; Cox, 1991; Cox and Blake, 1991). On the other hand, workforce diversity can also have negative implications. Some researchers have observed that groups characterized by high degrees of cultural diversity have lower levels of employee satisfaction and worse performance than in more homogenous groups (O'Reilly et al., 1989; Watson et al., 1993; Richard et al., 2003).

Diversity as perceived by organizational members

The focus of this case is in on the issue of how Danvita employees experience cultural diversity encouraged by the company's diversity strategy. 'As with many things in life, perception is reality' claim Allen et al. (2008: 22). Individual perceptions influence the way individuals interact with their colleagues and participate in the life of organization. Based on their perceptions, organizational members participate actively or passively in the implementation of the company's strategies as well as support or oppose organizational change. Knowledge of how organizational members perceive diversity opens a possibility for improvement and a dialogue.

The case data was obtained by means of 17 qualitative interviews with seven Danish and ten international employees. Their narratives, however, should not be understood separately from the environment where the stories and events took place. Thus the narratives were supplemented with direct observations of diversity training sessions and with documents containing the new diversity strategy, managerial speeches and company annual reports. In this way information about the social context in which the employees' perceptions of cultural diversity were constructed and reconstructed on an everyday basis was obtained.

D.2 Denmark and Danish

The context in which the diversity case is unfolding contains elements of both national and organizational culture. Although there is a considerable overlap, it is important to distinguish them. Despite its commitment to diversity and inclusion of international employees, the head office of Danvita is still operating in a broader context of Denmark. In Denmark the historical and religious development of the society led to the formation of a very particular institutional environment in which the state plays a significant role. Denmark has a well-developed welfare state that redistributes wealth and that ensures inequalities are relatively limited (Andersen and Svarer, 2007). The role of the Danish language as a uniting and protecting mechanism in Danish society must be acknowledged. Historically the Danish language is an indicator of membership of and belonging to Danish society. Its significance for inclusiveness means that it may also function as a mechanism of exclusion of non-Danish speakers. This factor co-exists with Denmark's membership of the European Union and its policy of welcoming well-qualified professionals to work in Denmark.

D.3 Danvita and the HR challenges it is facing

The aim is to create a culture where all employees feel valued and have the opportunity to reach their full potential. (Diversity strategy, Danvita)

Briefly about Danvita

Danvita is a company that has been a leader in the industry in which it operates. Annual reports indicate increased profits for 2009–2011. In March 2012 Danvita had more than 32,800 employees worldwide distributed across affiliates and offices located in 75 countries. Just over 40 per cent of its employees are located in Denmark. In order to function successfully as an MNC Danvita believes that it has to attract, develop and retain competent people from any location in the world. In 2009 it started a diversity initiative. At the core of this initiative is the operational guideline for HR which states that the company will provide:

equal opportunities to all present and future people, regardless of gender, age, race, religion, nationality, cultural and social origin, disability, political or sexual orientation and family status. (Danvita)

In 2009 when the diversity strategy was launched, about 700 of Danvita's employees in Denmark were foreigners. Although 68 nationalities were represented it should be noted that half of the foreign employees were from a handful of countries: the UK, the USA, Germany and Sweden.

The highest percentage of the international employees was among the professionals and specialists. An effort was necessary to make these employees feel welcome and willing to stay. The turnover rate for international specialists was three times higher than that among the specialists from Denmark. These numbers are not necessarily alarming since employees change jobs and employers frequently and international employees return home after rotations and expatriation. Nevertheless, through feeling welcome and happy with their working environment, international employees can contribute to higher retention rates in the organization which claims to be in need of workforce. Thus the diversity strategy was developed.

Guiding principles

The guiding principles of Danvita's diversity strategy attempt to lay the foundation for equal treatment of all the organizational members. These principles highlight the strategy's focus on providing equal opportunities and selecting the best-qualified candidates in order to attract and keep talent from all over the world.

Supporting initiatives

A number of supporting initiatives contribute to the creation of a culture of inclusion. There is an International Club which is run on a voluntary basis and which aims at creating a network for foreign employees. The idea is that foreign employees have the opportunity to meet in a non-work atmosphere and to experience the traditions and leisure activities of the host country. It also provides an arena to talk through their frustrations with more experienced colleagues.

Corporate way of speaking about diversity

Drawing on company documents we now present three company discourses on diversity.

Business and business needs

The first discourse emphasizes the business needs of the company. Diversity is a way of dealing with these needs. The discourse portrays the company as 'a global company', having an 'expanding presence in the world'. The key issue is: 'as we expand where are we going to find the people (we need)?' A representative of the top management team emphasizes the current growth and success of the company which is going to be 'even larger and more global' and articulates the need for attracting talent: 'We want to be among the most attractive companies so that we can continue to attract – and retain – the talent we need'. The business discourse constructs diversity as the necessary attribute for sustainable growth with satisfying the needs of international recruits as the means to this end.

Equality

The second discourse emphasizes diversity as an expression of equality. This discourse views diversity as a product of emphasizing talent regardless of any other considerations.

> We need to make a greater and more systematic effort to identify women and non-Danes with leadership potential when we are filling a management position . . .. The company will never use either negative or positive discrimination. We

will always choose the best individual for a vacant position. (Interview with top management team representative, Employee magazine)

The discourse sees selection of the 'best' individuals for positions as the guiding principle with the provision of equal opportunities to all as the means to this end.

Inclusion

The third discourse involves how the company talks about diversity as inclusion. This discourse presents inclusion as a precondition for achieving diversity: 'Inclusion is an integral element of the diversity strategy, as this is about how to value and utilize all the differences among our people' (Danvita Diversity strategy). While emphasizing inclusion this way of talking about diversity constructs diversity in terms of differences. In the Annual Report for 2008:

> inclusion of men, women, locals and non-locals must be considered for succession list for all key positions. Mentorship will be offered and supportive network initiatives including expatriate networks and a 'family-buddy' system are being set up.

These three main corporate ways of speaking about diversity coexist in the organizational space of the company. Of the three the business discourse is the most pronounced discourse and the inclusion discourse by far the least pronounced.

D.4 Cultural diversity as perceived by employees

Cultural diversity as a social construct

An overview of respondent data is presented in Table D.1.

The overall perception of cultural diversity among the respondents can be narrowed down to two groups of employees: Danes and non-Danes. It is seen from the examples below where two employees express their perceptions of cultural diversity in Danvita as consisting primarily of Danes and international people (Respondent 2) and as Danes and non-Danes who do not speak the Danish language (Respondent 14's quote):

> Awareness will take time, definitely. Of the three diversity training sessions we have had, the majority who attended were international people, but there were Danes who were there as well. (Respondent 2)

Table D.1 Respondent data

Gender	7 respondents – male
	10 respondents – female
Position	7 respondents – HR
	7 respondents – specialists
	3 respondents – administrative positions
Geographies	7 respondents – Denmark
	4 respondents – USA
	2 respondents – Germany
	1 respondent – Brazil
	1 respondent – Spain
	1 respondent – India
	1 respondent – Portugal
Age	2 respondents – 20–30 years old
	8 respondents – 30–40 years old
	5 respondents – 40–50 years old
	1 respondent – 50–60 years old
	1 respondent – over 60 years old

We do not typically write in English. We say that the company language is English, but normally we would write in Danish. Recently we found out that we have some standard operational procedures in our department that are only in Danish and nobody thought of actually translating them into English. It's just the mindset has been very Danish and suddenly we all of a sudden become aware: 'Oh, there are some people that are not Danes and do not speak Danish.' (Respondent 14)

It might sound quite natural to refer to different groups of organizational members as Danes and non-Danes or locals and international people. However, the perception of the workforce in terms of categories carries the inherited danger of reinforcing stereotypes (Litvin, 1997). These perceptions of organizational members as divided into categories reinforce constructs of being local and non-local as fixed entities with characteristics that are believed to accompany those categories. For instance, interviews suggest that Danish employees are sometimes perceived as being better colleagues and employees because they speak Danish and understand how social relations work in Denmark, and also because they possess country-specific knowledge that international employees lack. On the other hand, international employees are frequently perceived as not speaking the Danish language and being rather formal in communication, which makes it complicated to socialize and interact, while social relations at work are perceived as highly important in Denmark. Being international and therefore lacking knowledge of Danish laws and regulation is perceived as a disadvantage.

This perception of individuals as first of all belonging to one or the other group and possessing certain characteristics (speaking Danish, understanding the way social relations work, etc.) reinforces stereotypes (for example, that Danish colleagues are better colleagues and employees) since attention is being paid to the category into which the individual is locked in.

However, the interviews from Danvita also reveal an appreciation among organizational members that the company is attempting to create space for multifaceted difference. The right to be a unique individual and not to be ascribed to one of the predefined categories is valued and acknowledged by many organizational members.

> I am a bit special myself, I am a Jehovah Witness. It is a bit special religion here in Denmark. People do not know it very well. In relation to this, I think it is nice that there are differences. I like that the company does not have prejudices, and I myself try not to judge others. (Respondent 4)

> I am gay and I am a foreigner and I did not speak Danish and I did have the qualifications that they were looking for. By them accepting all these things was very-very important to me as a person. Because not only that they welcomed me as a professional, a foreigner but they welcomed me privately . . .. They were willing to see me as an individual beyond my private life, beyond my culture, beyond anything else. (Respondent 6)

As shown in the citations above, some of the interviewed organizational members perceive themselves as unique individuals with characteristics crossing over a number of categories. These employees prefer to be seen and appreciated for the complexity of the characteristics and qualities they embody.

However, the company continues to run two introductory programs for new employees: one in Danish and one in English. While the rationale that new employees should choose the language program they are most comfortable with, it does mean that nearly all of the international employees will choose the English language version. Thus, from the very outset of their Danvita careers employees are entering the organization as belonging to one of two groups – the Danes and the non-Danes.

Language as an exclusion mechanism

The use of the Danish language is often perceived as an exclusion mechanism.

I can point to incidents like our CEO's speech at the annual event that was in Danish; often communication is in Danish because people have not thought of it. It is still a part of a shifting mind-set . . .. Even small things like forwarding an e-mail from one person to another and asking for comments. Since it has been sent in Danish some people might not see what is written. Small things like that. (Respondent 1)

Others say that they feel the use of Danish language makes them feel unwelcome:

I am usually the one who says: 'Hello, can you speak English?' but sometimes you do not do that because people usually point at you saying: 'He is the one who always does this.' And you get tired that people always find you the annoying person that makes them change into English. (Respondent 3)

Mostly my communication would be in Danish: with my boss, with my colleagues . . . even though there are foreigners as well . . . When our Indian colleagues join us at lunch sometimes people continue in Danish. I am sorry to say that. (Respondent 9)

The employment interview often sets the expectations regarding the company's corporate language:

[The interviewee is referring to his employment interview] I said: 'I am not Danish, I do not speak Danish, I do not look like a Danish person and I would be working mostly with Danes. Is that a problem?' He said: 'Not at all. You do not even need to learn Danish because the corporate language is English and we do not want you to become Danish. We want to have your different perspective, your different point of view.' I took it as a statement and that's what I am following. (Respondent 2)

On day one of starting at Danvita:

A manager started speaking to me in Danish and then I said: 'Sorry, I do not speak Danish. Would you mind speaking in English?' 'Oh, but how long have you been here?' I said: 'That does not matter. The company language is English . . .. I was told that Danish is not a requirement for my position.' . . . That annoyed me that a person would not make an effort to be more inclusive. (Respondent 2)

As illustrated in the quotes above some international organizational members have a perception that organizational reality does not coincide with the message of English being a corporate language.

On the other hand, we observed that some international employees take it for granted that the corporate language is Danish. These employees willingly learn Danish and do not see any contradiction between what they were promised during the employment interview and the reality:

> During the interview we agreed that the working language would actually be Danish and that I therefore would have to learn Danish. (Respondent 7)

Some Danish employees also perceive Danish as the corporate language, not because they have been told so but because they take it for granted.

Reverse discrimination?

In Danvita there is a general belief that most of the Danish employees speak good English and are as comfortable in working and socializing in English as they are in Danish. However, some of our interviews with Danish employees indicated that these perceptions are not always correct:

> I do not really like to speak English but it will be ok. I will practice. (Respondent 4)

> If you go to the product sites there are many Danes working there who do not know English or the English they have is very limited, basic. So they would feel intimidated if there was a person from another country coming and they were forced to speak English. They would feel a little bit annoyed that it would disturb their routine in the group. So it depends where you are. (Respondent 14)

> I have experienced that for instance in IT they have employed a lot of people from other countries than Denmark. So when you have an IT problem it could be very difficult to communicate so we both understand what we are talking about . . .. That can be quite challenging. (Respondent 11)

> I hold back. Mostly because I get a little bit embarrassed what if I say words wrong or what if the grammar is not right and it sounds ridiculous when I speak (. . .) something like that. Sometimes I choke on the words. (Respondent 15)

The quotes above suggest that some local employees feel awkward when they are forced to speak a foreign language in order to include international employees. These organizational members refer to the necessity of speaking English as 'challenging', 'annoying' and 'embarrassing'. They feel rather 'intimidated' when they have to do it. In other words, some of the Danish employees perceive themselves in a situation of reverse discrimination because they feel at a disadvantage when they have to communicate with the international employees.

However, speaking English on an everyday basis is not only a challenge for the local employees. For most of the international employees English is also a foreign language and makes communication challenging to the same degree.

Preventing segregation

Mentoring and the creation of social networks are perceived by a number of organizational members as a way to welcome new employees from abroad and contribute to the creation of a positive and inclusive climate for cultural diversity. The initiatives are also perceived as a way of creating a meeting point for locals and non-locals – a bridge allowing people to get to know each other better and to find common points of interests. The International Club is an existing example of a social network run by employees, which is perceived as giving a helping hand to international employees:

> It can mean one hell of a lot to have colleagues that are open-minded and show that support and extend that hand to you as a foreigner when you come to the organization. So in a way if we start at the lowest level of the organization we could create that awareness and create it together. (Respondent 13)

However, the concern was also raised regarding the existing danger of segmenting people into categories and those people cultivating their own networks separate from other organizational members. International employees need to feel included and welcome, also with their families. This includes practical assistance to establish their life in a new environment.

> I would like to interact with all kinds of people despite their mindset, political thoughts, sexual orientation and so on. For me it is the person that counts. That is what I think is important. Personally I do not want to put people into boxes. (Respondent 15)

> They [Danish colleagues] should be part of this [International Club] to make it successful. Otherwise they are doing exactly the same as Danvita in Denmark, not integrating people. If the international people coming here are not integrated by Danish people into their activities it is just more of the same, isn't it? That's a dilemma really. (Respondent 8)

> Honestly, I think that mentoring is one thing but another thing is the hard facts and the basic help you need with the things that matter for everyday life. Imagine

people coming here with families . . .. You really have to address these needs if people are going to really feel 'OK, we feel good here. We are happy here'. (Respondent 13)

D.5 Creating the environment for cultural diversity

The following section reflects on what Danvita's approach to diversity means for organizational members' perception of cultural diversity.

Not wishful thinking

The goal of Danvita's diversity strategy is to have non-locals in all senior management teams within five years. These intentions are welcomed by most of the employees for numerous reasons:

> Diversity is something I have not felt until now. They are starting to think about diversity (. . .) Ok, we want to be international, so we have to show it also from inside to appear international. (Respondent 3)

> If we have more and more international employees everywhere people will be more aware and not scared that either we [international employees] are taking their jobs or making their life more difficult. It is fine to have people from everywhere. We need also to send people from the headquarters to the affiliates and that we are doing more and more. So, both ways, we need to bring non-locals and we need to export Danes to the affiliates. (Respondent 2)

> Of course, it is more demanding on you because you have to be aware: 'Oops, can't speak Danish now' but I think it enriches you as a person as well because when you talk to other people hopefully you benefit from it. They can teach me something. (Respondent 14)

Only a small number of the respondents perceive the change that is needed in terms of attitudinal, behavioral and structural changes:

> It is very good, it is needed, but it is difficult just to say: 'This is what we are going to do and we have to do this' because I think it has to come naturally. You cannot force it on people. (Respondent 14)

> It is good when it comes from top management but still it's a long process (. . .) Again diversity should be more than just: 'Now we will do this that, that and this.' It should be the mindset, but I know that that takes time. (Respondent 15)

Some of our informants perceive the diversity strategy as a matter of finally achieving fairness and had little sympathy with the locals:

> I was astonished to hear that Danes are saying, 'Ok, this means that we do not have a future in this company at all'. I say to them 'Welcome to our world!' If I were to face the barrier of nationality and then just give up, I would not be where I am today. Come on, get over it and work well, be competent in your job, perform well, and you'll be recognized. (Respondent 2)

Cultivating a diversity-valuing mindset

The corporate initiatives designed to raise awareness of cross-cultural differences among employees are the so-called Managing Across Cultures seminars. During the seminars one can observe the same over-representation of non-local employees as we witnessed at so many other diversity events:

> I am aware of these things so it was not for me an eye-opener or whatever. It is always fun to discuss and there are of course some interesting points how Danes sometimes appear mute and about how we perceive foreigners but as such (. . .) I probably was not a target audience, but I think it is needed. (Respondent 16)

The fact that the majority of the locals choose not to attend the diversity-related corporate initiatives does not go unnoticed in the eyes of many international employees. It raises a wave of disappointment and disapproval. The international employees see participation of all organizational members without exclusion as crucially important for creating a good organizational climate for diversity where awareness, understanding and empathy prevail. Some of the international employees perceive this absence of locals as a sign of unwillingness to participate in the construction and support of the valuing diversity mindset, which they perceive as a common assignment for all organizational members:

> This seminar should be done for the Danish community. I think it was aimed for the Danish community but I do not know what has happened and in the end there are a lot of international people that are well aware. (Respondent 3)

> What I really see missing to make this piece work in particularly is actually engagement from everyone in the organization. These diversity issues do not only affect foreigners. We need to wake up in the organization and realize that it also affects our Danish colleagues as well. If we are going to be a global company, it is global together, not just the foreigners who have to roll their sleeves and work and assimilate . . .. I do not see it working now. For example, when I attended

the first cultural session there I was extremely disappointed to see that a lot of the management members who were invited from our organization and who are Danish did not show up. (Respondent 13)

In line with this perception, diversity is something that cannot be measured by numbers or achieved by fulfilling quotas or goals. Instead, acceptance and appreciation of people from different backgrounds are ingrained in the organizational way of thinking as Respondent 15 expresses below:

> I do believe that diversity should be something that is penetrating what we are doing instead of saying: 'Ok, now we have to explore diversity for 3 days'. At some point we had diversity in our balance score cards and in some areas we have it as a kind of a tick-off exercise instead of really going in depth with what it means. (Respondent 15)

We observed that most of local employees perceive the company Christmas dinner as an occasion for meeting colleagues. Despite its name – 'Christmas' dinner – most of the respondents from Denmark cannot see any religious connotation in this festivity. However, two of our respondents perceived this corporate tradition as unfair and excluding. These employees wondered why it could not be called a 'New Year' celebration in order to avoid any connection to religion.

When we discussed this issue with locals some of them argued that it is necessary to keep traditions. They further argued that the dinner has nothing to do with religion and that the international employees would have to adjust to the host country and its ways. It was often assumed by these locals that the two objectors to 'Christmas' dinner were Muslims. However, in reality one was a Jehovah's Witness and the other a Jew.

Hiring the best

One key aspect to the diversity strategy at Danvita is that jobs are to go to the 'best' qualified candidate regardless of any other factors.

> The company will never promote anyone just because they are a woman or a non-Dane. We will not do that, but on the other hand we will not discriminate equal candidates for the same position because they are non-Danes or of the other gender. (Respondent 2)

However, what is understood by 'best' is not necessarily straightforward. For instance, being a manager from abroad and not being familiar with how things function in Denmark was referred to as a disadvantage by one of the respondents:

> If you go to marketing it is very diverse out there. Sometimes they even have problems that they are too diverse because it can be difficult for foreign managers if they do not know about Danish labor law and things like that (. . .) and nobody can help them because all around are non-locals. Then it can be a tough job for HR partner to learn them how we do things here in DK. (Respondent 9)

However, few organizational members show any awareness that 'best' may be a matter of perception:

> Every time you hear about this strategy you also hear: 'But of course we should employ the best'. Try to remember that or try to be aware of this. (Respondent 15)

D.6 Why workforce diversity?

A number of respondents that we interviewed perceive cultural diversity as beneficial for organizational creativity and problem-solving because it brings new perspectives and alternative views:

> the fact that they are from different cultural backgrounds gives a new view of things. If we have another project, and are there people from different countries or from different educational backgrounds, everybody has a different view of things and helps to generate ideas. (Respondent 12)

However, some respondents felt that it is only after the international employees have 'fit in' to the local working environment that they can become 'good' organizational members:

> I have heard from my own boss that he would not have hired me if I had not [fit in] (. . .) He told me that there were many good candidates – there are always many good candidates – and so he knew that I was very well qualified, but he just wanted to know whether my Danish was good enough (. . .). The social part in the working environment in Denmark is very important so you have to fit in. If you do not fit in there is not a good atmosphere at work (. . .). It was important that people should not have to switch in English during the lunch time and other events. It is just easier. (Respondent 17)

> if you want to live in another country, work in another country, you have to do whatever you can to understand the language and speak the language. Not that

I am saying that it is not ok that they [international employees] do not do it, but please make an effort. (Respondent 11)

The economic rationale

In the empirical material we found that most of the respondents perceive the need for more balance between locals and non-locals, understand that it is a process that takes time, and express willingness to work in a more culturally diverse organization in the near future. Personal interest and motivation in working with people from all over the world as well as knowledge sharing are mentioned by Respondents 16 and 5 in the quotes below:

It [more cultural diversity] will make it more interesting for me to be here. I would find it a more interesting place to work in if I could see that it is truly global. (Respondent 16)

Our director told us that they would work on that more people would come from our affiliates to work for some time here in the headquarters so that we could learn from each other. It is a good way of in-house training, so we could learn about diversity, about language, about our affiliates and their challenges. (Respondent 5)

A number of the respondents also perceive the need for cultural diversity in the case company as directly connected to globalization of businesses where a large part of production and sales takes place abroad. Besides perceiving cultural diversity as enriching organizational processes with new perspectives, the need for human capital is also perceived as one of the reasons for having cultural diversity in the company:

Everybody knows that it is not up for questioning that all resources cannot come from Denmark and from Danes alone. They simply have to include expertise from the outside world. Business relies on that and top management knows that. (Respondent 13)

The moral argument

While respondents' perceptions reveal adherence towards the economic rationale for cultural diversity, the moral underpinning – valuing and welcoming diversity in order to make it inclusive and fair for all organizational members – is rather limited in the way employees talk about cultural diversity and reasons for it. Instead, a number of international organizational members perceive themselves and some of their colleagues as being excluded and thus treated unfairly from time to time. For instance, respondents 17 and

3 refer to the occasions when local employees are not making an effort to be inclusive and speak Danish in the presence of their international colleagues:

> I find it hard to believe that you do not notice that there is someone who does not understand for half an hour . . .. It is the attitude like 'it is not my responsibility to make this person feel welcome'. (Respondent 17)

Respondent 17 is referring to a situation in which an Indian colleague sat isolated during a lunch break in the canteen, while the local employees were speaking the local language among themselves. The Indian colleague was thus simply excluded from the conversation.

Respondent 3 refers to his experience of meetings and the way he sometimes feels completely excluded when Danish takes over:

> Obviously I am not important for them. Do they really care about me? They only care about certain people in the team that are able to speak the language and if you are not one of them – good luck and that's it. Of course, it de-motivates a whole lot. (Respondent 3)

To summarize we noted several aspects to perceptions relating to cultural diversity. One was about being valued for whom one is as an individual rather than being identified with a group that possesses a set of ascribed qualities. Another concerned the issue of reverse discrimination. A third involved the stimulation of working with colleagues from diverse cultures. Finally, there was the rejection of responsibility by some of employees for contributing to making diversity actually work.

D.7 Two employee stories

Despite the substantial tendency to operate with a divide between Danes and non-Danes there are contrasting cases even within the same group. We have chosen two contrasting stories about being included and being excluded among the internationals.

The story of feeling valued and willingness to make others feel the same

> I spoke to my boss and we said: 'There are a lot of foreigners here right now. We need to do something so that we can all break down this imaginary wall of culture of oddness.' I think it was very odd that there was this sort of feeling in the air that we could not break and be able to walk and say: 'Hey, good morning!

How are you? How is it going? How is your family?' . . . My boss asked: 'What
do you know about Denmark? About us? Our traditions?' And I answered: 'Not
much'. The first diversity training session started during a national holiday.
Everyone who was Danish in the department took time to explain what that
tradition was about, what they ate. . . . It was in November. Out of this course
I learnt so many things. I was really motivated and so I came back and more
international employees were hired in December. I spoke to my boss again and
then I said: 'Well, maybe we should bring this course to our whole department.'
(Respondent 6)

Respondent 6 has been working in the company for several years and perceives the company as open towards foreigners. His employment interview
was held by an American and a Turkish person and this expression of cultural
diversity left a positive impression on Respondent 6:

I was interviewed by a girl from California and another lady from Turkey. So, just
the very principle that it was not a Danish person. There were two foreigners as
well that were interviewing me. One of them was from my own country. So, it
made me feel more at home, made me feel: 'Ok, such diversity (. . .) I am not the
only American running around in this building'. (Respondent 6)

Besides perceiving the case company as open and welcoming to international employees like himself, Respondent 6 expresses appreciation for
the company's ability to welcome and value him, first of all as an individual with his skills and qualities, notwithstanding a different nationality
and a gay sexual orientation. Respondent 6 feels valued and supported
and is ready to support his colleagues when needed. He views his team
which comprises five nationalities as somewhere he can acquire valuable
knowledge and improve both his personal people skills but also his work
performance. According to Respondent 6 he has developed in terms of
adaptability, sensitivity, tolerance and developed an acceptance of different
viewpoints.

For Respondent 6 it has been important to learn Danish and to get to know
Denmark. He takes private Danish lessons and practices his Danish every
day: 'We can speak English, but it does not harm you to speak Danish and
you live in Denmark, so. . .' (Respondent 6). In order to get to know his colleagues at the beginning he would every morning make a point of walking
around his department to try and greet everybody. Respondent 6 wants to
create a welcoming environment for all of his colleagues and is proactive
about doing that.

The story about feeling excluded

Respondent 3 has been living abroad for quite some time. First in the UK, then for a couple of years in Germany and for the last couple of years Respondent 3 has been working in Danvita in Denmark. Respondent 3 found it difficult to settle in Denmark and preferred to live in Sweden and commute across the border to work.

> When there are other people around and you are speaking a language they do not know (Danish) you are excluding. You are excluding them from communication, from belonging to the group; and when people use the language, they do not realize how much power is involved. (Respondent 3)

Respondent 3 does not perceive her working place as culturally diverse yet, but acknowledges the importance for having diversity in the organization as a means to getting Danvita to live up to the image it is trying to project: 'We want to be international, so we have to show it also from inside' (Respondent 3). She experiences feelings of exclusion and not belonging to the group of her colleagues. Respondent 3 expresses a lot of emotion connected to those times when Danish colleagues revert to their local language. She finds it unfair, and it presents a real challenge for her that she has to cope with it on an everyday basis:

> My team is very Danish, which means if there is any excuse for not speaking English, people won't speak English. It is a problem for me. (Respondent 3)

Realizing that it is a problem for her, Respondent 3 used to make her colleagues aware that she could not understand what they were saying and felt excluded. Also during larger events and department meetings Respondent 3 perceives resentment towards using English. Because these occasions of language-based exclusion have not become less frequent Respondent 3 is about to give up and tends to believe that the organization does not care about international people like herself. She is de-motivated, disappointed and embarrassed because she believes that her colleagues find her annoying since she makes them switch from Danish into English:

> Well, what am I gaining from all this? I could be in the other country, or my country, or here and not having to go through all this that I have to cope with. (Respondent 3)

D.8 Conclusion

While most of the respondents in Danvita appreciate being valued as individuals, they perceive cultural diversity predominantly in terms of fixed categories. The feeling of inclusion is perceived by all the respondents as fundamental for creating an inclusive, culturally diverse organization. However, one key factor impeding this is the perception of the role of language. It is not just the international employees that feel excluded by the use of Danish. Some of the local employees perceive themselves as placed in a disadvantaged situation as well when they have to use English. The mentoring and networking initiatives are perceived as possible solutions to overcome exclusion, but in practice these initiatives might lead to the segregation of international employees. However, despite the division into Danish and non-Danish employees, the case provided two stories of international employees, one of them feeling included and another one feeling excluded.

Cultural diversity is primarily perceived as related to attracting a larger number of colleagues from abroad and thereafter about quotas. Cultural diversity is seldom perceived in terms of a behavioral and attitudinal change accompanied by a diversity-valuing mindset. The business rationale dominates both the corporate way of speaking about diversity as well as the organizational members' perceptions. Indeed some respondents perceive the international employees as having to fit into the local culture.

? DISCUSSION QUESTIONS

1 Specify the challenges Danvita meets on the way to embracing cultural diversity.
2 Which theoretical models can be applied to explain cultural differences between Denmark, USA, Germany, Brazil and Spain?
3 Based on the discussion of theoretical models describe limitations of these models.
4 What actions can Danvita perform to implement the diversity strategy? What measurable results should it aim at achieving?
5 Based on the Danvita case, discuss the concept of culture at these three levels: national, organizational and individual.

6

HRM in multinational companies

6.1 Introduction

Kostova and Roth (2002) have argued that an important source of competitive advantage for MNCs is the utilization of their organizational capabilities on a worldwide basis through the leveraging of their management practices across their subsidiaries. In order to get to grips with the substance of cross-national HRM we will first specify how it differs from domestic HRM. Thereafter we will present a model for studying and analysing cross-national HRM within MNCs. The model differentiates between corporate and subsidiary level factors and between macro- and micro-level forces in order to account for the degree of similarity of HRM systems between parent and subsidiary. The framework signals the need for international managers to develop not just an awareness of cultural distance but also an awareness of socio-economic and institutional distance.

The chapter has a particular focus on institutional differences between countries. Results from a study of the degree to which US subsidiaries of MNCs adapt their management of human resources to their host country settings are presented. Practical lessons are discussed: to what extent should one expect that HRM can be transferred from corporate headquarters to subsidiaries? Finally, 'genuine' transfer of HRM from corporate headquarters to the subsidiary is differentiated from three other generic outcomes: 'translation', 'ceremonial adoption', and 'corruption'.

6.2 Brief background

A rapidly increasing number of firms are moving from being purely domestic players to being cross-national players. The majority are doing this through mergers and acquisitions. A major challenge for these firms is how to create a common identity across their operations. One response to this is to ensure that all HRM practices contribute to the overall strategy of the MNC.

Schuler et al. (1993) define the MNC's International Human Resource Management (IHRM) system as the set of distinct activities, functions, and processes that are directed at attracting, developing, and maintaining an MNC's human resources. Thus, strategic IHRM (SIHRM) comprises 'human resource management issues, functions, and policies and practices that result from the strategic activities of multinational enterprises and that impact the international concerns and goals of those enterprises' (Taylor et al., 1996: 961).

In a cross-national context it is paramount that managers at corporate headquarters recognize that their ways of managing human resources have evolved in relation to the cultural and institutional conditions that are specific to their particular countries of origin. What is more, their particular, idiosyncratic style of management cannot readily be applied to subsidiaries operating in dissimilar cultures and institutional settings. Given this, it is important for these managers to fully accept that their HRM systems and practices are not necessarily superior. Furthermore, they must be sensitive not just to the cultural setting but also to the institutional setting of the subsidiary. It is also important for them bear in mind that in many foreign contexts there is considerable risk attached to mismanaging human resources. This is because MNCs usually have a higher visibility and a higher exposure to both formal and informal monitoring than their indigenous counterparts. For instance, if a country has a policy requiring that host country personnel are to be preferred for specific positions, the MNC swiftly risks losing its legitimacy if it is perceived as having failed to respond.

6.3   The substance of cross-national HRM

Managing human resources embraces a variety of tasks. These may be categorized into five broad, but interrelated HRM areas: the acquisition of human resources, human resource development, compensation, design of work systems, and labor relations.

- Human resource acquisition encompasses both the internal and the external selection and recruitment of individuals to jobs. In addition, it includes the hiring of temporary employees and the use of external consultants.
- Human resource development includes not only the development of competences among employees but also their maintenance.
- Compensation embraces a wide spectrum of employee rewards and incentives. In this chapter we focus on extrinsic or externally controlled rewards, that is wages and employee stock ownership plans.

- The design of work systems refers to the ways in which tasks and responsibilities in the firm are structured and distributed, and the extent to which there are clear borderlines between jobs.
- Labor relations span the negotiations with the work force that are necessary in order to put into practice all of the above.

Although these areas are common to both domestic and cross-national HRM, foreign environments often make for a higher degree of complexity because of the cultural, socio-economic and – a particular focus of this chapter – the institutional dissimilarities involved. One important consequence of this complexity is that it may be more difficult to specify tasks and define and reward performance levels than is the case in purely domestic environments. To succeed, managers with cross-national human resource responsibilities must be equipped with a broader cognitive perspective and more knowledge than their purely domestic counterparts. There is a need for managers who are capable of coping with uncertainty and ambiguity and who are equipped with the ability to develop negotiated solutions to problems that may even lack clear-cut definitions. Schuler and Jackson (2005: 28) contend that:

> The practice of (SIHRM) involves the management of inter-unit linkages and internal operations (Bartlett and Ghoshal, 1989). Managing inter-unit linkages is needed to integrate, control and coordinate the units of a firm that are scattered throughout the globe . . . Internal operations, on the other hand, encompass the remaining issues. For example, internal operations include the way a unit operates in concert with the laws, culture, society, politics, economy, and general environment of a particular location.

Schuler and Jackson emphasize that this context for developing internal operations is much more complex and multi-faceted than that of firms operating in a single country. Compared to domestic HRM, SIHRM involves more uncertainties and more variation in the external settings. Furthermore, SIHRM includes a wider array of functions and activities related to human resources. If these managerial challenges cannot be successfully addressed the inter-unit linkages across the MNC may be critically weakened. For example how can an MNC align subsidiaries with its strategies if all of them employ significantly different rewards systems and all have dissimilar perceptions of what talent is? As a starting point for addressing these challenges, Schuler and Jackson argue that MNCs need an SIHRM framework. In the next section we will present a comprehensive SIHRM framework that encompasses both the management of inter-unit linkages and internal operations.

6.4 A framework for SIHRM

Adler and Ghadar (1990: 245) have argued that '[t]he central issue for MNCs is not to identify the best international HRM policy per se, but rather to find the best fit between the firm's external environment, its overall strategy, and its HRM policy and implementation'. On the other hand other researchers (for example Schuler and Jackson, 2005) caution that as neither the external environment nor the overall strategy are static there is a need for flexibility as well as fit. In particular this manifests itself as an ongoing tension between the need for MNC integration (that is inter-unit linkages) and differentiation (that is the need for each subsidiary to adapt to its local environment).

Taylor et al. (1996) have developed a model of the determinants of the SIHRM system of an MNC which we, with modifications, will adopt because of its sensitivity to this integration–local adaptation tension (see Figure 6.1). The model enables us to analyse why the HRM systems at the subsidiary level may 'deviate' significantly from HRM at corporate headquarters.

The principal dependent variable in Figure 6.1 is the degree of similarity between corporate parent company and subsidiary HRM systems. The first part of this two-fold model is at the level of the parent company and has as its focus the parent company's SIHRM orientation. By SIHRM orientation Taylor et al. (1996: 966) mean 'the general philosophy or approach taken by top management of the MNC in the design of its overall IHRM system,

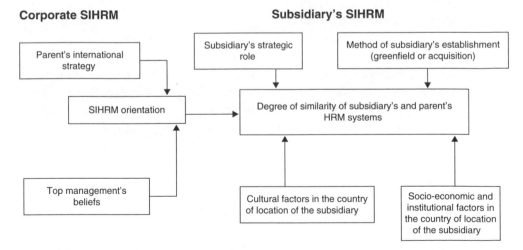

Source: Adapted from Taylor et al. (1996: 965) and reproduced with permission.

Figure 6.1 A model for analyzing SIHRM

particularly the HRM systems to be used in its overseas affiliates'. This approach will, for example, determine whether the MNC will have an IHRM director at headquarters or whether HRM will be decentralized. It will also determine whether there will be mechanisms designed to enable sharing of HRM policies and practices with and between subsidiaries. The MNC's SIHRM orientation determines its overall approach to managing the tension between the need for integration and the pressure for local adaptation.

Taylor et al. argue that the choice of SIHRM orientation is the product of the firm's international strategy coupled to top management's beliefs concerning the existence and context generalizability of its HRM competence. Let us start with the role of MNC strategy.

The role of MNC strategy

As we indicated in Chapter 3 it is common to differentiate four generic international strategies: the simple international, the multidomestic, the global, and the transnational. In light of HRM in MNCs, it is helpful to contrast multidomestic and global strategies as these represent diametrical opposites in terms of needs and challenges. Each is associated with specific structures and specific forms of SIHRM.

MNCs pursuing local adaptation grant considerable latitude to their subsidiaries, not only to develop products but also to develop their own HRM practices in line with their local needs. Although there are indications that many of these MNCs are seeking to move away from an overtly multidomestic strategy to a more integrated strategy, any transition from the multidomestic strategy is usually a slow process (see Chapter 3). Subsidiary managers used to running local fiefdoms rarely give up their prerogative to forge their own local strategies and HRM practices willingly. This differs from HRM in firms with global strategies as the major line of authority lies with parent company product managers who have a global responsibility for their product line. Subsidiaries are therefore managed largely according to the MNC's management principles.

The role of top management's beliefs

Taylor et al. (1996: 969) define top management's perception of HRM as 'the belief, expressed in corporate as well as personal communications, that the firm's way of managing its employees gives the company an advantage over its competitors'. However, in addition to this perception of HRM competence is the issue of whether top management believes that this competence is relevant beyond its national borders. A lack of such a belief would mean that there will be no attempt to apply its HRM competence in its subsidiaries. This is often a characteristic of multidomestic MNCs, just as a belief in the efficacy of its HRM applied beyond its borders is associated with global MNCs. In other words top management beliefs will usually precede and determine strategy formulation.

The resultant SIHRM orientation

The interaction of top management's HRM beliefs and choice of strategy results in characteristic SIHRM orientations. Taylor et al. (1996) distinguish between three different forms of SIHRM orientation: adaptive, exportive, and integrative.

An adaptive SIHRM orientation is one in which the top management of the MNC encourages the development of HRM systems that reflect subsidiary local environment (low degree of global integration and high degree of local responsiveness). In MNCs utilizing this approach there would be little or no transfer of HRM philosophy, policies or practices either from the parent firm to its foreign subsidiaries, or between its subsidiaries. It is an approach that is very much evident in multidomestic MNCs.

An exportive SIHRM orientation is one in which top management of the MNC prefers a comprehensive transfer of the parent firm's HRM system to its foreign subsidiaries (high degree of global integration and low degree of local responsiveness). In effect the aim is to replicate HRM policies and practices across subsidiaries with the parent determining those policies and practices. In short, unlike MNCs with an adaptive SIHRM approach, there is a high degree of control by the parent company over a subsidiary's system. In general this is the approach adopted by global MNCs, particularly in their early phase.

MNCs with an integrative SIHRM orientation attempt to take HRM 'best practices' regardless of whether they have originated in the parent firm or in the subsidiaries and apply them throughout the organization, while also allowing for some local differentiation, in the creation of a worldwide HRM system (high degree of global integration and high degree of local responsiveness). Thus, transfer of HRM policies and practices occurs, but it is just as likely to occur between foreign subsidiaries as between the parent company and its subsidiaries. In other words, transfers can go in any direction. This SIHRM orientation is associated with the transnational MNC and involves moderate control by the parent company over the subsidiary's HRM system.

MNCs do not necessarily retain their SIHRM orientation throughout their lifespan. First the beliefs of top management concerning the value and context specificity of parent company HRM competence can change as a result of international experience. Second, the firm may change its international strategy as a response to new technological opportunities or competitive pressures. Thus, for example, ABB is today pursuing a global strategy rather than the transnational strategy it pursued in the early 1990s. However, with this proviso, SIHRM orientations are reasonably stable not least because changes to strategy involve costs.

The subsidiary's HRM system

The second part of Taylor et al.'s SIHRM model is concerned with subsidiary level influences. The main point of this part of the model is to point out that because of subsidiary level influences the SIHRM orientation will not be applied uniformly to all subsidiaries. In Chapter 3 we distinguished subsidiaries in terms of the degree of knowledge resources they possess and the learning contribution of the subsidiary to the MNC.

The resource dependence of the parent company on its subsidiaries is highest for those subsidiaries with the greatest outflow of resources to the rest of the MNC: enhancers and centers of excellence. At the same time, greater reliance by the parent company on the subsidiary will increase the power of the subsidiary over the parent company. Hence, the parent company will attempt to exercise high levels of control over these subsidiaries, but these subsidiaries will simultaneously have the power to resist these control efforts. In the case of powerful centers of excellence – powerful in the sense that there is little resource dependence on the parent company combined with resource dependence of the parent on the subsidiary – there will only be a moderate degree of similarity of subsidiary and parent's HRM systems.

In addition to the strategic role of the subsidiary, the degree of similarity between the parent company's and subsidiary HRM systems will be influenced by a second subsidiary level factor: the method of the establishment of the subsidiary. Because greenfield sites have no past and therefore no established HRM practices it is easier to introduce those HRM practices favored by corporate headquarters than is the case for subsidiaries that have been acquired. Finally, Figure 6.1 includes macro-level factors that constrain what types of HRM practices an MNC can implement in its subsidiaries. One of these is the cultural context of the subsidiary: the national cultural differences we have discussed in Chapter 5 will impact on what types of HRM practices are readily acceptable in subsidiary. In addition both socio-economic and institutional factors may inhibit what HRM practices a MNC can introduce to a subsidiary. We will now examine these macro influences in detail.

6.5 Macro influences

Given the significance of host country conditions for the transfer of HRM practices we shall now further extend our perspective by developing a detailed focus on how elements in subsidiaries' macro-environments impact on their HRM systems and practices. Table 6.1 provides an overview of the presentation.

Table 6.1 Macro-environmental influences on HRM in subsidiaries of MNCs

HRM Functions	Macro-Environmental Factors		
	Socio-Economic	Institutional	Cultural
HR Acquisition:			
Recruitment and selection	External labor markets	Pressure to recruit locals	Women's position in society
Use of headhunters	Availability of services	Legal regulations	Recruitment ethics
HR Development:			
Employee training	Access to skilled people in the country	Public educational policy	Values attached to learning
Management development	Access to managerial competence	Supply of relevant external programs	Degree of bureaucracy in society
Compensation and Incentives:			
Individual performance appraisal	Degree of social inequality	Attitudes of national unions	Degree of egalitarianism
Wages	Local average wages	Minimum wage policies	Degree of materialism
Employee stock ownership plans	Level and distribution of income	Union policies on ESOPs	Ownership traditions
Work System:			
Teamwork	Authority and status relations	National traditions of organizing work	Degree of individualism
Labor Relations:			
Employee influence	Social stratification	Labor laws and regulations	Power distance in society

Human resource acquisition

For most subsidiaries of MNCs the local or regional external labor market is one of the most vital socio-economic factors for their operations. However, the size of the local pools of qualified individuals in relation to the jobs that have to be filled can be highly variable across different countries and regions. Another problem facing subsidiaries is that national educational systems and traditions are often very dissimilar to those of the parent country. This creates difficulties for subsidiaries of MNCs when they set about selecting the right type of personnel for various work tasks, since the credentials may be difficult to 'translate' into the standards of the parent country.

Moreover, the educational background locally deemed necessary for a person to become a manager may vary substantially. In Germany managers often have a technical, engineering background, in France managers usually have a grande école track or a university education, in Spain many managers have studied law or economics, in the USA an MBA is common for managers, whereas in the UK managers are recruited from a broad range of educational backgrounds. Recruiting local managers to subsidiaries without the credentials deemed locally necessary may well create difficulties for the subsidiary in its dealings with other local firms and the authorities.

A key question that every subsidiary faces is the issue of whether managers are to be recruited from the local labor market or as expatriates from other parts of the MNC (see Chapter 8). The choices MNCs make in this respect partly depend on their need to execute control over their subsidiaries. If this need is important then they tend to use parent-country managers. However, this decision is also affected by the amount of locally available managerial talent. Scarcity of local labor possessing the skills required may force the subsidiary to hire managers from the home country or from third countries. This may, however, involve problems since knowledge about the specific foreign culture may be crucial in order to operate effectively. Acquiring such knowledge may be both difficult and costly, depending on the cultural distance between the countries in question. Consequently, it may be necessary to recruit and train managers from the local labor market.

Political conditions are yet another factor that may play a key role in recruitment decisions. In some countries or regions it is expected that foreign companies recruit both ordinary employees and managers from the local population. A weaker version of this demand exists when recruitment of managers or specialists from third countries is negatively sanctioned in the local environment, whereas recruitment from the subsidiary's parent country is not. Many foreign companies may, for instance, find it cumbersome to hire personnel in China if they have to go through government agencies.

As noted by Schneider and Barsoux (1997: 134–135), in countries characterized by a high degree of collectivism, various kinds of nepotism follow from the widespread interdependencies among people: 'When an employer takes on a person, a moral commitment is established. There is an implicit understanding that the employer will look after the employee and quite possibly his/her family too. Family ties in turn provide social controls that are often more powerful than the organizational hierarchy.' India is a country characterized by high collectivism and related practices of selective recruitment of personnel. Budhwar and Sparrow (1998) noted that social relationships and political connections play a significant role in the selection, promotion and transfer of employees in Indian organizations. This is largely a function of the caste consciousness in substantial parts of the country's population.

Ethical norms relating to the recruitment of employees is also an important factor to observe. These differ across national borders and constitute an important cultural factor in the macro-environment and are often visible in local legislation. For example, some countries have legislation on equality of employment opportunity in relation to gender, race, and age, whereas in other countries issues of this type are hardly on the agenda at all.

Finally, in some areas, such as the Arab world and parts of Asia, there may be culturally based limitations on the recruitment of female managers. This is often due to religiously sanctioned convictions that women have a subordinate status. Yet in countries like Taiwan and Japan some companies, including MNCs, have been able to turn such a situation to their own advantage by systematically recruiting women who often have university degrees and who demonstrate above-average work performance (Adler, 1987).

The use of headhunting firms to recruit managers in foreign subsidiaries of MNCs is also subject to socio-economic, institutional, and cultural influences. The availability and quality of such services may have an impact along with ethical codes, implying that it is unethical to 'steal' employees from other companies.

Human resource development

A subsidiary's opportunity to develop its human resources can be severely restricted by shortcomings in the local education system (cf. Judy, 2002).

For example the experience of subsidiaries of Japanese electronics companies in the 1990s in Brazil was that they were only able to partly disseminate their TQM (total quality management) systems and practices. The reason was the insufficient numerical skills among local employees who were therefore unable to perform the required range of work tasks that the TQM system demands (Humphrey, 1995). Likewise, German MNCs will encounter problems when trying to implement their characteristic functional flexibility in countries where educational standards are significantly weaker than in Germany.

Turning to the institutional level, in some instances support is given by national authorities to facilitate human resource development in firms. Financial support or tax incentives may, for instance, be available for certain types of training and research and development. In France the training regime is characterized not so much by incentives as financial sanctions that are applied to companies that fail to spend an amount on training that corresponds to a certain percentage of the total wages bill.

Cultural factors that affect human resource development in general and employee training in particular include the local values and status attached to individual acquisition of competencies and development of human resources. These values are closely related to the host population's attitude to knowledge and learning in general.

When it comes to management development, this is partly affected by the actual access to managerial competence in the local or regional labor market. As pointed out earlier in this chapter, this often determines whether a subsidiary chooses to import managers from the home country or a third country, or whether it opts for developing local managerial talent.

A cultural factor that affects development activities in subsidiaries is the local preferred style of learning. As noted by Schneider and Barsoux (1997: 139), German and Swiss managers tend to favor structured learning environments with clear pedagogical objectives, course outline and schedule, and the 'right answer' or superior solution. This is markedly different to the learning style of British managers: 'Most British participants despise too much structure. They like open ended learning situations with vague objectives, broad assignments and no timetables at all. The suggestion that there could be only one correct answer is taboo with them' (Saner and Yiu, 1994: 962). Hayes and Allinson (1988) have concluded that learning environments and learning activities that promote effective learning in one culture may be quite ineffective in other cultures.

Compensation and incentives

The use of performance appraisal and, with it, performance-related pay, is an HRM practice that is considered to be particularly sensitive to socio-economic, institutional, and cultural conditions. Such systems appear to be easier to implement in countries characterized by substantial income inequalities among the working population than in countries with a more equal income distribution. Among the most influential institutional factors are the strength and attitudes of local unions. As we have observed above in Scandinavian work life, which is characterized both by relatively small income inequalities and strong unions opposed to individual performance pay, the use of performance appraisal and individualized pay is much less widespread than in the UK.

Individual measures of performance are also to some degree determined by the presence of egalitarian values in society. The designs and levels of wage systems in subsidiaries will also normally be influenced by specific socio-economic conditions in the country of location. One of the most important of these is the general income level that restricts subsidiaries' degrees of freedom by setting standards that may be difficult to violate. Another is the class structure and degree of socio-economic inequality in the population. If, for instance, a subsidiary located in a country with very low labor costs pays its employees according to the standards in the parent country, it would distort the local social hierarchy and at worst create a widespread hostility towards the MNC.

The motivational role of economic and other material rewards varies across cultures and may thus influence the design of incentive systems. In some countries, such as the United States, there is a strong belief in business life that employee motivation and thereby also organizational performance can be improved by offering co-ownership to employees. On an international basis, however, variations in levels and distributions of income may determine the relevance of such arrangements. Given that employees receive stocks in lieu of wages, such arrangements would be irrelevant to employees in countries with modest levels of earnings.

Finally, differences in general societal values may affect the viability of co-ownership as a means of stimulating motivation and commitment among employees. In countries where there is a strict, inherited social order the underlying authoritarian values will constitute an obstacle to employee co-ownership since this will be regarded as a threat against existing class or caste boundaries.

Work systems

Decisions regarding the organization of labor and the distribution of work tasks are crucial for organizational performance. The knowledge and skills possessed by employees are important socio-economic premises underlying such decisions. Variations in competencies or the actual mix of skills available in the local labor market may lead to variations in how work systems are designed and implemented across countries. This also applies to legal restrictions regarding safety in the workplace and regulations regarding working hours. One example of the possible impact of the local mix of skills on the use or non-use of teamwork is that German companies in some foreign settings have problems developing efficient teamwork involving functional flexibility, due to insufficient competencies among local employees (Pinnington and Edwards, 2000).

On the institutional level, the national traditions on performing tasks in groups may have an impact. So may also the actual structure and practices that are embedded in the national system of employee relations:

> In German and British plants of the same company, German team members have been found to be more positive about teamwork than their British counterparts. Attitude to teamwork appears to be influenced by the national institutional structure of employee relations, the traditional British adversarial system having negative effects on worker participation and team contribution (Murakami, 1998). On the other hand, direct employee involvement practices are less dependent on the existence of extra-firm supportive structures and, hence, there is more scope for their diffusion. (Pinnington and Edwards, 2000: 253)

A cultural factor that has consequences for the design of work systems is the degree of individualism or collectivism in the national culture of the host country (Hofstede, 1980a). An interesting illustration of this is the use of job analysis in HRM. This tool is frequently used in firms in the Western world because the strong sense of individual job ownership among employees means that individuals are regarded as the basic units of organization. In other words it is meaningful to split work processes into discrete work tasks. However, in Japan job analysis is non-existent. This is because behavior is largely group-oriented (Ishida, 1986), so that in Japanese work life it is the group that is the basic building block and not the individual employee. Thus work processes are designed for groups rather than single individuals.

Non-discussables or work taboos provide an additional illustration of how the work system can be influenced by variations in cultural values. In some countries, religious and social norms set limitations on who can carry out certain tasks. For instance, an effect of the Indian caste system is that only casteless persons are allowed to undertake work that religious belief defines as unclean. However, it should be pointed out that Indian law does not sanction this.

At the cultural level, the degree of individualism or collectivism will have at least some impact on how widespread teamwork is. In cultures characterized by high collectivism it will generally be easier to implement than in more individualistic cultures since most people are used to solving problems in group contexts. The opposite applies for employee autonomy. In addition, this will be affected by the degree of power distance in society, that is, the degree to which differences in status and power are accepted by the population. In cultures with high power distance people are used to being told what to do and in many cases do not want to become empowered or to enjoy a greater degree of individual autonomy (see Chapter 5).

Labor relations

The degree of social stratification and inequality in the host country affects the autonomy subsidiaries of MNCs enjoy in respect to implementing employee influence and participation. In cases where there are extensive differences between classes or castes, granting low-status employees substantial influence on decision making may be highly problematic. On the institutional level, it may be observed that a country's corporate and labor legislation will affect the degree of employee influence. According to corporate law, in the Scandinavian countries, for example, employees are granted the right to select among themselves one third of the board members in firms that employ 50 or more employees. A cultural factor that is critical to the implementation of employee influence arrangements is that of power distance. The greater the power distance, the more difficult it will normally be to introduce considerable employee influence.

Sources of change to subsidiary HRM

It should be borne in mind that just as the parent company's SIHRM orientation may be subject to change, so the subsidiary's HRM system does not necessarily remain static. The strategic role of the subsidiary may change with server subsidiaries evolving into centers of excellence, or centers of excellence losing their cutting edge technological advantage and becoming server subsidiaries. In terms of the macro factors, culture changes only slowly. However, radical changes can take place to the socio-economic context as economic growth changes living standards and therefore employee expectations. Significant changes can also occur to the institutional environment as new employment laws are enacted and the balance of power between employer and employee changes. In the next section we develop a further focus on the impact of institutions. By institution we are referring to 'social structures that have attained a high degree of social resilience' (Scott, 2001: 48). They cannot be ignored without risking a critical loss of 'legitimacy'. Furthermore, although there are aspects to institutions that overlap with culture, there are other aspects such as employment laws and the influence of trade unions that do not. In other words, institutions are more tangible and less stable than culture. In short institutions must not be confused with culture.

Institutional distance

Kostova and Roth (2002: 215) point to the need subsidiaries of MNCs have to achieve and maintain legitimacy in the environment in which they operate (Gooderham et al., 2006). That is they experience pressure to adopt local practices and become isomorphic with the local institutional context. Hereby there lies a tension between the need for global integration, on the one hand, and local adaptation, on the other. At the subsidiary level this is experienced as two sets of pressures. They are both confronted by an external host country institutional environment and by pressures from within the organization to become isomorphic to the parent organization's norms (Harzing, 2002: 213). Tension will be particularly acute when the MNC is trying to establish a subsidiary in an institutional context that is markedly different to its own and when it is not prepared to accept a multidomestic solution with comprehensive local responsiveness and little in the way of global integration.

Hall and Soskice (2001) have developed an influential approach to studying cross-national institutional differences that is known as the 'Varieties of Capitalism'. It distinguishes among developed capitalist economies by reference to the means firms and other actors use to coordinate their endeavors. It suggests that nations cluster into identifiable groups based on the extent to which firms rely on market or strategic (institutional) modes of coordination and that important complementarities can exist between institutions in different spheres of the political economy. Hall and Soskice distinguish between two clusters: liberal market economies (LMEs) and coordinated market economies (CMEs).

Hall and Gingerich (2004) developed a measure of coordination, placing 20 nations along a continuum between 'pure' LMEs (0) and 'pure' CMEs (1). At one end of the continuum are the LMEs where relations between firms and

Table 6.2 The coordination index (Hall and Gingerich, 2004)

Austria	1.0	'Pure' CME
Germany	0.95	
Italy	0.87	
Norway	0.76	
Belgium	0.74	
Denmark	0.70	
Finland	0.72	
France	0.69	
Sweden	0.69	
Netherlands	0.66	
Ireland	0.29	
Australia	0.36	
Canada	0.13	
United Kingdom	0.07	
United States	0.0	'Pure' LME

other actors are coordinated primarily by competitive markets. At the other end are the CMEs where firms typically engage in more strategic interaction with trade unions, suppliers of finance, and other external stakeholders.

Table 6.2 indicates that there is substantial 'institutional distance' between the Anglo-Saxon countries and Western European countries including the Scandinavian countries. In particular there are two important components of institutional distance: employment legislation and the influence of trade unions. The two should be considered together because in the absence of well-functioning courts of law and skilled lawyers, trade unions are often the only effective important guarantor of the enforcement of employment legislation.

Employment legislation may be analysed in terms of:

1. the protection of permanent workers against (individual) dismissal length,
2. specific requirements for the collective,
3. regulation on temporary employment.

Employing these three aspects to employment legislation the OECD has developed a measure of employment protection (Venn, 2009) that includes many LMEs and CMEs as well as countries that fall outside the 'Varieties of Capitalism' index. Figures 6.2a and 6.2b provide an overview of employment protection in selected countries.

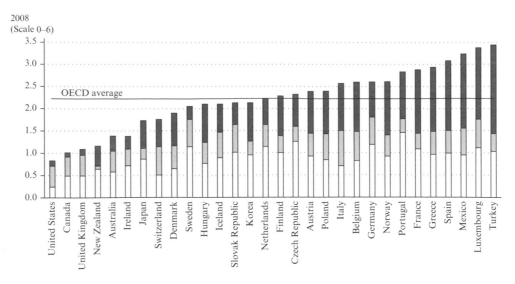

Note: Data shown are version 3 of the employment protection summary indicator. [a] 2009 for France and Portugal

Source: Venn (2009).

Figure 6.2a Strictness of employment protection in OECD countries (2008)[a]

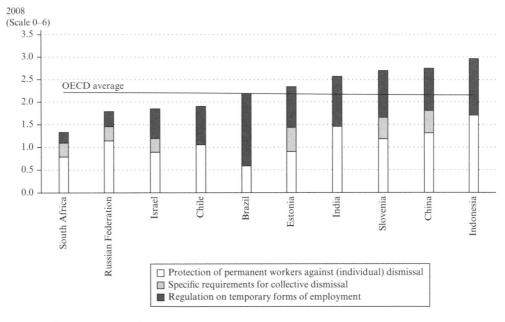

☐ Protection of permanent workers against (individual) dismissal
▨ Specific requirements for collective dismissal
■ Regulation on temporary forms of employment

Note: Data shown are version 3 of the employment protection summary indicator. [a] 2009 for France and Portugal

Source: Venn (2009).

Figure 6.2b Strictness of employment protection in other selected countries (2008)[a]

Table 6.3 indicates that most European countries are more heavily unionized in terms of union membership than the USA. However, in reality trade union influence cannot be gauged sufficiently by focusing on trade union density rates. A more important issue is that of trade union recognition, that is whether the employer deals with a trade union in a collective bargaining relationship that sets terms and conditions for all or most of the employees. It is in this respect that CME countries diverge to a considerable degree from the prototypical LME country, the USA. In countries such as France and the Benelux countries, there is legislation in place requiring employers over a certain size to recognize unions for consultative purposes. In the case of Germany there have been significant falls in trade union membership and bargaining coverage since the late 1980s. The issue is therefore whether Germany is undergoing institutional change and becoming more of an LME. However, it should be noted that Germany still has powerful unions within particular sectors of its economy and that they exert considerable influence in determining salaries and conditions. For example the IG Metall Engineering Union represents 3.4 million German workers in annual industry-wide negotiations that have a significant impact on wage setting in

Table 6.3 Trade union density and bargaining coverage as a proportion of wage and salaried earners

	Union Density Rate	Bargaining Coverage
Austria	35	95
Belgium	93	96
Canada	31	29
Denmark	99	96
Finland	68	98
France	8	98
Germany	20	36
Italy	97	98
Mexico	17	11
Netherlands	21	80*
Norway	53	75
Portugal	20	38
Spain	14	67
Sweden	74	90*
Turkey	25	26
UK	28	34
United States	12	13

Note: *Authors' estimate based on 2001 data from International Labor Office.

Source: Hayter and Stoevska (2011).

Germany in general. In addition works councils remain widespread. Thus Germany remains a CME.

Calculative HRM

Gooderham et al. (1999) have noted that 'calculative' HRM practices such as individual performance-related pay and individual performance appraisals operate more easily in some national settings than in others: while it is generally accepted in Anglo-Saxon business cultures, it is less widely accepted in Germany, or Scandinavia. Particularly in Scandinavia there is a resistance to the idea that individual members of the group should excel in a way that reveals the shortcoming of others. In addition these countries have powerful trade unions and, in the case of Germany, work councils that narrow the scope for implementing calculative HRM practices. However, although Scandinavia and Germany are institutionally more similar to one another than they are to the UK, there are also significant differences.

Employment law in Germany is so elaborate that traditionally the work of personnel departments has been largely restricted to ensuring that the firm is not in breach of any of the numerous regulations that constitute national employment law and agreements. Thus personnel or HR managers have a highly operative focus that inhibits their experimenting with the design of HRM. At the firm level in Scandinavia the legislative framework is more general, meaning that there is more latitude for the HR function to develop new HRM systems once trust between management and the local union has been reaffirmed. This means that on the one hand there remains engrained in Scandinavian work-life the assumption of divergent and conflicting interests between employer and employees and, therefore, an ongoing resistance to management-initiated calculative HRM practices; on the other hand there is the opportunity for collaborative local HRM innovation given that management and unions trust one another. This is a particular theme in the case that accompanies this chapter.

When in Rome, do MNCs do as the Romans?

In their pursuit of being effective global competitors, MNCs will typically seek 'the unimpeded right to coordinate and control all aspects of the company on a worldwide basis' (Bartlett and Ghoshal, 1995: 119). That is, MNCs will attempt to apply the management practices they are most familiar with regardless of the location of their subsidiary. However, in order to maintain legitimacy MNCs also have to take into account the demands and expectations of their various host environments. These may necessitate the modification of their management processes.

The Cranet data set (www.cranet.org) enables us to contrast the use of calculative HRM practices by US MNCs in four different European contexts: the UK; Ireland; Denmark and Norway combined; and Germany. Figure 6.3 indicates that indigenous or native firms in the UK make significant use of calculative HRM particularly in relation to Denmark and Norway. The figure further indicates that the subsidiaries of US MNCs make significantly more use of calculative HRM practices in Denmark/Norway and Germany than their indigenous counterparts. However, their use is less than in the calculative HRM-friendly UK. In short, in Denmark/Norway and Germany US MNCs are succumbing to cultural and institutional pressures to moderate their use of calculative HRM practices. This process of semi-adaptation results in hybrid organizational practices that are partly rooted in practices emanating from headquarters, and partly rooted in local cultural and institutional conditions.

Figure 6.3 also shows that Ireland displays significantly more divergence between native firms and subsidiaries of US MNCs. This is a product of the lack of institutional restrictions placed on MNCs that operate in Ireland.

Source: Gooderham et al. (2006).

Figure 6.3
Deployment of calculative HRM practices among US subsidiaries in the UK, Ireland, Denmark/ Norway (Den/Nor) and Germany and their native counterparts controlled for size, industry and age of establishment

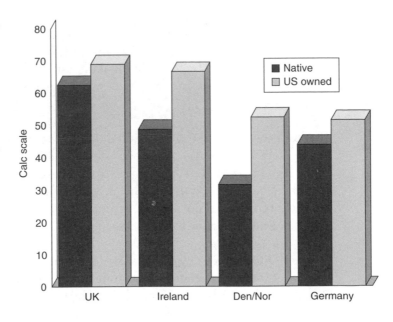

6.6   Practical lessons

The environments subsidiaries of MNCs operate in exert substantial influence on managerial decisions. This may undermine the efforts of the individual MNC to make decisions it perceives as rational in relation to human
resource acquisition, development, compensation, labor relations, and in the
design of work systems.

In practical terms it is critical for the MNC to be able to identify and assess
the significance of the conditions in the various environments in which it
operates. The analytical model outlined in this chapter can be applied to
environmental factors that influence the future operation of the subsidiary. Particularly before establishing a subsidiary or joint venture in a foreign
environment, it is essential that information about environmental factors
is compiled and that, on this basis, both possible and probable problems
relating to HRM in this specific environment are clarified. Such an analysis
may strengthen the MNC's ability to act proactively with regard to human
resource issues.

Customization and internalization

So far we have treated HRM practices almost as constants: they are either
transferred or not. However, HRM practices may be subject to local customization by the subsidiary. As Lozeau et al. (2002) have noted, in any
transfer there is always some degree of customization necessary to the
local context. Czarniawska and Joerges (1996) remind us that ideas are
transformed as they are transferred. Given any significant degree of difference in context, transfer requires not just the encoding and movement
of knowledge about practices, but making use of this knowledge and local
knowledge to construct new practices which function in the context of local
affordances.

Kostova and Roth (2002) have noted that the extent to which practices are
fully internalized locally versus only superficially adopted, varies considerably; high internalization being more likely where the local institutional and
cultural context is receptive to what is being transferred. Coercive pressures
to adopt transferred knowing and practice, in the absence of a receptive local
context, lead most often to purely ceremonial adoption.

Fenton-O'Creevy et al. (2011) have developed a categorization of outcomes of transfer attempts, as illustrated in Figure 6.4. Where the original
context and the context of transfer are highly similar in salient features,

and where there is considerable exposure to shared cognitive social processes and shared goals, we might expect that transfer of knowledge and practices could be achieved with little customization. While we would argue that there is always some reconstruction of practices in relation to local affordances, in practice two contexts may share such similarities and common assumptions that this work is quite small. Thus for this case we retain the term 'transfer'.

However, shared goals and effective engagement between contexts may, given that there is recognition that significant local customization of knowing and practice is required, result in significant effort being made to translate knowing and practice into the local context. We refer to this as 'translation'; as what is implied is new meanings consistent with the original purpose of transfer. New practices are constructed with similar goals, drawing on both local knowledge and knowledge carried from the original context.

Either a lack of exposure to shared cognitive social processes or the absence of shared goals may lead to low internalization. This may lead to a purely 'ceremonial adoption' in a 'box-ticking' approach characterized by no real identification with or understanding of the knowledge or practice.

The low internalization case may also be marked by significant efforts at customization, but in this case local efforts are largely directed at co-option of knowing and practice to secure the status quo or reinforce purely local objectives. We follow Lozeau et al. (2002) in describing this as 'corruption' of the original practice, since the original intent of the practice is corrupted.

Source: Fenton-O'Creevy et al. (2011).

Figure 6.4 Outcomes of knowledge transfer

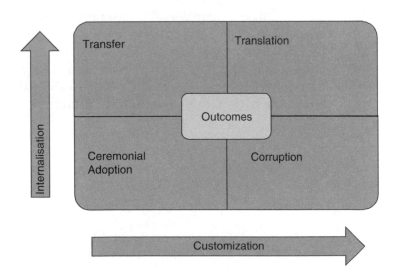

6.7   Summary

In this chapter we have highlighted the fundamental differences between domestic and cross-national HRM. It has explored SIHRM on the basis of a model which distinguishes the parent company's SIHRM orientation and subsidiary level influences. In regard to the first part of the model we emphasized the parent company strategy. This is crucial to gaining an understanding of the degree of MNC-wide integration of HRM systems and practices. In the context of MNCs pursuing a multidomestic strategy we should expect to be able to observe many locally determined variants of HRM, whereas for MNCs with a global strategy there will be considerable MNC-wide integration of HRM. Furthermore, in multidomestic MNCs corporate HR departments will be relatively small and there will be a more limited range of activities (Scullion and Starkey, 2000). This chapter has emphasized that to focus purely on the SIHRM orientation of the parent company is inadequate for an understanding of MNC-wide HRM. There are a number of subsidiary level influences which must be taken into account. The first of these involves the resource dependence of the parent company on its subsidiaries: centers of excellence have the power to resist integration, whereas global offshores and servers do not. The second involves entry mode: acquisitions are generally considerably more of a challenge in terms of integration than Greenfield subsidiaries. However, when MNCs design HRM systems for their subsidiaries, the model indicates that they invariably will have to consider host country culture, socio-economic conditions, and institutional constraints. Finally, in analysing the transfer of HRM to subsidiaries it is critical to distinguish 'genuine' transfer from other outcomes.

The case that accompanies this chapter is about a Norwegian bank that attempted to import a set of HRM practices designed to stimulate sales from the USA. The authors view the outcome as one of 'translation'. As the case indicates, the outcome could have been very different. Equally, the case illustrates how elastic the concept of translation is and in doing so raises the issue of when practices have gone beyond translation to something fundamentally different.

Case E

Gained in translation: the import, translation and development of a US sales and management concept

Martin Gjelsvik, Odd Nordhaug and Paul N. Gooderham

E.1 Introduction

This case offers a detailed description on how a Norwegian organization, SR-Bank, was suddenly confronted with a fundamental turnaround challenge brought about by profound changes to its external environment. The case tracks the adoption, translation and implementation by SR Bank of a sales program developed in the US. The program – 'SESAM' – had strong implications for human resource management (HRM), learning and organizational development. The story goes back to the latter part of the 1980s when the institutional rules of Norwegian banks were turned upside down. The deregulation and liberalization of the financial markets swiftly and radically altered the rules of the game in the banking industry. This development coincided with a serious downturn of the economy, causing big losses for the banks. The case presented here deals with a bank and its people that survived what may be coined a close-to-death experience, as the bank was on the verge of bankruptcy in 1991. Since then, the bank, with its roots back to 1839, has reinvented itself through a strong belief in linking its overall strategies to a human resource policy of continuously enhancing the knowledge and skills of the employees, close and long-term customer relations and a strong physical presence in the region. The bank is a learning organization where management consciously facilitates and encourages learning opportunities.

It is thus a story of an organization being forced to leave the shelter of strict, predictable government regulation and cartel-based non-competition to face and ride through the storms caused by deregulation. This story has repeated itself in many industries all over Europe. Like other businesses exposed to dramatic changes, the bank had to learn how to compete more or less from scratch. The bank decided to base its turnaround on a redefinition of the former roles of the employees and their managers through a comprehensive organizational development project. Developing the human resources became an integral part of the strategy. What was then conceived of as a program or a project, is today a continuing process to leverage the knowledge and skills of all employees; and turning those competencies into sales and solid profits. The story centers on SESAM that in 2012 had been running for 22 consecutive years and survived four CEOs.

E.2   Cultural context

In this section we briefly describe the historical, cultural and institutional context SR-Bank operates in. It should be borne in mind that the Norwegian context is not static. In 2012 there is a much greater acceptance of market-based solutions than was the case in 1990. Although Norway remains a relatively equal society with a comprehensive welfare state there are also increases in wealth disparity. In Norway the emphasis on equality has gone hand in hand with high levels of unionization. Powerful local and national unions have played, and still play, active parts in the public arena. Even in banks and insurance companies unions have played a significant role and even today the principle of job security is defended and wage differentials regarded with skepticism. Traditionally unions have opposed individual performance assessments, and compensation has to a substantial degree been determined through collective bargaining.

Banks have been among the most conservative work organizations in Norway. This is partly due to their shelter from competition through cartel agreements that determined interest rates and prices. In 1977 a new Savings Banks Act was implemented in which the savings banks such as SR-Bank were granted practically identical competitive conditions to the commercial banks. Yet the ownership structure remained very different. Furthermore, the savings banks were not obliged to keep mandatory capital ratios. There was no need for such requirements since losses were virtually non-existent. The lack of mandatory capital ratios turned the banks into vulnerable organizations when the bank crisis struck in the latter part of the 1980s. In addition, the banks had no systems for analysing or measuring the overall credit risk they were exposed to. The financial industry was in other words unprepared for the turmoil the subsequent deregulation and the economic downturn would bring about.

The post-1977 regime provided the foundation for a strong expansion in the savings banks' operations. The product range was substantially widened, and savings banks became full service banks for business and households. Compared to the rest of Europe, Norwegian savings banks command a unique position in their domestic market. However, the temptation to stretch for opportunities beyond the competencies of the employees and the capabilities of the organization proved to be too great. The consequences of this dash for growth were exposed in the late 1980s and early 1990s when several banks went bankrupt.

E.3 SR-Bank's strategy

Even with the rise of internet banking SR-Bank in 2012 still commanded a dense network of local branch offices. This is an expensive distribution strategy. It provides a very high level of customer service that is built on providing access to highly competent personnel. Investments in employees have been considerable throughout the years. During the past ten years the bank has expanded geographically from the county of Rogaland to the whole of the southwestern part of Norway. The main office is located in Stavanger, the oil capital of Norway.

E.4 Key financial figures

We present the financial results of SR-Bank for the past 22 years in Table E.1. All figures are shown as a percentage of average assets from the time of the introduction of the organizational development program.

In particular we may note the impact of the financial crisis that started in 1989 and that by 1991 had resulted in a disastrous performance. The long-term trend of slender interest margins had to be partly substituted by off balance sales (other than loans and bank savings). This trend has been strong motivator for SESAM which aims at supporting the bank's efforts

Table E.1 Key financial figures (figures shown as a percentage of average)

	2011	2010	2007	2000	1991	1989
Net interest margin	1.31	1.35	1.42	2.46	3.14	3.78
Other operating income	1.13	1.30	1.36	0.70	1.02	1.24
Total operating income	2.44	2.65	2.78	3.16	4.16	5.02
Total operating costs	1.22	1.22	1.44	1.76	3.56	3.43
Profit before losses and write-downs	1.22	1.43	1.34	1.40	0.60	1.59
Losses and write-downs	0.10	0.18	0.01	−0.18	3.96	1.50
Result of ordinary activities	1.12	1.25	1.33	1.58	−3.36	0.09

to sell other products and services. We may also note the strong decrease in the operating costs since 1989–1991, an indication of a considerable productivity gain achieved by the introduction and investment in state-of-the art technology. What the figure does not show, though, is that this development has been combined with a growth in both the number of branches and employees.

E.5 SESAM: the antecedents

The decision to keep and develop the branch network was made during the crisis in 1989–1993. SR-Bank has stayed with this strategy even with the introduction of internet banking. The strategy is costly and is dependent on SR-Bank's ability to generate higher revenues. Back in 1989 this ability simply was not in place because bank employees were simply not sales people. On the contrary, the most prevalent motive for seeking a job in a bank had been the desire to obtain a stable income and a secure job.

The decision to view the well-developed branch network as a part of the bank's strategy rather than as an unsustainable overhead was not an obvious decision. Indeed in 1989 it was the subject of a heated debate. The introduction of ATMs (automatic teller machines) together with an electronic payment transfer system significantly reduced the customers' need to visit the bank in person. Consequently, there were good reasons for downsizing the branch network. The recommendations from the experts and consultants were also straightforward: Get rid of the bricks and mortar!

In the internal discussion, two opposing points of view were present:

1. The bank needs to cut costs. Since the branch network incurs large costs, it must be reduced as much as possible. This is also in line with what our competitors are doing. The basis for this line of reasoning is purely cost oriented. The contribution of bank employees to revenues was not taken into consideration.
2. The branch network, including both the physical and human resources it comprises, represents a unique competitive advantage. No competitor has a similar distribution system. Such an advantage must be developed and exploited, not dismantled.
3. Associated with the argument above, a humanistic point of view was present at that time: We are responsible for our employees and their jobs. The challenge is: How can we use these strategic resources more efficiently than in the past?

When the smoke subsided, the two latter points of view surfaced as winners. However, the distribution network had to be modernized both physically and by enhancing the employees' communication skills and product knowledge. At this point in time, there was no appreciation on the part of employees that SR-Bank was facing a long-term crisis and that there was a real need for change. The notion of improving the knowledge and competence of employees as well as providing high quality service was easily agreed, but the process of transforming these ideas and intentions into practical actions gave rise to considerable differences of opinion. For example there were very different opinions as to whether there was need for a recruitment policy, career procedures and reward systems.

The case of lending is very illustrative of the way things had been done. In determining the salary of employees working for the retail market (individuals and households), the traditional practice involved linking salary to the amount of loans the employee was authorized to grant. Lending provided high internal status, leveraged authority and power vis-à-vis the customer, and it meant more pay at the end of the month. Lending was associated with more status than deposits, which in turn ensured more status than working with payment transactions. 'Sales' was a four-letter word.

A common shorthand description of bank employees engaged in work with private customers was 'order takers'. This kind of reactive work behavior was adequate as long as there was no reason for a customer to frequent more than one bank; as long as the customer, regardless of the service required, had to physically visit the bank. In the not too distant past, the banks offered the same products at practically identical prices. In addition, switching costs were high. But as the scale of the crisis became obvious and the awareness that the bank market had now changed radically, the main questions were: How could a sales-oriented culture be developed? How could prevalent attitudes and work behavior be changed? What kind of knowledge and skills do the employees and managers need? Do we have any tools or systems to aid us in this process?

There was dearth of answers. For several years the management had preached 'We must get better at selling' and 'We must become better at understanding customers' needs'. There was no end to what the employees had to become better at doing. But can anyone be expected to improve without having the relevant tools or instructions indicating *how* this is to come about?

The first step was to stake out a path by formulating a special strategy for the retail market. This was outlined by the division's management as follows:

1. We shall turn profitable customers into total customer relations by:
   - providing a full range of financial services
   - offering products and services for all phases of the life cycle
   - being an active problem solver for the customer
   - developing customer loyalty through cross-selling
2. We shall develop our customer orientation through:
   - increased professional skills
   - high service quality
   - needs-oriented sales
   - specifically focused market communication
3. We shall provide speedy and efficient customer service through
   - simplicity
   - easy availability
   - self-service
4. We shall develop profitable customer segments through
   - pricing
   - needs orientation
   - automation and standardization of mass-markets products

The notion of 'needs-oriented sales' was introduced to distance the employees from the common perception of an aggressive insurance salesperson; a salesperson more interested in his or her bonuses than in the customer's needs. 'Soft sell' was the buzzword; the starting point was always to meet the customer's actual needs. People had to be convinced that 'over-selling' would backfire in the form of complaints about poor and sloppy financial advice.

The human resource (HR) department assumed responsibility for arranging sales courses. These courses were typically one day or weekend courses aimed at teaching employees various sales techniques. However, this approach was unsuccessful. The reasons were plenty. The courses were not specifically directed at sales in banks: the ideals and techniques were copied from traditional retail business. The concepts of 'soft sell' and the focus on long-term customer relations were not at the forefront. Moreover, it had to be acknowledged that courses that were not part of a larger organizational context would easily result in only short-term enthusiasm among the participants, at best. The need for structural changes that could facilitate learning with lasting effects through organizational capabilities such as improved routines and revised computer programs became increasingly evident. The instructor's job was completed when the course was completed; he or she had no responsibility for either the use or implementation and follow-up of the individual learning that had taken place. And there was no system to indicate what had been learned and if performance in any substantial way had actually improved.

E.6   SESAM: the initial steps through knowledge import

At this time, during the course of business trip to the USA, the manager of the retail market happened to come across a sales training program that seemed to be answer to the whole issue of how to develop the skills needed to create a sales culture. The program had an excellent track record in US financial institutions and the designer of the program managed to convince him that what worked in the US could work in Norway.

On his return to Norway he attempted to convince colleagues that the program was the way forward for SR-Bank. Needless to say, this turned out to be rather difficult. Comments such as 'this will be expensive' and 'the US is different from Norway' were indications of a profound skepticism. On the other hand, colleagues did accept that the program was tailor-made for banks and that it had a proven track record. Furthermore, it was based on practice and not just some abstract theory.

After a good year of internal discussions a contract was finally signed with the American developer of the program. A pivotal condition was that the program was not only to be translated into Norwegian, but also adapted to SR-Bank's culture and strategy.

American businesses, not least in the banking industry, are characterized by a higher degree of management by directive than are businesses based on the more participative Scandinavian model. Therefore, bank employees in the USA typically have less autonomous jobs than their Norwegian counterparts. Employee behavior is directed more through detailed manuals and hierarchy than through development-oriented, cooperative projects as is the case in Norway where empowerment has a long tradition. In addition, the distance between Norwegian managers and employees in terms of both salaries and mentality is smaller than in the US. This is illustrated by the fact that SR-Bank's management was far more active and visible participants at all stages of the project than had been the case for US banks. Through their involvement in the training programs they disseminated the 'new sales language' and discussed further developments of the project in the top management team.

There was another important reservation regarding the original US version of the program. SR-Bank management and a number of employees observed from its reliance on detailed manuals and consultants in intensive training sessions that the program was explicitly based on behavioristic theory and assumptions. This provided considerable opportunity for managerial manipulation of employees. A prominent organizational psychologist was asked to consider the ethical implications of the program. He advised that the program was ethically sound given that the employees were informed about the measures taken and the tools to be used.

A new position as coordinator for the entire program was established on a contract basis. The coordinator, an external consultant, and the bank manager in charge of the retail market division completed an intensive two-week training session in the USA. They then 'Norwegianized' it.

E.7 SESAM: the explicit face

Having been 'Norwegianized', the program was implemented for all employees in the retail market division, including managers at all levels. More than 500 employees were involved. The program thus constituted a comprehensive organizational development process.

The primary objective was to offer a tool and a learning environment that provided understanding and opportunities to utilize the process of communication between the customer and the bank employees providing services to the customer. The aim was to develop the skills to determine the customer's present and future needs and to suggest the right products and services to fulfill these needs.

The sales and organizational development project was labeled SESAM, the Norwegian acronym for Salg Er SAMarbeid (sales is cooperation). The emphasis on the collaborative aspect was related to the customers' tendency to perceive the bank branches as one single bank. The customer wants to be recognized, regardless of whom they approach in the bank. It became crucial to stress the significance of intra-organizational cooperation, also across departmental boundaries. For example, information about the customer must be exchanged and made available to all customer service and support personnel.

The SESAM project had a long-term perspective. The organization was to be transformed from an 'order-taking station' into a 'proactive sales train'. Notwithstanding this, the process was called a project, indicating a temporary perspective. The process consisted of a number of training manuals defining the new roles of employees and managers combined with 2–3 days of training sessions. In terms of Nonaka and Takeuchi (1995) the introductory year may be referred to as 'the explicit phase'. The new roles and the related necessary skills were explicitly formulated in manuals. The training sessions were designed to transform this explicit knowledge into practice. The employees were expected to learn the content in the manuals in two ways, by repeating their contents, and by internalizing the content through learning by doing. The latter process, 'internalization', involves transforming explicit knowledge into tacit knowledge (Polanyi, 1966). When knowledge becomes tacit is hard to copy and therefore may constitute a basis for sustainable competitive advantage (Barney, 1991).

Below we offer detailed descriptions of two of the new roles, the one for tellers and the one for the manager of the retail division. Thus we illustrate their complementarities. Each individual employee's role was defined through the so-called 'winning plays'. These plays were used for tellers, financial advisors and support personnel. All levels of management were also equipped with winning plays, from the first-line managers ('sales leaders' in the new language) to the managing director. The sales leader of a bank outlet (for instance the local branch manager) was familiar with his subordinates' winning plays. Conversely, employees also knew their superior's winning play. Thus the different levels could check each other, and measures were generated so that everybody could continuously perfect his or her role performance. Table E.2 illustrates how the new role for the teller was defined.

The winning play revealed a very important and previously controversial point for the tellers' role. The tellers themselves were not asked to cross-sell, they were asked to refer the customer to a financial advisor if an opportunity for cross-selling arose. However, the tellers had previously responded negatively to any suggestion that they assume a more proactive attitude towards sales. They claimed that sales activity would 'only lead to long lines at the counters'. The management had until now been unable to provide any specific suggestions as to how these two seemingly conflicting demands, prompt service and active cross selling, could be met simultaneously. The paradox had finally been resolved, and the tellers' attitudes towards sales immediately became more positive.

The second example of a winning play was designed for the general manager of the Retail Market division, as illustrated in Table E.3. Note the hierarchical system of roles and their complementarity.

Considerable emphasis was placed on measurable behavior. Behavioral change was to be observed and reinforced through various forms of rewards:

Table E.2 The new role for tellers in SR-Bank

Winning play for tellers

1. Greeting and presentation	• Greet the customer politely so that he or she feels important and welcome • Look up, smile and establish eye contact • Even if you are busy with something else, greet the customer by saying something, nodding or waving • Ask how you may be of assistance
2. Carry out the customer's wishes	• Deal with the customer's requests in a competent and polite fashion • Use your knowledge to deal with requests, be precise and effective • Address the customer by name • Draw the customer into conversation – establish contact
3. Uncover needs	• Discover what PNO's[1] a customer may have, show interest and consideration • Comment as you serve the customer • Listen for sales opportunities in what the customer says
4. Give recommendations	• Find out which service best suits the customer and recommend it • Explain the solution • Use brochures actively • Recommend that the customer talk with a member of the customer service personnel
5. Refer the customer to relevant colleagues	• Use a customer presentation card • Write the customer's name, the services you suggested and your name on the card • Enclose your business card and any other relevant documents • Refer the customer to the right person • If possible, escort the customer and introduce him or her • If you are unable to escort the customer, explain who he or she is to see and give the customer the customer presentation card
6. Conclusion	• Thank the customer politely, using his or her name • If possible, shake hands • Welcome the customer back and offer your help in the future

Note: PNO: Problems, Needs and Opportunities. The rationale is that the customer comes to the bank with a problem that may be transformed into a need, which is a sales opportunity for the bank.

attention, praise and prizes. Reinforcing positive behavior was a priority. During the first year, managers were instructed not to react negatively towards those employees that did not succeed. Realizing that the project would lead to considerable changes in behavior, the first year was designated to be a trial-and-error period. Employees being unable to adjust were

Table E.3 The new role for general managers in the Retail Market Division of SRBank

Winning play for the division General Manager

1. Define and communicate the results you expect from each manager	• Establish 'Winning plays for sales managers' as a standard for sales management and training • Set targets together with the managers • Obtain acceptance for expected actions and set targets, both for superiors and subordinates, so that the desired behavior is measurable
2. Be a good example	• Practice what you preach • Be optimistic and enthusiastic • Practice the three C's (Competence, Courtesy and Consideration) • Demonstrate correct customer service when you are involved in sales yourself • Use the winning play • Be consistent
3. Empower your employees	• Share information • Arrange monthly follow-up meetings with your managers • Give your managers opportunities for individual development • Delegate authority and responsibility • Remove sales barriers • LISTEN! LISTEN! LISTEN!
4. Build team spirit	• Set goals for the region • Communicate goals and results • Map progress in the region • Don't forget the humorous side of things
5. Check on your expectations	• Execute hands-on management by visiting the local banks and branches • Review the local bank's results monthly with each manager, using the sales reports • Ask the customers if they are satisfied with the bank • Go through customer messages, letters etc
6. Reward and recognize	• At your monthly meetings, reward and recognize those who have achieved good results • Reward and recognize both individual employees and teams • Express your approval for a well-done job on a daily basis • Catch your employees doing a good job

helped to overcome their problems in their current job or transferred to another job.

'Catch your employees doing a good job' expressed the positive team spirit the organization sought to nurture. This proved to be a great challenge, especially for managers. Contrary to the US, Norwegians are introvert and seldom brag about their peers let alone themselves. The so-called 'Law of Jante' means that in Norway there should be no tall poppies.

Employee sentiments were mixed. Many wanted to demonstrate and visualize their own skills, for example as expressed in sales figures. Others, particularly the more union oriented, were skeptical. They partly expressed concern with the assumed 'weak' performers, and partly argued on the basis of their legal right to stick to the main provisions of the National Bank Agreement, which prohibited individual performance measurements. Evaluations at the group level were accepted, on the condition that nothing could be traced back to the individual employee. The bank's management contested this formal argument, however, since the point in question was included under the main section in the National Bank Agreement dealing with electronically based systems. The management claimed that registration using an electronic medium was forbidden, while manual recordings and measurements were allowed.

Many possible avenues to compromises were attempted. One suggestion was that manual measurements of individual employee performance could be carried out at the workplace and the results then collected by the closest line manager. Union representatives opposed this suggestion, even though the employees in many divisions found this solution desirable. However, the management was not interested in letting the issue evolve into an open conflict. A project that otherwise had been so positively received was not to be spoiled by a feature not considered vital to the success of the project.

Ultimately, the following agreement was reached: each individual employee should manually record his or her own sales figures every week. These were in turn registered on a form without specifying the actual persons. The sales leader added up the figures and calculated the results of the branch/department. The individual employee could then benchmark him or herself against the average sales scores.

SESAM did not challenge the organizational hierarchy as such, but it did change roles at all levels. Whereas the requirements and expectations previously had been diffuse and ambiguous, and had created uncertainty and insecurity among employees, clear instructions about what was expected and how it was to be accomplished were now provided. Demands were now explicit, measurable and precise.

The responsibility for training employees at the operational level was assumed by their immediate superior, the sales leader. An external consultant trained the 60 sales leaders. He was also in charge of training 20 bank employees to act as on-the-job instructors. These instructors assisted the sales leader in training their personnel.

E.8 Branches and departments: the new learning communities

The most important and encompassing learning process took place in the local branches and support departments. The sales leaders were responsible for arranging weekly personnel meetings. These meetings were held in the morning before the bank opened for customers. Typically they lasted for half an hour. The meeting followed a fixed pattern in one-month periods. Two meetings were designated for service improvement, one meeting for product knowledge, and one for presentation and discussion of sales targets. The cycle was repeated every month. This responsibility was a new challenge for the sales leader, and the quality and results of the meetings varied greatly. Some attempts were made to avoid the meetings all together on the grounds of practical excuses, but no deviation from the plan was accepted. Management simply required that these arrangements were part of the sales leader's job, something he or she was committed to through SESAM.

The weekly meetings were regarded as an appropriate vehicle to institution-alize the learning process at the organizational level as well as with the individual employee and manager. It was an important tool for the transition from project to organization, from experiment to organizational routine. Learning was to be an organizational capability to leverage the competitive position of the bank.

The weekly meetings were always based on local experiences. Employees were encouraged to present good or bad examples of customer service or responses. These examples served as the basis for a discussion of improvements, changes, needs for new system solutions and advertising material. This institutionalized arena for learning through experience transfer was also important for political and ethical reasons. Local learning based on the team's own experience could serve as an important counterbalance to the more centralized and behaviorist learning model on which the project was originally founded. This local learning, which became increasingly significant, led to a 'democratization' of the organizational development that took place, and successful agendas for weekly meetings were exchanged among the sales leaders.

The weekly meetings represent a telling example of what Nonaka and Takeuchi (1995) have coined the 'socialization' process in the knowledge creation spiral. At the individual level explicit knowledge (the SESAM manuals and the winning plays) was internalized through learning-by-doing in their respective jobs and communications with customers and peers. Explicit knowledge becomes embodied in new skills and attitudes, and gradually part of the individual's automatic routines, and thus made tacit. Since tacit knowledge is context-specific and difficult to formalize, transferring tacit knowledge requires sharing the same experience through joint activities and spending time together. Thus the weekly meeting became a supplement to the formal training sessions. The combined learning arenas facilitate the blend of internalization and socialization processes that allow for leveraging both from the explicit and tacit knowledge potential.

As we will see in the following sections, learning from experience became the dominant knowledge creation method in the bank. Gradually, the explicit and formal manuals were replaced with broad socialization processes across all levels of the bank.

E.9   SESAM in 1991

The first test of the viability of the program came with the new MD of the bank in 1991. The main structure of the program was then in place and likewise the outcome of the rather cumbersome negotiations with the union as to performance measurements and the policies towards those employees that did not want to change their roles. The new MD was recruited from outside the banking industry. At the time of his arrival SR-Bank was close to bankruptcy (see Table E.1).

Contrary to the development at other banks in similar situations he reiterated the commitment to keep all branch offices as part of a strategy to stay close to the customer. He quickly became convinced of the potential of the SESAM program, and dedicated much of his time to be visible at training sessions. His message was clear and straightforward: 'We have SESAM, now let's really use it to move forward.' He also made it clear that without increased sales efforts and tangible results, bank offices would have had to shut down and employees would be laid off.

The position as SESAM leader became a two-year assignment with high status and high visibility. The candidate was handpicked from the very highest ranks in the bank. Sales improved and with it the bank's financial results.

E.10 SESAM 12 years later: best practice in practice

In 2001 SESAM was still very much alive. It had survived three MDs all of whom had been very enthusiastic about the program. SESAM had been expanded to involve the whole organization. SR-Bank had outperformed every savings bank in Norway and it regarded SESAM as a critical element to this success.

When SESAM was first introduced the aim was to transform bank employees from order takers to proactive sales people. In 2001 this was no longer an issue. The employees had learned how to sell and the leaders at all levels knew how to motivate their employees to do just that. The objective in 2001 was to improve the performance of the existing roles, not to create new ones. The winning play outlined above was no longer in use as an explicit template. Instead the routine had become an internalized competence. Instead learning focused on learning from practice – positive and negative experiences. The MD in 2001 argued that this learning required learning arenas that would enable employees to share and reflect upon their own experiences. Two formal arenas served this purpose: the weekly local meetings in the branch offices under the leadership of the sales leader, and the training sessions under the leadership of the SESAM manager.

The program initially included only the retail bank but by 2001 the entire bank was covered. As such SESAM had contributed to developing a common experience across the bank and therefore a common culture. All bank managers were expected to perform as sales leaders. They were not allowed to withdraw to their paperwork in secluded offices. They were expected to serve as good examples as sales leaders and relentless motivators of their colleagues. These middle managers were all a vital part of SR-Bank's 'training arm', as illustrated in Figure E.1.

The arm may look like a modest attempt to demolish the traditional pyramid and hierarchical order. We have all encountered the advice of consultants to turn the pyramid on its head. Such advice is often embraced but is seldom

Figure E.1 The training arm

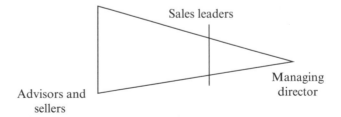

Sales leaders

Managing director

Advisors and sellers

implemented beyond window dressing. According to the bank in 2001, however, its sales organization actually worked horizontally. The managing director, the sales leaders and the advisors/sellers supported and served each other throughout the value chain.

Sales leaders were evaluated on an annual basis. Two dimensions were significant:

1. Sales results over time.
2. Feedback from the employees, by means of an annual internal appraisal and analysis. The analysis included leadership and organizational qualities like climate, job satisfaction, openness, and trust. In addition a score of individual capacity was provided.

In other words, the sales leader's performance was evaluated in terms of quantitative sales statistics and more qualitative dimensions at both the organizational as well as the individual level. If the sales leader did not perform as expected, he or she would be offered other opportunities in the bank.

The MD actively supported the program, took part in the training sessions, and challenged the employees to propose chores for him to do in order to support them. He frequently asked, 'What can I do to make you perform a better job?' And the employees were responsive: 'We want better systems, we need more people, and we want a more visible leader'.

The MD took care not to control the process. He put his head on the block in the same way as the sales leaders and employees in their common efforts to improve their sales capabilities and relational processes. This was the logic of the 'training arm' illustrating that the strength of the arm is dependent on everybody playing their respective roles to serve the customers.

E.11 SESAM in 2012

In 2012 we observed that the program had been managed by a series of dedicated SESAM leaders and that the two year position remained highly regarded. For some the position had been a stepping stone to top jobs in SR-Bank, for others it had been a time out from their normal careers.

The SESAM leader coordinated all of the corporate training activities of the bank. That included the management and administration of two core and very comprehensive activities that encompassed all leaders and employees: training of sales leaders and financial advisors/sellers. The SESAM leader reported to a steering committee that included the directors of the retail and corporate market, the marketing and the HR manager. This group took the formal decisions as to the content of the SESAM program. Before a proposition is presented to this committee, a broad process has taken place. First, the SESAM leader consults with top management and the marketing and the human resource departments. Of even more importance, groups representing all organizational levels and geographical areas of the bank provide input as to what they view as the main competitive pressures and the areas they regard as requiring more knowledge and training. They are also consulted on the methods to be used at the training sessions and the need for external consultants. The SESAM leader triggers the work of these groups, summarizes and further discusses their views in a feedback session before presenting the proposed content of the SESAM session to the steering committee. This process ensures that the goals and processes of SESAM are firmly rooted in the needs and experiences of the employees as well as with the strategies of management.

The issue of performance measurement

Ever since SESAM was introduced performance measurement has been a significant issue. In the early years any form of performance measurement was at odds with the SR-Bank culture. Not only did the unions make their demands but management was uncomfortable with what it also regarded as a US approach to management.

The negotiations with the union ended in a compromise: measuring sales at the branch level was accepted, but not at the individual level. A selection of products was to be measured. In accordance with the principles of the 'training arm' (see Figure E.1) the branch offices were, after consultations with the marketing department and the top management group, to decide on which products were to be measured. The range of products was narrow because SR-Bank wanted to focus on prioritized initiatives. Typically these coincided with marketing campaigns, seasonal sales or the utilization of new technologies such as internet banking. The mix of products could change from one quarter to another and the relative weighting of products could also change.

Compared with the original US program the connection between sales performance and economic incentives was fairly intricate and definitively not pitched at the individual level. On a monthly basis branches that reached their sales budgets would receive 50 euros per employee. Branches that achieved their quarterly budgets were granted a bonus of 200 euros per employee. The budgets and sales goals were stipulated on the basis of a combination of three factors: the bank's overall ambitions, the average of comparable branches, and the local conditions and opportunities. Thus a centrally prepared algorithm was used to define differentiated goals for the respective branches.

An internal competition was introduced between the branch offices by rewarding the five best performing branches with 400 euros per employee and the subsequent five best branches (numbers 6–10) 70 euros per employee. In addition to these regular bonuses, economic incentives were used for certain campaigns. All in all the employees in the very best sales branches could pocket an added 10 per cent to their annual wage. However, we emphasize that this was not a product of individual-level measurement but branch-level measurement.

To avoid complacency the bank implemented various schemes for bench-marking at three levels:

- Internally between the branches of SR-Bank
- Between SR-Bank and the other member banks of the savings bank alliance
- Nationally through Gallup polls

The effects of this performance measurement system were indisputable. In relation to comparable banks there was no doubting that SR-Bank had the superior sales organization. Within the bank it was noted that products and services included in the SESAM measurement scheme outperform those not included. This raised a new issue: economic incentives produced a short-term motivation. Remove a product from the basket of measured products and sales performance declines. This was at odds with SR-Bank's desire to achieve long-term motivation in line with its ambition to have long-terms customers. Indeed it emerged that there was evidence of overly aggressive selling of products in the current measurement scheme.

The management was surprised that economic, external incentives were such powerful motivators. Performance measurement set in motion power-ful emotional and competitive forces. Management began to try to balance these unintended consequences by stressing ethics and norms as the most viable basis for good customer relations. A balanced scorecard (Kaplan and Norton, 1996) was introduced as a means to developing a broader measure-ment system.

In 2001 the SESAM leader listed the following challenges for SESAM:

1. The conflict between short-term performance measures and the goal of long-term and profitable customer relationships needs to be resolved. Solutions are not obvious. A potential path is to focus on the drivers of sales, not the actual sales output. Sales referrals, teambuilding and the quality of the financial advice may serve as potential candidates. Needless to say, the discovery and documentation of such drivers are no easy task.
2. Developing the role of the sales leader. The sales leader is the key performer on the stage of sales actors. They need to internalize their role and the expectations from management, employees and customers. The sales leader has the responsibility to define the right quality of their services and employees to serve their local market effectively. To become a better leader they must have the courage to become more explicit in their feedback to the sales force. This leads to the third issue of
3. Goal and development assessment talks with the employees, including the ability and courage to raise difficult issues and resolve controversies.
4. Develop the human and social relations at the work place and within the sales teams. A caring organization is the best basis for open and honest experience transfer and knowledge creation.
5. Develop stretch targets. Stretch targets go beyond the budgets and reflect the hopes and ambitions of teams and individuals. In peoples' efforts to reach such targets the bank is tolerant of failure. The main point is to get employees to be more creative and more ambitious in what they are aiming for, and to try and think about how they can get there.

In the course of pursuing these challenges substantial changes took place to HRM in SR-Bank.

By 2012 in order to more fully and visibly integrate sales with the overall strategy of the bank, the sales figures are now fully integrated into a balanced scorecard. On a monthly basis the balanced score card measures four dimensions:

- The relations with customers and the market
- The quality of internal processes
- The quality of management and employees
- Financial results

Although the department manager knows the scores of each individual the agreement with the union is that the results are only ever to be published on the team/department level. The scores are actively used by departments to benchmark themselves against other departments and therefore to learn from one another. However, by 2012 there are monthly celebrations of the top ten individual sales performers. As you will recall, for many years any open recognition or rewarding of individual performance was blocked by the union. Now the union has changed its position. In Scandinavia at the firm level the legislative framework is so general that HR departments are not burdened with having to oversee the mass of detail that, for example, their German counterparts have to deal with. Employment law is sufficiently general to permit HR departments to experiment with and implement local HRM practices that are well received by employees. Concomitantly, the law preserves the rights of unions to withdraw their cooperation in the case of disagreement with local management. As SR-Bank employees have developed a liking for being measured and for competing internally the union has responded by withdrawing its objections. This collaborative and local nature to Scandinavian HRM is particularly discernible in another innovation that is specifically about fostering team spirit. Not only are 'goals' registered but also 'goal-creating passes' are registered. SR-Bank has introduced the terms 'passes' (that is recommendations) in order to record and measure collaboration between the branches. A branch gets a credit when it recommends a customer to another part of the bank, and the receiving branch records the recommendation as a pass.

In 2012 SR-Bank has become a very transparent organization with pervasive performance measures. However, equally it remains an organization with a strong union that has to be consulted.

? DISCUSSION QUESTIONS

1 Discuss the reasons why the SESAM program was modified when it was introduced into SR-Bank. Would these reasons apply elsewhere or are they peculiar to the Scandinavian context?

2 Discuss the modifications to the SESAM program at its launch. In relation to the performance of SR-Bank, were these modifications positive? If they were positive, could these modifications be applied universally?

3 Discuss the changes to the SESAM program. Have these changes caused SESAM to become more 'American' in character, or does it remain a fundamentally Scandinavian approach?

4 What lessons are there for US MNCs entering Scandinavia, or for Scandinavian MNCs entering the US?

7

Competencies and knowledge transfer

7.1   Introduction

The rise and fall of Nokia is a dramatic illustration of the difficulty in main-taining competitive advantage on the basis of a particular technology. From 1998 to 2012 it was the world's largest vendor of mobile phones. However, from 2007 it began to suffer declining market share as a result of the growing use of smartphones. While at the end of 2007 it had been worth more than Euro 110bn, by April 2012 its market valuation was just Euro 14.7bn. For any MNC both imitation and innovation by other MNCs are a constant threat. Patents provide only a measure of protection. Research we conducted as long ago as the mid-1990s indicates that firms in general have been conscious of the fragility of technology, as well as financial resources, as a source of competitive advantage for some time (Nordhaug and Gooderham, 1996). Instead it is the competencies and knowledge of their employees that they view as the most significant source of long-term competitive advantage.

The purpose of this chapter is twofold. First we introduce a typology for classifying competencies in MNCs. We develop a sixfold classification of employee competencies in MNCs. The ways in which these critical human resources can be generated are also discussed, together with their signifi-cance for MNCs. Potential practical applications of the typology are also discussed. Second we present a conceptual framework or model for ana-lyzing knowledge transfer and sharing within MNCs. One key aspect to our perspective on knowledge transfer in MNCs is the role social capital plays. In this chapter we further develop the concept and discuss how social capital can be developed by MNCs. The model we develop clarifies the ini-tiatives required for cultivating social capital in order to achieve knowledge synergies.

7.2   The MNC as a knowledge network

In Chapter 1 we discussed Dunning's (1981, 2009) eclectic approach or 'OLI theory'. To recap: The central idea of this approach is that three conditions (ownership, location and internalization) must hold for a firm to engage in FDI. In addition to the advantage of possessing superior competencies or other valuable and rare assets, there must be reasons why geographically separated production within the same firm is preferred to centralized production. The fundamental trade-off is between economies of scale on the plant level and potential decentralization advantages such as lower factor costs, transport costs or trade barriers. Finally, the firm needs to prefer internalizing production rather than, for example, licensing production to a local firm. This could be due, for example, to difficulties in writing a licensing contract that gives the parent firm sufficient protection.

However, by the 1990s Dunning was arguing that the OLI paradigm needed to be radically supplemented because:

> increasingly, firms are investing abroad to protect or augment their core
> competencies. In such cases, they are 'buying into' foreign created assets (notably
> technological capacity, information, human creativity, and markets) some of which
> are proprietary to particular foreign firms [hence the pronounced trend towards
> acquisition of foreign firms, rather than greenfield investment] and others are
> more generally accessible to corporations, but immobile across geographical space.
> (Dunning, 1997: 64) [our insertion]

In other words MNCs are no longer simply developing products at home and transferring these innovations to foreign subsidiaries, they are increasingly seeking to optimize their global innovative capabilities by incorporating subsidiary-specific advantages in different countries, sometimes engaging in major research at the subsidiary level (Davis and Meyer, 2004). In Chapter 3 we pointed out that one can increasingly discern subsidiaries with a developmental capacity, that is subsidiaries that not only have the capability to adapt products, but which also have the resources to enhance them or even the capability to single-handedly develop new products (Kuemmerle, 1997). In the latter case it is the subsidiary that is the center of excellence within the firm for particular products and technologies (Birkinshaw, 1997). As a consequence it is no longer sufficient to analyse the competitive advantage of the MNC solely in terms of location advantages in its home country (cf. Porter's 'diamond' framework, 1990a).

Given that the essence of the competitive advantage possessed by MNCs lies in their potential to combine geographically distributed competencies, the management of these competencies is now regarded as a key challenge. Not only do these competencies have to be generated but they also have to be transferred across spatial and national boundaries. But what are the constituents of these competencies? In our view the concept of 'core competencies' (Prahalad and Hamel, 1990) is useful but too abstract for management purposes. What is needed is a typology of the various competencies carried by employees, not least because it is these that form the building blocks for the development of core competencies. Because competencies are dispersed across individuals they are best analysed as sub-individual units. This approach has several advantages. Among these is the opportunity to aggregate competences across individuals. This is reflected in the use of concepts such as competence stocks, competence portfolios, competence configurations, team competencies and organizational competence (Winter, 1987; Hamel and Heene, 1994; Nordhaug, 1994). In addition, it is analytically useful to conceive of organizations needing specific types of competencies rather than specific individuals.

7.3 Classification of competencies

When work-related competencies are to be classified as sub-individual units of analysis, valuable insights are offered by economic human capital theory. It was originally economists such as Becker (1983/1964) and Schultz (1981) who launched the notion of 'human resource specificity' in conjunction with what is known as human capital theory. At the core of human capital theory is a distinction between those competencies that are firm-specific and which have little or no applicability beyond the individual firm, and those which are firm non-specific and which may apply across firms. According to human capital theory, firms will tend to avoid investing in the latter. Furthermore, firms develop internal labor markets in order to encourage employees to invest in firm-specific competencies despite their lock-in effect.

Useful as the distinction between firm-specific and firm non-specific competencies is, it fails to take into account task-related differences at the micro level (Nordhaug, 1994, 1998). In other words there is a need to add a task-specificity dimension. We shall define task specificity as the degree to which competencies are linked to the performance of a narrow range of work tasks. Low task specificity is characteristic of competencies that are not particularly relevant to any one particular task. Instead they have a bearing on the successful performance of a wide range of different tasks. They include, for example, analytical skills, problem-solving capacity, social skills, and the ability to work independently. However, when the degree of task specificity is high, competencies are linked to one specific task only and cannot be deployed for the performance of other tasks. For example, 'touch-method' typing can only be applied to the task of operating a standard keyboard. In contrast, social skills may be utilized across a wide spectrum of tasks.

If a competence can be used in one firm only, it is firm-specific and, by definition, has little or no potential value for other firms. In contrast competencies that are not firm-specific can be sold in external labor markets. Firm specificity is thus fundamentally different from the dimension of task specificity in that it is defined in relation to the external environment of the firm.

Because MNCs have subsidiaries there is a need to supplement firm or MNC specificity with the notion of subsidiary specificity. This is particularly necessary when subsidiaries are 'enhancers' or 'centers of excellence' (see Chapter 3) and have strong competencies of their own that are important to the MNC as a whole

In Figure 7.1 the dimensions of task specificity, MNC specificity and subsidiary specificity have been combined to form a three-dimensional competence typology comprising six cells. The cells contain different variants of competence idiosyncrasy and thus dissimilar types of competencies within cross-national settings.

The first competence type (I) is both MNC and subsidiary non-specific. It encompasses a broad range of knowledge, skills and aptitudes. Examples are literacy skills, learning capacity, analytical capabilities, creativity, knowledge

	SUBSIDIARY SPECIFICITY		
	Low	Low	High
Low	Meta competencies (I)	Intra organizational MNC competencies (II)	Intra organizational Subsidiary competencies (III)
High	Standard technical competencies (IV)	Technical MNC competencies (V)	Subsidiary-unique technical competencies (VI)
	Low	High	Low
		MNC SPECIFICITY	

TASK SPECIFICITY

Figure 7.1 Classification of competencies in MNCs

of foreign languages and cultures, the ability to perceive and process environmental signals and events, the capacity to tolerate and master uncertainty, the ability to communicate and to co-operate with others, general negotiation skills, and ability to adjust to change. We label these forms of competencies meta competencies, because of their relevance for the accomplishment of a variety of different tasks.

The second competence category (II) is characterized by low task specificity, low subsidiary specificity but high MNC specificity. Because this category contains those competencies that denote familiarity with the MNC as an organization, it can be labeled intra-organizational MNC competence. Illustrations of intra-organizational MNC competencies include knowledge about the company's history, its strategy and goals, its structure, its market position, its culture and its overall range of products or services. Additionally it includes knowledge of those persons, networks and alliances that are critical for getting decisions made. A further illustration is familiarity with the different subunits and their operational conditions which is developed through measures such as job rotation and comprehensive courses for new employees. The aim of this is to provide a broad overview of the MNC and its subsidiaries. The nurturing of managerial generalists within MNCs, that is employees who possess a substantial amount of MNC-specific, intra-organizational competencies, is a particular feature of Japanese companies, many of which have extensive job-rotation arrangements.

Type III competencies incorporate competencies that exhibit low task specificity, low MNC specificity and high subsidiary specificity. Consequently, we can call them intra-organizational subsidiary competencies. Although they are essentially the same as the types of competencies associated with MNC-specific competencies, they are different in that their value is restricted to one and only one subsidiary. Examples include knowledge of the subsidiary's organizational culture (for example, its symbols, subcultures, history, norms, organizational dialect or code, and ethical standards), its communication channels, informal networks and internal political conditions.

High task specificity, low MNC specificity and low subsidiary specificity are characteristic of type IV competencies, which may be labeled standard technical competencies. These embrace a wide range of operatively oriented competencies. Examples include the ability to operate PC keyboards ('typing'), knowledge of generic budgeting and accounting principles and methods, skills in computer programming, knowledge of standard computer software, and craft skills and professional task-oriented skills that can be applied across companies and industries.

Type V comprises those competencies that are task-specific, MNC-specific but subsidiary non-specific. Technical MNC competencies can only be used to accomplish a limited number of work tasks and are not portable across companies. They include the skills that are required to operate an individual MNC's IT, budgeting and accounting systems. These have usually been developed to meet the unique needs of the individual MNC and are rarely duplicated in other MNCs.

Type VI, subsidiary-unique technical competencies, can only be applied to solve a limited number of tasks within one particular subsidiary. They include the knowledge and skills required to operate the unique elements in an individual subsidiary's technology and routines. Examples are skills related to the use of specialized tools crafted in the subsidiary, knowledge about procedures and recipes developed exclusively within the subsidiary, skills in repairing unique technology and in operating specialized local filing or data systems as well as skills related to the administration and maintenance of organizationally idiosyncratic routines or procedures in general. The six competence types will now be discussed more thoroughly.

Meta competencies

The importance of meta competencies lies in their broad applicability. As such they form a crucial foundation for work and organizational performance in general. Not only are they critical in regard to most current tasks, but they also constitute a potential for mastering future tasks. That is, meta competencies constitute a potential for facilitating organizational and strategic change. It is not only managers who need to be equipped with meta competencies, but they are needed wherever in the organization change is necessary.

Traditionally, the formal educational system has been the main source of meta competencies. However, there are now many other important sources. One example is that of the training programs many MNCs have aimed at facilitating the cross-national transfer of their personnel. These comprise a variety of activities whose main aim is the development or refinement of employees' meta competencies. Indeed most listings of the competencies needed for management in cross-national settings comprise only meta competencies. For example Alkhafaji (1995) lists the following as those abilities that are essential skills for global managers:

- The ability to perform in a team setting
- The ability to manage change and transition
- The ability to manage work force diversity

- The ability to communicate in various cultural settings
- Proficiency in developing global strategic skills and turning ideas into action (implementation)
- The ability to change the way he or she thinks and operates
- The ability to be creative, learn, and transfer knowledge
- The expertise to form joint ventures or strategic alliances and to operate with a high degree of personal integrity and honesty

In addition to this, relational skills that make it possible to develop relationships with host country nationals and to find mentors in the MNC's HQ also frequently figure in this literature. Likewise perceptual skills that relate to being able to understand how host country nationals think and behave as well as the ability to be non-judgmental when confronted with confusing situations are often included.

Intra organizational MNC competencies

As with meta competencies, the importance of intra organizational competencies (IOMCs) has been discussed in the management and leadership literature but also within politically oriented organization theory concerned with power relations (for example, Kotter, 1982; Pfeffer, 1992; Clegg et al., 2006). The focus has been on internal networking capabilities, knowledge of and capacity to manage firm-specific symbols, and familiarity with the culture of different parts of the organization. In addition, the significance of knowing how key individuals and coalitions of individuals think and operate is emphasized.

IOMCs are inextricably linked to the organizational culture of the MNC and vice versa. The corporate culture of an MNC comprises knowledge about past successes and failures that is communicated to and learned by new members. This acquired knowledge becomes generalized through successive communication and reinforcement processes.

It should be noted that certain meta competencies are of no value unless they are combined with relevant intra-organizational competencies. For instance, there is a need to blend general leadership skills with knowledge about specific organizational conditions, especially an understanding of internal power structures. In order to act effectively in the organization, the employee needs to be politically adept.

Whereas meta competencies can be transferred to different contexts, IOMCs have to be acquired anew when individuals move to other companies. A period of several years may be needed to develop the necessary network of contacts. As noted by Whitley (1989: 213), the search for general properties of managerial work per se has tended to play down the organizational specificity of managerial tasks: 'This specificity means that managerial problems are not easily abstracted from their contexts for solution with general models and procedures. It also suggests that the generalizability of successful practices in one situation to other contexts – across space, time, and cultures – is limited.'

To further illuminate the difference between meta competencies and IOMCs, we may say that acquiring knowledge of the basic principles of strategic analysis represents an example of the former, whereas the ability to analyse the specific competitive conditions of the MNC per se is an example of the latter. Familiarity with the MNC is developed mainly through experience gained while working within it.

Normally, it is employees in managerial and higher-level professional positions who possess most of the IOMCs. However, it is increasingly the case that it is advantageous for the MNC if employees at lower levels also possess basic knowledge about its mission, strategy and policies, its products, competitive situation and competitors. This is particularly the case in service industries where front-line employees have to cope with a variety of dissimilar situations that cannot be encapsulated in work manuals.

IOMCs are mainly acquired through day-to-day interaction with and observation of colleagues. However, companies usually also take steps to enhance IOMCs by implementing job rotation, trainee and mentoring programs, on-the-job coaching, internal executive-development programs, and campaigns aimed at disseminating core values and information about the MNC's goals.

IOMCs need to be generated and maintained. Introduction programs for new recruits are a common example of the former. The aim is to start the internalization of company norms and values. For example, many MNCs have 'universities' or internal schools where their newly recruited employees are immediately sent to go through such programs. Maintenance of IOMCs is the purpose of mentoring for expatriates. The mentor is an experienced person who remains at the MNC corporate headquarters and keeps the expatriate posted on those developments that may be critical for his or her future career development.

Intra-organizational subsidiary competencies

Intra-organizational subsidiary competencies (IOSCs) are normally tacit and are acquired within the subsidiary through interaction with other members of the subsidiary. While they are critical for the operation of the subsidiary, they are of limited immediate value beyond its boundaries. For example, the ability to interact with personnel in one particular subsidiary is of little direct value in other contexts.

As we have indicated, most of the training programs designed for expatriates are intended to enhance their meta competencies. However, some companies also try to disseminate IOSCs to personnel prior to their expatriation by locating some of their training to the subsidiary. This gives incoming expatriates an opportunity to get to know managers within the subsidiary and to acquire some knowledge of its products, processes, organization and culture. Other possible arrangements are field trips to the subsidiary in question and internships. Many companies also use former expatriates to brief new expatriates about the specifics of the various subsidiaries.

Standard technical competencies

The leadership literature distinguishes technical competencies such as knowledge about procedures and techniques for performing a specialized activity, and the ability to use tools and operate equipment related to that activity, as a competency category. However, our classification goes further by subdividing technical competencies into three distinct categories:

- Standard technical competencies
- Technical MNC competencies
- Subsidiary-unique technical competencies

Standard technical competencies embrace a wide range of operatively oriented competencies. Examples include knowledge of generic budgeting and accounting principles and methods, skills in computer programming, knowledge of standard computer software, and craft skills and professional task-oriented skills that can be applied across industries.

Important generators of standard technical competencies are the educational system, adult vocational education and training, parts of company in-house training programs and apprenticeship arrangements. Another source of standard technical competencies is the training provided by suppliers of information and communication technology.

Technical MNC competencies

Technical MNC competencies are those competencies that are specific to the technology of the MNC. Some of these are critical assets while others, such as company-specific routines and policies, are of more marginal value. What they have in common is that they have little immediate value beyond the individual MNC.

Typical ways of generating technical MNC competencies are through vocational training specific to the task-related needs and technology of the individual MNC. Common examples are company trainee programs and apprenticeship arrangements and, not least, experience gained through concrete, practical work within the MNC. In addition, training aimed at making people knowledgeable about MNC-specific routines and procedures may provide an illustration of this. Together with intra-organizational MNC competencies, technical MNC competencies may create an organizational lock-in of employees if their possession of these competencies is high relative to their meta competencies and standard technical competencies.

Subsidiary-unique technical competencies

The narrowest type of technical competence in our classification is that of subsidiary-unique technical competencies (SUTCs). Their immediate relevance is exclusive to that of the subsidiary. The main significance of SUTCs lie more in their contributions to generating congruence between personnel and tasks than in their contribution to facilitating change and mobility within the MNC. Idiosyncratic technical competencies are typically generated within the one subsidiary and are developed through channels such as informal learning, job rotation, in-house training and apprenticeship arrangements.

It is therefore SUTCs that have the greatest potential for creating lock-in of employees, since their value is not only confined to one organizational unit, but to a narrow range of work tasks. Employees whose competencies are primarily located within this category cannot be deployed in other subsidiaries without substantial supplementary training. This is often the case for the local employees of subsidiaries located in developing countries because most of the training they receive is narrowly subsidiary-specific.

However, in a dynamic perspective it must be emphasized that SUTCs may become MNC-specific if they form the basis for technology or product development that is disseminated to other parts of the MNC whether these are other subsidiaries or corporate headquarters. This is the case for enhancer and center-of-excellence subsidiaries.

Some implications

The typology may be applied as a tool for internal analyses and assessments of the existing pool of competencies in the organization. For example, subsidiaries can apply it as a means for assessing their latent adaptability. Using the typology may expose an over-investment in developing standard technical competencies, technical MNC competencies and subsidiary-unique technical competencies, and an under-investment in meta competencies, and intra organizational MNC competencies.

Four important lessons in particular for competence development in MNCs can be derived from the typology. First, many jobs can no longer be reduced to a bundle of discrete operational tasks, each demanding easily definable task-specific competencies. Their successful execution involves overarching competencies, for example, those related to communication and co-operation with colleagues as well as to adjustment to working in teams. Second, jobs are enclosed in wider organizational contexts that affect employees, job content and performance standards. These contexts require that employees go beyond technically correct job performance. There is now an increasing need to communicate with colleagues either in one's own department or in other departments or subsidiaries. Knowing whom one should approach to develop a solution to a problem is thus vital. Third, if subsidiaries of MNCs only invest in the development of subsidiary-specific technical competencies, inflexibility may be the outcome. Fourth, it is important that individual employees possess a broad range of competencies.

Managers of subsidiaries, for example, need both meta competencies, such as communication skills and co-operative abilities, and intra-organizational competencies such as knowledge about informal communication channels and power structures together with knowledge about central persons in the company. The need to blend competencies may be triggered by the recognition on the part of the MNC that there is a need to integrate certain classes of complex and sophisticated knowledge. This requires employees who not only are highly competent in their own fields but who also concomitantly possess intra-organizational MNC competencies such as knowledge about the overall strategy as well as the MNC's organizational procedures and routines.

We will now address the issue of how knowledge can be transferred among units of the MNC. It should be borne in mind that for an increasingly significant proportion of MNCs knowledge transfer is not necessarily unidirectional (from corporate headquarters to subsidiaries), but bi-directional, or even multi-directional between knowledge-rich equals (cf. Cantwell, 1989, 1994). This notion of the MNC as a knowledge network has given rise to concepts such as 'heterarchy' (Hedlund, 1986).

7.4   Knowledge transfer in MNCs

While the possession of knowledge-based assets endows an MNC with the potential to derive advantageous synergies, a distinct ability to transfer knowledge and other competencies efficiently is also required. The application of social capital theory has contributed important insights into the processes underlying knowledge transfer within the MNC. However, this perspective needs to be supplemented in two ways. First, there is a need to take into account the influence of the external environment and second, there is a need to specify the capabilities, in the form of management-initiated practices, required to promote and maintain capital. The latter include transmission channels, socialization mechanisms and motivational mechanisms. These mechanisms represent the key modifiable elements in facilitating knowledge flows. In the following, we present a conceptual model for the study of intra-MNC knowledge transfer that embraces the various facets of social capital, the influence of the external environment and modifiable practices (Gooderham, 2007).

Background

Internalization theory explains the existence of MNCs in terms of firm boundary questions. For example Buckley and Casson (1976) argued that because the market for knowledge-based assets was flawed, the cost of internalization is less than the cost of using the market. Thus firms become MNCs as they internalize the markets for their knowledge assets in multiple locations. Internalization remains the solution as long as the cost of internalization is less than the cost of using the market. However, more recently the evolutionary theory of the MNC (see Chapter 1) proposes that rather than focusing on the causes of and consequences of market failure, greater emphasis should be given to the advantages firms have over markets: '(the firm) should be understood as a social community specializing in the speed and efficiency in the creation and transfer of knowledge' (Kogut and Zander, 1996: 503). That is, organizations have the potential to develop particular dynamic capabilities that enable them to share knowledge in a way that is superior to that of the market.

However, the possession by MNCs of these knowledge transfer capabilities cannot be taken for granted. This is of particular significance because a growing body of research argues that MNCs that have these knowledge transfer capabilities are more productive than those lacking them (Tsai and Ghoshal, 1998; Inkpen and Tsang, 2005). Thus it is important to consider those practices or mechanisms that reduce the difficulties in transferring knowledge from one unit of an MNC to another. For successful knowledge transfer to occur there must be significant internal coordination in the sense of organizational capabilities that are consistent over time and that promote linkages across units. These dynamic capabilities consist of specific strategic and organizational commitments to particular practices and processes that enable the MNC to design and implement new resource configurations (Eisenhardt and Martin, 2000).

Four types of knowledge

Polanyi (1962) distinguished explicit and tacit knowledge. The former is objective in the sense that it can be codified in, for example, scientific formulas and manuals, whereas the latter is subjective and experiential and therefore hard to formalize (Nonaka, 1994; Nonaka et al., 2000). Because explicit knowledge is easily transmitted it is readily imitated by competitors and therefore unlikely to be a source of competitive advantage. In contrast tacit knowledge, because it is non-codifiable, is difficult to assess from the outside and has therefore a stronger potential to generate distinctive competitive positions abroad. However, it is precisely tacit knowledge that is difficult to transfer particularly when the knowledge overlap between the source and recipient is limited (Szulanski, 1996).

Kogut and Zander (1992: 386) employ a similar distinction. They use the terms 'know-what' for relatively articulable knowledge (that is explicit knowledge or information), and 'know-how' for 'the accumulated practical skill or expertise that allows one to do something smoothly and efficiently' (that is tacit knowledge). Gupta and Govindarajan (2000) have further elaborated this distinction by viewing 'know-how' as 'procedural' types of knowledge including: (i) marketing know-how, (ii) distribution know-how, (iii) packaging-design technology, (iv) product designs, (v) process designs, (vi) purchasing designs, and (vii) management systems and procedures. These contrast with 'declarative' types of knowledge such as monthly financial data. The focus in our context is effectively on these forms of 'procedural' or 'know-how' types of knowledge.

In the case attached to Chapter 3 we introduced Spender's knowledge-based theory of the firm. In addition to distinguishing explicit and tacit knowledge, Spender argues that one should distinguish individual from social knowledge.

	Individual	Social
Explicit	Conscious	Objectified
Implicit	Automatic	Collective

Figure 7.2 Different types of organizational knowledge

This results in four generic knowledge types (Figure 7.2). Drawing on Fenton-O'Creevy et al. (2011) we will now distinguish these four forms of knowledge.

Conscious knowledge is held by individuals and comprises established standards of practice that are a product of their technical training. Automatic knowledge is also held by individuals but is more psychological in the sense that it comprises the hunches, intuition and automatic skills of individuals. The objectified knowledge of a firm comprises its intellectual property such as its patents and registered designs, as well as its canonical knowledge embodied in forms, manuals, databases and IT systems. Finally, the collective knowledge of a firm comprises key aspects of its organizational culture that involve distinct, firm-specific, processes of knowledge production underpinned by emergent idiosyncratic practices and rules. Such knowledge may be relatively unknown from individual actors but is accessible and sustained through their interaction (Spender, 1994).

For a given firm these four elements collectively constitute its intellectual capital. While these four elements are interdependent, Nahapiet and Ghoshal (1998) distinguish the two types of social knowledge in their analysis of what constitutes a firm's organizational advantage. Further, they argue that it is the two types of social knowledge that distinguish individuals working within an organization from individuals working at arm's length across a hypothetical market. Spender (1996: 52) himself is even more precise in terms of organizational advantage, suggesting that 'it is collective knowledge [that] is the most secure and strategically significant kind of organizational knowledge'.

Its strategic significance lies in that it influences individual learning to such an extent that individuals can only be proficient once they are 'socialized' into the organization and 'have acquired much of the collective knowledge that underpins "the way things are done around here"' (Spender, 1996: 54). In other words the 'travel of ideas' (Czarniawska and Joerges, 1996) within a firm is dependent on sustained exposure to collective knowledge. Not only does this imply that without that exposure cognitive hurdles will prevent knowledge exchange, but it also implies that parties must be politically motivated to engage in that process of exposure.

Knowledge transfer

In line with Bresman et al. (1999) we use the concept of transfer of knowledge to refer to the accumulation or assimilation of new knowledge in the receiving unit. However, like Minbaeva et al. (2003: 587), we would also specify that: 'The key element in knowledge transfer is not the underlying (original) knowledge, but rather the extent to which the receiver acquires potentially useful knowledge and utilizes this knowledge in its own operations'. In other words for transfer to have taken place, not only has some change in knowledge or performance in the recipient unit occurred (Inkpen and Tsang, 2005) but through social interaction the underlying or original knowledge may have undergone profound change that affects both transfer and recipient. As such 'knowledge sharing' rather than 'knowledge transfer' may be a more appropriate concept.

7.5   Determinants of knowledge transfer

Theorization on the determinants of knowledge transfer in MNCs has focused both on the MNC's external environment and on its internal environment. In terms of the latter, building on existing knowledge-based theories of the firm, Nahapiet and Ghoshal (1998) argue that social capital theory provides a sound basis for identifying the capabilities organizations are uniquely equipped to develop for the sharing of knowledge. Social capital, they contend, increases the efficiency of knowledge transfer because it encourages cooperative behavior. They propose that differences between firms in terms of knowledge transfer may represent differences in their ability to create and exploit social capital. They distinguish three dimensions of social capital: the relational, the cognitive and the structural.

The relational dimension of social capital refers to such facets of personal relationships as trust, obligations, respect and even friendship, which together increase the motivation to engage in knowledge exchange and teamwork. The significance of this dimension of social capital as a driver of knowledge flows has received empirical support through case studies conducted by Bresman et al. (1999) of three MNCs that had acquired companies with the main objective of gaining access to and utilizing the acquired companies' R&D knowledge. Their analysis indicates that in the early stages of an acquisition the lack of personal relationships between acquirer and acquisition made it very difficult for either party to trust in the abilities of the others. In this phase knowledge transfer is limited to imposed, unidirectional knowledge transfer of a 'know-what' type from the parent to the subsidiary. It is not until the acquired company is fully integrated in the sense that trust has been established and that there is therefore a perception that 'the risk of opportunistic behavior is low' (1999: 442) that a high level of reciprocal knowledge flow of a 'know-how' variety occurs.

This clearly underscores the significance of the relational dimension of social capital for knowledge transfer. Using data from the subsidiary units of a large multinational electronics company, Tsai and Ghoshal (1998) also indicate support for this relationship. Finally, Hansen and Løvås's (2004) research on knowledge transfer from new product development teams situated in a focal subsidiary of a large US high-technology MNC supports the notion that good informal relations are of critical importance for these teams to engage in competence transfers with subsidiaries without related competences. In short, the greater the degree of relational social capital that has been developed across the MNC, the greater the degree of knowledge transfer.

The cognitive dimension refers to shared interpretations and systems of meaning, and shared language and codes that provide the foundation for communication. Tsai and Ghoshal (1998) found empirical support that the role of the cognitive dimension of social capital lies in effectuating the development of the relational dimension of social capital rather than directly on knowledge transfer. In other words sharing 'a view of the world' is a necessary prerequisite for sufficient levels of trust to be developed that in turn stimulates knowledge exchange. The greater the degree of cognitive social capital that has been developed between units, the greater the degree of relational social capital between them.

Nahapiet and Ghoshal's (1998) concept of social capital contains a third dimension, that of structural capital. The structural dimension of social capital refers to the presence or absence of specific network or social interaction ties between units of the MNC and the overall configuration of these ties. As such it is not directly associated with the transfer of knowledge. Instead its significance for the transfer of knowledge is through the ways in which it 'influences the development of the relational and cognitive dimensions of social capital' (1998: 251–252). Network ties facilitate social interaction which in turn stimulates the development of the cognitive and relational dimensions of social capital. Thus a precondition for the development and maintenance of relational and cognitive dimensions of social capital is that of sustained social interaction. Moreover, particularly rich patterns of interaction are important when the knowledge to be transferred is not codified.

Empirical support for the importance of social interaction ties can be found in the case studies conducted by Bresman et al. (1999). They found that technological know-how is best transferred through intensive communication, with many visits and meetings, because it facilitates the development of a common set of beliefs and values. In other words social interaction is a key mechanism for the leveraging of knowledge because it effectuates the development of the cognitive and relational dimensions of social capital. Further, the structural dimension of social capital is a necessary prerequisite for the emergence of the cognitive dimension of social capital which in turn facilitates the development of the relational dimension of capital which leads to the transfer and exchange of 'know-how'.

If it is the case that sufficient degrees of relational social capital must be in place to enable the transfer of 'know-how' and that this is dependent on a sufficient degree of cognitive social capital and structural social capital, the issue is then how best to develop these two latter forms of social capital. However, prior to examining this issue we shall consider the impact of the external environment on the formation of these two forms of social capital.

7.6   The external environment of the MNC

In terms of the external environment, Ghemawat's (2001) CAGE distance framework that we introduced in Chapter 1 distinguishes various dimensions that impact on the formation of inter-unit MNC social capital including geographic distance, cultural distance and economic distance. Hansen and Løvås's (2004) study referred to above does indeed confirm that large spatial distance reduces the tendency for the facilitation of competence transfers even when the transferor and the receiver have related competences. Thus it remains the case that because long-distance travel is expensive and time-consuming geographical distance is a barrier to developing structural social capital.

Cultural distance, in the sense of a common language and a common administrative heritage (colony/colonizer), is also reported as a critical dimension for cross-border economic activity (Ghemawat and Mallick, 2003). In other words there are initial steep costs involved in moving out of one's culturally proximate area because of the difficulties in creating a common language and shared interpretations. Thus Bresman et al. (1999) found that in the early stages of an acquisition the lack of cognitive social capital is accentuated by cultural distance. For US MNCs the costs in terms of performance stemming from cultural distance appear to manifest themselves as an inverted J-curve (Gomes and Ramaswamy, 1999). This is because while initially US MNCs tend to locate foreign activities in Canada, the UK and Australia, that is, culturally proximate areas, a performance decline sets in when they move outside of these areas. The curve appears to be different for Western European MNCs in that Ruigrok and Wagner's (2003) research indicates a U-form in terms of performance for German MNCs. German firms have only very limited culturally proximate areas to move into (Austria and parts of Switzerland) and are therefore immediately confronted by cultural non-proximity when engaging in foreign activities. As such German MNCs expect to and therefore have experience of making the effort required for the development of a shared language and a common vision regardless of setting (McFadyen and Cannella, 2004). However, as cultural distance increases, the investment in creating social capital means that the first stage of the 'U' becomes steadily deeper and more prolonged.

Economic distance also appears to play a significant role in regard to the formation of cognitive social capital. Gupta and Govindarajan's (2000) investigation of parent–subsidiary knowledge flows suggests that effectuating the flow is actually significantly more challenging when the subsidiary is an acquisition in a country with a relatively high per capita income. At first sight this is a strange finding. However, given that high per capita income is usually associated with high levels of education and therefore self-confidence it may be the case that the 'not-invented-here' syndrome kicks in in these locations.

7.7 The role of management-initiated practices

Given the impact of the external environment on inter-unit social interaction and the formation of cognitive social capital, having dynamic capabilities in the form of routines and practices that negate the impact of the external environment and which promote the development and maintenance of social interaction and the cognitive facets of social capital, is critical. Without such routines knowledge synergies will be difficult, if not impossible, to achieve (Eisenhardt and Martin, 2000; Nonaka et al., 2000). Indeed both De Meyer's (1995) and Reger's (1997) research indicated a considerable amount of effort by MNCs in developing mechanisms and practices that facilitate social interaction and the development of common sets of meaning. All in all the research indicates three sets of practices or mechanisms that MNCs apply in varying degrees: transmission channels, motivational mechanisms and socialization mechanisms.

The first set of practices, transmission channels, features prominently in Gupta and Govindarajan's (2000) study of knowledge flows within MNCs and is of primary importance for social interaction. By transmission channels they mean formal integrative mechanisms such as liaison personnel, inter-unit task forces and permanent international committees. Using the concept of formal proximity in the sense of units being formally grouped together and reporting to the same business or divisional manager, Hansen and Løvås's (2004) study also supports the significance of transmission channels in generating social interaction in the face of spatial distance.

Additionally one may observe the use and significance of intranet systems as transmission channels. As early as 2000 Teigland's study of a multinational IT company noted the importance of intranet 'communities' as sources of knowledge for technical employees. He records that: 'This is a curious discovery because these "communities" exhibit many of the characteristics of communities of practice – reciprocity, identity, and so on – but the individuals have typically never met' (Teigland, 2000: 143). The emergence of the intranet as a transmission channel has also been documented by IBM (2004). In 2003 71 per cent of IBM's employees regarded the IBM corporate intranet, 'w3', as vital to their jobs as opposed to only 28 per cent in 1997 (IBM, 2004). One effect of 'w3' is that it has spawned 'communities of practice', that is global communities of IBM professionals centered on particular domains of knowledge and focused on sharing both 'know-what' and 'know-how' across organizational boundaries. These are supplemented by 'BluePages' that list employees worldwide and their areas of expertise, 'World Jam Sessions' (virtual brainstorming events centered around a selected topic over a 72 hour period which employees are obliged to participate in), 'Buddy Networks' (virtual social communities), e-mail and telephone conferences. IBM also employs a number of more traditional communication channels such as global forums, face-to-face meetings and workshops. It is hence likely that the greater the magnitude of transmission channels between MNC parent and subsidiary, the greater the degree of structural social capital between them.

We have argued that the structural social capital dimension influences the cognitive dimension of social capital. However, social interaction ties in themselves may not be sufficient for a shared language and shared systems of meaning to emerge. The implication is that the development of the cognitive dimension of social capital requires particular attention by MNC managers. A number of researchers have observed the importance of mechanisms that promote the internalization of MNC-wide shared goals and mutual understandings. These socialization mechanisms have to be so potent that they are effective despite the impact of cultural distance and the 'not-invented-here' mentality MNCs often confront. One approach is to organize diversity training designed to help employees work effectively as part of a culturally heterogeneous workforce, to become aware of group-based differences among employees, and to decrease negative stereotyping and prejudice. Another involves training key employees in all host countries in the common language of the company (Caligiuri et al., 2005). Gupta and Govindarajan (2000) identify vertical mechanisms such as job transfers to corporate headquarters and participation in corporate mentoring programs as playing an important role in employee socialization into the MNC corporate culture. Tsang's (2001) case studies of Singapore-owned operations in China indicated the importance of Chinese managers not only spending time at corporate headquarters but also in other parts of the MNC. Supplementing these training initiatives is the design of performance appraisal that enables individuals to reflect on behaviors that are inconsistent with the shared corporate goals (Björkman et al., 2004; Minbaeva et al., 2003). Early mentoring of new employees by experienced veterans of the firm is also used by, for example, IBM. Kyriakidou (2005: 112) cautions that:

> Developing integrating competencies and skills in a diverse group should not be an attempt to make it more homogeneous; rather these capacities should create a mechanism where individuals can retain their dimensions of diversity (which are inherently valuable for a variety of group tasks), while at the same time avoiding such damaging processes as dysfunctional interpersonal conflict, miscommunication, higher levels of stress, slower decision making and problems with group cohesiveness.

Whereas socialization mechanisms involve occasional, formalized programs and are aimed at groups of employees, motivational mechanisms are much more constant and are often aimed at individual employees. The motivational disposition to the sender and the receiver are key elements in successful knowledge transfer (Gupta and Govindarajan, 2000). By rewarding certain types of behavior, motivational mechanisms contribute to a common understanding of what matters to the MNC. Motivational mechanisms may be divided into the use of extrinsic and intrinsic rewards. Several studies investigating the role of the use of extrinsic rewards for knowledge transfer indicate that they are counterproductive because they undermine the development of social capital (Frey, 1997; Bock et al., 2005). One explanation for this phenomenon might be that when pecuniary rewards are introduced, an incentive for the individual to withhold knowledge for future gains is also introduced. In short, the implication is that knowledge-sharing behavior cannot be paid for. Osterloh and Frey (2000) argue that only intrinsic motivation such as the expectation that knowledge contributions will be acknowledged by colleagues and superiors facilitates knowledge transfer. Gooderham et al. (2011) compared the impact of intrinsic and extrinsic rewards on social capital and knowledge transfer in MNCs. They found strong empirical support for the benefit for social capital of using intrinsic rewards whereas extrinsic rewards had detrimental consequences.

7.8   Conceptual model

Figure 7.3 summarizes our discussion of knowledge transfer in MNCs. Although the model is conceived in linear terms, this is obviously somewhat simplistic. Undoubtedly one could posit a bi-directional effect between

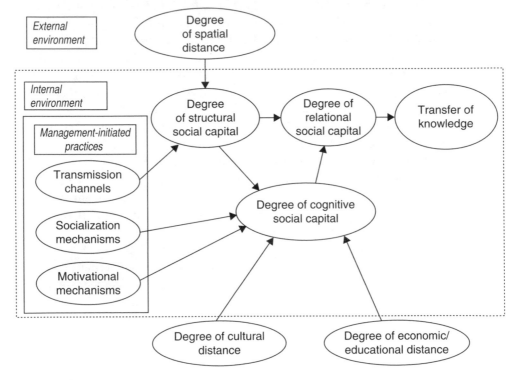

Source: Gooderham (2007).

Figure 7.3 A dynamic capabilities-driven conceptual model of the determinants of knowledge transfer in MNCs

for example the transfer of 'know-how' and the degree of relational social capital and between the degree of cognitive social capital and the degree of relational social capital.

The model proposes that successful leveraging of 'know-how' through its transfer across MNCs is directly dependent on the development of the relational dimension of social capital characterized not least by trust between units. The model further proposes that this relational dimension of social capital is in part a product of the degree of structural social capital and cognitive social capital that have been developed. This is largely congruent with the work of Nahapiet and Ghoshal (1998) and Tsai and Ghoshal (1998). However, the model also takes into account the impact of the external environment in relation to the formation of structural and cognitive social capital.

Finally, our model also specifies a number of practices that can be developed and applied by managers in order to develop the dynamic capabilities required for the augmentation of the structural and cognitive dimensions of social capital. Thus, whereas the degree of parent–subsidiary cultural, spatial and economic distance is fixed, the model proposes that the selection and application of transmission channels, socialization mechanisms and appropriate motivational mechanisms are factors that can be influenced by managers. Not only can they determine the degree of social interaction and the development of a common language and set of meanings, they can also indirectly mitigate the impact of cultural, geographic and economic distance. Thus at the core of our model of the leveraging of 'know-how' is a management perspective in the sense that it is the purposeful design, selection and combination of transmission channels, socialization mechanisms and intrinsic motivational mechanisms that are the key to developing the various dimensions of social capital that are key to knowledge transfer.

From a practitioner perspective the model may, in an initial phase, be used as a means to identify and calibrate existing management-initiated practices aimed at creating the foundation for the transfer of 'know-how'. Thereafter it can be used by practitioners to guide them in their future efforts and investments for the achievement of those social capital foundations that extant research indicates are of significance for knowledge transfer within MNCs. This latter use of the model means that it has the added potential to function as a decision-making tool in relation to the acquisition of knowledge-rich subsidiaries by clarifying the initiatives required for knowledge synergies.

7.9   Summary

In this chapter we have classified competencies carried by employees in MNCs and their subsidiaries. The classification was based on three dimensions: task specificity, MNC specificity and subsidiary specificity. On the basis of these three dimensions a typology of employee competencies in MNCs and their subsidiaries was derived that included meta competencies, standard technical competencies, organizational MNC competencies, technical MNC competencies, intra-organizational subsidiary competencies and subsidiary-unique technical competencies.

These human resources constitute opportunities for building unique capabilities that are difficult to imitate and that create competitive advantage. However, in building these capabilities there is always an inherent danger of creating rigidities that may hamper change processes and mobility across subsidiaries in the MNC. This is particularly the case for the development of subsidiary-specific knowledge and skills.

In the second part of the chapter, our focus was on knowledge transfer in MNCs and their subsidiaries. A model that explains key sources of variation in the ability of MNCs to transfer and share knowledge in the face of spatial, cultural, economic and educational distance was developed. The model not only considers the relationship between the three dimensions of social capital but also delineates the dynamic capabilities that condition the development of a social context that promotes knowledge transfer. The development of these dynamic capabilities is dependent on purposeful action and investment, not least on the part of MNC managers. Thus the model is not only a response to the need to understand variations in knowledge transfer but also a response to practitioner needs to augment their understanding of those organizational mechanisms and practices that enhance the efficient intra-MNC transfer of knowledge. The model may be used to analyse the case that follows this chapter, that of Siemens and its efforts at creating a global knowledge-sharing system.

Case F

Five steps to creating a global knowledge-sharing system: Siemens ShareNet

Sven C. Voelpel, Malte Dous and Thomas H. Davenport[1]

F.1 Introduction

Knowledge-sharing systems have been implemented in various global companies during the last few years. However, many of them have failed because they were limited to technical solutions and did not consider the organizational and cross-cultural factors that are necessary to make a knowledge-sharing platform successful. We identified Siemens – a major player in the electronic industry – as a benchmark company in the global transfer of management knowledge. Based on in-depth interviews with executives within Siemens, we describe the five steps with which Siemens successfully established its global knowledge-sharing system 'ShareNet'. The examination of Siemens' strategies for coping with the organizational and cross-cultural challenges that arose in each phase should be instructive to other organizations using or aiming to create a global knowledge-sharing system.

F.2 Siemens ShareNet: five steps to creating a global knowledge-sharing system

Siemens, a Munich-based global electronics giant, is involved in information and communication systems, products and services, semiconductors, passive and electromechanical components, transportation, energy, health care, household appliances, lighting, and other businesses. It has a decentralized corporate structure with every unit having its own executive management, supervisory groups, regional and corporate units and services. Because Siemens was a global, highly diversified organization with an increasing customer demand for complex 'total solutions', knowledge management had already become very important for the company by the mid-1990s (Davenport and Probst, 2000).

In 1998, Joachim Döring, President of Group Strategy at Siemens' largest group Information and Communication Networks (ICN) faced a dramatic change in the telecommunications industry. Especially the deregulation in its core market, Germany, confronted Siemens with growing competition and the challenge to transform from a 'simple' product seller to a complex, customer-oriented organization that provided customized solutions and services globally. Novel competencies were necessary, and this urged Siemens to carry out a comprehensive restructuring. Information and Communication Networks (ICN) was one of the newly named groups which united the carrier and the enterprise branches of Siemens' Telecom Networks. The new group encompassed the Wireline Networks Group, Communications on Air, IP/Data Networks, Transport Networks, Manufacturing and Logistics, and Service and Carrier Networks.

As an incumbent and long-time leader in this industry, the group understood that they had a rich body of experience. ICN needed to tap into and rejuvenate its large number of employees' comprehensive expertise in order to put their combined knowledge to work.

The path Siemens had taken since 1998 resulted in a well-established and beneficial knowledge-sharing system. The following sections describe the procedure and challenges Siemens faced on their way to establishing ShareNet, and discuss their solution's key learning outcomes and limitations.

Step 1: Defining the concept

To foster the sharing of knowledge, Döring and his team decided to establish a knowledge initiative for ICN's Sales and Marketing organization. A knowledge management system had to network the 17,000 sales and marketing employees, which would enable a Sales and Marketing team in a local company to profit from the experience of an ICN team in another part of the globe, if that local team was involved in a similar deal. The knowledge-receiving team could then increase the speed and quality of their bid.

The concept of creating a knowledge management system was nothing extraordinary, although most of the existing systems dealt only with codified or explicit knowledge and thus resembled data repositories. Döring's idea was to create a system that was able to handle not only explicit knowledge, but also help externalize the individuals' tacit knowledge. Such a solution is also referred to as a 'codification' strategy. With a codification strategy, the firm's knowledge is organized into reusable assets that are stored in a formal KMS and knowledge is shared through the reuse of these assets

(Hansen et al., 1999; Grover and Davenport, 2001). A codification strategy is best suited for organizations that reuse the same knowledge repeatedly, and therefore require a scalable knowledge-sharing approach that enables efficient knowledge transfer (Zack, 1999; Dixon, 2000).

Döring gathered ICN's most successful sales persons to map the solution-selling process that covered everything from general business development to the preparation of individual bids as well as the creation of specific solutions. This team had to identify the broad classifications of knowledge as well as the questions relevant to each step in order to establish a structure for organizing the knowledge content. To overcome the stumbling blocks of traditional, repository-based knowledge management systems, the new system had to be designed to integrate components, such as a knowledge library, a forum for urgent requests, and platforms for knowledge sharing, that would enable a higher 'richness' of knowledge transmission channels. The latter had to include community news bulletin boards, discussion groups for certain topics, and live chat rooms. The ensuing product was called ShareNet.

The knowledge library, which would be composed of thousands of knowledge bids, served as the central component of the required initiative. These bids would be constructed to categorize the experience gained from ongoing and completed projects. Project team participants would enter the details of each bid by means of web-based entry forms.

The questionnaire-type design was important; Andreas Manuth, ShareNet manager at ICN, remarked: 'We knew we needed to capture some of the "tacit" knowledge that managers had in their heads – the "real life" tested pros and cons of a solution. We had to ask questions that managers wouldn't necessarily think about after just completing a bid or project document.'

The 'urgent request' platform was to be ShareNet's second most important component. Here it would be possible to enter urgent questions for answer by other users who would regularly scan through this forum to check if they could answer questions such as: 'Does anyone have a list of recent network projects by this competitor?', or 'My customer needs a business case to implement this new router technology by next Thursday. Can anyone help?' In practice this component revealed its value when, for example, for insurance purposes an ICN project manager in South America tried to discover how dangerous it was to lay cables in the Amazon rainforest. He posted an urgent request asking for help from anyone with a similar project in a similar environment. A project manager in Senegal responded within several hours. The ShareNet manager estimated that obtaining the right information before the cables went underground saved Siemens approximately 1 million dollars.

The initial gathering of the ShareNet initiators was followed by ten more meetings until the end of 1998. Döring used this time to gather competent and motivated members for his ShareNet core team, who would start mapping out the detailed plan of how ShareNet's technological and managerial processes ought to operate.

The first ShareNet version was developed with the help of an external web-development company. Subsequently, pilot projects were carried out in Australia, China, Malaysia, and Portugal from April to August 1999 to gain cross-cultural insights from those users who were far from the headquarters in Munich and who would have to rely on the system the most. The ShareNet team therefore wanted to avoid the usual Siemens practice of rolling out initiatives from Munich to the rest of the company across the globe, as this procedure had not always been successful.

In July 1999, Döring gathered 60 managers – from every country in which ICN was represented – in a boot camp to elaborate on their operation procedure. A ShareNet committee of 11 members – mainly users from different regions, but one from ICN's board, and two from ICN's Group Strategy board – took responsibility for ShareNet's further strategic direction.

This opportunity to consider the views of managers and employees from all the countries where ShareNet would be launched was crucial for the success of the conception phase. It ensured that the system would benefit from the integration of a rich source of cross-cultural competencies at an early stage, which would serve as a cornerstone of the subsequent global rollout.

Step 2: Global rollout

In August 1999, when the first version of ShareNet was launched in 39 countries, the core question was how to tackle the global character of ShareNet. The Munich-based headquarters of the ShareNet team could definitely not manage the launch and the later supervision of ShareNet in all 39 countries on its own. Furthermore, it is widely acknowledged that knowledge is context sensitive, which means that the management of cross-cultural flows is the key to the global leveraging of knowledge (Glisby and Holden, 2003). Bresman et al. (1999) assert that creating mutual trust between cross-cultural knowledge-sharing partners is a prerequisite in that respect. A motivating global corporate culture furthermore helps to control the limitations of and frustrations with cross-cultural knowledge transfer (Davenport and Prusak, 1998).

Siemens decided to address the bias of both global integration and local responsiveness by an approach that can be described as 'glocal'. While the headquarters and local branches would jointly define ShareNet's strategic direction, it would be centrally maintained at the Munich headquarters. The joint definition and the central strategic maintenance of the system would then revert to the local companies. ShareNet managers were therefore appointed to the local subsidiaries to help the initiative access the culturally embedded knowledge there.

Andreas Manuth described the 'glocal' way of diffusing ShareNet to ICN's worldwide subsidiaries as follows:

> To jump-start the network, we held two- to three-day workshops in the local countries to get each local company on board, to get them used to the system and interface, and to convince them of its value. We had an exercise we'd run at every workshop. At the beginning of the sessions, we'd ask them: 'You must have some problem that isn't solved – that you left sitting on your desk before you came here. Put that up on the system as an urgent request.' Without fail, by the end of the day, that posting would get at least one reply, and inevitably, the effect was that the person who had posted it would be stunned. And everyone else in the room would see the effect too.

In addition, ShareNet managers were selected to represent their local company and promote the initiative within their regions. These had to be people who were intrinsically motivated by the idea that a knowledge-sharing system would yield benefits. They were assigned to supervise local level usage, but also tackled many of the urgent requests at the start of the initiative. This international group of ShareNet managers was a major cornerstone for leveraging the knowledge-sharing idea globally. They served as the nucleus in their local organizations to convince people who had not known much about the value of sharing their knowledge before.

Bringing together the expertise and cultural assumptions of both headquartered and local ShareNet managers emerged as an appropriate way of handling the rollout cross-culturally. According to Holden, the interaction and shared experience between individuals with specific cultural knowledge gives rise to active (implementational) know-how, fosters participative competence, and stimulates cross-cultural collaborative learning (Holden, 2002).

ShareNet consultants were employed to provide support in each of the countries represented, to organize and manage conferences, and to interface

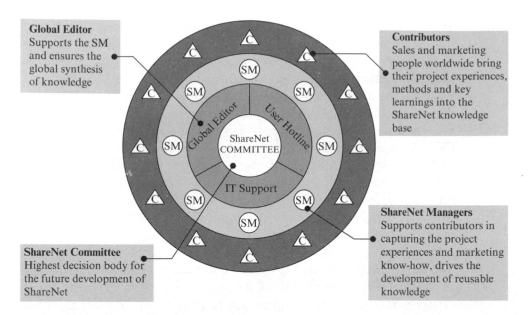

Global Editor
Supports the SM and ensures the global synthesis of knowledge

Contributors
Sales and marketing people worldwide bring their project experiences, methods and key learnings into the ShareNet knowledge base

ShareNet Managers
Supports contributors in capturing the project experiences and marketing know-how, drives the development of reusable knowledge

ShareNet Committee
Highest decision body for the future development of ShareNet

Source: Siemens ICN.

Figure F.1 The ShareNet organization

with the ShareNet managers once a country's system was running. They also monitored the network and its contributions for quality and bid feedback, where suitable. Figure F.1 depicts the 'glocal' ShareNet organization, including global editors, 'local' ShareNet managers, the global ShareNet committee and worldwide contributors. The global editors were ultimately responsible for the quality of the content. They had to ensure the clarity and usefulness of contributions, and review ways in which entered solutions could be understood and reused efficiently.

In the course of time, the endeavors at the start of the project began to pay off. Every local workshop was followed by an increase in urgent request postings from that country and introduced a flow of knowledge bids. As anticipated, the benefits almost immediately became obvious, especially in ICN's more remote regions. Towards the end of 1999 ShareNet had 3,800 registered users. Manuth remembered:

> For example, we had an official hotline for engineers in the field to call in to get technical help for one of our switches. If someone in Vietnam had a problem with the switch, they were supposed to call the hotline. Over and over again, we heard 'No one ever calls me back. We're too small.' But with urgent requests, ShareNet gave them access to other people struggling with switch problems out in the field – people who would call them back or at least drop them an email.

The fact that the users recognized the direct value that they obtained from the system for their business problems also helped to overcome language and cultural problems – even at remote subsidiaries, as long as they had sufficient proficiency in English to participate independently. In Germany, however, the attitude towards the English-only ShareNet was negative at first. Although the English literacy at Siemens Germany was sufficiently high, many employees still did not dare to post a question in a forum where several thousand people could see their grammar or spelling mistakes. Others were of the opinion that in a Germany-based company the first language should still be German. Fortunately there were relatively few users with such an attitude. The ShareNet team furthermore observed that these language problems were mitigated over time when these users too saw the personal benefit of sharing and receiving knowledge.

The lack of proficiency in English and other cultural particularities became more evident in China – one of the fastest growing markets for Siemens. The literature has adequately discussed cultural particularities in China from various perspectives. The cultural aspects concerning knowledge management in China were tackled, for example, by Chow et al. (2000). Based on the culture-related research of Hofstede and Schwartz, their investigation concerns the impact of cultural dimensions, for example Confucian dynamism (long-term orientation) and concern regarding 'face', on knowledge-sharing behavior by comparing China and the USA (see Hofstede, 1980a; Schwartz, 1994).

Regarding these dimensions, Siemens had to face major cross-cultural particularities when implementing the ShareNet idea in the company's most important Asian market. The ShareNet case in China is outlined in the following box.

BOX F.1

Particularities of Siemens ShareNet in China

Since all of Siemens' worldwide business divisions are active in China, the organization has more than 50 companies and 27 regional offices in the country, with a workforce totaling 25,000 people. ShareNet had already been introduced to Siemens' ICN division's Chinese subsidiaries during the system's pilot stage in 1999. In the fiscal year 2000–2001, with 16.7 knowledge objects per contributor, China ranked 10th of the 58 countries participating in the ShareNet system (Voelpel and Han, 2005).

Chow et al.'s results suggest that in comparison with US nationals, Chinese nationals have a relatively high willingness to share

➡

knowledge, even knowledge that involves a conflict between self-interest and the collective interest. The Siemens case study affirms this finding. The Siemens ShareNet statistics of the fiscal year 2000–2001 shows that the average number of posted knowledge objects per contributor in China (16.67 per contributor) is much higher than in the US (3.29 per contributor). Table F.1 illustrates this argument when comparing it to Hofstede's indices of Individualism and Long-Term Orientation.

Table F.1 Siemens' knowledge-sharing behavior vs. Hofstede's cultural index

	Average number of posted knowledge objects per contributor	Hofstede's Long-Term Orientation Index
China	16.67	114
USA	3.29	29

Confucian dynamism, which largely shapes the Chinese culture, emphasizes long-term consequences and objectives. Among the appreciated values of Confucian dynamism, 'personal steadiness' and 'respect for tradition' support knowledge-sharing behavior best. The interviewees' responses support this argument, since 'gaining peer respect' and 'building on reputation' are frequently mentioned motivators for making a contribution to ShareNet.

Another reason for the comparably high contribution rate of Chinese employees can be found in the attractiveness of the rewards for knowledge sharing. As we will discuss later in this chapter, Siemens employed a premium-based reward scheme. Our findings suggest that these rewards were more desirable to the Chinese than the Americans, and were therefore partly responsible for the comparatively high per capita contribution rate.

Furthermore, the high number of individual contributions is due to the fact that in China, contributions are often aggregated to single contributors. Our research reveals that the current Chinese ShareNet contributors are mainly middle and upper management levels who usually have adequate English language skills, while the lower management level's participation is very limited. With respect to cultural barriers to successful knowledge-sharing, this indicates that the 'concern for face' negatively influences Chinese employees' knowledge-sharing behavior. 'Face' is defined as what other people think of you (Ho, 1976). The Chinese culture strongly emphasizes 'face saving', thus employees who are highly sensitive in respect of 'face saving' and feel insecure with their ability to write English, are reluctant to make contributions. They are afraid that grammar and spelling mistakes might harm their 'face' in the company.

Siemens, however, did not immediately grasp this phenomenon. Only in 2001 were efforts were made to foster the proliferation of ShareNet among lower management levels. Measures included additional workshops for local ShareNet managers as well as a Chinese version of the user handbook. Contributions in the Chinese language were allowed, but contributors were asked to classify their contributions' key terms into predefined English categories in order to facilitate the capturing of Chinese knowledge and make it available to the global knowledge-sharing community.

The ICN headquarters fully funded the specific efforts in China – as it did the whole ShareNet initiative. Because ICN's product divisions and local companies offered the service gratis, users could simply log on and start utilizing the system. Manuth noticed the immense benefits of this approach: 'Nobody has to obtain a signature to spend money to use ShareNet. For example, in Brunei there is just one technical sales person. Via ShareNet, he is connected to all the other ICN technical sales people, which would not be possible if we billed him for system use.'

Step 3: Bringing momentum into the system

Getting Siemens people to collaborate, and thus to continually contribute to and rely on ShareNet for solutions, was a significant challenge. The ShareNet management team never stopped injecting energy and resources into getting people to use the system. They soon realized that Siemens needed to substantially change its organizational and individual knowledge-sharing culture. Siemens' corporate structure could not be used as a cornerstone, as the single business units were separate instead of networked, and the leading governance paradigm relied mainly on hierarchy instead of cross-unit collaboration.

Gerhard Hirschler, Director of the Center of Competence Europe and Middle East at ICN Carrier Sales, who was one of ShareNet's first chosen managers, recalled that:

> there were always excuses. People said, 'I don't have the time to spend on this.' Others were reluctant to share. The network consultants, for example, said, 'Sure, we have knowledge, but it's for sale, it's not for free.' Still others said 'Everyone has a certain clarity regarding their own projects in their heads, but it won't translate well for others.'

The ShareNet team was also concerned about managing people's expectations – employees might be disappointed with their first interactions and not use ShareNet. This also implied the need to change people's opinion in respect of the negative perception of 'reuse' by actively encouraging them to use – or copy – the knowledge that was offered by ShareNet.

De Long and Fahey (2000) also observed such phenomena in their research on 50 companies pursuing knowledge management projects. They assert that a corporation's knowledge culture in terms of interactivity, collaboration, and attitude towards reusing existing knowledge, dictates what knowledge belongs to the organization and what knowledge remains in the individual's control. Companies should therefore examine whether their organizational culture enhances or hinders knowledge-sharing behavior, and thereafter derive appropriate measures to foster trust, sharing and teaching, as well as collaboration among their employees.

Siemens' ShareNet team decided to introduce incentives that would motivate employees to use the virtual knowledge network. The first system was called 'Bonus-On-Top'. It provided incentives for local country managers, and rewarded a country's overall participation in knowledge sharing. If a country's sales team managed to secure a certain amount of business with the help of international knowledge sharing, they received a bonus. The bonus was applicable to both the country that had contributed the knowledge and the country that used it.

With this kind of incentive, Siemens made a significant investment in ShareNet. Nevertheless, although a considerable number of country managers did receive the bonus, there was no guarantee that ShareNet would ultimately benefit from this reward system. ShareNet managers recognized that receiving direct recognition of how much an employee's daily job is appreciated, motivates him far more than receiving some reward (Gibbert et al., 2000). Consequently, the managers decided to focus more on the users themselves. This was realized by means of a web-based incentive system in early 2000. Users received ShareNet 'shares', which were, in fact, bonus points as in an airline mileage system, for a valuable contribution. Contributors gained shares for entering knowledge bids into the library, for reusing knowledge, for responding to urgent requests and for appraising one another's contributions. Users earned, for example, ten shares for technology, market or customer bids. For a project, technical solution or service, or a functional solution component as well as for contributing a success story, 20 shares were allocated. For answering an urgent request they gained three shares. Later an award system was introduced in which shares could be redeemed for various gifts and prizes, such as textbooks, Siemens mobile phones, or even trips to knowledge exchange partners.

The conversion of shares into premiums was gradually adapted to each region's local income levels. However, the ShareNet team made a critical observation with regard to material rewards in economically emerging countries such as China and India. In India, for example, ShareNet users were enthusiastic about the system and the underlying reward scheme. The desire to receive an award, such as a mobile phone, was high, as the employees did not only use their awards to benefit themselves, but also actively traded in them. This skewed motivation for participating in ShareNet led to people tending to share their knowledge without reference to business needs and to neglecting their actual jobs. Knowing that contributions would decrease if the reward system were to be terminated, the ShareNet team decided to change the premiums in India towards less expensive and tradable goods such as books and accessories.

In 2000, more than 396,000 shares were awarded. The scheme had therefore significantly accelerated the growth of the number of contributions. However, quality problems started to occur that drove the ShareNet team to establish a rating measure. Subsequently, the users themselves had to evaluate contributions with the number of stars allocated reflecting the contributions' usefulness. The rating of contributions was also rewarded with shares to encourage users to evaluate the bids they had utilized. Moreover, whenever a user wanted to redeem his shares, global editors evaluated his contributions and ratings before authorizing an appropriate award.

During July 2001, 2,328 contributions were posted in contrast with the slightly more than 600 the previous October. Likewise, 76,075 shares were gained in this month compared to the 19,330 the previous October. Despite accumulating large numbers of shares, however, few users than ever converted them into prizes. ShareNet managers speculated that the knowledge had become its own reward, and users did not want to relinquish the status of a high share total by redeeming it. Ardichvili et al. (2003) made a similar observation in their study on motivation in knowledge-sharing communities of practice. They too confirmed the insight that employees feel the need to establish themselves as experts, for example, by gaining formal expert status by contributing to the community, or by gaining informal recognition through multiple postings and contributions to the community.

Step 4: Expanding group-wide

By 2001, ShareNet's success had extended beyond the marketing and sales department at ICN. Like Joachim Döring a few years before, the head of the Wireline Network Development Group at Siemens ICN, Jürgen Klunker, saw ShareNet's potential and promoted the idea of using the system in his research and development (R&D) division as well.

Siemens ICN's Wireline Network product development was run by 3,000 employees at Siemens' headquarters in Munich. The unit concentrated on developing core platforms for telephony and data network switching systems. At Regional Development Centers (RDC) these platforms were adapted to local market needs for each of 300 customers in more than 100 countries. Situated in countries such as Belgium, Brazil, Greece, Hungary, India, Portugal, Russia, Slovenia, South Africa, and Thailand, these RDCs employed approximately 460 employees, mostly regional engineers.

Jürgen Klunker decided to adapt ShareNet's Sales and Marketing version for the R&D organization. The structure of the knowledge library architecture remained almost unchanged, although it had to be adapted to reflect a knowledge base appropriate for R&D, which mainly concerned the relevant criteria and parameters when contributing a knowledge object. This adaptation recognized the fact that R&D knowledge is more specific and complex than in other organizational units, which is one reason for its 'stickiness' and problematic transfer ability (Reed and DeFillippi, 1990).

In February 2002, the inaugural version of R&D ShareNet was launched. The major challenge was to encourage people to contribute without an initial marketing campaign, as the R&D ShareNet team wanted to proceed carefully. But by May 2002 only 50 knowledge bids had been posted and again a strong endeavor was necessary to foster contributions. The reasons for this meager participation might have been the lack of marketing effort, but more probably this was due to the ShareNet team being confronted with a different context in the R&D department. This issue is also known in theory, with the literature explaining that protectiveness and 'shielding mechanisms' by the source of knowledge can hinder the knowledge flow between different R&D units (Simonin, 1999).

Siemens had to cope with an organizational culture at ICN R&D that was less supportive of knowledge sharing than at the Sales and Marketing department. It was more or less a lack of 'care' within the R&D organization – 'care', according to von Krogh, consists of values like trust, empathy, help, lenient judgment, and courage that are responsible for the evolvement of a knowledge-friendly organizational culture (Von Krogh, 1998; Kostova, 1999).

For the ICN R&D group, such cultural barriers within the organization were harder to overcome than geographical or language barriers. The most important object to achieve was to get the knowledge that was concentrated in the headquarters in Munich to those engineers who needed that knowledge. The people in the labs – in Klunker's group, for example – already had their own informal information networks established and already belonged to communities of experts. The ShareNet team had to communicate knowledge-oriented cultural values, such as openness and trust as well as the personal benefit of knowledge sharing, to the engineers at ICN R&D. Klunker affirmed:

> The developers are the owners of the knowledge, and, for the most part, they are not aware that others might need some part of this knowledge. We had to convince them that even though writing an answer to a question doesn't seem to yield any immediate return, it's worth participating and being part of the community. This is not an advantage that counts in the next quarter of an hour, but it will definitely pay off after a certain length of time.

Interesting, however, is that the engineers located outside the Munich headquarters recognized the system's strengths far better. They depended on knowledge from outside and therefore realized the value of the system faster than the engineers in Munich. In the end, this observation again contributed to the insight that there is hardly any better incentive to bring knowledge transfer into action than its value for the knowledge receiver.

Step 5: Consolidating and sustaining performance

By July 2002, ShareNet was utilized by more than 19,000 registered users in more than 80 countries. They were supported by 53 ShareNet managers from different nations all over the world. More than 20,000 knowledge bids populated the system, half of which had been published within the previous year. Over 2.5 million ShareNet shares had been distributed with almost 300 users within reach of an award.

But, with the economic downturn, especially in the telecommunications industry, the corporate mood took a turn for the worse. Siemens too was not spared. At the end of 2001 reorganization and staff reductions affected every division, especially in the Information and Communication group. During January 2002 a restructuring was carried out within ICN, as a result of which ShareNet was positioned within the newly established Competence and Knowledge Management department. The ShareNet team was trimmed to include only Manuth, three ShareNet consultants, the global editor, and a few full-time IT experts.

ShareNet's users had also adapted their contribution behavior during the crisis. The number of new entries in the knowledge library decreased dramatically and the discussion forums too were less frequented. Surprisingly, the urgent requests maintained their previous level. Contrary to contributing to the knowledge library, which costs time and does not yield the contributor an immediate profit, the urgent requests help problem-solving

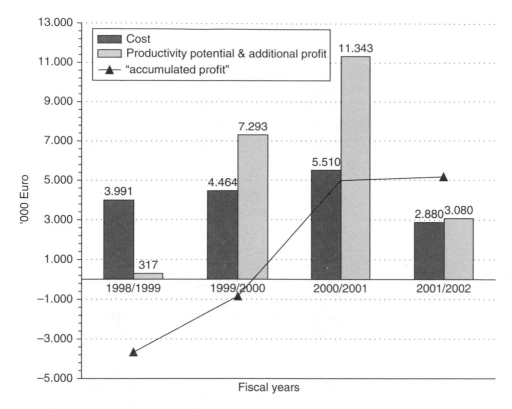

Source: Siemens ICN.

Figure F.2 The ShareNet business case

directly and could contribute to a decisive business transaction during tough times.

Discussions on the performance and value of ShareNet led the ShareNet team to try to demonstrate the system's worth. Consequently, Döring began to document the impact that ShareNet had had on ICN's businesses since its implementation. The ShareNet consultants appealed to local country managers to provide details of projects in which ShareNet had had an important influence on the performance of a contract during the financial year 2000–2001. They further asked managers to provide documentation of every case in which Siemens had truly obtained earnings from customers. After a comprehensive investigation and a compilation of the savings and business opportunities associated with the use of ShareNet, the Business Case (see Figure F.2) revealed that the accumulated profit the knowledge-sharing system had generated for ICN accrued to approximately €5,000,000 since its implementation in 1998.

On the profit side of the calculation, contracts that, for example, had been gained with the support of other divisions, or savings like the previously mentioned cable project in South America were included. A contribution key, determined by a questionnaire-like form that the ShareNet Managers had to fill out, determined the proportion that ShareNet had contributed to the success of each initiative. Thereafter the central ShareNet team in Munich cross-checked the benefit ratio. Since spillover effects, like the size of the knowledge library as an organizational learning resource, or the increase in the employees' potential willingness to share their knowledge, had not been included, the aggregate value of €5,000,000 does not seem too impressive. On the other hand, Siemens executives avoided the drawing of too rosy a picture that would be hard to justify if questions arose.

On the cost side, the man-days of the Munich ShareNet team and the locations worldwide were calculated on the basis of internal charge rates. Additional costs, like traveling expenses and the efforts of the ShareNet Shares incentive program, were also added. However, hard-to-define indirect items, like opportunity costs, or an employee's time spent on searching the knowledge base, or answering an urgent request, were not included in the business case.

These omissions make the absolute validity of the business case nearly impossible to prove. This constellation is also mentioned in management literature. The fundamental premise is that a knowledge-sharing system that is actively used by its employees can improve performance and may produce a long-term sustainable competitive advantage for the organization (Spender and Grant, 1996). At present, however, this premise is only based on theoretical considerations and anecdotal evidence (Alavi and Leidner, 2001). At Siemens the lack of accuracy was traded off against the opportunity to show that an overall, cross-checked balance sheet of the ShareNet initiative was positive up to that point. The use of the performance measurement was rather to identify cost and benefit drivers and to communicate the outcome group-wide for further optimization and expansion of the initiative.

F.3 Learning outcomes from Siemens and implications for global practice

In the ShareNet case study we described how Siemens managed to establish a global knowledge management system. In ex-post contemplation, Siemens' procedure can be structured into five steps that the company had to master towards the sustainable establishment of the knowledge initiative.

Note: 'Size' stands for the ShareNet participation level in terms of knowledge bids, urgent requests and discussion forum entries.

Figure F.3 The five steps of creating a global knowledge-sharing system

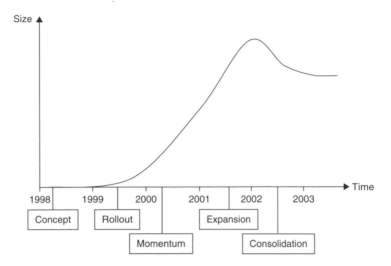

The first three phases focused on the systematic methods of implementing a knowledge-sharing system. Although these steps seem rather generic and well known from standard project management, there are, in fact, some crucial aspects to consider when implementing a knowledge-sharing system globally. Global knowledge sharing was furthermore sufficiently counter-cultural within Siemens ICN to require considerable and ongoing efforts to bring about organizational change.

The crucial task for Siemens, however, has been to manage the crisis resulting from the economic downturn. Although ShareNet shrank to an operational minimum at the time of general budget cutbacks, the system has shown that even with minimum costs, it is able to create value for the company and gain its users' acceptance. The path that led to ShareNet's sustainability can be depicted as a slope as in Figure F.3.

Siemens now faces the challenge of maintaining the steady level that it achieved after consolidation. At this stage gaining further experience and capturing lessons learned will serve as a preparation for ShareNet's second growth wave once the crisis has been overcome and customer projects increase again.

The ShareNet path was framed by key insights that occurred in each of the five steps of implementation. The following insights could serve as a guideline for other companies that intend to establish a knowledge-sharing system in a global environment, see Table F.2.

Table F.2 Learning outcomes from the Siemens ShareNet implementation

Steps of creation	Learning outcomes
1. Conceptual phase	• Knowledge-sharing systems need 'rich' interactive elements to help people externalize tacit knowledge. The 'urgent request' platform served Siemens as a cornerstone in this respect. • Departments such as marketing or business development make the knowledge-sharing results visible immediately, e.g., through a gained customer, or avoided mistakes in a market entry. These 'quick wins' are needed to communicate the system within the organization. • Global acceptance of the system requires a global procedure for its development. At Siemens it was important that a joint approach resulted from integrating different views from both the headquarters and the subsidiaries. • Knowledge management initiatives need a creative leader and driver for change. Joachim Döring and his team's dedication was crucial and served as the project's nucleus.
2. Global rollout	• A 'glocal' approach with a central strategic supervision and decentralized local ShareNet managers pools the knowledge resources globally while considering cross-cultural particularities. The local managers' personal role serves as social 'glue', thus helping to access context-specific knowledge. • Even though a knowledge-sharing system's right to exist should be based on whether it can provide its users with the help needed, marketing and communication initiatives do have to be undertaken in the rollout phase in order to achieve a critical mass of users. • In order to leverage the full potential of knowledge sharing in China, mechanisms to overcome particularities, like the lower hierarchies' fear of losing 'face' due to insufficient English language skills, have to be installed. A practicable solution would be the permission to allow contributions in Chinese, combined with the indexation of English key words.
3. Bringing momentum into the system	• Incentive systems can fully develop their motivational potential if they reward knowledge contributors individually, premiums are adapted to the local cultural context, and if a quality control mechanism is applied. • Transparency regarding the number and quality of contributions reveals the contributors' 'expert status' and therefore fosters peer motivation.
4. Expanding group-wide	• Cultural context matters, also in an organizational respect: knowledge tends to be more 'sticky', for example, in R&D than in other units, and 'shielding mechanisms' have to be overcome through more concentrated personal effort.

Table F.2 (continued)

Steps of creation	Learning outcomes
5. Consolidating and sustaining performance	• In business functions like R&D, knowledge-sharing systems have limited potential to support the transfer of context-bound knowledge. Instead, more interactive, media rich, or even face-to-face methods have to be employed to build the trust and 'care' necessary to enable successful knowledge sharing in such domains. • The establishment of a broad basis and user acceptance within the organization during favorable times helps knowledge-sharing initiatives to survive difficult environments. • The ability to demonstrate the benefits of a knowledge-sharing initiative through references as well as through an illustrative business case facilitates top management support and the budget necessary for further operations.

The limitation for generalization of these observations lies, of course, in the environmental conditions with which a knowledge-sharing initiative is confronted. It seems obvious that the launch of an entirely new project would have been difficult to accomplish during economically bad times such as in 2001/2002. In fact, the knowledge management 'Zeitgeist' at the end of the 1990s provided ShareNet with favorable times during which it was comparatively easy to dedicate resources to bring momentum into the system (see Davenport et al., 2003 for a description of 'Zeitgeist'). The insight is that profiting from such an enabling context and anchoring the system within the organization are necessary actions to survive when contrary winds are encountered. Without references and success cases that demonstrate the value of a knowledge-sharing initiative, times are dire indeed, but if substance can be achieved, the chances increase that those responsible for budgets will be willing to maintain the initiative until times turn more favorable.

F.4 Limitations and future challenges

While some authors have argued that an IT-based knowledge sharing strategy cannot improve performance (see for example McDermott, 1999), others argue that the just in time delivery of context-specific knowledge can significantly improve performance (see for example Davenport and Glasser, 2002). The Siemens case supports the second view as it reveals that a thoughtful implementation of a knowledge-sharing system enhances the transfer of knowledge within a global organization and can therefore create value. However, a system like ShareNet also has certain limitations that are hard to overcome. On the financial side, maintaining a knowledge-sharing system will remain a significant cost, as the supervision can only be automated to a certain degree. This means that personnel resources have to be dedicated. At Siemens, ShareNet's global editors still have to do content management manually. Some automated solutions have already been implemented, but the current state of technology still makes maintaining consistent terminology and overall quality within a global knowledge-sharing system an extensive task.

The ShareNet case also revealed that the sharing of tacit knowledge through a virtual medium has limitations. Alavi and Leidner (2001: 122) assert that:

> the institutionalization of best practices by embedding them into IT might facilitate efficient handling of routine, predictable situations during stable and incrementally changing environments. When change is radical or discontinuous, however, there is persistent need for continual renewal of the basic premises underlying the practices achieved in the knowledge repositories.

When transferring specific, contextual (that is 'sticky') knowledge for product or business model innovation, rich mechanisms, like face-to-face contact, are required (Subramaniam and Venkatraman, 2001).

The personal interaction that might be necessary for the knowledge receiver to understand the knowledge source's context can only be promoted by a system, but not guaranteed. Tacit knowledge, however, is one of the most important drivers of innovation, as is demonstrated within this article and in all the concepts referred to. Various approaches to tackling the problem of enhancing innovation through global knowledge transfer and creation have been introduced in the management literature, some of which can already be found in practice (Von Krogh et al. 2000; Kirkman et al., 2002).

Hansen (2002) points out that the limitation of virtual knowledge platforms is that they only enable 'weak ties' within the organization, since their lack of media richness does not provide an enabling context for creating 'strong ties'. Hansen's findings suggest that weak inter-unit ties help a project team search for useful knowledge in other subunits, but impede the transfer of complex knowledge, which tends to require a strong tie between two parties. He therefore proposes the introduction of personal 'knowledge networks' to provide a rich mechanism for strong ties and, thus, for the transfer of complex, context-specific knowledge. Such personal networks may also contribute to a shared cultural context and therefore to a higher cross-cultural empathy among the members of global organizations.

More intense sharing of tacit knowledge to foster collaboration and innovation is what Siemens is aiming at as well. Based on the success of ShareNet, Siemens is currently establishing PeopleShareNet, a system that serves as a virtual expert marketplace for facilitating the creation of cross-cultural teams composed of members with specific knowledge and competencies. Such teams or knowledge networks can become the global cornerstones for the leveraging of knowledge in future. In this respect, both systems should help to realize what Heinrich von Pierer, President and CEO of Siemens AG, desired: to truly release this 'treasure trove of experience . . . one of our key competitive advantages' (Davenport and Probst, 2000: foreword).

DISCUSSION QUESTIONS

When responding to these questions it will be helpful to do so with reference to Figure 7.3.

1　Describe the five steps with which Siemens successfully established its global knowledge-sharing system 'ShareNet'.
2　Discuss Siemens' strategies for coping with the organizational and cross-cultural challenges that arose in each phase.
3　One conclusion in the case (see Table F.2) is that in regard to 'business functions like R&D, knowledge-sharing systems have limited potential to support the transfer of context-bound knowledge. Instead, more interactive, media rich, or even face-to-face methods have to be employed to build the trust and 'care' necessary to enable successful knowledge sharing in such domains.' Discuss whether the costs of interaction will outweigh the benefits.
4　What incentives are required to motivate employees to share knowledge?

NOTE

1　This is an abridged version of the case that was previously published in the *Academy of Management Executive* (see Voelpel et al., 2005).

Appendix: Research approach for case

This case and its conclusions regarding the Siemens ShareNet case are derived from a two-stage research approach. As a first stage, the foundation of this article was laid by a seven-year research study involving 116 in-depth expert interviews with leading authorities in knowledge-intensive industries, such as high tech and consulting industries. Our research focused on knowledge-sharing systems that enhance the effectiveness of knowledge's global transfer and encompassed large and small companies headquartered in North America (including Accenture, Boston Consulting Group, Cap Gemini Ernst & Young, DHL, McKinsey), Europe (Bayer, DaimlerChrysler, Infineon, Novartis, Roche, Siemens) and Asia (Motorola, NTT DoCoMo, Sony).

From the understanding and the findings of the first stage, we identified Siemens ShareNet as a best practice knowledge management system (see Davenport and Voelpel, 2001; Ewing, 2001). In the second stage, we particularly focused on Siemens ShareNet with a longitudinal case research approach (Eisenhardt, 1989; Yin, 1994; Stake, 1995). This stage explored the implementation process and global establishment of ShareNet in detail, which suggested the need for a longitudinal approach that would provide extensive access to the individuals involved in the knowledge initiative. Between 2001 and 2004 we conducted 35 semi-structured interviews on global knowledge management with executives, general managers, and line managers within different units at the Siemens headquarters in Munich as well as in China. We also used participant and direct observation as a primary data source (see Whyte, 1991). Secondary data such as internal documents, project manuals, presentations, annual reports, and internal company presentations were used to support our research foundation. This type of triangulation minimizes the personal perspective bias and enhances the information's validity (see Yin, 1981, 1994).

Finally, concerns for external validity (particularly statistical generalizability) were traded off against the opportunity to gain in-depth insights, but precedent cross-case analysis was used to at least ensure analytical generalizability due to the wide range of companies and industries studied.

8

Expatriation and repatriation

8.1 Introduction

The objective of this chapter is to introduce the concepts of expatriation and repatriation and discuss key challenges related to the internal transfer of resources and capabilities. Factors influencing the individual and organizational outcomes will also be discussed with a particular emphasis on selection and retention processes.

8.2 What is expatriation and why invest in it?

Expatriation is a term used when MNCs assign human resources to foreign locations for a set period of time, typically lasting two to five years (Harzing, 2001). The expatriates become embedded in the daily business of their assigned foreign location, which sets this cross-border interaction apart from shorter term business travel and project work. With the increased focus on globalization of business, firms' investments in expatriates have become more common (Bolino, 2007).

MNCs utilize expatriation for a variety of reasons and the lengths of assignments vary according to the purpose and internal needs. The reasons for expatriation are typically grouped into three main categories: (1) filling a position when local talent is lacking, (2) developing the organization, and (3) developing future leaders (Edstrom and Galbraith, 1977; Shay and Baack, 2004; Brock et al., 2008). Filling a position for immediate business needs requires individuals with specified competencies and skills that can transfer these to the local business context. Expatriates with such roles and responsibilities are usually expected to invest significant time in supporting and training the local organization by contributing with their specific knowledge (for example technical or process knowledge). Expatriates are also used for organizational development purposes to improve internal coordination by facilitating the transfer of organizational systems, processes and technologies across the geographically dispersed organization. Expatriates can further-more enhance direct control through behavior and outcome monitoring as well as indirect control by fostering shared values and culture. Many MNCs also use expatriation as a tool to develop future managers by exposing them to cross-cultural situations and thus develop a stronger understanding of global business needs and the complexities of cross-border organizations.

Just as the reasons for investing in expatriates differ, the ideal candidates and expected long-term effects also vary. For instance, filling a position nar-rowly targets the requirement for specific competencies and skills. While this reason is critical to meet immediate business demands, learning opportuni-ties for the expatriate and the long-term strategic importance may be lower than when expatriation is motivated by organizational or leadership develop-ment. When the expatriation is motivated by organizational learning, techni-cal skills must to a greater extent be balanced by social skills to enable the development of long-term organizational benefits such as shared values and internal networks. Similarly, expatriation motivated by leadership develop-ment requires that the identified individuals possess the necessary business, cognitive and social skills necessary to learn from the organization.

Since estimates of the cost of an expatriate range somewhere between 2–10 times higher than if the position was filled locally (Black and Gregersen, 1999; Carraher et al., 2008), there is an assumption that the investment, particularly in organizational and leadership development, will result in some form of value creation for the MNC. However, research on the actual value creation is still inconclusive. Studies suggest that CEOs with experience from interna-tional assignments tend to be more effective and perform better than those who were not expatriated (Bolino, 2007; Shay and Baack, 2004; Tan and Mahoney, 2007). There is no clear empirical support, however, for the rela-tionship between number of expatriate managers and degree of knowledge transfer from subsidiaries to other corporate units (Björkman et al., 2004).

Mobility can also add value for recruitment and retention of employees. Mobility is not limited to the assignment of headquarter personnel to foreign subsidiaries, but also includes assignments from foreign subsidiaries to the home country as well as between foreign units. Some distinguish between expatriation and inpatriation where expatriation entails sending people from headquarters to foreign subsidiaries and inpatriation entails sending people from the foreign subsidiaries to headquarters (Harzing, 2001). Although inpatriation can also be driven by similar motives, it will likely exhibit few control motives. In this chapter, the term expatriation will be used for both forms of foreign assignments.

8.3   The importance of repatriation

Repatriation occurs when employees return from their foreign assignments and reintegrate into the organization in their home country. This process is extremely important for MNCs to ensure that the organization taps into, and makes use of, the valuable experience and expertise gained during the expatriation period. The repatriates become important vehicles for knowledge transfer and organizational learning (Lazarova and Cerdin, 2007).

Despite its importance, however, many employees are disappointed when repatriated. This dissatisfaction is rooted almost entirely in the repatriation process (Jassawalla and Sashittal, 2009; Reiche et al., 2009). The expectations of repatriates are often unfulfilled and there is no clear link identified between an expatriate assignment and subsequent career success (Bolino, 2007). Some repatriates have even claimed that they would have been better off career-wise without the expatriate experience, as the positions are often not left open during their absence and some experience a loss of their internal connectivity.

Organizations that have invested in expatriates are also often dissatisfied (Bolino, 2007). The dissatisfaction from both the individual and organization can be seen in the dismal statistics suggesting that as many as 20–50 per cent of repatriates leave the firm within a year of their return (Jassawalla and Sashittal, 2009). In their earlier groundbreaking study of 750 MNCs from the EU, Japan, and the USA, Black and Gregersen (1999) found that the average turnover within three months after repatriation was 25 per cent. As many as 75 per cent of repatriates felt that their permanent position when returning home was a demotion from their position abroad, and 61 per cent felt they lacked opportunities to put their experiences to work.

Successful repatriation requires planning and preparation prior to the actual return of the individuals, and retaining people becomes one of the greatest HRM challenges. When repatriates leave the MNE, the organization not only loses valuable knowledge and skills, but also potentially loses it to a competitor. Disappointed repatriates may also deter other employees from wanting to take on international assignments.

8.4   How managerial mindsets impact staffing policies

The MNC characteristics and approach to staffing is often rooted in the managerial perceptions and mindsets. We commonly refer to three distinct mindsets to help us understand strategic decisions in MNCs and their approaches to staffing policies: ethnocentric, polycentric and geocentric (Perlmutter, 1969; Reiche et al., 2009). Although these mindsets are distinct they may to some extent coexist within the same MNC, especially if the success of a geographically spread organization requires internal differentiation in the approach to managing and staffing foreign operations.

Ethnocentric mindsets

Ethnocentric mindsets reflect a management approach that is deeply rooted in the home-country culture and 'ways of doing things'. Top management seeks to project competencies and capabilities (including processes and procedures) from headquarters to the rest of the organization, reflecting a unidirectional flow of resources and information (Johnson et al., 2006). Staffing policies in ethnocentric MNCs are characterized by extensive use of expatriates to manage foreign subsidiaries and transfer knowledge throughout the organization. Local employees in foreign subsidiaries are typically viewed as the recipients of knowledge and often find it difficult to excel into higher management positions as these are entrusted expatriates from headquarters.

The benefits of ethnocentric mindsets include a greater degree of control in geographically dispersed organizations by staffing key management positions with expatriates and directly influencing 'ways of doing things' in the foreign subsidiaries. This can also enable the development of a shared organizational culture that largely reflects the home-country organizational culture. The benefits are greatest when host markets lack qualified managers or employees to fill positions or when competencies and capabilities have tacit characteristics that are otherwise difficult to codify and transfer.

Ethnocentric mindsets can trigger resistance in the foreign subsidiaries. Local employees may feel disgruntled by perceived limitations to their career development if top management positions are continuously filled by expatriates rather than locals and perceptions of imposed norms and values. This may result in lower productivity and high turnover, and at worst lead to self-fulfilling prophecies that reinforce headquarters' perceptions that key positions can only be trusted to individuals with close ties and proven loyalty to the parent organization. Furthermore, inherent limitations to headquarters' ability to identify and understand local needs may result in lost business opportunities and management decisions that are not well adapted to the local business context. A lack of recognition of competencies and capabilities outside headquarters can also influence repatriation by creating barriers to receptivity (Oddou et al., 2009).

Polycentric mindsets

Polycentric mindsets, in contrast, value local adaptation and seek to develop the foreign operations to 'think locally'. These MNCs value localized 'ways of doing things' and management positions in foreign subsidiaries are preferably filled by locals. The polycentric mindset is compatible with multi-domestic strategies where foreign operations experience greater levels of autonomy. Communication across organizational boundaries is lower, often limited to financial and accounting reports from the subsidiaries to headquarters, rather than transfers of competencies and capabilities. Staffing policies in polycentric MNEs are characterized by more restrictive use of expatriates since cross-border organizational and leadership development is less emphasized.

Many of the advantages of polycentric mindsets address the identified disadvantages of ethnocentric mindsets. Local employees see better opportunities for local career advancement, which also positively influences the attractiveness when recruiting new talent. The local organization can more easily develop important local networks and communicate better both internally and externally as managers are fully embedded in the local culture. It hinders the danger of 'cultural imperialism' that may clash with local traditions. The local management is also better able to identify and respond to local business challenges and opportunities. Additional benefits include less resistance locally (both politically and socially) when the organization is perceived as 'local', and avoiding the high costs of large numbers of expatriates.

The main disadvantages of polycentric mindsets include the difficulties of achieving synergies and efficiencies in geographically dispersed organizations' globalization of markets. The increased globalization of markets has pushed many MNCs to become more cost-efficient by tapping into location advantages such as low-cost labor and build scale economies through geographically dispersed but closely integrated value chain activities. Localizing activities with minimal control and coordination hinders such competitive advantages and the MNC may suffer from inefficiencies in the organization. Limiting the use of expatriates can make the foreign subsidiaries more detached from headquarters, resulting in managers and employees that lack an understanding of 'global business' and overlook opportunities for cross-border value creation. In addition, opportunities for local employees to gain international experience through foreign assignments or work with headquarters, qualities that often make MNCs attractive, may be limited.

Geocentric mindsets

Contrary to ethnocentric and polycentric mindsets which emphasize the importance of a specific geographical location, geocentric mindsets seek to build on best practices from all parts of the organization. Geocentric mindsets thus reflect multidirectional transfers of resources and capabilities (Reiche et al., 2009). Staffing policies using this approach are characterized by selecting the best candidates for the positions, regardless of organizational or geographical origin. As such, subsidiary managers may be staffed by expatriates from anywhere in the organization, based on the alignment of organizational needs and individual qualifications.

Key advantages of geocentric mindsets include the ability to tap into a larger pool of resources for expatriation and thereby make better use of the organization's human resources. It can also facilitate the development of internal networks, transfer of core competencies and build a unified organizational culture that is not perceived imposed by headquarters. This should ideally reduce the resistance to perceptions of 'cultural imperialism' while also recognize needs for local adaptation. Geocentric mindsets can thus facilitate the development of a greater pool of future leaders with a sound understanding of global business needs, as the selection criteria and international appointments are not rooted in geographical considerations. Individuals may also more easily transfer from assignment to assignment across organizational units, extending their expatriate careers while ensuring cross-border value creation in the MNC.

One could question why all MNCs do not strive to become geocentric, with the apparent benefits it can generate. First of all, true geocentric mindsets require extensive coordination and an ability to identify both organizational needs and individual qualifications. The diversity of international assignments can also result in difficulties when developing compensation structures, training programs and development plans. This is particularly challenging as dual career families make longer expatriate assignments increasingly difficult. Further, challenges in the foreign subsidiaries may still exist if key management positions are continuously filled by expatriates from other parts of the organization rather than locally recruited individuals.

Can managerial mindsets change?

Some argue that managerial mindsets are influenced by the MNCs home-country national culture. Japanese firms in particular, have been examined extensively to determine if they exhibit ethnocentric mindsets and invest in expatriates primarily to exert home-country 'ways of doing things' (Brock et al., 2008). While Japanese firms do use expatriation extensively for top management positions in foreign subsidiaries, the reasons for this are inconclusive. Mixed effects of ethnocentrism and a contingency approach have been identified in Japanese firms where decisions are also contingent upon strategic issues such as the emphasis on inter-firm ties or the local market orientation and perceived strategic importance of the foreign subsidiary (Belderbos and Heijltjes, 2005).

Several MNCs purposefully hire top managers with different experiences and perspectives to infuse different mindsets into the organization. This is particularly visible in MNCs with polycentric mindsets that feel increasing competitive pressures as markets become more globalized and competitors tap into low-cost countries to achieve efficiencies. Increasing the investment in expatriates for the purposes of organizational and leadership development can also gradually influence the managerial mindsets as a new generation of managers with extensive international experience takes on key positions. Ownership structures also influence managerial mindsets. It may be more fitting for state-owned enterprises, for instance, to maintain ethnocentric mindsets where the hiring of foreigners into top management positions can generate resistance among key stakeholders. International joint ventures and mergers will also likely influence managerial mindsets, making ethnocentric mindsets more difficult to maintain.

8.5 Enabling the expatriate

Accepting a foreign assignment exposes the individual to many new challenges such as a new work environment as well as differences in both organizational and national cultures (Shay and Baack, 2004). The expatriate must thus overcome a number of challenges to achieve anticipated career advancements and opportunities for personal development associated with foreign assignments. There has been extensive research on how expatriates can increase their effectiveness and suggestions for how to ensure their assignments are successful. One of the most important areas to clarify early is the alignment of expectations. Organizational and personal expectations do not necessarily align. It can be helpful for an expatriate to understand the motivations behind the foreign assignment to better align expectations (Shay and Baack, 2004). If the assignment is motivated by filling an immediate business need, fewer expectations will be placed on learning and contributing to informal control mechanisms. At the same time, filling an immediate business need may also have less of an impact on the individual's career advancement (Bolino, 2007).

Most research to date has focused on adjustments at the individual level without linking it to performance outcomes. The performance of the individual undoubtedly has a huge impact on the organization's value creation. Knowledge transfer, for instance, is highly contingent on the expatriates' ability and motivation to accumulate and share knowledge (Reiche et al., 2009). Achieving satisfactory embeddedness in both the home organization and the local organization to enable valuable knowledge transfer is challenging. MNCs can support individuals by establishing formal communication channels. These should ideally enable the expatriate to communicate and transfer knowledge throughout the assignment and not be limited to repatriation (Carraher et al., 2008). The role of expatriates' local social networks also impact adjustment and performance. A study of expatriates in China found that successful interactions with host country nationals play a significant role in the success of expatriate assignments (Bruning et al., 2012). Repatriation adjustment assistance and engaging with the expatriate in career development plans also supports successful outcomes. Many expatriates express concerns about losing touch with the home country as they fear being 'out of sight, out of mind' might affect their career opportunities when repatriating (Reiche et al., 2009).

Since the roles and responsibilities of many expatriates require extensive experience and expertise, individuals are often at a stage of life with family situations where partners and children are also directly affected by the foreign assignment. Adjustment difficulties among family members have long been recognized as one of the most common reason for expatriate dissatisfaction and shortened assignments. In their recent study of how expatriates could best succeed in their foreign assignment, Clouse and Watkins (2009) suggested that expatriates should first of all establish the family foundation (or support networks) before focusing on embedding in the workplace.

The previous discussion of managerial mindsets is naturally not limited to managers making staffing decisions. Mindsets of the individual expatriates also impact the success and outcomes of an assignment. The ability to accumulate and share information is critical, requiring openness and appreciation for information that is perceived as 'foreign' and difficult to grasp. Expatriates with strong ethnocentric mindsets may exhibit less willingness and ability to recognize valuable local knowledge. As previously discussed, clarifying the reasons behind the assignment may enable the expatriates to better understand their roles and responsibilities and create an opportunity to build on strengths and develop weaknesses to better meet communicated expectations. Many MNCs also work with potential expatriate candidates to assess individual mindsets and develop a plan for building the necessary skills and capabilities to tackle the expatriate assignment (Javidan et al., 2010).

8.6   Capturing the value of repatriates

Since the expatriate's accumulated knowledge and experience is believed to have high value for the organization, the ability to transfer knowledge and reintegrate repatriated individuals is critical (Reiche et al., 2009). One of the key managerial challenges is thus related to minimizing repatriation failure rates. Although the estimated costs and failure rates of expatriation vary across studies (Carraher et al., 2008), there is nevertheless agreement that the costs of expatriates are significantly higher than the costs of local hires with empirical evidence supporting concerns about failure rates.

Repatriates frequently express dissatisfaction with unfulfilled expectations regarding their career opportunities upon their return (Bolino, 2007). So why have decades of debate and research on the topic not resulted in significantly lower failure rates? MNCs are still characterized as 'too focused on expatriation instead of repatriation, too ad hoc and opportunistic instead of strategic in their behaviors, and too disorganized to implement post repatriation-related programs scholars recommend' (Jassawalla and Sashittal, 2009: 770).

To fully capture the value of repatriates, MNCs must recognize that cross-cultural transfers of human resources generate added complexities compared to domestic transfers. The accumulated knowledge is often perceived as 'foreign' and difficult to understand by the home-organization, requiring organizational capabilities to receive such information (Oddou et al., 2009). But as Lazarova and Tarique point out, 'not all knowledge is easy to capture . . . individuals and organizations do not necessarily have coinciding goals with respect to using knowledge as a basis for developing a competitive advantage' (2005: 362). This requires a fit between the repatriate's type of knowledge and motivation and the organizational capability to capture knowledge and create appropriate incentives for repatriates to share their knowledge. The re-socialization process may also be more extensive due to geographical and cultural distances. This is an area that is frequently overlooked by human resource departments.

Selecting the right individuals for foreign assignments can have a huge impact on the outcomes. MNCs should therefore seek to send people on foreign assignments 'for the right reasons'. A good technical track record in the home country may not serve as a good success recipe for future international leaders. Technical skills do not necessarily reflect the ability to understand business at a global level, if the person is open to new ideas and experiences, or has the ability to build trusting relationships in cross-cultural settings (Javidan et al., 2010). In a study of Japanese expatriates, intercultural personality traits identified before the assignment were positively related to the expatriates' abilities to acquire competencies when expatriated and subsequent abilities to transfer these competencies when repatriated (Furuya et al., 2009).

Many firms, such as Siemens, also try to avoid expatriation becoming financially motivated and focus on setting fair conditions that enable employees to maintain equivalent living standards but not 'gain economically' from it (Russwurm et al., 2011). In general, there is not one specific type of person that is most suitable for expatriation. Different people fit with different reasons for expatriation. As a consequence, resourceful organizations such as Royal Dutch Shell invest tremendously in HRM systems that will enhance the selection and fit between individual characteristics and needs and the organization's immediate and long-term needs (Sucher and Corsi, 2011). Clarifying the reasons for an expatriation will thus enable the organization to ensure best fit with potential candidates.

There is an inherent assumption that if expats are well adjusted, they will also be effective (Shay and Baack 2004). Mentoring has been identified as a tool to enhance the adjustment and effectiveness of expatriates. The mentorships should ideally be connected to both the home country and host country (Carraher et al., 2008). Accordingly, host-country mentors are particularly helpful with cultural adaptation while home-country mentors create important links back to organization in home country and ease various repatriation issues. Formal mentoring programs can thus be beneficial to avoid negative outcomes of international assignments.

The knowledge acquired during expatriation (such as procedures, ideas, experiences, models developed over time that guide actions and decisions) is particularly valuable in a global business environment where learning generates competitive advantages. If MNCs fail to capture value from their repatriates, they miss opportunities for competitive advantages and risk 'losing their investment' if repatriates leave (Oddou et al., 2009). There are two key reasons why MNCs have problems retaining repatriates. First, repatriates become dissatisfied when their organizations do not express any interest in utilizing their newly acquired expertise. Second, repatriates may also be proactive in managing their own careers and evaluate career opportunities outside the company (Suutari and Brewster, 2003). Thus, turnover does not merely reflect dissatisfaction with the repatriation process and career opportunities; expatriates may also be assessing the overall attractiveness of future opportunities (Lazarova and Tarique, 2005). A study of Finnish expatriates found that

65 per cent received external job offers while still expatriated and 60 per cent received external job offers after repatriation (Suutari and Brewster, 2003).

8.7 What can we learn from best practices?

With the dismal statistics discussed earlier showing dissatisfaction with outcomes both at the organizational and individual level, learning from best practices can be valuable. Despite the many reasons for expatriation, filling immediate business demands has long represented the most common driver for expatriation (Black and Gregersen, 1999). While this addresses immediate business needs, it may not result in long-term effective human resource management or organizational development. MNCs continuously need to consider their long-term goals in terms of knowledge creation and leadership development which also requires an investment in structured repatriation. Just as the reasons behind expatriation differ, the type of knowledge accumulated will vary depending on the nature of the responsibilities and degree of interaction involved in the position (Lazarova and Tarique, 2005).

Successful companies have been found to emphasize three key practices for international assignments. First, knowledge creation and global leadership development are emphasized to ensure that the assignment creates long-term value for the MNC. Although filling an immediate business need with an expatriate may not be motivated by learning, the MNC should strive to use expatriation foremost as a learning opportunity. Second, MNCs must invest in identifying the right candidates by ensuring that any technical skills are matched or exceeded by cross-cultural abilities. The ability to absorb and transfer knowledge in cross-cultural contexts requires cognitive and social capabilities. Selection processes should thus value specific technical skills as one of many necessary expatriate qualities. Finally, successful MNCs have deliberate and well prepared repatriation processes that start well in advance of the physical repatriation (Black and Gregersen, 1999).

8.8 Future challenges and alternatives to expatriation

This chapter shows that success from the perspective of individuals may differ from perceptions of success from an organizational level. This bodes the question whether we need to reconsider how we define successful expatriation and (Lazarova and Cerdin, 2007). We tend to assume that retention implies positive organizational outcomes and that individual benefits translate into organizational benefits. When re-examining the three main reasons for expatriation, however, one could argue that not all turnover is negative as assignments vary in their long-term strategic importance for the organization.

It must also be recognized that despite their individual qualities and leadership potential, not all individuals are interested or able to accept international assignments. Dual income families are frequently referred to as one of the main challenges of expatriation, although the reasons are many. These barriers to accepting foreign assignments can in some instances be addressed by the length of the assignment. The typical length of an assignment still falls within a two- to five-year period which is costly for the organization and may deter individuals who are less mobile (Harzing, 2001). Firms, such as Walmart and Samsung, are increasingly focusing on shorter assignments to also enable people who are earlier in their careers or who have difficulties moving for longer periods to gain global experience (Russwurm et al., 2011). Shorter assignments are by no means new, but have received greater attention lately as a strategic tool to reduce costs and expose attractive candidates for international experiences (Bonache et al, 2010).

In addition to revisiting the length of assignments, the following alternatives have been identified as interesting alternative approaches to consider: self-initiated expatriates, commuter assignments, frequent traveling and virtual working (Bonache et al., 2010). The effectiveness of expatriation versus more centralized control as well as investments in training, diversified projects and task forces have also been debated without clear empirical evidence. Some of the proposed alternatives may better address certain aspects of organizational development, however, rather than satisfy the needs for knowledge transfer or management development (Harzing, 2001). Clarifying the reason behind a proposed expatriation assignment will help managers when comparing the costs and benefits of alternative arrangements.

Finally, as MNCs increasingly grow through mergers and acquisitions (UNCTAD, 2011), new challenges may arise for expatriation. Most research to date has primarily focused on expatriation in wholly-owned MNCs while the international ownership structures increasingly exhibit variations of joint ventures and strategic alliances. MNCs must carefully consider how the role of expatriates fits with their international strategies and ownership structures (Harzing, 2001).

8.9 Summary

Expatriation is common in MNCs and typically motivated by immediate business needs, organizational development or leadership development.

This chapter has highlighted some of the key challenges associated with expatriation, particularly related to the ability to transfer valuable international experience from the individual to the organization. The discussion shows that although individuals can actively work on their ability and motivation to accumulate and share knowledge, organizational characteristics have been found to impact both the individual's career success and the achievement of expected organizational outcomes (Bolino, 2007). Success, as perceived by both the individual and organization, relies on the combination of the expatriates' experience (for example success and type of posting), career development practices (for example structured development and internal connectivity), and parent-organization contexts (for example mindsets, international strategy and international experience of the CEO and top management). Case G following the chapter exemplifies how LVMH approached the international mobility of personnel and highlights common challenges facing MNCs.

Case G

LVMH: career development through international mobility

Jean-Luc Cerdin

G.1 Introduction

LVMH – Louis Vuitton Moët Hennessy, is the leading luxury brand conglomerate in the world. Based in Paris, it employs 56, 000 people, 63 per cent of whom are outside France. With more than 1, 400 stores worldwide and sales of €12 billion for the year 2000 (84 per cent outside France), LVMH is a global giant.

Created in 1987, it has a portfolio of 50 prestigious luxury brands. Each one of these brands has its unique history and culture. Among them are famous names such as Château d'Yquem founded in 1593, Moët & Chandon in 1743, Hennessy in 1765, Guerlain in 1828 and Louis Vuitton in 1854. LVMH is a financial and commercial group specialized in the profitable market of luxury goods. LVMH is a young group based on timeless brands, and endeavors to preserve the authenticity of all of them. Because of the strength of these brands, LVMH chose to be a decentralized organization. It is also a growing and evolving organization, constantly acquiring new businesses.

From its creation, LVMH was an international business, but its human resources were sometimes lacking in international experience. Competing in a global environment, LVMH must attract, develop and retain managers with global competence. By 2001, it had 260 expatriates and 650 other employees working in a country not their own.

G.2 History

The creation of Moët Hennessy in 1971 was a first step towards the creation of a larger group in 1987 under the name LVMH, as illustrated in Figure G.1. In 1989, the Groupe Arnault, as shown in Figure G.2 became a

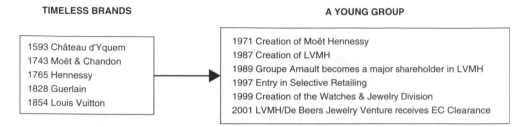

TIMELESS BRANDS

1593 Château d'Yquem
1743 Moët & Chandon
1765 Hennessy
1828 Guerlain
1854 Louis Vuitton

A YOUNG GROUP

1971 Creation of Moët Hennessy
1987 Creation of LVMH
1989 Groupe Arnault becomes a major shareholder in LVMH
1997 Entry in Selective Retailing
1999 Creation of the Watches & Jewelry Division
2001 LVMH/De Beers Jewelry Venture receives EC Clearance

Figure G.1 History: a young group

majority shareholder in LVMH. In 1997, LVMH entered the selective retailing market to better control the distribution of its goods. In 1999, it entered the Watches & Jewelry business. LVMH is organized in five business groups. In addition to Watches & Jewelry and Selective Retailing, LVMH's activities include Wines & Spirits, Fashion & Leather Goods and Perfumes & Cosmetics. The sales level of these activities is given in Figure G.3. The list of all of LVMH's companies can be found in Figure G.4.

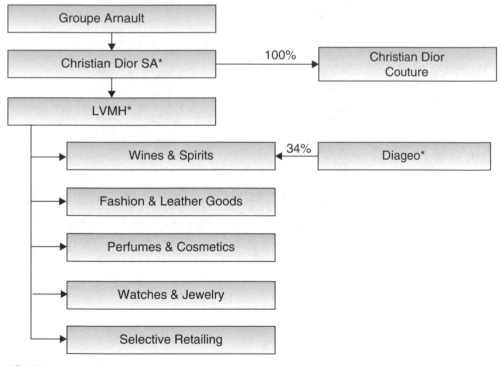

Groupe Arnault

Christian Dior SA* ——100%——> Christian Dior Couture

LVMH*

Wines & Spirits <——34%—— Diageo*

Fashion & Leather Goods

Perfumes & Cosmetics

Watches & Jewelry

Selective Retailing

Public companies

Figure G.2 Group structure

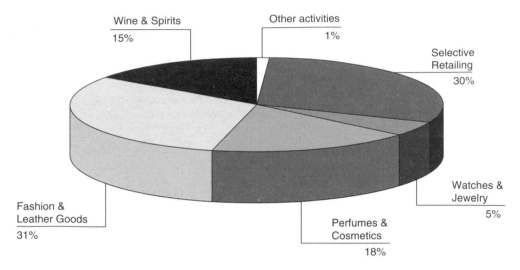

Figure G.3 Balanced portfolio of activities (% first half 2001 sales)

16th

1593 Château d'Yquem

18th

1729 Ruinart
1743 Moët & Chandon
1763 Hine
1765 Hennessy
1772 Veuve Clicquot
1780 Chaumet
1796 Phillips

19th

1828 Guerlain
1836 Pommery
1843 Krug
1846 Loewe
1852 Le Bon Marché
1854 Louis Vuitton
1858 Mercier
1860 Heuer
1865 Zenith
1868 Canard Duchêne
1870 La Cote Desfossés
1870 La Samaritaine
1895 Berluti

20th

1911 Ebel
1925 Omas
1925 Fendi
1930 Acqua di Parma
1936 Dom Pérignon
1936 Fred
1945 Celine
1947 Parfums Christian Dior
1952 Givenchy
1952 Connaissance des Arts
1957 Parfums Givenchy
1958 Emilio Pucci
1960 DFS
1963 Miami Cruiseline Services
1970 Kenzo
1970 Etude Tajan
1972 MountAdam
1973 Domaine Chandon
1973 Sephora
1974 Investir
1976 Cape Mentelle
1978 Newton
1979 Art & Auction
1981 Pacific Echo
1983 Radio Classique
1984 Thomas Pink
1984 Marc Jacobs
1984 Donna Karan
1985 La Tribune del'Economie
1985 Cloudy Bay
1985 Benedom- CD Montres
1987 Christian Lacroix
1987 Parfums Kenzo
1987 Laflachère
1989 Make Up For Ever

1991 Fresh
1991 StefanoBi
1995 Hard Candy
1995 BeneFit Cosmetics
1996 Bliss
1996 Urban Decay
1997 Chandon Estates
1999 Solstice
2000 eLuxury

21st
2001 LVMH/De Beers joint venture

Figure G.4 History: a world-class portfolio of brands

Today the group defines its core values as 'being creative and innovative', 'aiming for product excellence', 'promoting our brands with passion', 'acting as entrepreneurs' and 'striving to be the best in all we do.'

G.3 Group structure

The group's roots are French, and most of the headquarters of LVMH's companies are located in France. Yet, LVMH believes that its management must be multicultural. The group is structured around five business groups. Each business group is a collection of several strong brands, as shown in Figure G.5. LVMH is an aggregate, a 'confederacy' of brands, in the words of LVMH's CEO Bernard Arnault. This organization is atypical because it is a young structure that aggregates several brands, sometimes very old and independent. The strength of each brand stems from a unique culture which translates into relatively autonomous brand management.

The group is made up of 50 companies managing 450 subsidiaries. These companies are the foundation of the group. Each company has its President and its Executive Committee. Each company has its subsidiaries which report directly to it either through the President or through an International Director in charge of supervising the activities of the company's subsidiaries.

LVMH's leadership is based on its balanced presence in several key sectors of luxury goods and an even geographical split of its activities between Europe,

Wines & Spirits	Fashion & Leather Goods	Perfumes & Cosmetics	Selective Retailing	Watches & Jewelry	Other Businesses
Moët & Chandon	Louis Vuitton	Parfum Christian Dior	DFS	TAG Heuer	Phillips, de Pury &
Dom Pérignon	Céline	Parfums	Miami Cruiseline	Montres	Luxembourg
Mercier	Loewe	Guerlain	Sephora	Christian Dior	Etude Taja
Ruinart	Kenzo	Kenzo Parfums	Sephora AA	Ebe	D.I Group
Veuve Clicquot	Givenchy	Hard Candy	Le Bon Marché	Zenith	Investir
Ponsardin	Christian Dior*	Fresh	Solstic	Omas	Radio Classique
Canard-Duchên	Christian	Laflachèr	La Samaritaine	Chaumet	La Tribune
Pommery	Marc Jacobs	Bliss		Fred	Jazzman
Krug	Berluti	Urban Decay		LVMH/ De	Le Monde de la
Chandon Estates	Fendi	Make Up For Ever		joint venture	Musique
Cloudy Bay	StefanoBi	BeneFit Cosmetics			System TV
Cape Mentelle	Thomas Pink	Acqua diParma			Connaissance des Arts
Newton	Emilio Pucci				Art & Auction
MountAdam	Donna Karan				Sephora.com
Hennessy					eLuxury
Hine					
Château d'Yquem					

*Christian Dior is one of the indirect holders of LVMH.

Figure G.5 Organization in five business groups

Asia and the Americas. It pursues an aggressive growth strategy based on a high level of innovation, control over distribution and sustained advertising and promotion.

G.4   HR structure

LVMH organizes its human resource management around five main world zones, namely, France, Europe, the Americas, Pacific Asia and Japan. France and Japan are regarded as country/zones because of the size of their market, see Figure G.6.

Corporate HR policy is more than compulsory rules imposed on the business groups and on the companies. Through adaptable guidelines, it also provides management support to the companies. The role of corporate HR is to normalize certain procedures, to define strategy and to give an impetus to companies' HR teams. Regarding guidelines, corporate HR proposes but seldom imposes.

An employee deals directly with the company he or she works for; this company in turn deals with the business group which reports to corporate headquarters. Roughly 50–60 per cent of moves are handled by companies, the others being managed by the business groups or corporate.

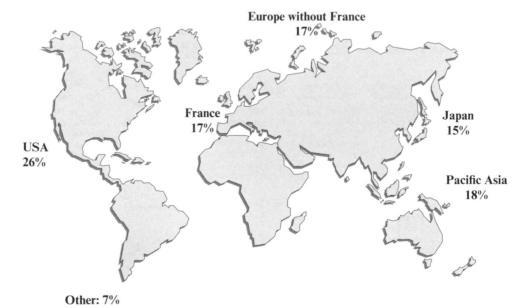

Figure G.6 World sales

There are four types of HR managers at LVMH. Following the group's structure, they operate on four levels: corporate, regional, business group and company level. The subsidiary HR Director, or the person acting as such, reports to the subsidiary's President. The subsidiary's HR Director gets advice and support from his company. The business group's HR Director coordinates his companies' HR Directors through monthly meetings. The purpose of these meetings is to identify vacant positions throughout the world and to study the list of the potential candidates for these positions, amongst which are the 'Ready to move'. Being a 'Ready to move' does not mean that a candidate has formally expressed a desire to move, but that the organization has identified him or her as having the potential to progress through a new assignment within the year.

The main goal of corporate HR management is to ensure information flow and to harmonize procedures, while leaving final decisions to the company, up to a point. The regional HR Director ensures that internal rules are coherently applied within his or her zone. For subsidiaries with no HR Director, recruitment is done by the Regional HR Director.

G.5 Career development and international mobility

LVMH was a global business from the start, however it soon realized that its human resources often lacked international skills. In 1987, too many managers were not fluent in English. Since then, LVMH has sought to create a pool of global managers, with a working knowledge of international markets. The head of LVMH's Compensation & Benefits (C&B) defines a global manager as a person with the training or the experience needed to manage a global business. He or she can perform from any place in the world thanks to a global vision and skills in managing multilingual and multicultural teams. To achieve such abilities, one must have worked in several countries so that his or her potential can be released, and noticed.

LVMH believes that the best way to develop its employees is not formal training but mobility. This includes vertical, horizontal and geographical moves within the organization. In order to facilitate mobility, employees' seniority is valued at the group level. International mobility is but one form of mobility, it accounts for one out of five moves.

Basic principles of LVMH's policy for international mobility

LVMH prefers to use the term 'international mobility', rather than expatriation. Contrary to the concept of international mobility which suggests perpetual movement, the term expatriation suggests systematic repatriation. For example, a Dane leaving a Danish subsidiary of 15 people to take on an international assignment will not be expatriated. He will sign a local contract in the country of his assignment. He will be considered 'internationally mobile' because it is most unlikely that he will ever work again in Denmark for LVMH. The skills he will have acquired abroad will largely surpass the competence needed in Denmark.

The international mobility policy is part of a career development scheme which requires the training of global managers on a limited time basis. LVMH does not want to create a legion of expatriates who live out their careers outside their home base, often in the same country, maintaining their benefits. In such cases, expatriates are disconnected from their home base. Moreover, such practices are not cost effective.

LVMH strives to attract managers to international assignments through exciting career development prospects and not through economic incentives, even though its incentive program is competitive. HR convinces a manager to become 'internationally mobile' by offering him or her a more challenging job with more freedom to perform his or her task than at home.

LVMH does not dispatch expatriates because of a lack of local talent. Most of its expatriates fit two profiles: those sent out by the corporate HQ to control its subsidiaries and protect its interests (internal auditors and financial staff) and those sent out to develop their skills. Organization development accounts for a quarter of expatriates while the rest is part of a management development scheme. Most expatriates are in charge of small subsidiaries for three years on average, very few of them stay longer. They are senior expatriates whose role is to manage the local business, train the host-country nationals and transfer corporate culture. Clearly some expatriations result from specific needs. For example, certain designers in leather goods are very hard to find and must be expatriated.

International talents

International mobility is an integral part of each high potential's career path. International mobility mainly aims at developing managers. Many expatriates are high potentials. International mobility is likely to entail a radical functional move. The head of HR development recalls the case of a French insurance specialist in the fashion business unit who was sent to Romania to head a shoe factory. LVMH recognizes the need to take risks in order to develop high potentials. It wants to put them in new situations to help them develop new skills and prove their mettle.

LVMH's career development goal is to make the mobility process smoother, particularly international moves. Indeed, HR is well aware that top management is somewhat ethnocentric. Half of LVMH's senior executives and 40 per cent of managerial staff are French, whereas the French account for 37 per cent of the group's global workforce. Ideally, HR wants to develop more foreign global managers so that they can in turn globalize top management. However, LVMH's mobility process works thanks to a network of HR teams mainly staffed with locals. Many heads of subsidiaries are French. Italians are also well represented at LVMH, as they are historical key players in the luxury business. The Board of Directors features French, Italian and American nationals.

Until recently, LVMH defined two types of high potentials, HP1 and HP2. An HP1 is an individual likely to achieve a top management position such as a member of Board committees, Regional President or Subsidiary President. An HP2 is an employee likely to go up one or two steps in the hierarchy. For corporate HR this definition of high potential is too broad and is more relevant for flat structures. It is now considering narrowing it. It would retain the definition of HP1 and include those who are considered to be experts in their domain.

The LVMH performance appraisal system is not only based on results but also on the ability to propose and implement new ideas. The group's growth and financial might allows these projects to come to life. LVMH has a career management process called Organizational and Management Review (OMR). This annual process aims at reviewing HR objectives and results. The OMR is an essential tool for LVMH's human resource planning, taking into consideration the organization's needs for the next three years. It defines succession planning and HP and 'Ready to move' lists. Employees identified on these lists are given developmental experiences which include international assignments, in order to prepare them for top management positions. The OMR particularly looks back on the previous year's objectives for HPs and those 'Ready to move' and assesses their current development. LVMH manages to staff internally two out of three executive positions.

Up until recently, the typical career path included showing one's mettle in France, moving from position to position within France in order to master the corporate culture. Once these conditions were met, the employee could be expatriated. LVMH is now willing to make expatriation happen earlier. It recognizes the risks involved in such a policy but believes that these risks are offset by the development of a young and adventurous global workforce.

International recruitment

In order to build a pool of global managers, LVMH must be able to have a worldwide recruiting process and to send its employees on global assignments. LVMH is a very attractive company for French prospects, however it is not as successful on international labor markets. Once having achieved global recruitment, LVMH must succeed in developing its employee's global skills. Expatriation is an integral part of LVMH's HRM policy.

LVMH's natural labor market is France. LVMH is a very attractive company for early career professionals and is very active on French business campuses. An early career professional is an individual with less than five years of professional experience. Today, roughly 70 per cent of early career professionals at LVMH are recruited in France.

LVMH would like to expand its labor source to a more international level. Being a decentralized organization, their website is their main source of candidates along with on-campus job fairs. Through this website, candidates from any country can apply directly to any of LVMH's subsidiaries in a country not their own and obtain a local employment contract.

In order to support international business growth, the number of employees involved in international transfers is increasing. However, this does not mean that a rise in the number of French expatriates will drive this trend. Rather LVMH's pool of global managers will grow through third-country nationals and mostly multicultural profiles.

LVMH wants to recruit more individuals with international profiles. The ideal candidate is a person who has been immersed in several cultures, has traveled extensively, speaks at least three languages and has an open mind.

Today the number of expatriates at LVMH is 260 and rising, 79 per cent of them are French. Inpatriates (foreigners in France) represent 5.5 per cent and third country nationals 15.5 per cent of employees on international assignment. The average age of expatriates is 36 years, 48 per cent of them are under 35 and 5 per cent are over 50. General managers, area managers and brand managers account for 35.5 per cent of expatriates, finance and

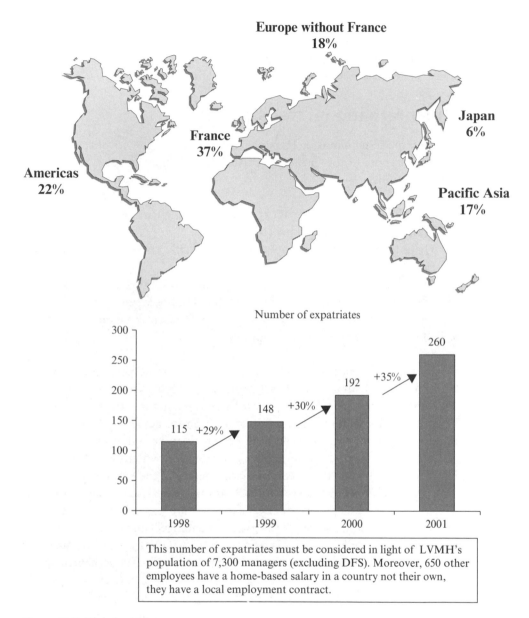

Figure G.7 Global workforce

audit staff for 17.5 per cent, marketing for 12 per cent, store managers and HR staff each account for 4 per cent of expatriates, and the remaining 27 per cent includes other positions. In the past years the number of expatriates has grown by approximately 30 per cent each year while the overall population of managers has grown by 20 per cent each year (see Figure G.7).

In addition to these expatriates per se, 650 other employees have a home-based salary in a country not their own, they have a local employment contract. For example, an Australian recruited in France, and still working there, is not an expatriate and is not on global assignment.

G.6 The international transfer policy

The International Transfer Department operates at the corporate level to provide support to the group's companies. It defines its role through five main functions:

- Determining expatriate packages in order to guarantee internal equity between the group's various companies
- Helping the group's companies address specific issues regarding international transfers
- Providing information and advice on the evolution of 'external rules' which govern international transfers, that is labor laws
- Conducting, spreading and explaining LVMH's internal mobility policy
- Monitoring of international mobility data

Corporate HR's purpose is to define clear and simple principles that can be applied to all subsidiaries in all countries. In order to facilitate mobility within the group, LVMH is trying to harmonize its practices to allow for a more global workforce. The prime condition for achieving this goal is to make equity a priority, between both countries and employees. LVMH did not choose to set up an international corporation which would centralize HRM and would dictate the compensation policy of the entire organization. The organization would like to avoid situations where line managers are confronted with the frustrations of expatriates earning less than their colleagues in the same position. As a result the manager could feel uneasy and would not know how to cope with such discrepancies. LVMH has chosen to maintain a decentralized organization where corporate HR defines general principles.

LVMH's corporate policy of international mobility is very recent. Before 1987, each company proceeded according to its own international transfer policy. The foundation of the corporate policy was laid out at the group's creation. The companies gradually adopted this policy which was eventually formalized in July 2000. Today, each company HR possesses a copy of the 'International Transfer Policy' charter which covers all main aspects of international mobility. The charter does not focus on career development but rather on the formal procedures related to international mobility. It encompasses all the aspects pertaining to an expatriate package. It is meant to be used by company HR directors. Some technical annexes are for the use of the companies' C&B staff so as to facilitate communication with the International Transfer Department and to provide answers to potential expatriates' concerns. Indirectly, this charter helps expatriates understand their package.

The charter was first published as a paper document. It structures and formalizes past practices and tries to build a common policy. The International Transfer Department is now considering broadening its information supply to HR companies through the use of its intranet.

The expatriate package

LVMH does not aim to attract expatriates through high compensation levels. The group is striving for cost efficiency. It is aware that a 'good' package is necessary, but that it is not the main incentive to go abroad. Research on French expatriates shows that compensation is not the main motive for accepting an international assignment, as shown in Table G.1.

The basic balance-sheet approach for compensation package is based on the principle that expatriates should neither lose nor gain from their move. LVMH's C&B department has retained this approach as a guide for its compensation package policy.

The home-based salary is marked up at the time of departure according to the international assignment. It will increase during the length of the assignment. It is used as a base for the calculation of social security and pension contributions. The mobility salary is compared to local labor market averages in compatible

Table G.1 French managers' motives for expatriation

Ranking of French managers' motives for expatriation (293 expatriates working for 12 organizations in 44 countries were asked to express their motives to go and work abroad)

Motive	Rank	%
Desire for change	1	77.7
Personal experience in another culture	2	75.3
Increased prospects of future promotion	3	49.8
Compensation	4	37.8
Immediate promotion	5	18.3
Desire to escape home country's economic and social environment	6	16.2
To distance one's self from certain personal problems	7	6.2

Source: Cerdin, J-L. (2002). *L'expatriation*. Editions d'Organisation, p. 65.

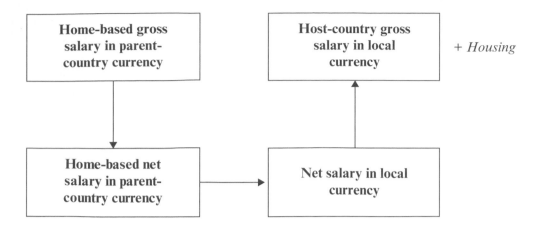

Figure G.8 Basic balance sheet approach

countries. LVMH delineated two types of countries, the 'compatible' countries, roughly including OECD countries, and the 'incompatible' countries.

In order to calculate expatriates' gross salary in local currency, that is the mobility salary, LVMH's C&B department first considers their home-based gross salary in parent-country currency, then it calculates their net salary (by deducting theoretical home tax, social security and compulsory pension contribution). Then a cost of living allowance (COLA) and various family allowance differentials are added to or subtracted from this net salary in parent-country currency. A foreign premium service can also be granted. The net figure obtained is then expressed in local currency. The net salary is then 'grossed up' by adding taxes and the social contribution of the host country. See Figure G.8 for an overview.

LVMH's C&B department has adapted the balance sheet approach for its housing policy. A consultancy provides them with the housing market rate for the host country. LVMH's local correspondents verify this information. Potential expatriates may also have their own knowledge of market rates. As a rule, all the parties involved are honest, but they might not always understand each other perfectly. As a company HR put it:

> Having local correspondents is one thing, understanding each other is another one. For instance, an apartment of 125 square meters in Hong Kong refers to the

surface area of the apartment itself plus a proportion of the communal parts area. This is less than 125 square meters of living space. The same apartment surface might appear larger to a person used to areas where only living space is taken into account.

Once the local market rate is agreed on, LVMH will compensate the expatriates but they have to contribute 15 per cent of their home-based gross salary. For example, a French expatriate in New York will be paid an amount in US dollars equal to the average monthly market rate times 12, minus an amount in dollars equal to 15 per cent of his/her yearly gross salary in France as expressed in Euros. This 15 per cent contribution is based on the assumption than a French employee's housing costs amount to roughly 15 per cent of his/her gross salary. LVMH believes that this estimate is below the cost effectively paid by most employees. The rationale behind this contribution is that employees have to pay a percentage of their salary on housing at home and must also do so abroad. LVMH can directly provide housing to the expatriates or it can grant them an allowance by using the above principle. This housing allowance is also 'grossed up'. The expatriates are responsible for the cost of utilities. They are granted a relocation allowance equivalent to one month's worth of gross salary upon arrival in the host country, where they must work, and after return to the home country, whence they were expatriated.

LVMH works with consulting firms specialized in overseas Cost of Living Allowances (COLA) calculation. It uses a positive index to protect its employees from losing money when they move to a country with a higher cost of living. It uses a negative index when they move to a country with a lower cost of living. Here the balance-sheet approach is strictly applied. C&B corporate relies on the internal exchange rate used by the corporate finance department, in order to avoid any complaints from financial expatriates. The calculation of the cost-of-living differential is based on the assumption that all employees, regardless of their family situation, save 30 per cent of their home-based net salary. The COLA is set at the time of departure.

C&B does not rely on outside consultancies to determine its incentive allowances. A foreign service premium is calculated by taking into account four criteria, namely: the environment (health facilities, pollution, climate), personal security, social amenities and the everyday quality of life. The granted premiums range from 0 to 30 per cent depending on the home country and the host country. For instance, for an expatriate from France, whatever his or her nationality, the premium is null when the move is within the European Zone or towards the USA. It achieves its maximum, 30 per cent, for a host country such as India.

LVMH's appeal to global managers does not rely mainly on its mobility salary but on its home-based salary, from which the mobility salary is calculated. This appeal is also greatly increased by the role of international mobility in career paths. International mobility is like an investment; the return on investment for the expatriate will be the high future incomes generated by a promotion achieved through successful international assignments.

The mobility salary also includes other aspects such as compensation of other social benefits (like family support). It also compensates for the possible loss of profit-sharing benefits resulting from a move from one successful subsidiary to a less successful one. Indeed, no profit-sharing schemes exist at the corporate level.

Expatriates are also entitled to additional benefits such as paid education for children, paid home-leaves, temporary housing for up to 30 days, loans for housing deposits or for purchasing a vehicle. Costs of moving are also covered. According to French labor laws, in addition to their five-week vacation, French managers, except top executives, are entitled to have more days off. Some countries are far less advantageous in terms of vacation time. LVMH grants four-week vacations in the USA and five-week vacations elsewhere.

The expatriate package is prepared at the corporate level but the final decision is left up to the companies. As the companies are the ones that must pay the expatriates, they have some leeway. For instance, as expressed by a C&B manager:

> Some of them are going to give higher housing allowances, they may offer more generous home-leave allowances than those favored by the Group, such as business-class air fare instead of less expensive economy-class ones.

The International Transfer Department defines clear procedures; however, implementing them requires some flexibility. At the company level, policies often end up being tailor-made to cope with expatriates' specific concerns. The group's policy is to treat expatriates as locals when they are sent to compatible countries. Nevertheless, when it wishes to send an employee on an international assignment, it may have to meet his or her specific needs. A corporate manager recalls the concerns of some expatriates:

> My children have a French culture and education, and I want them to be in an international school.

> My wife has health problems, so I'd like to get this particular kind of health insurance.
>
> I was used to a 180 square meter apartment in Rome and for the same price, I can only afford a 35 square meter one in New York.

Negotiation with expatriates might appear time-consuming and much too focused on details for a company's HR staff. Indeed, international assignments often entail specialized, strategic and key positions, for which the company must be more flexible. This is also due to the HR structure which allows potential expatriates to negotiate, in rare instances, some non-technical aspects of the compensation package at the company level.

Harmonizing the package in the group's various companies remains a high priority. Each company is responsible for its budget. The companies can rely on the group's expertise to address certain issues, but they are the ones that implement the policies.

Expatriate compensation policies of other multinational companies may appear more advantageous than the one defined by LVMH, particularly with respect to housing allowances, car allowances and club membership allowances. The package facilitates mobility, in so far as it avoids having employees cling to a country in the hope of keeping favorable benefits. It is also a cost-effective practice and has not yet failed to attract the needed talents.

Home-based salaries may differ between individuals depending on the country and on the business group they come from. As reported by an HR manager:

> Global cash compensation for equivalent positions vary depending on the business group and on the country. Some business groups offer historically higher or lower wages than others. The purpose of LVMH's compensation policy is to reduce these differences between the various companies in the same country. Some countries offer higher wages than others because of specific labor market conditions. As a result the salary for a specific international assignment may vary according to the expatriate's previous position.

LVMH is very sensitive to international compensation market rates. It is striving to offer competitive compensation with regard to local practices. For equal qualifications, wages in the USA are much higher than in France. Relying solely on the balance sheet approach to determine the salary of a French employee sent to America would result in a low salary, not at all competitive on the American market. LVMH takes into account the local market, but does not always align its compensation with it. The reverse situation of an American sent to France is equally problematic for LVMH. The balance sheet approach implies that he or she must accept a lower gross salary: according to the cost of living differential, buying power is maintained for a lower salary. Compensation first follows the balance sheet approach but then illustrates a hybrid approach in order to combine cost of living, exchange rate, housing and labor market conditions.

Security benefits

LVMH will not compromise over its expatriates' peace of mind concerning security benefits. The principle is that the chosen schemes will not penalize expatriates, that is they will have access to security benefits as good as those available in their home country.

Many countries have, because of their own social history, unique retirement plans. This requires the security benefits aspect of the compensation package to take into account the retirement plans expatriates have contributed to. Building compensation packages for French expatriates is particularly difficult due to the unique nature of the French retirement system.

The French retirement system is partly linked to the social security system. It is not based on capitalization like a self-funded pension scheme, but rather on a principle of wealth sharing with a contributory 'pay-as-you-go' pension scheme. Employees and employers on French territory have a legal obligation to contribute to the retirement system. In order to be eligible for full retirement benefits, a French worker must contribute to the system for 40 years. Provided that they contribute, French workers believe they are guaranteed good retirement at no risk. A French expatriate may wish to stick to the French system, particularly if he or she is to experience but one international assignment within the group. This is especially the case for older employees who have been contributing to the French system for many years. Things are different for a young graduate who is about to begin contributing to the French social security. In compatible countries, he or she can opt for another, more satisfactory, system.

Maintaining continuity between the different systems is a priority for expatriates. LVMH deems it its own responsibility. When no agreement exists between the French social security system and the host country's social security system, such as in Japan, a double contribution has to be paid. LVMH pays the French contribution to maintain the expatriates' right to retirement in France and must pay the contribution in Japan, because the Japanese system does not recognize the French one.

Most third-country nationals are dealt with differently, because many countries have implemented pension funds. LVMH analyses the employer's contribution to a retirement fund before an expatriation, it then compares it to the retirement plan of the host country. When it can find neither a solution to maintain the expatriate within the parent-country system, nor a solution in the host country, it uses an 'offshore' system. This 'offshore' or international fund has no anchor in the countries involved in the move. LVMH acknowledges that there is no ideal response to the retirement issue. Generally, the parent-country scheme is maintained.

LVMH is attentive to its employees' health benefits. As a rule, the group will opt for the insurance schemes available in the host country only if they offer coverage as wide as those prevailing in the parent country. When in doubt, they provide expatriates and their families an international insurance. Many of the group's companies have adopted this scheme. Roughly 95 per cent of the group's expatriates are covered by it. According to a C&B manager:

> Our plan is very competitive. Besides, because health is part of daily expenses and because expatriates exchange information, having various reimbursement levels would create pointless frustrations.

For life insurance and disability protection, LVMH also ensures that the level of protection is at least as good as the one before the move.

Unemployment insurance benefits reveal some intricacies. Within Europe, because of European regulation, it is not possible to maintain the system of the parent country. An employee is only entitled to receive unemployment compensation from the country he or she is working in. For a move from Europe to another country, options will depend on the host country's regulations. The group has not yet ruled on a common private scheme for all of its employees.

Logistical support

International transfer policy provides expatriates with acceptable logistical support needed to ensure smooth relocation. This amounts to support in housing search and administrative procedures, such as the lease, utilities and hook-up, etc. Relocation services also help families find schools and help them with the enrollment procedures.

International transfer experts are now working to expand their relocation services offering. Indeed, expatriates need help in finding good, experienced suppliers, such as furniture movers. It aims to provide more than financial support. These experts are writing up requirements for relocation services suppliers in order to assist companies.

Support for spouse

Very few employees turn down an international assignment. Nevertheless, LVMH acknowledges that certain employee characteristics impede their mobility. Indeed, some expatriates are hesitant to accept such a move. LVMH puts out feelers to assess employee willingness to take on international assignments. It prefers not to offer an international mobility when it anticipates reluctance or potential problems.

The issue of dual careers has become increasingly critical for any organization willing to expatriate employees. The willingness of the French to go and work abroad is rather weak compared to other nationalities in Europe. In order to cope with this issue, LVMH has agreements with other French multinational companies, which include résumé exchanges. However, they do not integrate the spouse in one of their companies to avoid any problems.

The process of identifying potential expatriates does not take into account marital and family status. Young graduates, mostly single, are keen to accept international assignments because they understand their developmental purpose. So far, most senior expatriates are males married to a non-working spouse. LVMH is well aware that this is a legacy of the past. Today, an increasing number of women are committed to their career. Now 25 per cent of LVMH's expatriates are women, and in addition more and more women are being appointed to high-profile positions within the group. Consequently, the number of female expatriates will rise.

Intercultural training

Intercultural training is more of a project than a reality. So far, intercultural training was not perceived as a priority because of the international profile of the expatriates. As a rule, when a candidate is sent on an international assignment, he or she has had some previous international exposure, for instance through his or her studies, or through earlier professional experience. Moreover, luxury

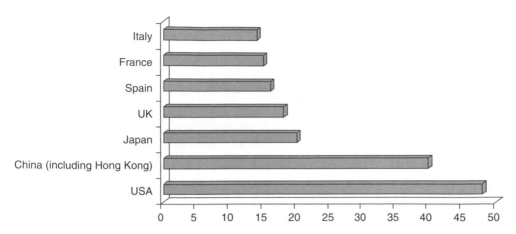

Figure G.9 Key destinations/number of expatriates

businesses are set up in prominent locations, such as large capitals or cities like New York, Hong Kong, Singapore, Tokyo or Paris, as shown in Figure G.9.

LVMH is increasingly feeling the pressure to prepare its expatriates for international assignments in order to facilitate cross-cultural adjustment. As a result, the cross-cultural adjustment process will be accelerated. It is moving towards extending training to both the employee and his or her family. For the time being, both pre-departure and post-arrival training amounts to language courses. Moreover, an international position usually has to be filled very quickly, which leaves little time for intercultural training. Therefore very little training is provided, even for 'culturally tough' countries like Brazil or Mexico, where people are expected to adjust on their own. However, they are not pressured to perform as quickly as if they had had rigorous training. Preparatory field trips are paid for and, in some cases, subsidiaries provide help to newcomers. Often, the size of the subsidiary does not allow for HR staff devoted to helping newcomers.

When intercultural training is provided, it is mainly on an ad hoc basis. It is proposed at the corporate level and some companies offer it depending on past practices or the characteristics of the host country. An HR Manager stresses that:

> On international assignments, French expatriates are most likely to find other French or European expatriates, particularly in the North America, Asia and Japan zones. To some extent, the expatriates can rely on the experience of other already adjusted expatriates.

Repatriation

Regardless of the nature of an employee's international assignment, be it an expatriation per se or a local contract, there is always the willful limitation of the length of the assignment. LVMH has always warned its companies not to create permanent expatriates. These expatriates tend to lose contact with their home country, which makes their repatriation difficult. In order to facilitate the next move or repatriation, assignments are customarily limited to a period of two to three years.

When one begins a career within the LVMH group, in most cases he or she is anchored to a home base. Throughout this career and in spite of many international moves, the home base country usually remains the same.

Even when expatriates are compensated like locals, they have a theoretical home-based salary in order to facilitate their return home. Expatriates are clearly informed that LVMH will use this theoretical home-based salary as the basis for the calculation of the return compensation. The home-based anchor is upgraded each year. Upon returning home, the compensation of the international assignment is not a referent. When a promotion is granted, the home-based salary is upgraded accordingly. The theoretical home-based salary acts as a minimum guarantee referent. The repatriation process begins at least six months to one year before the return home. It chiefly tackles career issues by addressing expatriates' concerns about return positions and career progression.

Sometimes, the anticipated return is altered into another move toward a third country. Such a situation is captured by the following example:

> The Business Group Perfumes & Cosmetics recently transferred a young French expatriate from Givenchy in Sydney to manage the business group in Hong Kong. He will be on the Givenchy payroll, because the business group has no legal entity.

The times when each company would send their employees only to their own subsidiaries are over. Thanks to the 'Ready to move' list, moves are now more frequent within a business group or between business groups. For instance, transferring employees from Veuve Clicquot France to Louis Vuitton Pacific exemplifies this inter-business group mobility. The corporate level ensures that the prevalent logic is group strategy.

G.7 Looking to the future

In spite of its young age, LVMH has already acquired an impressive expertise in international assignment policy. The International Transfer Department relies on the information flowing from LVMH's vast international networks to better determine the needs of HR decision makers. International transfer experts can then provide a helpful framework of reference on which HR companies can rely. Corporate HR hopes to build a global HR information system designed to provide updated and upgraded information and guidelines for HR staff around the world.

As the number of international assignments rises, the group is considering its future needs. It is looking for ways to strengthen its expertise and its ability to assist companies' HR teams. LVMH is pondering over the future of its corporate HR structure which has to cope with the group's growth and with the rising number of expatriates.

International transfer policy is an integral part of LVMH's management philosophy. It has a clear mandate to spread the group's key values which are preserving autonomy and encouraging entrepreneurship. It is also part of the process by which LVMH tries to define its future policy of career development.

The group is thinking about new ways to develop its international mobility policy so that it may better support a larger career development policy. Ultimately, the question for LVMH is to find out how such a career development strategy can better serve its strategy of international development.

? DISCUSSION QUESTIONS

1 What are the challenges faced by LVMH regarding international mobility?
2 Why did LVMH draw up its 'International Transfer Policy' charter? Was such a policy inevitable?
3 How does LVMH tackle the issue of international adjustment? How is its international transfer policy different from those of other multinational organizations?
4 Acting as a consultant, what could be your input in order to improve LVMH's strategy of career development through international mobility?

9

Ethical, social and environmental responsibilities in MNCs

Leighton Wilks and Odd Nordhaug

9.1 Introduction

The rapid growth in the number of MNCs, together with their increased economic and political power, has strongly accentuated the issue of their ethical, social and environmental responsibilities. This chapter will discuss why MNCs should focus on ethical, social and environmental responsibilities in efforts to satisfy stakeholder expectations and create long-term competitive advantage. We will highlight core challenges that MNCs face when striving to act ethically and responsibly. Corporate social responsibility is first defined and placed in the historical context of globalization. We then elaborate on why an MNC would want to consider its ethical, social and environmental responsibilities to various stakeholder groups and address the key question of whether or not an MNC can 'do well by doing good'. We conclude the chapter by discussing current issues that MNCs face including corruption and bribery, child labour, and discrimination.

9.2 Defining ethical, social and environmental responsibility

An MNC's ethical, social, and environmental responsibility to society has been referred to by many similar, yet subtly different terms that include corporate social activity, global corporate citizenship, global citizenship behaviour, and corporate social responsiveness. Despite the multitude of terms and their nuanced differences, most academics and members of the business community currently refer to an MNC's duty to meet the ethical, social, and environmental expectations of society as its corporate social responsibility (CSR).[1] Although a definitive definition of CSR remains elusive, Dahlsrud

(2006) examined the most commonly used definitions of CSR as found in journal articles and on corporate websites. Of the 37 identified definitions, the most frequent dimensions of CSR include: (1) stakeholders, (2) social responsibility, (3) economic factors, (4) the voluntary nature of CSR-related activities, and (5) the environment. Over half of the definitions of CSR contained four or more of the identified dimensions, suggesting that although the exact wording of a universal definition of CSR has yet to be agreed upon, the basic foundations of ethical, social, and environmental responsibilities are consistent and somewhat universal.

The development of various global standards and guidelines including the Global Reporting Initiative (GRI) G3 Sustainability Reporting Guidelines (2006), and the International Standards Organization (ISO) 26000 Guidance on Social Responsibility (2010), have also shaped our understanding of the ethical, social and environmental responsibilities of an MNC. The GRI and the ISO 26000 are voluntary guidelines that can be adopted by any organization to assist with the reporting of social and environmental issues to various stakeholders. Both the GRI and the ISO 26000 adopt the definition of sustainable development put forth by the United Nations World Commission on Economic Development (WCED) in 1987 which holds that 'Sustainable development is development that meets the needs of the present without compromising the ability of future generations to meet their own needs'. The ISO 26000 goes one step further, and links sustainable development with social responsibility by stating that social responsibility reflects the organization's responsibility to the environment and society, while sustainable development sums up the broader expectations of society. As such, 'an organization's social responsibility should be to contribute to sustainable development' (ISO, 2010: 9).

Although the GRI G3 Sustainability Reporting Guidelines do not explicitly define CSR, the ISO 26000 has made a significant contribution to the field through its extensive definition of social responsibility as:

> The responsibility of an organization for the impacts of its decisions and activities on society and the environment through transparent and ethical behaviour that:
> - Contributes to sustainable development, including health and the welfare of society;
> - Takes into account the expectations of stakeholders;
> - Is in compliance with acceptable laws and consistent with international norms of behavior; and
> - Is integrated throughout the organization and is practiced in its relationships.
> (ISO 26000, 2010, p. 3)

Table 9.1 ISO 26000 core subjects and issues of social responsibility

Core Subject: Human Rights
Issues: Due diligence, human rights risk situations, avoidance of complicity, resolving grievances, discrimination and vulnerable groups, civil and political rights, fundamental principles and rights at work.

Core Subject: Labour Practices
Issues: Employment and employment relationships, conditions of work and social protection, social dialogue, health and safety at work, human development and training in the workplace.

Core Subject: The Environment
Issues: Prevention of pollution, sustainable resource use, climate change mitigation and adaption, protection of the environment, biodiversity and restoration of natural habitats.

Core Subject: Fair Operating Practices
Issues: Anti-corruption, responsible political involvement, fair competition, promoting social responsibility in the value chain, respect for property rights.

Core Subject: Consumer Issues
Issues: Fair marketing, factual and unbiased information and fair contractual practices, protecting consumer's health and safety, sustainable consumption, consumer service, support, and complaint and dispute resolution, consumer data protection and privacy, access to essential services, education and awareness.

Core Subject: Community Involvement and Development
Issues: Community involvement, education and culture, employment creation and skills development, technology development and access, wealth and income creation, health, social investment.

Source: ISO 26000 (2010).

The ISO 26000 elaborates upon six core subjects of social responsibility including: human rights, labour practices, the environment, fair operating practices, consumer issues, and community involvement and development (see Table 9.1). This results in a comprehensive guideline for socially responsible behaviour that expands the limits of what is traditionally thought of as being socially responsible, in an effort to address the ethical dilemmas faced by today's MNCs. For example, the subject of 'consumer issues' is progressive in its focus on topics such as data protection and privacy, customer service and dispute resolution, access to essential services, and fair marketing and contractual practices. Our increasingly connected and electronic world puts issues such as these at the forefront of the discussion of ethical practices, especially given the amount of electronic data that can now be collected, stored, and potentially used for less than ethical purposes.

In this chapter, we emphasize how the type of social or environmental activities will vary across firms and industries. We will therefore continue to use

CSR as an umbrella concept, but also emphasize that MNCs must determine which CSR activities are strategically important to create value for both the firm and society. It is important to note that differences across national borders related to institutional contexts, stakeholder expectations and regulatory environments can create ethical dilemmas and 'moral free space' for MNCs (Kolk and van Tulder, 2010). The economic, ethical, social, and environmental trade-offs MNCs make are directly affected by their managers' underlying attitudes and approaches to business ethics. The next section provides a historical overview of CSR, with a focus on how and why CSR became a significant factor in today's business environment.

9.3 The evolution of corporate social responsibility

With the end of World War II came unprecedented economic growth that led business schools to begin to look at the responsibility of business to the society in which it operates. The late 1950s gave rise to a new social consciousness, with citizens becoming more aware and less accepting of current economic, political, and social conditions. It is during this time that respected business schools such as Harvard, Columbia, Berkley, and Northwestern started to offer required courses in the area of 'business and society' (Epstein, 1998). Early debates in the field of business and society attempted to define what it meant to be a socially responsible business, and generally focused on expanding the responsibilities of business beyond what was economically and legally required.

The 1970s saw an increasing cynicism regarding corporate responsibility and society. Nobel Prize winning economist Milton Friedman famously stated in the *New York Times* that executives have a 'responsibility to conduct business in accordance with their [that is shareholders] desires, which will be to make as much money as possible while conforming to the basic rules of the society, both those embodied in law and those embodied by ethical custom' (1970: p. 33). Friedman makes several arguments against CSR including: (1) socially motivated goals will divert managers' attention from the primary goal of increasing shareholder wealth; (2) CSR-related activities are an expense to the firm that detracts from bottom line financial performance; (3) managers are 'woefully ignorant' when it comes to social issues, so will add little value to society by addressing social need; and (4) CSR is akin to taxation without representation, as shareholders are essentially 'taxed' through philanthropic donations yet have no say in where the money will be spent.

At the same time as Milton Freidman was vehemently arguing against the social responsibility of business, the business environment was undergoing significant change that was not conducive to social or environmental values. The beginning of globalization, increased competition from foreign firms, long-term wage stagnation, as well as an economic downturn in the late 1970s meant that companies were concentrating on simply surviving as opposed to their responsibility to society. Epstein (1998) argues that it was these very conditions that led to market manipulations, bribery, insider trading, and a disregard for environmental health and safety that characterized business in the early 1980s.

Criticism of the perceived moral and ethical decay in both business and politics in the early 1980s led to a renewed interest in business ethics, ethical codes of conduct, and corporate social responsibility. The early years of globalization resulted in MNCs having to face new ethical dilemmas on a global scale and, due in large part to improved technology and the internet, these ethical dilemmas often played out in the court of public opinion. International criticism in the early 1990s of the exploitation of those in developing countries by MNCs such as Shell, Nestlé, Gap, and Nike led to substantial changes in CSR-related practices and the way MNCs viewed their responsibility to society. Socially responsible practices were bolstered by academic work that sought to legitimize business practices that exceeded the minimal standards set by law. Freeman (1984) developed stakeholder theory, a major perspective in current CSR research that urges managers to consider the needs of various interest groups that are not directly connected to the corporation. In 1997 Elkington introduced the triple bottom line (economic, social, and environmental factors) as managers came to realize the increasing risk to both the financial and reputational value of their firms as a direct result of failing to behave in a socially responsible manner.

This century has seen a dramatic increase in the attention paid to ethical, social, and environmental responsibilities both by academics and by practitioners in MNCs. It now seems that the fundamental question has changed from 'Should an MNC be socially and environmentally responsible?' to 'How socially and environmentally responsible should an MNC be?'. MNCs are large, complex organizations that are now tasked with the equally large and complex challenge of being socially and environmentally responsible in a dynamic business environment. An MNC must balance profitability with a multitude of demands from stakeholders in the various environments in which it operates. The section that follows will explore current topics that MNCs face including the economic, legal, ethical, and social responsibilities of an MNC, the link between social responsibility and profitability, and strategically implemented CSR.

9.4 The economic, legal, ethical, and social responsibilities of an MNC

One self-evident consequence of increased globalization is that MNCs have broadened their sphere of power and influence. Some of the largest MNCs have so much economic power that in developing country settings they are capable of overshadowing local governments as the main engines of industrial development. This is one of the main reasons that ethical, social and environmental demands are increasingly being directed at MNCs. That is not to say that such demands are not levelled at purely domestic firms but that they are particularly pronounced for globally visible MNCs. The legitimate demands placed on MNCs by various stakeholders raises an interesting and fundamental question – What are the economic, legal, ethical, and social, responsibilities of an MNC?

Carroll (1991) attempted to answer this question by proposing his widely cited pyramid of corporate social responsibility (Figure 9.1). For Carroll, CSR consists of four hierarchical responsibilities: economic, legal, ethical, and philanthropic. The foundation of any business is its economic responsibility to society, which includes being profitable, providing employment

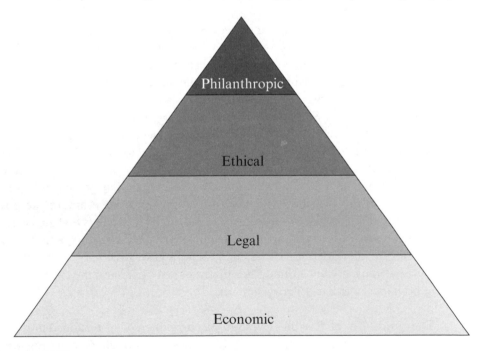

Source: Carroll (1991).

Figure 9.1 Carroll's pyramid of corporate social responsibility

opportunities, and generating taxes. MNCs are often criticized for placing profit maximization over social responsibility, yet it is important to keep in mind that the primary function of business in modern society is to be the economic engine for the world economy. In the current hypercompetitive global economy, the economic reality is that MNCs who do not focus on generating profits will soon find themselves forced out of the market.

As an MNC strives to meet its primary goal of making a profit, it must also meet or exceed the minimum legal responsibilities set by various local and federal governments. Carroll (1991) states that it is important to operate in a manner that is consistent with the expectations of government and law, but MNCs that operate in several countries are often faced with a difficult question – Whose laws do we obey? As MNCs expand overseas in an effort to reduce costs and gain market share they are often faced with different, and often less stringent laws regarding labour practices and environmental protection. This raises both ethical and operational questions, as managers must decide if they will abide by the laws and regulations of the country in which they are headquartered, or will they abide by the laws of the host country and perhaps become the target of criticism from stakeholders and non-governmental organizations (NGOs).

In some countries it may even be difficult to determine which level of government to deal with, and even who the legitimate government is. This issue is particularly salient when looking at the amount of taxes paid to both federal and local governments. For example, in some African countries dictators come to power through brute military strength, often as the result of a bloody civil war. Some stakeholders and NGOs question the legitimacy of these governments, and MNCs have been accused of helping to fund civil wars simply because they paid taxes to the legitimate (although often temporary) federal government. Yet another issue arises when an MNC pays taxes to the federal government of a developing nation, and that government fails to distribute the funds to various local governments despite having protocol in place to do so. As a result, many local areas that are rich in natural resources see very little tax benefit when MNCs begin operations. In an effort to alleviate these issues, many MNCs have gone to great lengths to increase transparency around the amount of taxes paid and the expectations of both local and federal governments.

The third level of Carroll's pyramid of corporate social responsibility is a company's ethical responsibilities to society. Although Carroll suggests that managers should abide by ethical standards that are consistent with the morals and standards of society, he fails to explicitly state the extent of these obligations. Margolis and Walsh (2003) help to clarify this issue by looking at a company's moral duty to aid and respond. The first moral duty occurs when a firm directly contributes to or causes a certain condition. This duty suggests that if a firm causes harm such as environmental pollution, or even the potential to do harm, such as dangerous working conditions, then the firm has the duty to respond and should prevent these conditions from affecting others in society. Often MNCs run into trouble when they shirk this basic duty, and become the target of various stakeholder and NGO actions.

The second duty to respond occurs when the firm benefits from an unjust condition to which it did not contribute. An example of this type of duty would be paying a living wage to employees in developing countries. MNCs do not set the standards for minimum wage in these countries, yet they may benefit from paying extremely low wages to employees. This moral principle suggests that it would be unethical for an MNC to exploit workers by paying less than a living wage while contributing to long hours of work with a low standard of living. Another example would be a firm that sells a product that is banned in one country for safety reasons to consumers in another country with lower safety regulations. As an example, the province of Quebec in Canada has recently come under fire for the continued operation of four asbestos mines. Until 2010, Quebec produced up to 150,000 tonnes of asbestos annually, with 90 per cent of the carcinogenic material being sold to developing countries (CBC, 2012b). Production of asbestos continues in limited quantities in Quebec, despite the fact that the material has not been widely utilized in Canada since the 1980s due to the well-documented health effects from exposure.

Eells and Walton (1974), two pioneers in the field of social responsibility, suggest that CSR should be thought of as 'good neighbourliness' involving two distinct processes: (1) not doing things to spoil the neighbourhood, and (2) volunteering to help solve neighbourhood problems. The aforementioned moral duties to respond when a firm benefits from an unjust condition to which it did not contribute will help guide an MNC in its effort to 'not do things to spoil the neighbourhood'. However, MNCs are also faced with the expectation from various stakeholders to 'help solve neighbourhood problems'. The idea that an MNC has an ethical or moral responsibility to solve neighbourhood problems remains controversial, and reflects a third ethical duty to respond out of benevolence.

Acting in a benevolent manner reflects the philanthropic responsibilities of Carroll's (1991) pyramid of corporate social responsibility, which suggests that firms should be good corporate citizens and contribute resources to the community to provide social benefit. However, unfocused corporate philanthropy has been criticized by many, including neoclassical economist Milton Freidman, as simply being an expense to the MNC with little to no return on investment. Although these critics may have a valid point, several scholars, most notably Michael Porter and Mark Kramer (2002, 2006, 2011) argue that strategically implemented CSR practices can represent a win/win situation in which value is created for both society and the MNC. This chapter will now look at why an MNC should take seriously its ethical, social and environmental responsibilities. Selected topics include the increasing importance of stakeholders, the link between social responsibility and financial performance, and the mutual value created to both the firm and society when an MNC strategically implements its CSR practices.

9.5 Why an MNC should focus on ethical, social, and environmental responsibilities

Stakeholders

Freeman's (1984) stakeholder theory highlights the importance of considering the needs of various groups that are affected by the daily operation of an MNC. Stakeholder theory is an important development in the social responsibility of a MNC as it shifted the focus from profit maximization to gaining a social license to operate through engaging with various stakeholder groups. The basic argument is that an MNC will not be able to make a profit if society does not grant it a social license to operate. Thus, stakeholder theory is gaining in legitimacy in the business world, as it suggests that meeting the needs of various stakeholder groups is essential for the economic performance of the firm (Clarkson 1995; Donaldson and Preston, 1995).

As 'global corporate citizens' MNCs have to accept that they may be held accountable for their impact on the economic and political development of the local communities in which operate. Given the negative attention that MNCs such as Nike and Royal Dutch Shell received from NGOs for perceived ethical violations in the 1990s, most MNCs now recognize the importance of engaging with a wider range of stakeholder, particularly those MNCs with valuable and correspondingly vulnerable brand names. However, meeting the needs of stakeholders is not an easy task, particularly for an MNC that operates in many countries, as stakeholders may have conflicting or competing views with regard to how an MNC should approach its responsibility to society.

The primary criticism of stakeholder theory is that it suggests that managers should focus on satisfying the needs of various stakeholder groups, but fails to provide recommendations as to which stakeholder groups are most important. The ISO 26000 provides a very broad definition of a stakeholder as an 'individual or group that has any interest in any decision or activity of an organization' (ISO, 2010: 4). This definition suggests that practically any group or individual should be considered a stakeholder, and leaves few prescriptive recommendations for manager of MNCs.

Mitchell et al. (1997) have aided managers by suggesting that stakeholder groups can be prioritized on the basis of the power, urgency, and legitimacy of their claims. Yang and Rivers (2009), looking at CSR within MNC subsidiaries, identify a comprehensive list of relevant stakeholders. Two relevant groups of stakeholders emerge: those involved in the social context in which the firm operates including formal institutions, the community, NGOs and industry bodies; and those groups that are part of the organizational context including consumers, shareholders, employees, and parent firms. Despite the best efforts of both academics and practitioners, significant issues still remain surrounding how MNCs should best address the needs of various stakeholder groups.

NGOs: A unique stakeholder

There is no doubt that action taken by NGOs against corporations such as Nike, Gap, and Royal Dutch Shell helped to reshape the meaning of ethical, social, and environmental responsibility in the 1990s. Social and environmental advocacy from NGOs will continue so long as MNCs are willing to push ethical boundaries. However, partnerships between these former adversaries are becoming an increasingly popular means of strategically implementing CSR-related initiatives (Peloza and Falkenberg, 2009; Yaziji and Doh, 2009). When MNCs and NGOs work together they can utilize each other's core competencies, and may even develop new core competencies that would be costly, inefficient, and time-consuming for either MNCs or NGOs to develop in their own.

Yaziji (2004) suggests that NGOs have four key strengths that make them viable partners for MNCs. First, NGOs have a sense of legitimacy, which is to say that they legitimately care about a social issue and are committed to providing value to society. By partnering with an NGO, an MNC can show that it also legitimately cares about the same social issue. Second, NGOs have a keen awareness of social forces. By partnering with an NGO an MNC may be more in tune with social and environmental shifts in consumer preference and demand, resulting in a competitive advantage. Third, NGOs have distinct networks that are different from the traditional networks found in MNCs. Not only do NGOs have access to regulators, lobbyists, other NGOs, and legislators, they are also very efficient at gathering and disseminating information throughout these networks. Partnering with an NGO will provide an MNC with access to these non-traditional networks. Finally, and perhaps most importantly, NGOs have vast specialized technical expertise. Lawyers, scientists, technical experts, and policy analysts, many of whom have advanced graduate degrees, are employed by NGOs. An MNC may be able to partner with an NGO, and utilize the knowledge held within for the betterment of society.

Strategic partnerships between two MNCs are significantly complex to manage, even though both partners have the same goal – to make a profit. The level of complexity is multiplied in MNC/NGO partnerships, as one partner is seeking to increase value to the firm, while the other partner is seeking to add value to society. MNCs bring technical expertise as well as human and financial capital to the partnership, while NGOs bring human capital as well as social and technical expertise. However, the potentially adversarial nature of these partnerships makes for strange bedfellows. NGOs, much like MNCs, have valuable brands, and both brands may become damaged if either partner reneges on its promises. Berger et al. (2004) suggest that selecting the right NGO to partner with is essential to the survival and productivity of the partnership. Much like an alliance between MNCs, both the NGO and MNC must look at the strategic fit of the partner with regard to mission, resources, management, workforce, objective, product or cause, corporate culture, time lines, and definition of project success. Through successful partnerships, both the NGOs and MNCs have much to gain, with society being the ultimate benefactor in this unlikely union.

Doing well by doing good

The reputation and brand of an MNC is an intangible asset that can be worth much more than the physical assets of the firm. Roberts and Dowling (2002) claim empirical proof of a strong link between positive reputation and the financial performance of a firm, whereas Calvano (2007) views reputation to be a competitive advantage by preserving the firm's ability to operate effectively within the local community. History has shown that some multinationals have suffered reputational and financial consequences when they acted in a socially irresponsible fashion, making it clear that socially irresponsible behaviour may bring with it substantial costs. Although the financial and reputational damage to an MNC for even perceived unethical behaviour is undeniable, what is less clear is whether or not socially responsible firms do better financially in the long run.

The 'holy grail' of research on social responsibility is establishing the link between economic performance and socially responsibility. The basic question that researchers are trying to answer is 'Can an MNC do well through doing good?'. Meta-analyses by Margolis and Walsh (2003) and Orlitzky et al. (2003) provide some support of the link between social responsibility and financial performance. However, evidence of the link between financial performance and social responsibility is far from conclusive, perhaps due to the varying definitions of CSR utilized in the studies as well as different metrics for capturing financial data.

Neoclassical economists many very well have a point in their criticism of corporate philanthropy as a cost with no benefit to the MNC. However, research suggests that firms that strategically implement CSR could see greater financial performance. Hillman and Keim (2001) found CSR that addresses stakeholder needs to be positively correlated to financial performance, whereas CSR consisting of philanthropic donations did not have the same correlation. McWilliams and Siegel (2001) suggested that consumers are willing to pay a premium for socially responsible goods, and that an optimum level of CSR can be identified that maximizes profits while at the same time meets stakeholders' demands. Indeed, companies such as TOMS Shoes have built their brands on a foundation of social responsible behaviour. In 2006 Blake Mycoskie founded TOMS shoes based on a shoe design worn by Argentinean farmers, with the intention of donating one pair of shoes to a child in need for every pair of shoes that were sold. Through 'Friends of TOMS', a non-profit affiliate of TOMS shoes, more than 2,000,000 pairs of shoes have been donated to children in more than 44 countries around the world. Most recently, TOMS has expanded its product line to include eyewear and has maintained its 'One for One' philosophy of social responsibility. Mycoskie, realizing that sight-related disabilities are in most cases solvable, has pledged a pair of glasses or a sight-saving surgery for every pair of TOMS eyewear that is sold. It could certainly be argued that companies such as TOMS shoes, the BodyShop, and Ben & Jerry's have utilized socially responsible business practices to build a strong brand. However, these companies are generally the exception to the rule and were established by entrepreneurs who specifically set out to develop a socially conscious product.

Strategically implemented CSR

A growing body of literature on CSR and MNCs revolves around the need to reconcile a global strategy with adapting to the local environment of the host countries in which the MNC operates. Researchers are now beginning to employ the international strategies in empirical research on CSR (see

Chapter 3 for an overview of international strategies). Christmann (2004) finds MNCs that follow a global strategy also implement globally standardized environmental policies, and that standardization of environmental performance standards, environmental policies, and environmental communications results from pressures from different groups in the institutional environment. Husted and Allen (2006) make the distinction between 'local CSR', which meets the needs of the local community, and 'global CSR', which focuses more on macro issues with a global impact. Through their study of MNC subsidiaries in Mexico, Husted and Allen find that most MNCs place importance on global issues such as the environment and human rights, but firms that employ a high degree of local responsiveness in their product market activities also focus more on local CSR issues.

Muller (2006) points out that a global strategy may lead to an efficient transmission of CSR practices, but that implementation at the local level may lack ownership and legitimacy within the local community. Further, CSR developed at the local level may better meet the needs of the local community while at the same time bringing the organization more legitimacy within the local environment, however these practices may be fragmented and reactive. Muller's research on subsidiaries in the automotive industry in Mexico finds the most proactive subsidiaries with regard to CSR are given the most autonomy by headquarters, yet still closely follow the CSR strategy set by headquarters. MNCs with highly centralized control over their subsidiaries have the lowest CSR performance. Finally, Jamali (2010) finds that managers of subsidiaries in Lebanon have considerable autonomy to implement CSR practices based on the global guidelines set buy headquarters. However, these guidelines are often detached from the needs of the local community, thus diluting the potential value of most CSR initiatives.

The strategic implementation of CSR is fast becoming a key issue as MNCs try to address their ethical, social, and environmental responsibilities. For more than a decade, Michael Porter and Mark Kramer have been suggesting that strategically implemented CSR will result in both increased financial returns to the MNC as well as greater benefit to society. According to Porter and Kramer (2002), the overlap between social value to society and economic value to the firm can be identified through a focus on location advantages in and across geographical locations, categorized by Porter (1990b) as a diamond model of national competiveness (for an in-depth discussion of the diamond model in the context of MNCs, see Verbeke, 2009). MNCs that want to be more strategic in the implementation of their CSR-related efforts should focus on CSR-related efforts in one or more dimensions of the diamond model (Figure 9.2).

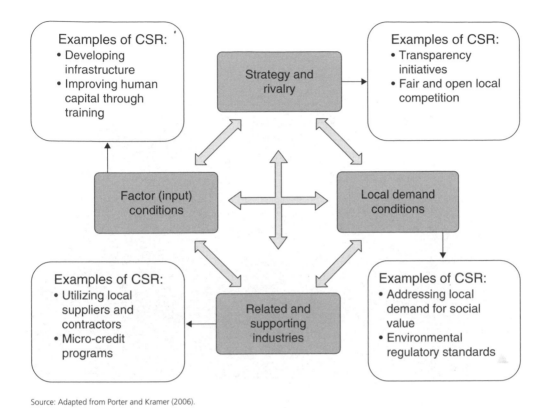

Source: Adapted from Porter and Kramer (2006).

Figure 9.2 Porter's (1990) diamond model and corporate social responsibility

An MNC may improve factor conditions through efforts such as employee training programs and investment in physical infrastructure within developing countries. Typically MNCs have focused CSR-related efforts on factor conditions, as investment in physical infrastructure is often required for the MNC to operate within developing countries. Second, an MNC may look at programs that increase demand conditions through efforts to expand the size and quality of local markets. An example addressing demand conditions includes something as simple as providing free wifi service (a social value) in an effort to attract more customers (value to the firm). Third, enhancing the context for strategy and rivalry can be done though efforts to increase transparency and reduce corruption. For example, the Extractive Industries Transparency Initiative (EITI) has been implemented by the extractive industry to ensure that payments to governments and government-linked entities are fully transparent. The EITI helps to ensure that host governments distribute taxes and revenue generated by mining and oil companies in a way that benefits those in the local community, while at the same time enhancing

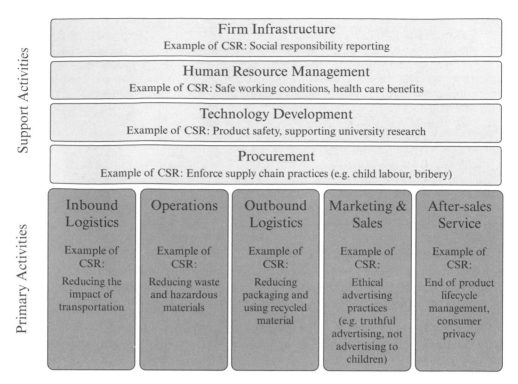

Source: Adapted from Porter and Kramer (2006).

Figure 9.3 The social impact of the value chain

the image and reputation of the industry. Finally, MNCs can strategically implement CSR by promoting related and supporting industries. Addressing related and supporting industries is often accomplished through working with local contractors in developing countries. Microfinance programs, which involve providing low interest loans to entrepreneurs in developing countries that would otherwise not qualify, are also an effective form of CSR that addresses related and supporting industries.

Porter and Kramer (2006) further expand on the idea of strategically implemented CSR by suggesting that each aspect of a firm's value chain can be infused with socially responsible practices that can add value to both the firm and society. Figure 9.3 shows how firms can be more socially responsible though the primary activities of inbound logistics, operations, outbound logistics, marketing and sales, and after service sales, as well as through support activities including firm infrastructure, human resource management, technology development, and procurement.

Infusing the value chain with CSR-related activities leads to improvements within the MNC, while concentrating on infusing the four factors of the diamond model with CSR will lead to improvements outside of the firm. In either case, the main point of strategically implemented CSR activities is that both the firm and society gain value. In their latest work on strategically implemented CSR, Porter and Kramer (2011) introduce the concept of shared value, which they define as 'policies and operating practices that enhance the competitiveness of a company while simultaneously advancing the economic and social conditions in the communities in which it operates' (p. 66). Porter and Kramer argue that the short-term economic approach to value creation held by most MNCs is outdated and comes at the expense of addressing the long-term needs and challenges faced by society. The authors suggest that the purpose of the corporation should be redefined as to create shared value, as this will bring long-term benefit to both the MNCs and to society.

9.6 Ethical issues that pose challenges across borders

Corruption and bribery

According to Transparency International (TI), an NGO that aims to fight corruption worldwide, corruption may be defined as the abuse of entrusted power for private gain. The organization differentiates between according-to-rule corruption and against-the-rule corruption: 'Facilitation payments, where a bribe is paid to receive preferential treatment for something that the bribe receiver is required to do by law, constitute the former. The latter, on the other hand, is a bribe paid to obtain services the bribe receiver is prohibited from providing' (www.transparency.org).

Transparency International was founded in 1993, being dedicated to increasing government accountability and curbing national and international corruption. It monitors and reports on global corruption and bribery and publishes its findings on an annual basis. Since 1995, TI has published the 'Corruption Perceptions Index' (CPI) which is based on several different surveys among business people, academics and risk analysts. According to the 2011 CPI rankings of 182 countries, the top ten least corrupt nations were New Zealand, Denmark, Finland, Sweden, Singapore, Norway, the Netherlands, Australia, Switzerland, and Canada (in that order). At the bottom of the ranking we find Somalia, North Korea, Myanmar, Afghanistan, Uzbekistan, Turkmenistan, Sudan, Iraq, Haiti, and Venezuela. There is an obvious pattern to the ranking. The lowest levels of corruption are found in wealthy, developed nations and the highest in poor, less developed countries. High levels of corruption tend to be a feature of countries that are undergoing profound transitions, such as many of the former communist bloc states in Eastern Europe. It is worth noting that the CPI only measures corruption involving public servants or officials, and that covert payments to finance political campaigns as well as money laundering and bribery involving MNCs are not included.

Corruption has multiple consequences and may be detrimental to goals such as peace, democracy, and execution of human rights. In economic terms corruption is regarded as hampering efficiency and growth, thus leading to a depletion of national wealth in the countries involved. The World Economic Forum's Partnering Against Corruption Initiative – Principles for Countering Bribery distinguishes between different categories of corruption:

- Bribes: bribery carried out directly or through third parties, including subsidiaries, joint ventures, agents, brokers, suppliers or any other intermediary under a company's effective control.
- Political contributions: direct or indirect contributions to political parties, party officials, candidates, or organizations involved in politics.
- Facilitation payments: small payments that are made to secure or speed up the performance of routine actions to which a company is already entitled.
- Gifts, hospitality and expenses: the offer and receipt of gifts, hospitality or expenses in cases where such arrangements could improperly affect, or is perceived to improperly affect, the outcome of business operations and transactions.

In some countries, corruption involving bribes is so widespread that it may be difficult or impossible for international companies to deal with the public authorities and local companies without becoming involved. In its most extreme form corruption is institutionalized to such an extent that public servants are dependent on such income in order to secure a standard of living above the subsistence level.

Child labour

It has been estimated that the exploitation of children through child labour occurs in more than two-thirds of all the countries in the world, with many of the children involved performing hazardous work tasks. In 2010 the International Labour Organization (ILO) estimated that approximately 306 million children between the ages of five and 17 were child labourers. Among these, 176 million were between five and 14 years old (Diallo et al., 2010). It is important to keep in mind that the concept of child labour refers to permanent employment that makes schooling either difficult or impossible, and not to children working part-time in family businesses or on farms while attending school. Child labour is in part a product of the fact that children lack the resources needed to establish unions or other types of organizations that could protect them and secure their rights. It also lies in the fact that as child labour often replaces adult labour, their unemployed or underemployed parents have no choice but to force them to work.

According to the ILO, child labour slated for abolition falls into the following three categories:

- Labour that is performed by a child who is under the minimum age specified for that kind of work (as defined by national legislation, in accordance with accepted international standards), and that is thus likely to impede the child's education and full development.
- Labour that jeopardizes the physical, mental or moral well-being of a child, either because of its nature or because of the conditions in which it is carried out, known as hazardous work.
- The unconditional worst forms of child labour, which are internationally defined as slavery, trafficking, debt bondage and other forms of forced labour, forced recruitment of children for use in armed conflict, prostitution and pornography, and illicit activities.

The push for the abolition of child labour is not without its critics, as this is a complex global issue for many in developing countries. The following stems from an editorial in *Business Week*:

> Culture can be a serious problem. Child labour in factories is opposed by anti-globalization forces, but in many countries it is a major source of income, keeping families together and girls out of prostitution. Besides, it is commonly accepted on American farms today and was legal during the long period when the U.S. itself was a developing country. . . . Imposing high 21st century labour and environmental standards on developing countries runs the risk of appearing hypocritical and undermining growth. (*Business Week*, 2001: 64)

Child labour itself is a not so distant phenomenon historically in western countries, and even the idea of universal schooling is relatively recent. Critics contend that automatically abolishing products made by child labour might be harmful to children, although it may make consumers feel morally good. As a consequence, children may be forced into more hazardous work such as prostitution and agriculture. A UNICEF report found that after the 'Child

Labour Deterrence Act' was introduced in the United States, an estimated 50,000 children were dismissed from garment industry jobs in Bangladesh. Many of them moved to jobs such as 'stone-crushing, street hustling, and prostitution'. According to the report, boycotts are viewed as 'blunt instruments with long-term consequences that can actually harm rather than help the children involved' (UNICEF, 1997).

Gender discrimination

In the United States and most European countries gender equality has been established in law, yet women are significantly underrepresented at managerial levels. Despite having full freedom of mobility and equal rights to education, the vast majority of women in these countries tend to earn significantly less than their male counterparts. Gender discrimination challenges can be difficult to address in even the most developed nations of the world, and MNCs face additional challenges in other countries due to cultural and religious norms. There is no doubt that subsidiaries of MNCs operating in fundamentalist Islamic countries or regions have virtually no degrees of freedom when it comes to treating female employees in more 'Western ways'. MNCs in Saudi Arabia cannot, for instance, insist that native female employees be allowed to drive cars because this is the norm in Western countries. Nor could an MNC demand that Saudi women and men work together in their Saudi Arabian subsidiary. Likewise a subsidiary of an Arab MNC located in the United States would be obliged to adhere to the Equal Employment Opportunity (EEO) regulations that permeate US work life. In this sense there is a set of 'givens' in all contexts in the form of legal imperatives that must be abided by. However, this does not mean that MNCs should not seek out opportunities to contribute to changing discriminatory conditions, for example by providing education and training for women and by providing equal compensation for equal work regardless of gender.

In particular, dilemmas occur when MNCs which have personnel policies that condemn gender discrimination and promote equal opportunities set up subsidiaries in countries or regions where social and cultural norms allow and perhaps even stimulate discrimination against women. In countries where gender inequalities are established by law, the company risks legal prosecution if it applies its domestic personnel policy in that country. Then it may choose not to operate in such countries, but that may involve substantial costs while at same time not contributing to helping women in these countries.

9.7 Summary

In this chapter, we have emphasized that the ethical, social and environmental responsibilities of an MNC have changed over time, and are indeed still changing to address important social issues on a global scale. An MNC must now look at its economic, legal, ethical, and social obligations to stakeholders in all of the countries in which it operates, and try to strike a balance between global policies and local adaptation. Although the economic case has been made that companies can 'do well through doing good', the future of CSR practices seems to be strategically aligning the creation of economic value with the creation of social value, representing a win–win situation for society. Finally, MNCs operate in a varied and dynamic global environment with differing laws, regulations, forms of government and cultural norms. Operating on a global scale means that MNCs will not only face complex ethical and social issues, but that the MNC will be looked at as both the cause and the solution to some of the world's largest issues.

Attached to this chapter is a case study featuring Cermaq, a Norwegian fish farm and feed company that came under both social and economic pressure for its CSR related policies. The case illuminates key ethical dilemmas that MNCs face including balancing profit making with social responsibility, facing pressure from NGOs and governments, reporting on social issues, and ultimately creating shared value through socially responsible business practices that ultimately increase bottom line financial performance.

NOTE

1   Even the term corporate social responsibility is falling out of favor, with many practitioners simply using the term social responsibility.

Case H

Cermaq: from activist target to sustainability leader

Sveinung Jørgensen and Lars Jacob Tynes Pedersen

H.1   Introduction

This case firstly describes the Norwegian fish farm and fish feed company Cermaq ASA (hereinafter referred to as Cermaq), especially focusing on (1) the crisis in the Chilean aquaculture industry in 2007, (2) the critique directed at Cermaq, and (3) the substantial measures Cermaq has since undertaken in order to make the company and the industry more sustainable. Secondly, the case discusses these changes in light of a corporate social responsibility (CSR) framework, which focuses on the 'why?', 'how?' and 'so what?' of corporate responsibility (Jørgensen and Pedersen 2011: 2013). Finally, the case offers recommendations for future operations based on the analysis of the motivation (why?), integration (how?) and the effect (so what?) of CSR initiatives initiated by Cermaq after the fish health crisis in Chile.

The case is set in 2012, five years after the initial crisis, and we look back at the time before and after Cermaq's turnaround. The Cermaq crisis is a relevant case in this regard because it involves a multinational corporation (MNC) that was exposed to pressure from activists and non-governmental organizations (NGOs), thus triggering a CSR crisis. The reason that Cermaq became a target for the activists was its poor environmental performance with regard to fish health and control of fish populations. In a word, Cermaq's core activities were claimed to be unsustainable and environmentally destructive. The case is especially relevant for CSR in an international context, since it involves the OECD and its Guidelines for Multinational Enterprises. These guidelines are described as:

> far reaching recommendations addressed by governments to multinational enterprises operating in or from adhering countries. They provide voluntary principles and standards for responsible business conduct in areas such as employment and

industrial relations, human rights, environment, information disclosure, combating bribery, consumer interests, science and technology, competition, and taxation. (OECD, 2011)

Norway, as a member of the OECD, is required to establish a National Contact Point (NCP) for Responsible Business, a so-called grievance mechanism.[1] The NCP handles complaints related to possible violations of the OECD guidelines. As we shall see, the NCP arranged for mediation between activists who targeted Cermaq and the company, which resulted in a joint statement concerning Cermaq, aquaculture and sustainability. Moreover, both the crisis in 2007 and the responsibility initiatives implemented by Cermaq thereafter, have received international attention. This may imply that other MNCs have been affected by Cermaq's 'best practice', both related to the integration of responsibility in its business model and how sustainability is expected to be an integrated part of its annual report.

In this case, we will focus specifically on Cermaq's role in the development of the fish health crisis in Chile in 2007 and how Cermaq managed it. We will do so by describing the content and the result of the mediation between Cermaq and the activists, and on the subsequent overhaul of the company's orientation.

H.2   Case overview

Cermaq is a Norwegian MNC that operates in Norway, Canada, Chile, Vietnam and the United Kingdom. It was founded in 1995 as a state-owned, grain-trading company called Statkorn Holding. The company soon moved into aquaculture, and according to the company web site it is today one of the 'global leading companies in farming of salmonides [that is production of Atlantic Salmon] and in fish feed production'. The company changed its name to Cermaq in 2001, and it was listed on the Oslo Stock Exchange in 2005. Currently, 43.5 per cent of the company is owned by the Government of Norway.

Cermaq's fish farming activities are branded Mainstream, while the brand name EWOS is used for the production of fish feed. Cermaq has about 4000 employees, and in 2011 Mainstream's total production of salmon was 108,500 tonnes, which is equivalent to a market share of 6 per cent. In the same year EWOS' total production of fish feed was 1,081,400 tonnes, which is equivalent to a market share of around 36 per cent. In total, this resulted in a revenue of NOK 11.634 billion (approximately €1,580 billion) and a net result of NOK 793 million (approximately €108 billion).

On May 19 2009 the Norwegian Contact Point for Responsible Business received a complaint from two NGOs: Friends of the Earth Norway and The Forum for Environment and Development (ForUM).[2] In this complaint, Cermaq was accused of violating OECD's Guidelines for Multinational Enterprises. At first, Cermaq rejected the complaint. Later, however, the Norwegian Contact Point for Responsible Business arranged for mediation between the two parties. This resulted in a joint statement that was presented on August 10 2011. Therein, Cermaq and the two NGOs agreed that:

1. The sustainable use of natural resources, including the precautionary principle and accountability in meeting social and environmental challenges, is crucial for the aquaculture industry's future.
2. The Chilean aquaculture industry, including Cermaq, should have been operated in a more sustainable manner before the fish health crisis in Chile in 2007. Since 2007 Cermaq has undertaken constructive measures in their own business operations and contributed in developing knowledge, making the industry more sustainable.
3. The complaint by Friends of the Earth Norway and ForUM included claims about Cermaq and its business that have been refuted.
4. Future cooperation and contacts shall be based on mutual trust and clarification of facts.

We will return to the content of this joint statement. First, however, we will turn the attention to 2007 and the fish health crisis in Chile that led to the activists' complaint in 2008. Cermaq's operations in Chile started in 2000, both with fish feed production and fish farming. In 2004, by an acquisition of the remaining shares in the Chilean farming company Salmones Andes, Cermaq became one of the largest producers of salmon in Chile. Until the fish health crisis in 2007, Chile experienced over a decade with huge growth in salmon aquaculture.[3] This made the country the second largest salmon and trout producer after Norway. In 2006, Chile produced 38 per cent, while Norway produced 39 per cent of the world's salmon volume. Thus, in 2006, salmon was Chile's third largest export product in terms of value, representing 3.9 per cent of their total exports. Then, in 2007, the Chilean salmon industry experienced a serious setback, as a result of an outbreak of a disease called infectious salmon anemia (ISA) (Godoy et al., 2008). In addition, there was a serious outbreak of sea lice, and Cermaq was also criticized for the use of antibiotics in fish farming. Finally, the company had experienced problems keeping the farmed fish inside the closed-off areas in which they are farmed, which may threaten non-farmed fish populations. As a result of the crisis, the production in Chile was reduced from 400,000 to 100,000 tonnes from 2005 to 2010.

At the time of the crisis, Cermaq was one of the dominating actors in the Chilean aquaculture industry. Hence, Cermaq's financial results were seriously affected by the fish disease, since as much as a whole year of salmon production was destroyed. The fish crisis also affected the price of salmon worldwide, and both Cermaq and the aquaculture industry were harmed by negative reputation effects and decreasing trust following the self-inflicted crisis. In the joint statement described above, Cermaq admit that they played an active role in the fish crisis. For instance, the two parties agree that '[t]he density of fish farms was too high in several places in . . . Chile, and the procedures required to prevent disease in fish were insufficient.' Moreover, both parties recognize that warnings were issued. In concrete terms, this implies that the fish crisis was in part created by the fish farming practices of Cermaq, wherein the conditions for fish health were poor and rather conducive for disease.

The statement also concludes that '[w]here government regulation does not ensure the sustainability of aquaculture, the industry should take its share of responsibility'. Thus, the joint statement expresses that Cermaq could and should have used the knowledge and the regulatory framework in Norway, since employing this competence in Chile could have led Cermaq to make efforts to influence legislation in Chile, and thus may have prevented the crisis. Cermaq were well aware of the dangers of high density, which allowed for higher production levels, but carried higher risk. Regardless, Cermaq chose to operate with lower standards in Chile than in their Norwegian production, and taking on this level of risk did not pay off.

In the joint statement, the NGOs recognize that Cermaq have now learned from the crisis and have made positive changes to prevent fish disease both in Chile and in Cermaq's global business. Both parties underline that best practices from one geographical area should be used across operations globally in order to ensure sustainability. Together, the two parties have developed a 'basis for sustainable aquaculture'. Therein, Cermaq states that the company has 'a responsibility for people, communities and environment affected by its activities, and that Cermaq activity should be organized so as not to undermine the potential for future production based on the same resources'.

In the joint statement, this is further explained by highlighting that Cermaq will aim for leadership in social responsibility in the aquaculture industry, and that it will strive for excellence on environmental initiatives in its industry by contributing to the development and use of environmentally friendly technology. The joint statement also focuses on the precautionary principle (as defined in the OECD Guidelines for Multinational Enterprises), as well as human rights and the rights of indigenous people and workers' rights. Finally, it is stated that:

> Cermaq will continue reporting against sustainability indicators, which are anchored at the level of its board, based on Global Reporting Initiative (GRI) and customized indicators specifically designed for the business of aquaculture. Cermaq intends to continue the practice of external verification by an independent third party. In the further development of its qualitative and quantitative indicators, Cermaq will draw on feedback from both internal and external sources, including groups who may be affected by the business.

As the title of this case reveals, only five years after the crisis in Chile, Cermaq is perceived as a sustainability leader. According to Cermaq's website, the company's slogan is 'Sustainable aquaculture', and their vision 'is to be an internationally leading company within aquaculture, with a particular focus on sustainable production of feed for salmon and trout, and the farming of salmon and trout'. They moreover argue that '[o]nly sustainable production can ensure a foundation for long-term production. We work with transparency and we engage in constructive dialogue with stakeholders to ensure the continuous improvement of our operations.'

This strategic approach and Cermaq's efforts to integrate responsibility and sustainability metrics in its annual reports has received much attention. In the July 2012 edition of Seafood Intelligence's benchmarking of the world's top 35 salmon and trout farming companies' endeavours on corporate, social and environmental responsibility (CSER) reporting, Cermaq is – for the second time – ranked as number one. In a comment on the price, CEO of Cermaq, Jon Hindar, claims that '[t]hrough transparent reporting we tell openly about our sustainability results and invite our stakeholders to make up their own opinion. Transparent reporting is the best basis for dialogue with stakeholders and continuous improvement. I encourage everyone to look at our reporting and results at www.report2011.cermaq.com'.

Seafood Intelligence describes how Cermaq's integrated annual and sustainability report is based on the Global Reporting Initiative (GRI). Moreover, it is expanded with customized indicators for aspects where GRI does not have indicators for fish farming and fish feed production, such as medicine use, sea lice, marine index, etc. (Seafood Intelligence, 2012). This means that Cermaq bases its performance measurement and management on the best practice of GRI, while at the same time breaking ground in developing its own appropriate measures. For this work, Cermaq was awarded the 'IR-Stockman prize 2012' in the category of small and medium-sized listed companies in Norway. In its assessment, the jury highlighted 'Cermaq's equal treatment of market participants, transparency and credibility in its information, and the environmental and social responsibility'.[4]

In the following section, we will introduce a theoretical framework of CSR. The framework will subsequently be used to discuss some of the main responsibility features of the Cermaq case introduced thus far.

H.3 Theoretical backdrop: the *why, how* and *so what* of CSR

There are three questions related to CSR that typically arise in conversation with business leaders, investors and others who are interested in corporate performance: (1) What is the rationale for businesses for actively taking responsibility? (2) How should companies who want to take responsibility do this fruitfully? And finally: (3) what effects can be expected? Will they be successful, and will the measures have a measurable impact on society and the environment?

These are all good questions, and they comply with several of the main lines of the CSR literature as discussed in Chapter 9. It is today commonly recognized that all organizations have a responsibility that extends beyond their economic and legal obligations.[5] However, there is still uncertainty regarding what this responsibility really entails. Consequently, there is no one universally accepted definition of CSR. A common theme found in the different understandings of CSR is that it is about a balancing of values. There may be a balancing of instrumental values (the organization's purpose, for example profit or other objectives) and moral values (for example justice, care, sustainability). In the corporate context, this balancing of values is typically illustrated by the logic of the triple bottom line, which reflects a balancing between economic values, social values and environmental values (see, for example, Elkington, 1998). The general idea is that socially responsible companies have the ability to balance these three types of values in their activities and thereby protect the interests of legitimate stakeholders.

Another significant feature of CSR is captured in Carroll's (1991) perspective on CSR and the tension in current discourse, as discussed in Chapter 9. Figure H.1 illustrates the three main positions: (1) Friedman's (1970) focus on limited responsibility, (2) the idea of extended (and unequivocal) responsibility to conduct its business in a manner that is consistent with sustainable social and ecological systems (see, for example, Zsolnai and Ims, 2006; Ingebrigtsen and Jakobsen, 2007), and (3) the central position of substantial

Substantial
responsibility

Limited
responsibility

Extended
responsibility

Figure H.1 Corporate responsibility: a tension between extremes – and a middle way

responsibility for addressing all legitimate stakeholders who are substantially affected by the organization's activities (Freeman, 1984).

What level of social responsibility one ascribes to organizations will naturally be related to which of these three positions one accepts. Moreover, which of the perspectives one accepts has far-reaching consequences for the way that organizations actually take responsibility for their actions. We propose that the differences in the perception of social responsibility are linked to the answers of these questions:

1. To whom is the organization responsible?
2. For what is the organization responsible?
3. What are the limits of the organization's responsibility?

The first question corresponds to the identification of the organization's stakeholders. The second question deals with what ways and to what extent the organization is accountable to those stakeholders. The third question – and perhaps the most difficult one – is about considering the limits of responsibility of the organization, and is thus a question about an assessment of what may reasonably be expected of an organization (see, for example, Messner, 2009).

Moreover, we argue that corporate responsibility is characterized by three essential properties of any corporate action (Jørgensen and Pedersen, 2013). First, there is the question of why firms invest in CSR. This is a question of motivation. Second, there is the question of how companies that invest in CSR integrate this into their corporate strategy and core activities. It is thus a question of integration. Finally, there is the question of so what – that is, how investments in CSR affect the company's performance. It is thus a question of efficacy.

The question of company performance may seem irrelevant in the context of responsibility. However, broadly speaking, we can say that the overarching question of business is: how can companies achieve high performance over time? In addition, we can add the strategically oriented question: why do some companies achieve higher performance than others? In traditional economic theory, these questions are entirely oriented towards economic performance – that is towards achieving competitive advantage that leads to sustained and growing profitability. In this case description, however, we operate with a multidimensional performance concept. Hence, in addition to assessing the company based on financial performance measures, we also consider it based on social and environmental performance metrics. This is in line with the triple bottom line logic, and thus implies an expansion of the corporate performance space.

In order to discuss the Cermaq case, we distinguish between three dimensions of CSR practices – motivation, integration and effect. We use these three dimensions to show how companies can invest in CSR for different reasons, in different ways and with different results. This is done to understand three elements of CSR practice: (1) why firms invest in CSR, for which we divide between intrinsic and extrinsic motivation, (2) how CSR initiatives are integrated in the enterprise, for which we distinguish between measures that affect the company's core activities and those that do not, and (3) the outcome of this for business, for which we distinguish between measures that have positive profitability and reputational effects for the company and those that do not. These three dimensions are visualized in Figure H.2 below:

Source: Based on Jørgensen and Pedersen (2013).

Figure H.2 Three dimensions of CSR

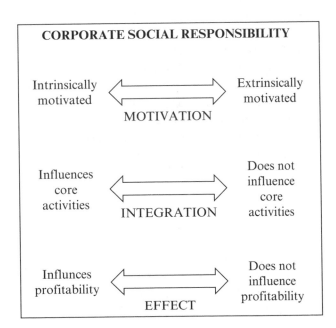

H.4   CSR analysis

In this section, we discuss the Cermaq case in light of corporate social responsibility. We base the discussion on the questions of the 'why?', 'how?' and 'so what?' of CSR, each of which is treated in the following. We thereby provide a theoretically informed discussion of Cermaq's turnaround, and the changes in their rationale, their strategies and operations, and how this led to new outcomes for the organization.

Motivation: why did Cermaq (not) invest in CSR?

It is nearly impossible to really know why people or organizations do the things they do. This implies that actors' intentions can only be interpreted. In turn, to a certain degree, we can only hypothesize on why Cermaq did not conduct their business operations responsibly before the crisis, and why they decided to invest in CSR afterwards. In other words, it is difficult to tell if these actions are intrinsically or extrinsically motivated. Intrinsically motivated actions are actions that are performed for their own sake, and where the motivation is thus inherent in the action itself, while externally motivated actions are performed as a means to achieve other goals or to avoid sanctions (Deci and Ryan, 2000).

We will approach Cermaq's motivation for CSR by exploring their expressed values before and after the crisis. We proposed above that what level of social responsibility one ascribes to organizations is dependent on which view one takes on the issue of responsibility. Here we distinguished between responsibility as either limited or extended, and we defined substantial responsibility as a middle way. We also argued that even though there are uncertainties regarding what CSR really entails, a common theme found in the different understandings of CSR is that it is about a balancing of values. Thus, there is a clear connection between the values that are prioritized by an organization, and its view of CSR. In the discussion below, we will illuminate how Cermaq's expressed values, as well as the company's view of responsibility, changed in only a few years' time.

In Cermaq's annual report for 2006, that is one year before the Chilean fish crisis, there are many signs that suggest that values like profit, growth and expansion dominated the company. It should, however, be noted that the concept 'sustainability' is mentioned (Cermaq, 2006). In the executive summary of the report, the first headline reads: 'Increased volume gives record result'. Thereafter, Cermaq's core values are spelled out, of which the first one claims: 'Our attention will always be concentrated on generating cash and opportunities for profit. All other goals come to naught if we fail.' Later in the report, the CEO at the time, Geir Isaksen, proudly announces that '2006 was Cermaq's best year so far. Our operating profit of NOK 1,311 million is more than twice as high as the previous record of NOK 636 million, set in 2005. This result puts us up with the absolute leaders with regards to fish farming efficiency and profitability.' Furthermore, Isaksen describes the future growth opportunities as bright, and claims that Cermaq's 'aim [is] to increase volumes by 20 percent in 2007'. At the same time, Isaksen and Cermaq explicitly argue that the company is balancing these economic values and objectives with sustainability, claiming that in order to be sustainable:

> [w]e have . . . adopted the Scouting motto as one of our core values, 'be prepared!' And we have chosen sustainable aquaculture as our vision. By sustainable, we mean that we will be able to withstand sharp economic fluctuations and act in a way which protects our long-term value creation. At the same time, our business will maintain a good balance with nature and society at large.

In retrospect, it is obvious that the values of growth and profit outbalanced the value sustainability, and that the scouting motto was not properly implemented in the company's operations. There are also traces that sustainability is considered a prerequisite for business success rather than a value in itself, and that their approach to sustainability was rather shallow. Hence, Cermaq was by no means prepared, and its business was not in balance with nature and society. The consequences were disastrous.

According to the annual report for 2007, that is the year of the crisis, the headline of CEO Isaksen's annual comment is 'a good, but demanding, year'. The devastating year was described as a good one for Cermaq because it 'achieved an operating result of 747 million, the second best in our history' (Cermaq, 2007: 10). Even after the fish health crisis, then, the main focus is on operating results. Later in the commentary, a description follows of what is denoted quite dissociated as 'the business situation' in Chile. Therein, it is stated that the so-called business situation 'has been much discussed in 2007', and that the focus of these discussions has been 'the spread of sea lice and the spread of ISA'. According to Isaksen and Cermaq, these 'problems have led to increased mortalities and lower growth rates in the fish. In this situation it has been difficult to anticipate production developments and in 2007 we have experienced significantly lower production volumes than expected at the start of the year'. It is also claimed that 'Chile will come back'.

In Cermaq's annual report for 2008, Cermaq and Isaksen admit that 2008 was a 'painful year' (Cermaq, 2008: 10): 'For our Chilean fish farming company, Mainstream Chile, this has brought about an operating loss of NOK 332 million. Two years ago, before the disease caught on, the same company showed a profit of NOK 555 million.' If we compare the CEO's comment at this time with the conclusion of the joint statement after the mediation with the NGOs, it is obvious that Cermaq at this point did not take the responsibility for the fish crisis. Rather, the crisis is described as an incident that 'caught on' and which has 'brought about' loss in profits. Hence, Cermaq's agency in creating the crisis is not acknowledged. This is in stark contrast to the joint statement from 2011, wherein Cermaq admits that it should have acted differently to avoid the crisis.

In the annual report of 2008, Isaksen also describes how the Chilean authorities and Cermaq 'co-operate in a comprehensive manner to change industry practices. [But it] will take a long time to implement these changes, and in the meantime, the production of Atlantic salmon in Chile will drop dramatically.' This suggests a view of responsibility that implies that Cermaq's only responsibility was to act in accordance with laws and regulations in Chile at the time. Moreover, the crisis is described as an exogenous factor, rather than an endogenous factor for which Cermaq was responsible, and which Cermaq could have prevented by behaving differently. In other words, Cermaq's perspective is reminiscent of what we earlier defined as a view of responsibility as 'limited'. Thus, there are few signs in this material of an intrinsically motivated approach to CSR.

Cermaq's view of responsibility may have changed in the subsequent period, that is after the complaint made by the NGOs. In Cermaq's annual report of 2009, the first of the core values has changed from 'Business mindedness' to 'Integrity', and Cermaq claims to 'adhere to a code of ethical values such as fairness, loyalty and respect, so that we maintain our pride and earn trust' (Cermaq, 2009). In 2009, the main headline of Isaksen's commentary – displayed on a background depicting a blue ocean – reads: 'Dedicated to sustainable aquaculture'. The following year, in 2010, Cermaq began communicating an integrated annual and sustainability report online, in which readers can navigate among key figures related to both financial performance and sustainability (cf. Cermaq, 2010). Such an integrated report was also made the following year (cf. Cermaq, 2011).

We will return to the content of these reports and the new CSR initiatives put forward by Cermaq below. Before we do so, we propose that there are reasons to believe that the annual reports from 2009, 2010 and 2011, together with the content of the joint statement from 2011, reveals that Cermaq's general view of responsibility has changed from 'limited' and extrinsically motivated, to a more intrinsically motivated and 'substantial' responsibility for addressing the legitimate stakeholders affected by the organization's activities. This means that Cermaq's values, and thereby its reasons for action, may have changed in this period. In the following, we will discuss how these changes have been integrated in Cermaq's business activities.

H.5   Integration: how did Cermaq (not) invest in CSR?

We now turn the attention to *how* CSR has been integrated in Cermaq previously, as well as the current state. We argued in the theoretical section above that differences in the perception of social responsibility (either limited, substantial or extended) are linked to the answers to the questions: (1) to whom is the organization responsible? (2) for what is the organization responsible? and (3) what are the limits of the organization's responsibility? These three questions are all directly related to 'the how' of CSR, that is the extent to which the CSR initiatives affect the company's core activities.

According to a case study of Norwegian aquaculture companies' CSR activities in Chile, there were relatively large differences between the manner in which the two Norwegian companies Cermaq and Fjord Seafood ASA integrated CSR in their core activities (Huemer, 2010). It should be noted that both companies have received complaints from trade unions and environmental groups. To illustrate the differences between the two companies, Huemer (ibid.: 271) claims that '[w]hile Fjord had approximately 5,000 people benefitting from its dental services, Mainstream offered toothbrushes to its employees'. Moreover, he refers to an interview with the Cermaq CEO, Geir Isaksen, who in 2007 claimed that being Norwegian in Chile is impossible, and that 'in Chile we must be Chileans'. Hence, according to the CEO, Cermaq could, for instance, not be expected to offer comparable standards in work conditions for its employees in Chile as in Norway.

We will not dig deeper into the working conditions for the Chilean employees in Cermaq, but we choose to use this as an example in order to show how integration of CSR relates to a balance between economic values, social values and environmental values (see, for example, Elkington, 1998). While prioritization of economic value and its influence on the environment is easily identified in the Cermaq case, the social dimension and the possible neglect of social values are perhaps more difficult to reveal. However, the three questions that we raise above are made in order to identify: (1) who the organization defines as its legitimate stakeholders, (2) in which way and to what extent the organization acknowledges that it is accountable to those stakeholders, and (3) what the organization thinks is reasonable for the stakeholders to expect from them. Thus, Huemer's (ibid.) empirical study of the two Norwegian aquaculture companies suggests that Cermaq originally, that is before the sustainable turnaround of the company, only to a limited extent defined the Chilean workers as legitimate stakeholders towards whom it had a substantial responsibility. This means that Cermaq only took limited responsibility for them, and compared to Fjord Seafood ASA, there are considerable differences in what is considered the domain of responsibility by Cermaq towards those stakeholders (cf. the example of dental health support). The same arguments may be put forward in relation to Cermaq's other stakeholders, for example the local authorities and the environment.

We will not delve further into the discussion of Cermaq's lack of responsibility before the fish health crisis in 2007 and immediately thereafter. Rather, we choose to focus our attention on how Cermaq integrated CSR after the crisis and how the company thereby increasingly has been able to find a balance between economic, social and environmental goal attainment. In 2011, Cermaq became a member of the United Nations Global Compact (UNGC), and they also decided to join the Nordic UNGC network. In the Cermaq Integrated Report 2011, it is claimed that '[t]hrough the membership in UNGC, Cermaq ASA is committed to aligning our operations and strategies with ten universally accepted principles in the areas of human rights, labour, environment and anti-corruption' (Cermaq, 2011). The report also describes and discusses the following ten principles from Global Compact:

1. Businesses should support and respect the protection of internationally proclaimed human rights; and
2. make sure that they are not complicit in human rights abuses.
3. Businesses should uphold the freedom of association and the effective recognition of the right to collective bargaining;
4. the elimination of all forms of forced and compulsory labour;
5. the effective abolition of child labour; and
6. the elimination of discrimination in respect of employment and occupation.
7. Businesses should support a precautionary approach to environmental challenges;
8. undertake initiatives to promote greater environmental responsibility; and
9. encourage the development and diffusion of environmentally friendly technologies.
10. Businesses should work against corruption in all its forms, including extortion and bribery.

In the integrated report from 2011, the information about the various parts of the report is tagged using these principles, which means that the reader of the report can use the symbols and read about how Cermaq deals with the four main issues in the UNGC: Human rights, Labour standards, Environmental impact and Anti-corruption. Visually, these four are represented by a symbol. In addition, there are two other symbols, representing Fish health and Community engagement. These symbols are displayed in Figure H.3 below:

Figure H.3 Symbols representing the main CSR issues for Cermaq

Human rights

Labour standards

Environmental impact

Anti-corruption

Fish health

Community engagement

In the report, Cermaq accounts for what it has done in order to live up to the principles in practice. For instance, in the GRI section 4.17, Cermaq openly provides examples of stakeholders (either directly involved or impacted by their industry) who have raised concerns during 2011, and how Cermaq have responded to them.[6] Examples of stakeholders that are mentioned are ForUM and Friends of the Earth Norway, WWF Norway, Norwegian Member of Parliament, LO – the Norwegian Labour Union Organisation and The Labour Direction in Puerto Aysen, Chile. These stakeholders' different concerns are described and Cermaq's responses to the concerns are accounted for. For example, WWF Norway have 'General concerns about the environmental impact of salmon farming', and 'Cermaq has engaged with WWF Norway through a series of meetings during 2011, providing detailed insight as to how Cermaq manages sustainability, and seeking areas of common interest and priorities'. This illustrates how Cermaq has moved from being a company in very limited contact with its primary stakeholder to a company that actively initiates and engages in stakeholder dialogues.

The report also describes 'Key impact on sustainability and effects on stakeholders', which is a materiality analysis that endeavors to identify the key risk factors and that describes what Cermaq is doing in order to address these factors. Here Cermaq defines, for example, 'Environmental compliance, Consumer Health & Safety and Corruption' as significant risk factors, and explains how different measures like ISO certification are undertaken in order to stern them.[7] Other risks, as for instance 'Biodiversity risk' and 'Occupational Health & Safety (OHS)' are evaluated as 'Insignificant risks', and arguments are provided to support these judgments. Such materiality analyses allow Cermaq both to identify the most urgent stakeholder interests at risk, as well as to communicate the judgments made and their justifications to the company's stakeholders. As such, this promotes transparency and accountability. Stakeholders are enabled to get access to Cermaq's assessments of risk factors and to raise concerns to the company.

Above we have shown examples of how Cermaq reports sustainability and responsibility issues in their integrated annual report. One may of course question whether or not the report really reflects the necessary changes. Cermaq ASA, Friends of the Earth Norway and (ForUM) shared their experiences with the mediation at Norwegian National Contact Point for Responsible Business with the annual meeting for all National Contact Points at the OECD in Paris on June 20th 2012. Here is an excerpt of the NGO's reflections about the process and the outcome: [8]

> Our immediate impression is that the company in recent years has changed its approach and attitude towards CSR in a fundamental way. It has become one of the best in implementing best practices in areas such as reporting on sustainable practices and fish hygiene. . . . However, we still do not have enough documentation to conclude that the company is complying to the agreed elements in the joint statement. The annual report of Cermaq, including its sustainability report, is not comprehensive in this respect, and there is no independent evaluation of the company's fulfillment of the joint statement. As an example we still lack information concerning the company's action on a critical topic such as indigenous peoples' rights.

This suggests that the NGOs are positive, but that they still have some critical questions concerning Cermaq's operations. For instance, there is some indication that Cermaq has done a more comprehensive job of tackling environmental issues than social issues. However, by using GRI as well as customized performance measures on the environmental dimension, Cermaq is to a much larger extent aware of, and able to monitor its performance in, these critical areas of environmental performance. Below, we will turn the attention to the possible outcomes of Cermaq's investments in CSR.

H.6 Outcome: what is the effect of Cermaq's investments in CSR?

In the theoretical backdrop, we distinguished between CSR measures that have positive profitability and reputational effects for the company and those that have not. In the following, we choose not to discuss further the negative effects of Cermaq's disinvestments in CSR before the crisis, since this has been treated in detail above. Rather, we will focus on how the integration of CSR in Cermaq's core activities has affected the company, both reputational and financial. Note, however, that we expand the corporate performance space by considering both financial performance measures and social and environmental performance metrics.

We have seen the many prizes Cermaq has been awarded and the positive attention this has created. No doubt, the reputational effects of Cermaq's transformation to sustainability leader have been substantial. Not least, there has been considerable positive attention in the press directed at Cermaq's innovative reporting system in which the sustainability report and the financial report are integrated. It is often said, and not without merit, that it takes only seconds to break down trust, but a very long time to rebuild it. In this sense, the transformation of Cermaq and the corresponding rebuilding of reputational capital is quite astonishing. Moreover, it is likely that much of the effect is yet to be seen, since only a few years have passed since the crisis and the subsequent changes in Cermaq.

Similarly, one might consider the possibility of financial effects of the turnaround. Reputational capital can lead to financial gains in at least two important ways. First, a good reputation can make the company more attractive to customers and other potential partners. Hence, a good reputation can promote financial performance through improving the value of the brand. Second, a good reputation often signifies trustworthiness, which implies that the transaction costs of the company could drop following a strengthening of reputation.

There may, however, also be financial effects that do not follow from the reputational effect. In a more direct sense, crises are also costly. Financial and organizational resources are put to use in managing the crises, and diverts attention from other, more productive, activities. This implies that companies who act responsibly and thus avoid crises in the first place actually avoid costs related to crisis management. Finally, there are numerous cases of companies that alter their organizational processes and activities in order to promote sustainability and that attain secondary positive effects, for

Table H.1 Key financial figures of Cermaq 2007–2011

Income statement, amounts in NOK 1000	2011	2010	2009	2008	2007
Operating revenues	11,634,344	9,990,528	8,971,715	8,715,572	7,721,204
EBITDA*	1,685,520	1,778,299	857,910	331,825	1,008,332
EBITDA margin (%)	14.50	17.80	9.60	3.80	13.10
Net result	792,834	1,514,669	295,959	−58,017	498,987

Note: *EBITDA – earnings before interest, taxes, depreciation and amortization.

instance in the form of cost reductions. Hence, there may also be processual effects that promote financial performance.

If we look at Cermaq's financial results in the five-year period since just before the crisis in Chile (cf. Table H.1), it is clear that their results took a massive drop in the first couple of years following the fish health crisis (that is in 2008 and 2009). For instance, their EBITDA margins dropped from 13 per cent to less than 4 per cent in the first year. Since the transformation of the company, however, their margins have reached, and even exceeded, their former margins. Revenues have increased substantially, as have the company's net result. It should be noted that there was a substantial drop in Cermaq's financial results from 2010 to 2011, but this was due to a drop in Atlantic salmon prices during the last six months of 2011. Hence, this was an event that was out of Cermaq's control, and it led to an increase in operating revenues, but in effect a fall in margins and net result.

There has been no research conducted on the financial results of Cermaq in this period and the role of their sustainability work in promoting results. However, the numbers paint a suggestive story that indicates the negative financial effect of the crisis (that is the lack of CSR) and the upsurge in financial results following the company's serious investments in CSR and sustainability thereafter. It seems likely that Cermaq's journey from activist target to sustainability leader has had considerable financial effects also.

Moreover, if we look at Cermaq's key sustainability figures, their social and environmental performance seem to be increasing as well. As indicated by Table H.2, their issues with non-compliance with regard to social and environmental regulations and standards have decreased considerably. This follows from their tackling of these issues both strategically and operationally.

Table H.2 Key sustainability figures of Cermaq 2008–2011

Sustainability Figures 2011	2011	2010	2009	2008
Employees (number)	4,047	3,533	3,277	4,072
Fatalities (number)	0	0	0	0*
Injury rate (injuries per 1,000,000 working hours)	31.1	31.0	27.4	34.1
Workforce absence rate (percentage of total work days)	32	3.1	3.0	5.0
Total energy consumption (GJ)	1,688,930	1,368,484	1,251,123	1,460,947
Global GHG emissions (Tonnes of CO_2e)	85,984	68,450	63,229	81,809
Non-compliance with environmental regulations	2	1	0	6
Non-compliance with food-safety regulations	0	1	1	1
Non-compliance with other societal regulations	2	6	3	16
Non-compliance with product and service regulations	0	0	–	–

Note: * In 2008, two contracted divers died while carrying out work for Mainstream Chile.

It should be noted, however, that the company's energy usage and CO_2 emissions have increased considerably, which likely follows from their increased market share. Hence, better performance in terms of production and sales also leads to a bigger ecological footprint. As such, this is an issue of environmental performance that Cermaq should take very seriously, and which is yet to be tackled properly.

The overall picture of Cermaq after the crisis does, however, seem to be one of a company that has reaped the benefits of working seriously with CSR and sustainability. It is tempting to argue that the very focused nature of Cermaq's work with developing performance measures and sustainability objectives has made it a visible force in the fish farming market, and thereby rebuilt its reputation quicker than one might have expected in advance. If we consider Cermaq in a multidimensional performance perspective, it is evident that the crisis has led the company to improve its performance along all three performance dimensions simultaneously. In this way, Cermaq has attained a position in the market which has allowed it to prosper further. In October 2012, Cermaq announced its purchase of the Chilean fish farming company Cultivos Marinos Chiloé for 110 million USD. This ensures Cermaq further growth in its core markets.

H.7 Summary

This case has illustrated Cermaq's journey from being an activist target due to unsustainable practices to becoming a sustainability leader that in many ways pioneered performance measurement, management and reporting in the fish farming industry. The case has moreover illustrated the role of the crisis in initiating this process in the company, and as such given insight into a case of sustainability forcing its way into the awareness of a company. It is very likely that many more such cases will follow in the years ahead.

? DISCUSSION QUESTIONS

1 What were the central issues of responsibility facing Cermaq?
2 What alternative courses of action were available to Cermaq?
3 What should Cermaq have done and what can we learn from the story of Cermaq?
4 Discuss the role of Cermaq's performance measurement and management system.

NOTES

1 More information about the NCP is available at: http://www.regjeringen.no/en/sub/styrer-rad-utvalg/ncp_norway.html?id=642292.
2 Norwegian National Contact Point for the OECD guidelines for Multinational Enterprises (2011).
3 National Commission for Scientific and Technological Research – Chile (2007).
4 See more information at: http://www.cermaq.com/portal/wps/wcm/connect/cermaqen/home/press/news/cermaq+awarded+the+ir-stockman-prize+2012.
5 Parts of this section are based on the theoretical discussion found in Jørgensen and Pedersen (2011).
6 http://www.report2011.cermaq.com/our-approach/sustainability-and-reporting-profile/.
7 http://www.iso.org/iso/home/standards/certification.htm.
8 http://www.forumfor.no/Artikler/6877.html.

10

Global industrial relations

Richard Croucher

10.1 Introduction

In this chapter we deal with an increasingly important set of issues for top managers in MNCs.[1] These are normally dealt with by a small circle of the most senior managers, who frequently regard them as strategic and unsuitable for delegation to lower levels. The chapter aims are first, to introduce the system of labor regulation at the global level, and show how it shapes industrial relations, and second, to provide the necessary background required to participate in strategic discussion of managing the risks involved in employing people across the world.

The chapter is structured as follows. In the following section, global industrial relations are defined and their significance elucidated. Next, we survey the varieties of trade unionism in the world, explaining how and why unions at national level affiliate to global bodies and drawing out some implications for MNCs. Our third section deals with the legal and paralegal system that regulates global labor issues. Finally, we conclude by examining why and how MNCs and Global Union Federations (GUFs) have entered dialogue.

The overall argument is that MNCs necessarily operate in a context of high, hard-to-manage risk on labor issues with little guidance. This is a consequence of the rapidity of the current wave of globalization, which has outpaced the capacities of longstanding historic institutions to deal comprehensively with the issues. Against this background, many MNCs have engaged in dialogues with GUFs. They have sometimes concluded formal agreements with them, but this is simply one formal part of a wider dialogical approach to dealing with these matters.

10.2 Global industrial relations and their importance

Defining global industrial relations

We use the 'global industrial relations' term here to mean relations between MNCs and the global level of union organization in the form of the GUFs (see below) and to a lesser extent the global union political organization: the International Trade Union Confederation (ITUC). Many MNCs have formal or informal relations with these bodies, which involves them in sensitive relationship management. For MNCs, this is part of a wider set of public affairs and corporate social responsibility (CSR) considerations, but it is a particularly specialized one. In many MNCs these relations assume great significance, and in a few they do not exist at all, but most large European-based and some American-based MNCs have dealings at this level (Croucher and Cotton, 2011). All MNCs have to navigate the global regulatory framework even if it is weak, and managing relations with the GUFs is integral to this.

Labor risk and the significance of global industrial relations

Revealingly, MNCs are sensitive to disclosing information on their labor affairs. Academics who audited the extent of disclosure by the several hundreds of MNCs who report to the Global Reporting Index (GRI), a CSR index which contains an HR section in which these rights are covered, found that 'In no HR category did a majority of companies disclose to any level' (Roper et al., 2011: 13). This is likely to be because they perceive considerable risks to their corporate image in the area (Croucher and Cotton, 2011). MNCs engage with global unions as one way of reducing and managing these risks, which we call 'labor risk'. We therefore proceed by describing what 'labor risk' entails.

Institutional theory argues that MNCs are engaged in a quest for legitimacy (DiMaggio and Powell, 1983). In short, senior MNC managers are compelled to attend to the 'political' question of their right to exist and operate across national boundaries, to employ nationals from other countries, to extract minerals from foreign countries' territories or to repatriate profits to their home country.

MNCs are exposed to high levels of risk from boycotts by consumers and refusal of contracts by governments where practices they are associated with are viewed as unacceptable. Hugely valuable brands may be reduced in value as a result. Many employment practices occur that are considered problematic by consumers, commentators and governments, when the world as a whole is considered, as many of the publications cited in this chapter demonstrate. MNCs must have the capacity to justify these practices convincingly to their stakeholders. While the practices may be acceptable in host countries, customers in the developed world may simply stop buying certain products if they disapprove of them. The Nike example is a relatively well-known one but is emblematic of others.

MNCs face certain challenges that are simply a result of the different national environments they operate in. Thus, societies riven by civil conflict, war, famine, corruption, disease and mass migration contain and create significant risks for MNCs. All of these phenomena impact the employment relationship. For example, migrant workers have a high incidence of HIV/AIDS, with obvious consequences for their employment and their employer who has to deal with the results of their sickness. As employers, MNCs have an interest in dealing with the issue. Moreover, there is external pressure on them to do so. They may find themselves accused of either doing too little to mitigate negative effects on employees, or of actively ignoring them.

MNCs have on occasion become associated with unacceptable behaviors in labor and human rights matters. In certain countries, notably Colombia, Guatemala and to a lesser extent others in Latin America, trade unionists are regularly murdered (Croucher and Cotton, 2011). This can expose MNCs to accusations that they are in some sense or another at least indirectly associated with these killings. When MNCs employ murdered unionists, the question has been posed of whether they were implicated.

Paradoxically, MNCs are frequently 'employers of choice' both in the developed and (even more markedly) in the developing world. They offer a wide range of opportunities within well-structured internal labor markets, interesting and varied work and extensive training opportunities. These jobs can often be used as the springboard to employment in other MNCs. In the developing world in particular, they tend to offer far better pay and conditions than local companies and a much better and healthier working life than in the 'informal sectors' that are the main prospect for many people. MNC remuneration packages may well include health care for their families and education for their children. Yet MNCs have themselves created certain risks. They are extremely active in extracting maximum value from their global value chains, and are major players in restructuring work by means of outsourcing and using agency and contract labor (Grenier, 2006).

The most obvious example of companies creating risk is that of extended value chains. The MNC sources products and services as cheaply as possible, creating long chains of contractors and sub-contractors. At the end of the chain, there may be slave, bonded or child labor. They do not escape scrutiny because they themselves may not be directly involved. As Cox (Cox, 2012: 32) argued when investigating Apple's outsourcing practices in China, 'Establishing an arm's length relationship (with suppliers: author) does not absolve a company from moral responsibility for the way its chosen partners treat workers'.

Child labor is a significant phenomenon in the world as a whole. Slave and bonded labor are also more than marginal phenomena, as Slavery International publicizes. MNCs claim that they are not connected to these practices, but although no reliable statistics exist, links have been established by researchers. Bales, in his graphic work *Disposable People* (2004) established several. He demonstrates, *inter alia*, how cars sold in Canada by MNCs used Brazilian steel manufactured using charcoal made by slaves in Brazil's interior.

In many cases, only a minority of those who work for MNCs are actually employed by them. It has been suggested that 70 per cent of those manufacturing, packaging and distributing products for the world's most profitable company, Nestlé, are not directly employed by that company (Cotton, 2011). Outsourcing trends operate in a similar direction: 60 per cent of Fortune 500 MNCs were outsourcing work to India in 2006 (Vagadia, 2007). This 'externalization' (Theron, 2005) policy is often enforced on local units by central MNC managers (Westney, 2008).

Where MNCs carry out mainly business-to-business operations, they are nevertheless likely to be exposed to labor risk even if is mitigated by the fact that they do not sell directly to customers in the developed world. MNCs often have to justify their practices to contract-awarding governments or Non-Governmental Organizations (NGOs) that are skeptical of their claims to have high CSR standards. Similarly, some companies only use suppliers that can demonstrate that they observe certain labor rights (Morrison et al., 2011). Managers from the developed world may themselves become de-motivated if they find that even some of those doing work for the MNC are being dealt with in ways that they would consider unethical by their personal standards.

These matters are judged in an environment of increasing skepticism about business practices in general. If the media expose a specific practice, MNCs are not judged in a court of law, according to legal criteria, but by the press and in the normative 'court of public opinion' where ideas of acceptable practice are often more widely and morally conceived.

These reasons explain why many MNCs have actively sought relations with union bodies at the global level. As union organizations, they may appear unlikely collaborators for MNCs, who might theoretically prefer (as some do) to seek out NGOs as partners. Yet solid grounds exist for MNC–GUF partnerships. First, GUFs are centers of profound expertise on labor issues internationally and these are, as we have begun to demonstrate, complex. Second, unions are unlikely to be accused of bias towards the company. Third, and perhaps most importantly, the GUFs are also more directly and accountably interested in the fate of MNC employees than NGOs. Union members do not wish their job security to be jeopardized by criticism of their employing MNCs that ignores their own interests as employees and they have well-established democratic channels for voicing concerns to their elected representatives that are lacking in NGOs. The GUFs have therefore not generally adopted the radical tactics of 'corporate campaigning' used by certain ad hoc campaigning bodies, some NGOs and some American trade unions. These campaigns systematically map and attack all of an MNC's external stakeholder relationships, making determined, 'no holds barred' efforts to bring MNCs to deal with them (Greven, 2006). In this sense, the GUFs are in comparison relatively benign (but not uncritical) interlocutors for MNCs because these companies are important actual or potential partners for them. The GUFs' futures are ultimately founded on MNCs' existence, and GUF staff are well aware of the growing importance of MNCs in the world economy. They do not wish to irrevocably alienate managements and indeed seek to build long-term relationships with them. These associative links are well-developed. The GUF General Secretaries are often known to senior MNC managers from meeting in global industrial conferences, the World Economic Forum and elsewhere.

10.3 Trade unions: structures, functions and cultures

The primary actors in global industrial relations are MNCs and trade unions. Since much of the rest of this text is concerned with MNCs themselves, we focus here on analysing trade unions. We begin at the national level, because it allows us to show first, that unions are highly diverse institutions, and second, because it helps us explain what the GUFs are and how they relate to the national level of trade unionism. In Figure 10.1 below, we provide a schematic representation of the structure of trade unionism in industrial sectors globally.

Individual trade unions at the national level may choose to affiliate to Global Union Federations; this is a matter of free choice on both sides and some are not affiliated. GUFs must offer tangible benefits to their affiliates to secure and maintain affiliations. The GUFs were first formed in the late nineteenth century as 'International Trade Secretariats' and were developed in the first half of the twentieth century by the large European (and later the American)

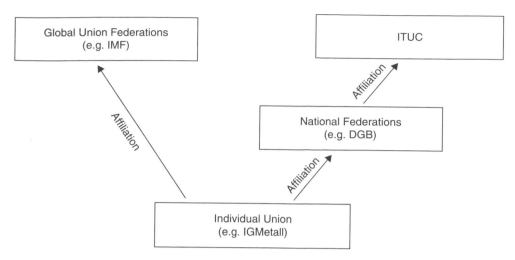

Figure 10.1 Trade union's two avenues for global affiliation

unions. Trade unions in the developing world have increasingly affiliated to the GUFs since the 1970s, hoping to access services that will help compensate for their weak bargaining power at national level.

The GUFs are coordinating bodies organized along industry lines; unlike their global sister organization the ITUC they are not primarily political organizations. National union federations, not individual unions, affiliate to the ITUC, the global political voice of labor. The ITUC relates primarily to international financial institutions such as the World Bank and World Trade Organization, governments and global bodies such as those in the United Nations 'family'. We pay little attention to the ITUC here, since it only deals directly with MNCs to a small extent. The two possible routes for union affiliation at the global level are shown in Figure 10.1, taking the German metalworkers' union IG Metall as an illustrative example.

Trade unions at national level

Despite declining membership, trade unions remain the world's largest membership organizations, represent the voice of organized labor and in some countries are considered the legitimate voice of working people more broadly. A trade union is defined here as a continuous association of wage earners dedicated to the advancement of its members' interests.

Incorrect assumptions about what a trade union is or does are potentially dangerous for managers operating on a global level. The definition given above helps one to understand why, because it is a wide one that encompasses many different functions and approaches by unions. However, it includes the significant phrase 'dedicated to the advancement of its members' interests' and this establishes a lowest common denominator. In some countries, trade unions have been subordinated to political parties or the interests of the state in such a way and to such an extent that they cannot be considered 'free' or 'independent' trade unions in any reasonable judgment. This is arguably the case in China and Belarus to give just two examples. In China, a country of undeniable significance for MNCs, unions are essentially Communist Party organizations, practicing surveillance on employees and they are not currently recognized internationally as members of the free trade union movement (Croucher and Cotton, 2011).

Thus, trade unions may be free and independent or they may be little more than government instruments. They may also be little more than employer-sponsored organizations, sometimes called 'yellow' unions. Management open themselves to criticism on human rights grounds where they encourage such organizations' development.

Free trade unions have very different structures and functions in different countries. A few indicative examples follow:

- Different structures: In Japan, Russia, the countries of the CIS, Mexico and Mauritius, most unions are essentially workplace organizations. In Russia, almost all members' subscriptions are held at the workplace and only small amounts are passed on to the regional and national levels. By contrast, in Germany, unions are essentially national, industry-based organizations with only an indirect role in most workplaces; they mainly exercise influence in workplaces by having their members operating as works councilors on legally-backed works councils. In France, Italy and Spain unions are politically based organizations. This means that different union confederations exist according to their political rather than their industrial orientation. Therefore many different confederations exist, including in the same workplace, a situation that is much less common in Northern Europe.
- Different functions: In Russia, although efforts are being made to change them, many unions are basically welfare organizations, distributing holiday and other vouchers to their members. In Latin America, many unions are essentially community campaigning organizations, carrying out a lot of public campaigning functions on their members' behalf (Murillo, 2001). In Latin American countries, general strikes are relatively common events rather than events that occur once in a century as for example in Britain.
- Different cultures and approaches: In the countries of Latin America,

unions often have a highly political approach (Murillo, 2001). These unions are 'social movement' bodies and some are capable of mobilizing whole communities on a large scale. On the other hand, in the Russian-speaking world this is rarely the case, and unions there do not usually have the same ability to mobilize members as in Latin America. In Western Europe, unions have become largely institutionalized; their cultures are much less politicized than their Latin American counterparts. The relatively routine and predictable dealings managers may have with West European or Russian unions will be no preparation for dealing with their much more volatile counterparts in Latin America.

Trade unions' bargaining spheres and membership levels

Trade unions generally bargain about wages and conditions, but the level at which they do so varies in different countries. Clearly, whether wages are bargained at the industry or company level matters a great deal to MNCs. In the former case, wages are taken out of competition in the national industries to which this applies, that is there is reduced scope for MNCs to compete for manual labor by offering different pay for the same level of skill. This is not the case, on the other hand, if wages are determined at the company level. MNCs' pay policies are strongly affected by this diversity because pay simply cannot be the same across countries where bargaining arrangements differ radically. In general, this forces MNCs to have little or nothing more than uniform general principles or even simply 'values' in terms of compensation policies at the global level. Where collective bargaining exists, we can be confident that the right to collective bargaining (an ILO core labor standard, see below) also exists in that country.

Proportions of national workforces in union membership also vary greatly between countries. Scandinavian levels are high but those in the USA are low. Union membership is also concentrated in certain industries such as mining, docks, manufacturing and certain types of service industries. Thus, although the USA has low union density at the national level, large manufacturing MNCs such as Boeing and General Motors contain strong trade unions. The situation is complicated by the fact that in some countries such as France and Australia, unions have historically enjoyed considerable legal support and can therefore exercise influence that goes well beyond the level their membership might suggest. One may also note the wide disparity between memberships in different countries. Although the USA is considered a low membership country, this tells us little about union power. American longshoremen, employed in a country with a low rate of unionization, have frequently supported their equivalents in other countries in their industrial action and they play a significant role (as do the Teamsters) in the International Transport Workers' Federation.

The GUFs themselves have a major task in reconciling and trying to group all of these different unions together in one global body. The GUFs are greatly assisted in their unifying task by referring to 'lowest common denominator' issues such as the right of unions to operate freely as this is something that all unions can agree on even if they operate in very different national contexts and in very different ways. MNCs experience this as an insistence on these basic rights.

Their intimate knowledge of this variegated picture means that GUFs are unique centers of expertise on the trade union picture across the world as well as on labor issues more widely, and these are significant reasons for trade unions to join them. They are also important reasons for MNCs entering into dialogue with them, as a single and authoritative source of information on a subject they may feel weakly informed about.

Trade unions at global level

The GUFs, with their memberships, are listed below in Table 10.1.

Most of the GUFs have their headquarters in Geneva, although the ITF has its headquarters in London. They also have regional offices all over the world. Their governance is dominated by the large, powerful unions, predominantly from the developed world, that make relatively large inputs to their resources. Their elected General Secretaries normally come from one of these developed country unions (Croucher and Cotton, 2011).

As indicated above, relations between unions at the national and regional (for example, European Union) level are complex and sometimes difficult. National unions expect GUFs to provide them with an effective service when dealing with MNCs, and may be critical towards GUFs if they feel that is not being delivered. GUFs, on the other hand, may reply when criticized along these lines that they cannot substitute for a lack of union power at the national level (Croucher and Cotton, 2011).

The GUFs' daily work is in supporting their affiliates and in taking initiatives that assist their affiliates in their dealings with MNCs. They defend the rights of unions to operate by pressurizing international organizations and national governments where these are threatened. They provide information to unions on company operations and give them bargaining information.

Table 10.1 Global union organizations in 2008

Organization	Estimated total membership (millions)	Total number of unions affiliated	Number of countries covered	Main sectors covered
Education International	30	394	171	Education
ITUC	168	311	155	Umbrella body
BWI	12	318	130	Construction and materials
ICEM	20	379	117	Chemicals, energy, mining, paper
IFJ	0.6	117	100	Journalism
IMF	25	200	100	Metalworking
ITGLWF	9	238	122	Textiles, garments, leather goods
ITF	4.5	654	148	Transport
IUF	2.6	375	127	Food, agriculture, catering, tourism
PSI	20	650	160	Public services
UNI	15.5	900	160	10

Source: Schwass (2004).

The GUFs conduct campaigns in particular MNCs where fundamental principles are concerned. Increasingly, they have direct dealings with the MNCs in their industrial sectors and their General Secretaries are very often in regular contact with CEOs. This often happens even when the MNCs are only weakly unionized because the MNCs are aware of the GUFs as important players in the labor relations and CSR areas and sometimes want to 'sound out' the General Secretaries on various issues.

10.4 Global labor regulation

The labor risk issues identified at the beginning of this chapter are not new. 'Globalization' has long existed but the issues have become more prominent as the current wave of globalization has proceeded, change has accelerated and the public has become more sensitized to these matters. Attempts have nevertheless been made to regulate them throughout the period since the end of the First World War and this section describes the accumulated results of these efforts.

The global system provides only weak constraints and elementary guidance for MNCs. Moreover, a common criticism of the International Labor Organization (ILO) is that it lacks a strong enforcement mechanism to back up its Conventions. Indeed, the entire system of global labor regulation has been described as 'weak and largely tokenistic' (Hyman, 2002: 1) and constitutes part of a hard-to-manage situation for MNCs. This means that companies have a good deal of latitude in the policies and practices they pursue in the area. Thus, in the case study of Anglo-American plc linked to this chapter, we discuss the actions taken by the company. Yet it is also important to recognize that its competitors followed different (much less successful) policies.

Key instruments of global labor regulation

We now introduce the key instruments that play a role in regulating labor issues. Table 10.2 shows these in a schematic way. The GUFs' regulatory role is dealt with separately below.

At the lowest level of compulsion, we find company self-regulation (Kolben, 2011). This is firstly carried out through Company Codes of Conduct, and secondly shades into 'private regulation' through reporting procedures and external monitors. We now consider these in turn.

Over 3,000 Company Codes of Conduct existed in 2004, making a wide range of statements about MNCs' policies (Wick, 2004). The number of Codes has probably grown since this report was published. They often cover numerous subjects such as the company's actions in regard to the environment or corruption and only occasionally contain sections on labor. These sections have been subjected to careful analysis and criticism on numerous grounds, notably that they evade central issues such

Table 10.2 Key instruments for regulating the employment relationship at global level

Global level	ILO Conventions
	OECD guidelines
Regional level	European Union Law
	Treaty Law (North American Free Trade Area)
National government	Statutes
'Private regulation'	NGO monitoring and reporting
	Agreements with GUFs
'Private regulation'	Self-regulation: Company Codes of Conduct

as the freedom of association and do not correspond to reality (Royle, 2010).

The second type of 'private' regulation takes a more collective form and is reflected in arrangements made through voluntary associations such as Social Accountability International, the Fair Labor Association, the Global Compact or the Global Reporting Initiative. Some of these bodies have a degree of independence from particular companies yet these have also been shown to have major shortcomings. A thorough academic survey identified three issues with all such systems. The first was transparency: it is often unclear how exactly they operate. The second was the monitors' independence. Third, the same study also concluded that improved accountability to workers and their organizations was one of several requirements that would need to be met if these systems were to make a meaningful contribution to labor regulation internationally (O'Rourke, 2003).

As O'Rourke (2003) points out, there are obvious problems with inspection systems, including how effective they can be even if they are fully independent. As O'Rourke argues, an ongoing improvement perspective is required that should involve employees who are on the ground all the time and are fully committed to working day-in, day-out in that workplace.

'Public' forms of regulation are those that are strictly external to companies. At the top of Table 10.2, we find arguably the most important of these, the International Labor Organization (ILO). Founded in 1919 by US President Woodrow Wilson in the aftermath of the Russian Revolution, it has become a leading authority on labor matters. In its own publicity, the ILO describes itself as 'responsible for drawing up and overseeing international labor standards' (International Labor Organization, 2012). Most countries in the world are members.

The ILO sets labor standards that constitute a 'floor' of basic rights, which are part of its wider 'decent work' agenda (Sengenberger, 2001). Following ILO standards is simply to observe certain basic 'hygiene factors'. Yet best practice demands more than not employing child or slave labor and the ILO standards are indeed basic. The standards (Conventions; see below) involved are those that a country agrees to pass into its own national labor law. ILO standards are sometimes used as benchmarks by MNCs, though they are strictly speaking not intended for that purpose.

The ILO is a tripartite body, that is it brings employers, unions and governments together to conclude and revise Conventions. Governments can choose whether or not to adopt (or 'ratify') ILO Conventions. When they do so, they agree to ensure that the law in their countries conforms to a Convention's principles. It is therefore a 'contracting-in' system. The ILO has a set of 'Core labor standards' which are deemed to be a minimum for all countries.

Many other ILO conventions exist and a total of 175 are currently in force. Many countries have adopted these standards, but some have not. Despite the existence of the Core labor standards, just 22 countries had actually ratified all eight of the fundamental Conventions as of May 2012. The countries that have contracted into the different standards are shown in a set of useful global maps produced by the International Centre for Trade Union Rights (ICTUR), based in London (www.ictur.org/).

A second important global body providing 'public' regulation and guidance is the Organisation for Economic Co-operation and Development (OECD). The OECD has an expert committee, the Trade Union Advisory Committee (TUAC). The OECD Guidelines for Multinational Corporations (2011) constitute a significant part of the global system of regulation on labor matters and more may be learned about their detail at www.sa8000.org. Complaints that the guidelines have not been followed may be made to the OECD's National Contact Points (NCPs), who are expert individuals nominated by governments to investigate such complaints.

We now show the system working in practice, demonstrating how a GUF campaign and a complaint to an OECD National Contact Point operated together to change Unilever's policy. This demonstrates that when these two elements of the system work in tandem, they can affect MNC practice. GUF campaigning combined with use of the global regulatory system can therefore pressure MNCs to change their practices. However, some MNCs, aware of this possibility and sensitive to their own reputations, have sought to pre-empt this type of pressure. They have taken a pro-active stance, and have sought advice and entered into dialogue with GUFs rather than being forced to react after the event.

10.5 Dialogue with GUFs and International Framework Agreements

Many MNCs have signed global labor agreements ('International Framework Agreements', sometimes called 'Global Framework Agreements') with GUFs. The initiative for these frequently comes from MNCs themselves (Croucher and Cotton, 2011). In mid-2008, there were 61 such agreements involving many large European-based MNCs, and there are now likely to be more although the rate of increase may have declined since the number of MNCs is not large and many agreements have been concluded (Croucher and Cotton, 2011). These agreements are usually concluded between GUFs and MNCs with the intermediation of major unions. They are generally simple statements of the company's agreement to observe ILO Conventions on fundamental issues such as the right of unions to organize and bargain collectively and the company's avoidance of child labor. They are one formal manifestation of the wider relationships and discussions between MNCs and GUFs that we refer to above.

The Building Workers' International BWI provides its perspective on this in the following passage taken from its website:

> MNCs signing Global Company Agreements with BWI commit themselves to respect workers' rights based on the core conventions of the International Labor Organization (ILO). In addition, the company should also agree to offer decent wages and working conditions as well as to provide a safe and healthy working environment; and in many cases they contain a complaint and/or monitoring system and cover also suppliers and subcontractors. Some consider framework agreements to be negotiated codes of conduct with complaints systems; however, this is not a useful way of looking at these agreements which are qualitatively different from codes of conduct. These framework agreements constitute a formal recognition of social partnership at the global level. These agreements provide a global framework for protecting trade union rights and encouraging social dialogue and collective bargaining. Therefore they complement and do not substitute for agreements at the national or local level.
>
> The purpose of International Framework Agreements (IFAs) is to assist affiliates to get recognized as unions and to start a social dialogue on the company and national level with MNCs, suppliers and subcontractors of BWI partner MNCs. This should lead to collective bargaining and finally to improved working conditions and better wages. However, the success of any global company agreement will depend on the strength of the unions at the national level and full implementation of the global agreements is only possible when workers are organized in free trade unions and are able to bargain collectively at the national and enterprise level.

For the BWI and other GUFs, these agreements are therefore a means to an end: to establish effective unions in MNCs' developing world operations where workers are normally in a very weak position vis-à-vis employers. Yet these agreements co-exist with, and are not a substitute for, dialogue between GUFs and MNCs.

These agreements may have positive functions for central MNC management. The top management of MNCs is often painfully aware of the limitations of information provided to them by lower levels of management, particularly in sites thousands of miles away that are located in very different institutional and cultural environments (Kristensen and Zeitlin, 2005). They are therefore often interested in what employee representatives have to say simply because it provides them with another source of information that does not come from people with a clear interest in telling senior managers what they want to hear. In addition, they may provide central MNC managements with a way of extending existing co-operative arrangements with employee representatives across their international operations (Schömann et al., 2008).

Such dialogues may be more or less formal and show different types of result. A positive type of relationship, explained in detail in our extended case study in this book was the basis for extended collaboration between the mining company Anglo-American plc and the International Federation of Chemical, Energy and Mineworkers Unions (ICEM). We simply note here that this dialogue transcended defensive considerations to achieve a strategic partnership. It brought considerable mutual gains to the company, the GUF and many thousands of workers on two continents.

Some MNCs and notably most US-based ones are reluctant to conclude formal agreements of this sort, or indeed to engage in wider dialogue, for two main reasons. First, they fear that the BWI's ambitions for them will be realized. This is most common among US-based MNCs (Croucher and Cotton, 2011), who are frequently hostile to unions *per se* and often fear an extension of unionization in their MNCs (very few MNCs are entirely union-free). Second, they are reluctant to commit themselves in writing to undertakings they feel they are unable to enforce throughout their supply chains. However, it is important to reiterate that MNCs themselves have often taken the initiative with GUFs to reach these agreements, feeling that they offer some protection against accusations of abusing labor. Thus, company attitudes vary widely.

10.6 Summary

All MNCs are exposed to serious and extensive labor risk, whether or not they deal directly with consumers. This is partly because of MNCs' quests for low costs. Extended supply or value chains tend to have at their end tiny units of production, often families working outside of the regulated economy. It is also partly because MNCs operate in very different national environments where norms of what is acceptable in employment terms may differ enormously. The global context is that the system of global labor 'regulation' is weak in relation to national systems, while 'private regulation' lacks wider credibility.

Across the world, a variegated and complex set of national trade unions with a plethora of structures and functions play a significant role in defending and seeking to develop labor regulation at all levels, especially in MNCs. Seeking a single, credible and global partner with whom to approach these matters, many MNCs have therefore engaged in dialogues with GUFs trying to draw on the latter's undoubted expertise in labor issues in their industrial sectors. Sometimes they have concluded formal agreements with them, but these are simply reflections of a much wider process of dialogue. MNCs, especially when they are Europe-based, have frequently concluded that such dialogues with GUFs constitute their 'least bad' option, because the GUFs are the only bodies with the public credibility, global reach and depth of expertise to act as effective global partners to minimize labor risk. In some cases, such as that of Anglo-American plc and the International Federation of Chemical, Energy and Mineworkers' Unions, which is investigated in depth in our case study, the mutual benefits to the MNC and GUF transcended risk management to bring substantial benefits to all involved.

NOTE

1 This chapter draws on Croucher and Cotton (2011), which provides much of the chapter's theoretical and empirical underpinning.

Case I

A GUF's relationship with a multinational company

Richard Croucher and Elizabeth Cotton

I.1 Introduction

This case study illustrates and expands on many of the themes developed and discussed earlier.[1] It is a case study of the International Federation of Chemical, Energy and Mineworkers Unions (ICEM)'s relationship with Anglo American plc (AA), analysing how the GUF, national unions in South Africa, Ghana and Colombia and the company interacted with positive results for all concerned. The main institutional players are represented in Figure I.1.

The case was selected for two reasons: first, because *prima facie* it allowed detailed examination of how a GUF acted as a major and indeed indispensable partner for an MNC. The MNC followed a conscious partnership strategy with the GUF at the latter's initiative, a path that differed radically from that taken by its competitors. Second, unusually high-quality longitudinal information was obtained through the long-term involvement of one of the authors, supplemented by unusually extensive project reports, company and union documentation.

The MNC greatly improved the effectiveness of its approach to HIV/AIDS in Africa, through its partnership with the ICEM. The GUF was the prime mover. We show how it developed a positive relationship with Anglo American by integrative bargaining on an issue of great significance both to it and to workers; this built company consent for distributive bargaining by affiliates in a different part of its operation on another continent. The narrative demonstrates the significance of strong articulation developed over many years between the national and international union levels, in part created and supported by a strong educational input. The GUF's role was crucial: none of the national unions in the case had previously related effectively to MNCs. The GUF learned from the process and transferred

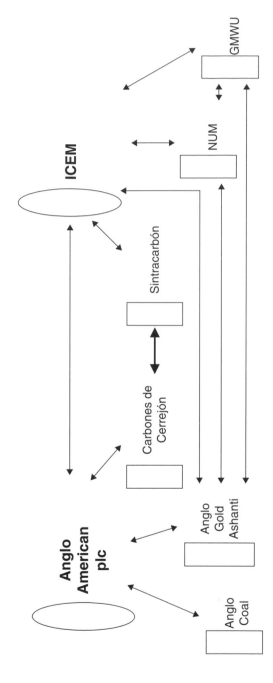

Figure I.1 Anglo American and its relationships to other main players

the approach elsewhere in the world. The case confirms that, contrary to Neuhaus's (1981) suggestion, GUFs can initiate significant developments and need not simply react to other actors' agendas.

The case is presented in three sections. The first introduces the company and its relationship with the ICEM. The second analyses work developed in Ghana around HIV/AIDS in the mining sector. The third section examines the dynamics of rebuilding union dialogue with mining companies in Colombia. Finally, we draw broad conclusions and examine the case's wider relevance.

I.2 The company, the ICEM, national trade unions and their relationships

Anglo American is one of the world's largest corporations, ranked 88 in the Financial Times Stock Exchange index of the world's largest 500 companies and employing 162,000 people worldwide in 2006. Its operations are focused on mining. The company, like other natural resources companies, has enjoyed rising prices for its products since 2000, and its increasing profits in that period are significant background to the case.

The company, although owned mainly by British financial institutions, operates in many countries but its main mining operations are in Sub-Saharan Africa and Latin America. It was for some time South Africa's largest conglomerate and a key corporate player in negotiating the post-apartheid employment settlement. It has a complex and highly devolved structure, claiming in response to criticisms of the activities of companies in which it has a sizeable interest (War on Want, 2007) that it does not have 'management control' of them (Anglo American, 2007). Following the practice of many such corporations, the associated companies have high levels of managerial autonomy and seek to establish internal leadership in both efficiency and CSR matters. In this sense it is typical of the modern MNC, and can be conceived of as a 'federation' (Andersson et al., 2007) or a grouping of companies linked by a range of methods including overlapping directorships and shareholdings.

Table I.1 shows the company's structure in February 2004. In 2004 it had a controlling financial interest in both Anglo Coal and Anglo Gold Ashanti (AGA). This interest was reduced to 41.8 per cent in April 2006; but until spring 2007, AA retained two directors on the AGA board. In 2000, AA bought a 33 per cent share in the Cerrejón mine in Colombia; by 2006 three companies, AA, BHP Billiton and Xstrata, were equal shareholders. AA works closely with Cerrejón management.

Table I.1 AA company overview (2004)

Business area	Main countries of operation	Key subsidiaries	Percentage ownership of subsidiaries
Platinum	South Africa	Anglo Platinum	74.1%
Gold	South Africa	Anglo Gold Ashanti	54.5% (17% in 2008)
Diamonds	South Africa	De Beers	45%
Coal	South Africa; Colombia	Anglo Coal	100%
Base metals	Chile	Anglo Base Metals	100%
Industrial minerals	UK, France, Belgium	Anglo Industrial Minerals	100%
Paper and packaging	South Africa; Russia	Anglo Paper and Packaging	100%
Ferrous metals and industries	South Africa, Australia	Anglo Ferrous Metals and Industries	100%

Source: Anglo American plc.: *The Business: An Overview*, 14 February, 2004.

Company relations with stakeholders have to be built on a long-term basis, Sir Mark Moody-Stuart, then chairman (now retired), argued to shareholders at the April 2008 AGM. Fixed sites and high front-end expenditure mean 'that we have to live with the judgements we make about our ability to operate ethically in particular locations' (Anglo American, 2008). 'Resource nationalism', the sentiment in countries that their national resources should bring them national benefits, increasingly means the company has to attend to its wider political profile throughout its operations. AA and AGA are highly engaged with international development, and since 2000 AA has made a considerable contribution to the UK government's Africa strategy. The company's CSR efforts are also reflected in its role in establishing and building the Global Business Coalition (GBC), set up to promote business responses to HIV/AIDS, which Sir Mark Moody-Stuart chaired. The GBC claims that it has supported over 1 million companies in implementing local AIDS workplace programmes.

AA has taken a 'business case' approach to HIV/AIDS provision, although there is considerable congruence between business and CSR rationales. AA's subsidiary Anglo Coal was one of the first companies in the world to calculate the precise economic benefits of providing antiretrovirals (ARVs), but this 'making disease management pay' (the phrase is that of Dr Richard Gaunt (2007) of AA's major competitor Rio Tinto) approach is becoming well established in mining companies. Research carried out in Anglo Coal showed in 2006 that it was economic to provide private medical insurance,

Table I.2 Anglo Coal: preliminary cost–benefit analysis of providing ART

Duration	ART Cost per month (South African Rand)	Absenteeism savings per month	Health care cost saving
Amount per month saved when compared to no Anti-Retro viral Therapy (ART) – 12 months	R2223	R1052	R755
Per month saved when compared to no ART – 18 months	R1652	R1093	R804
Per month saved when compared to no ART – 24 months	R1304	R1126	R837
Additional savings		R458	R396

Source: Ms D Muirhead, Aurum Institute for Health Research: presentation.

including possible VCT and ARVs, for all employees and their dependants rather than to provide nothing. The company's preliminary cost–benefit analysis shown in Table I.2 demonstrated that after the first year, the costs of providing drugs were estimated to decline relative to savings from absenteeism and healthcare. This calculation accompanied a move beyond the classic position taken by companies, whereby they deny any legal responsibility for workers' sexual health. The latter position clearly rejects any real responsibility for reducing risk, in order to limit potential liabilities (Weait, 2007).

The company has scope and reasons for improving both its health and safety record and its public image: in 2007 it reported that 44 people were killed in its mining operations, and its practices in relation to indigenous communities have been sharply criticised (War on Want, 2007). Part of its reply to War on Want's criticisms was to point to its record in publicly insisting that the Colombian government attend to the physical defence of trade unionists. Like many mining employers, AA is reconciled to trade unionism and almost all of its mining sites have a major union presence. The company has sought to construct positive relations with unions, including them in efforts to improve efficiency by cost reduction; union cooperation in health and safety has brought major benefits to the rate of return on capital employed. Their experience at the New Denmark mine in South Africa demonstrated this dramatically, when union partnership helped raise the return on capital employed from 24.7 per cent in 2001 to 43.2 per cent in 2003. Moody-Stuart used this experience as a model for others in the company to follow (Anglo American, 2003). Hence, the links between trade unionism, health and safety and profitability are well recognised at the top of the company. This is important background to the distinctive partnership path that the company took in relation to its main competitor companies.

Anglo Gold has robust long-term relations with the South African National Union of Mineworkers (NUM), based on AA's 'progressive positions' on recognising black unions in South Africa, and its part in the transition to democracy (Anglo American, 2003, 2008). The NUM itself had a central role in ending apartheid and enjoys great prestige within the trade union movement both in Africa and internationally, with strong bilateral links with other mining unions, and high-profile participation in the ICEM and the IMF. The NUM has long emphasised HIV/AIDS as an issue, having concluded an agreement with the South African Chamber of Mines on the subject in 1993 (N'Deba and Hodges-Aeberhard, 1998). The union has a broad political conception of its representative functions and has successfully negotiated protection for contract workers (von Holdt and Webster, 2005). The NUM has conducted personnel exchanges with many African mining unions and has had a long-term relationship with the Ghana Mineworkers Union (GMWU) based on personal contacts developed through the ICEM Regional Committee. The GMWU is itself a strong union within the well-developed Ghanaian trade union movement, and is therefore a relatively equal partner for the NUM. It is a highly politicized organization, focussed on dialogue with the state which until recently ran the mines. It was only therefore relatively recently that the GMWU had to negotiate with private management and the union stood to learn from a relationship with the NUM.

Exchanges between the ICEM and AA were partly based on the longstanding relationship between Fred Higgs (then ICEM general secretary, retired 2006) and Sir Mark Moody-Stuart. The two were in contact when Moody-Stuart held management positions at Royal Dutch Shell and Higgs was National Oil Industry Officer at the UK's Transport and General Workers Union. This contact continued through difficult years for Shell and for oil workers, including the 1995 Brent Spar incident. The relationship was renewed through their joint participation in the United Nations' Global Compact's Advisory Committee from that body's foundation in 2002. The committee was established to help the Global Compact develop speedily into a substantial CSR mechanism, working directly under Kofi Annan's office at the United Nations. Its membership included representatives of civil society, labor (GUFs and the ITUC) and business. Shortly after its creation, Moody-Stuart became AA chairman but retained his Advisory Committee position. The foundations of trust between Higgs and Moody-Stuart were built on the fact that, unlike other participants, both came from an industrial relations background. They held similar views on the minimum 'integrity measures' that would be credible for the Global Compact to be an effective body, based on their experience of industrial monitoring and complaints procedures. Their capacity for joint action was higher than either had with the non-governmental organizations involved and was another factor in building a distinctive partnership approach between the company and the GUF that marked the company out from its competitors.

There was also a long-term and complex web of relationships between the ICEM and its key affiliate the NUM, and of both with the CEO of Anglo Gold Ashanti, Bobby Godsell. Godsell is an exceptional business person. On his retirement from the company in 2008, he was credited by Moody-Stuart with a significant role in South Africa's transition to democracy (Anglo American, 2008). An industrial relations expert, he was hailed as an 'organic intellectual' of South African business (Handley, 2005) for his part in South Africa's transition. The editor of works on South Africa's future (Berger and Godsell, 1988), he persuaded a skeptical business community of the merits of the Labor Relations Act in its amended 2002 version, which improved legal cover for contract workers (Bidoli, 2004). In 2002, he surprised a business meeting in New York by wearing an NUM strike T-shirt (*ibid.*). Godsell had a close relationship with Cyril Ramaphosa, the first NUM president and subsequent secretary general of the ANC who became chairman of the Mondi paper and packaging group after its de-merger from AA (Bidoli, 2004; Mondi, 2007).

In West Africa, long-term relationships also existed between AGA management and medical staff, the ICEM and the Ghana Mineworkers Union (GMWU). The then GMWU president, John Brimpong, was the Ghana TUC's HIV/AIDS representative, and a member of the ICEM regional and international executives who was well known both within Ghanaian mining communities and to local mine management. Brimpong was at the center of a constellation of industry and community contacts built up over 40 years of union activity. An already close relationship between GMWU leadership, the ICEM and senior AGA medical staff was cemented through the latter's HIV/AIDS project.

I.3   The ICEM's HIV/AIDS pilot projects: background and significance

The ICEM was one of the first GUFs, with ITF and EI, to take a lead on promoting HIV/AIDS action by unions since workers in these sectors are disproportionately affected. From 2002 the ICEM worked with affiliates to develop a strategy and initial activity. The union problems identified when dealing with HIV/AIDS were defined as lack of leadership, the stigma around testing and a lack of sustainable funding for treatment. An additional barrier in Africa was the reluctance of workplace representatives, often from Christian backgrounds, to confront the issue. At that point virtually no ICEM affiliate, except those in South Africa, Ghana and Botswana, recognized HIV/AIDS as a union issue. In countries outside Africa, some ICEM affiliates, notably in Eastern Europe, strongly resisted the argument. The African affiliates could therefore potentially become international leaders to persuade others of the case for taking up the area of work.

Following six months of consultation with affiliates already active around the issue and experienced HIV/AIDS activists, the ICEM and these affiliates decided to promote medical provision and prevention programs, and to negotiate anti-discrimination policies through pilot schemes that could later be adopted elsewhere in the world. The agenda was therefore more ambitious than the earlier common union practice of simply carrying out awareness campaigns. It entailed developing core expertise, raising funds from new sources and dialogue with both employers and government.

HIV/AIDS is a central labor management concern for multinationals invested in Africa and Eastern Europe. In Sub-Saharan mining, infection rates are approximately double national averages and frequently higher. In Zambia the BBC (2006) reported a national infection rate of 14 per cent, and an estimated 50 per cent in mining communities. These high rates are explained by four factors. The first is the remoteness of mining operations and the communities surrounding them. Second, single sex workers' hostels, although reducing in number, are widespread. Third, many male migrant and contract workers are away from their partners, further stimulating high levels of prostitution and 'second families'. Fourth, stigma and denial around sexual practice and prevention of infection is widespread.

The private sector plays a significant role in general healthcare in these communities, making miners dependent on companies for health, and in some cases life, as well as work. The majority of clinics and hospitals in mining regions are to some extent privately supported or funded. Most miners working directly for multinationals at present are members of private medical insurance schemes which provide antiretroviral drugs, although this is a recent development and rarely applies to indirect or contract workers. Thus, companies play a considerable role in the diagnosis of HIV/AIDS and in providing access to treatment as well as in healthcare more broadly.

The diagnosis of HIV/AIDS raises significant dilemmas for management and workplace representatives alike and is therefore extremely demanding for individuals on both personal and professional levels. If a worker with HIV/AIDS is threatened with dismissal, this raises fundamental issues about that worker's future. Workers' fear of losing their jobs demands strong workplace representation by the union, since local management may take action against them despite statements by senior company staff thousands of miles away. The issue giving rise to the dismissal threat may not be the simple fact of the worker having HIV/AIDS. For example, a worker receiving antiretrovirals through a company medical scheme may face dismissal for a gross misconduct matter. The local manager and workplace representative will both have to take personal responsibility for evaluating the cost to the worker, his family and the community of him losing his job and, simultaneously, his access to treatment.

Workers must be convinced that testing will not lead to dismissal and, to a lesser degree, they also must be confident that it will lead to treatment. This must be seen in the context that until legislation changed in 2003, mining companies in South Africa practiced compulsory testing for workers at the point of recruitment, refusing those who tested positive (Kenny, 2004). The role of trade unions is important in negotiating, verifying and rigorously policing any assurances by securing anti-discrimination and anti-victimization protections in collective agreements, promoting and monitoring VCT provision and by convincing workers that they will not suffer if tested.

Most workers, even in highly infected areas, do not present themselves for testing. Only tiny percentages of workers normally volunteer, particularly if testing is offered by company doctors in company facilities. Companies draw a distinction between confidential and anonymous testing, arguing that they practice the latter, but this fails to reassure workers. Most employees in African mining companies have limited confidence in management's concern for their interests (von Holdt, 2005) and they require credible guarantees of protection from company action against them that only union involvement can offer.

I.4   Preparing for and implementing the projects

In September 2002, on the ICEM's initiative, an International Framework Agreement was signed between Anglo Gold, ICEM and the NUM, the first such agreement signed with a company operating in Africa. The accord was signed in public after the UN's World Summit in South Africa, and promoted as part of the company's sustainable development work. It had essentially symbolic rather than substantive significance in tackling HIV/ AIDS, because it contains no clause on the subject. It nevertheless symbolically cemented the relations between the three signatories and was relevant background to their cooperation in the HIV/AIDS field.

By 2004 the ICEM had launched an international HIV/AIDS initiative, designed to identify pilot workplaces where the GUF and its affiliates could develop workplace provision, with the support of employers, local hospitals and international funding. The project aimed to mainstream the issue in affiliates' policies and practice. It was decided to work in two Ghanaian mining regions, Obuasi and Tarkwa, with Anglo Gold Ashanti and its partner company with which it was merged in April 2004, Ashanti Goldfields, because of the working relationship with the companies and the GMWU's clear commitment to conduct the demanding program. Overall, the project worked within the comprehensive guidance offered by the ILO Code of Practice on HIV/AIDS in the Workplace; the immediate objective was to implement a strategy based on the Code. The pilot project aimed to secure, through negotiations with these key employers, the establishment or development of dedicated medical facilities for VCT and treatment, and adequate anti-discrimination and non-victimization clauses in agreements. The pilots would in due course identify other important needs, including a need for trained peer counselors from union cadres to support miners diagnosed positive. These counsel people before and after testing, helping them to make lifestyle changes and to manage their treatment.

These companies, unlike many others, have professional staff to manage HIV/AIDS to high technical standards. By 2004 the ICEM also had acquired dedicated HIV/AIDS coordinators. The experts responsible for CSR and HIV/AIDS in both the company and the GUF facilitated technical discussion between the partners. Technical staff involvement also helped build consensus within the companies since there was marked management resistance within them, as in other companies, to acquiring inherently difficult and open-ended responsibilities which generate considerable uncertainty about future costs and requirements. For all parties involved, there is no margin for error. Even small technical mistakes in HIV/AIDS testing and treatment programs are likely to reduce uptake and to make restoring miners' confidence very difficult.

It has been suggested that the most effective company strategy is to carry out in-house programs, without involving partners (Husted, 2003). Yet the AA companies rejected this option. Company engagement with the GUF and local unions occurred against the background of strong relationships outlined above, but its immediate cause was the practical issue of testing and the positive effect that the company felt the union could have. The huge scope for charismatic union leaders to influence workers' perceptions is difficult to envisage outside of the African mining context. Their role is highly significant well beyond the workplace, since they are seen as community, and not simply as workplace, leaders. This influence has frequently been referred to by AA managers. Thus, Brian Brink, AA's senior vice-president for health, referred to the partnership with other organizations including unions as 'crucial to success' in tackling HIV/AIDS (Business Action in Africa, 2007: 20).

Senzeni Zokwana, the president of the NUM (elected president of the ICEM at its Bangkok Congress in 2007) personally took the issue of HIV/AIDS to mines. He carried out awareness-raising activities and encouraged testing. He publicly submitted himself for personal testing at each mine, paving the way for successful testing drives. The union also undertook a wider educational effort to train peer educators and negotiators to bargain for protections for people living with HIV/AIDS.

HIV/AIDS programs are often reported in vague ways, but in the cases of AGA and AA more widely, tangible results could be reported. In AGA in 2004, 10 per cent of employees were being tested; in the company's 2006 annual report, 75 per cent were reported as having been tested. By June 2006, 34 per cent of AA's workers had been tested: of an estimated positive workforce of 28,294, 9,758 were enrolled in the company's HIV/AIDS program, 3,772 of whom were taking up antiretroviral treatment. In comparative terms, these are high take-up rates and a significant improvement on previous levels.

A further concrete result is identifiable, since the Ghana pilots triggered agreements with the employer and government. AGA signed a public–private partnership agreement with the Ghanaian Ministry of Health in 2005 to provide HIV/AIDS testing and treatment and malaria control in the Obuasi mining area, an initiative supported by the ICEM. In this 'co-investment' project (Vuckvic et al., 2005), the company donates the infrastructure of the hospital and available medical staff. It provides VCT and ART to its employees and their dependents at these facilities through an agreement with the Ghanaian government and with insurance company funding.

The project provided an essential first step in establishing the possibility of moving beyond an awareness-raising model by making material progress and showing concretely how that could be done. It also made the case to companies outside of those directly involved that union cooperation is a positive factor. The pilot initiative has been exported, at the time of writing, to other companies in Ghana and also to Botswana, Nigeria, Namibia, Democratic Republic of Congo, Côte d'Ivoire and Mali.

We now turn to the second element of the case study: ICEM–union–company relationships at the Cerrejón mine in Colombia.

Colombia

This part of the study focuses on relations between the Sintracarbon union and Carbones del Cerrejón, part-owned by AA. As indicated above, AA is closely involved in Cerrejón with regular visits to the mine by senior AA staff including Edward Bickham, executive vice president, external affairs. The African initiatives described above were essential background to developments in Colombia since they created awareness within the GUF and the company that positive relations on that continent were yielding benefits for both sides. It also shows how education played a significant role in building relationships between Colombian unions and generating union capacity to act locally in relation to AA and other companies.

For trade unionists, Colombia has long represented the most dangerous country in the world. The civil war has placed unions in a highly vulnerable position since they have to operate with and in the interstices between government, guerrillas, paramilitary forces, multinationals and criminals (Pearce, 2004). Hundreds of union leaders have been assassinated during the last decade, causing activists to reduce or abandon their union work, leaving small, isolated unions. At the time of writing, many trade unionists have again been forced into hiding by a wave of violence.

Overcoming problems of inter-union dialogue

Colombian unions have varied and powerful political orientations that tend to fragment them. Unions in the ICEM sectors are affiliated to the main center-left Colombian union federation, Central Unitaria de Trabajadores (CUT). They have a strong orientation towards political action, and the state has the legal right to intervene in their affairs. Up until 2000, none of the unions discussed below provided representative services to members and had only minimal experience of collective bargaining, while some resisted dialogue with employers on political grounds. Certain unions actively supported oppositional movements while others retained their historical basis in left-wing groups although there is no organizational or political link between the unions and the left-wing guerrilla organizations ELN or FARC. One union was built from the radical M19 grouping, although M19 was disbanded and no longer directs union strategy. Unions have strong factional dynamics and most unions experience mistrust between executive members that becomes acute at high points in the societal conflict.

Unions in the ICEM's industries also have significant industrial differences. For example the Sintraelecol union is a large public sector union, with the highest level of security threat for union leadership. Miners, among the first Colombian workers to organize in the early twentieth century, have a respected position, but are also exposed in relation to threats of violence against them. Sintraquim, by contrast, is a small, relatively moderate union representing a majority of women working in the chemicals and pharmaceuticals sectors, mainly concerned with the lack of secure jobs and factory closures. These differences make it difficult for unions to cooperate, both between themselves but also within the CUT and the ICEM. This reinforces their sense of isolation and weakness in relation to employers. It should be noted, however, that the ICEM affiliates have attempted to work in a coordinated way for ten years as the ICEM Colombia Committee, which reflects their increasingly important positioning within CUT and, more recently, with employers.

The ICEM's interventions

The foundations of the ICEM's work were educational, and projects moved through three overlapping stages: building the GUF–union relationship, reviewing the unions' own structures and ways of working and finally bargaining with companies.

The ICEM's work with Colombian unions began in the 1980s through the Education Department of the Miners International Federation (MIF), which merged with ICEF in 1995 to form the ICEM. Ann Browne, then MIF education officer, established contacts with the mining unions, initially informally, focusing on mining communities and child labor, which were priority issues for the MIF at that point. These contacts led to a relationship with the current leadership of the Sintracarbon (at that time Sintraintercor) union.

Sintracarbon and the Carbones del Cerrejón management were central to wider developments in Colombia. The Cerrejón mine is one of the largest open caste coal mines in the world and Sintracarbon is also an important ICEM affiliate. Its president, Jaime Deluquez, is a member of both the ICEM Latin American regional committee and its international executive committee. He is a well-respected and highly effective member of the international with a deep awareness of the possibilities and limits of international trade unionism, formulating clear requests to the ICEM and its affiliates in ways that could be readily understood and responded to. He is therefore in a strong position to represent the interests of his own union and the other ICEM Colombian affiliates at the international level. His reputation with management was that of a capable and focused leader. He played a key role in helping build the relationships between Sintracarbon, Carbones de Cerrejón and the ICEM.

In 1975 the state-owned company Carbones de Colombia (Carbocol) sold 50 per cent of the Cerrejón mine to Intercor, an ExxonMobil subsidiary. In the late 1990s the mine and the surrounding region suffered from poor health and safety conditions and in response to Colombian requests were included in the MIF's international Health and Safety Project for mining unions. Interestingly, the GMWU also participated in this successful Global Health & Safety Project. The project, in addition to campaigning for ratification of the ILO's mining safety convention, C176, provided education and consultancies for unions to develop their own health and safety capacity and to work with managements to build medical services. Significant gains were made by the union, including introducing the first occupational health testing system in the mine and creating a good working relationship with company medical staff. The doctor then in charge of the Cerrejón medical facilities established comprehensive systems for data collection and testing for occupational diseases.

This program ended in 1998 and simultaneously a dedicated educational methods program began, for ICEM affiliates in Colombia and those interested in affiliating. The consistent funding and support it received for 15 years from the Swedish metal and mining union Metall (now IFMetall) and LO-TCO was essential. From 1998 until 2004 the program was coordinated from Bogotá by the experienced trade unionist Carlos Bustos; his involvement continues. The high-quality work focused on educational methods for Colombian regional and national leaders, with particular emphasis on providing a safe and inclusive educational environment for national and local leaders. The project funded them to travel by air rather than by the inherently dangerous road routes and provided an important way for national leaders to meet their own regional and local activists.

Union educational methods provided democratic and safe contexts for trade unionists to debate and find solutions to highly threatening problems. The educational setting provides clear rules, participation and emphasizes equality between participants – exceptional emphases in the national context. For those that came from a highly politicized background, the experience of participatory education was initially very difficult to come to terms with, as they were accustomed to lecture-based, and position-taking modes of exchange. At first, classroom discussions were highly combative, leading to absenteeism. Less senior, female and younger trade unionists were initially unwilling to participate in joint activities, but this changed as the focus gradually shifted from aggressive political debate towards finding practical and practicable joint solutions to industrial relations problems.

Over time, participants grew to appreciate the educational environment, and the removal of restrictions and stress when they attended project activities. Attendance gradually improved. For many involved, the risks of congregating in one location meant that for attendance at project activities to be so consistent over the long term the benefits must have been significant. Education provided an opportunity to build social capital: friendships and good working relationships were formed between activists from the same and different unions. This had a long-term effect on their behavior at ICEM and other union events and also provided them with a firm social base from which to venture into trying to address their individual unions' ways of working. By 2004 the ICEM's six affiliates were all prepared to start reviewing their organizations.

A new phase of education was therefore directed to examining these issues. The unions perceived their problems to be recruiting new members, weak finances, corruption, and lack of education at any level, all contributing to organizational stagnation. Both joint and single union seminars were carried out using ICEM staff to initiate thinking around organizational change, focusing in particular on the difficult recruitment issue. Although this phase was relatively short, the discussions stimulated union executives to think beyond the immediate crisis that they faced, to consider longer-term objectives and to regard the possibilities of recruitment more positively. In brief, they began to take a more strategic approach, including in terms of their relations with employers.

Dialogue with employers

A final phase of the ICEM's educational work in Colombia turned to the core issue of dialogue with employers. By 2003 collective bargaining had effectively atrophied. Colombian law allows management and unions to extend collective bargaining agreements without revision at six monthly intervals, and the practice had become common. The level of danger for union leaderships is raised during negotiations with management, discouraging negotiators from resuming discussions. The education program was redirected towards a process of formally denominated social dialogue, directly mediated by the ICEM, involving the six ICEM affiliates and eight nominated MNCs.

The original MNCs identified were:

- Anglo American (UK)
- BHP Billiton (Australia)
- Xstrata (Switzerland)
- Linde (Germany)
- Codensa/Endesa (Spain)
- Owens Illinois (USA)
- Smurfitt (Ireland)
- Union FENOSA (Spain)

The related ICEM affiliates were:

- Sintraelecol (Elecric Power)
- Sintravidricol (Glass)
- Sintracarcol (Paper & Cardboard)
- Sintracarbon (Coal)
- Sintraquim (Chemicals & Pharmaceuticals)
- Fenaltec (Electrical Engineers)

One-day meetings occurred every quarter, preceded by ICEM affiliate meetings and facilitated by the ICEM leadership to agree areas for negotiation. Complementary research was commissioned by the ICEM on specific areas such as contract labor, and union-only and joint training activities were organized on new issues such as HIV/AIDS. The areas identified by the group for negotiation included security for trade unionists, health and safety, HIV/AIDS and contract labor.

A process of ICEM-mediated negotiations with employers was initiated around this agenda and carried on for several years with an increasing emphasis, encouraged by the ICEM, on bilateral negotiations between employers and unions. International mediation provided both sides with an externally created platform to restart direct collective bargaining. AA and the Spanish-owned utilities multinational Endesa (with whom the ICEM has an International Framework Agreement) were pivotal to company participants responding to central company prompting to become involved.

The security and health and safety agendas were especially attractive to these companies.

A framework for dialogue was agreed in the early stages, designed to provide clear mechanisms for unions and employers. The central commitment of both the companies and union partners was to seek common ground and agreement. Importantly, the partners committed to participation in the process regardless of any local disputes or ongoing collective bargaining. Partners were asked to nominate formally a small team of representatives responsible for maintaining dialogue within their organization. These were responsible for ensuring their consistent participation, for securing bilateral meetings at workplace level to debate areas of common interest, for maintaining regular communication with partners and the ICEM, and finally for contacting the ICEM general secretary if difficulties arose. The importance of continuity of personnel from both unions and companies was emphasized, to ensure that momentum was maintained.

In 2004, the process, still at an early stage, was buttressed by state involvement. The government appears to have been interested in closer relations with companies, and in discussing human rights issues both with them and with the ICEM. Employer and union partners attended regular meetings with the Ministry for Social Protection, to present the issues under negotiation and seek support from the ministry for the principles of their work. The meetings were headed by Jorge Leon Sanchez, vice-minister for social protection, and his staff, joined initially by government human rights specialists. Areas for future work were identified including promoting HIV/AIDS initiatives and developing tripartite dialogue on setting limits and standards on contract and agency labor. Importantly, the vice-minister committed himself to prioritize action when unions approached the ministry about union representatives' security.

The most significant outcome of the ICEM program was improved dialogue between Sintracarbon and Carbones del Cerrejón. On 1 December 2004 negotiations between Carbones del Cerrejón and Sintracarbon re-opened. The negotiations were closely watched by other companies and unions to see what could be achieved at a time when the level of violence against and murder of unionists was especially high. During the negotiation period the union negotiators and their families were threatened with extortion and assassination and the entire negotiating team was forced into hiding. Sintracarbon contacted the ICEM to inform them of the threats. The ICEM immediately contacted Sir Mark Moody-Stuart, and requested that they contact Cerrejón management to establish whether the company was in a position to minimize the risk. AA management and the union immediately issued a joint statement affirming their belief in fundamental labor rights and condemning intimidation. The company drew the threats to the attention of the vice president of Colombia, asking that the personal security of those involved be ensured. The negotiation process was able to continue; and although the threats did not entirely stop they diminished, and the negotiators and their families were unharmed throughout. Developing an HIV/AIDS pilot in the Cerrejón mine was discussed in 2006 with senior AA management as the final stage in this relationship. Although it is currently unclear whether this will succeed, it is testimony to the strength of relationships that such a complex issue could be broached in the context.

These negotiations brought some benefits for workers, and established a momentum that built on these. As a result of a subsequent wave of negotiations, an improved agreement was signed on 28 January 2007. The agreement brought salary increases for all workers including those in ancillary jobs and holding fixed-term contracts. The company pension scheme was opened for the first time to workers on fixed-term contracts of longer than six months. Also for the first time the company agreed to follow Colombian legislation by monitoring contract workers' conditions, and by jointly carrying out health and safety inspections within the mine with Sintracarbon representatives. In addition, the agreement covered social issues such as education and family benefits.

Sintracarbon's achievements provided motivation for other unions to embark on renewed collective bargaining. Thus, for example, coordinated bargaining was subsequently secured in the glass sector after many years of stalling by key employer Owens Illinois. The results of these negotiations were uneven, but overall workers' conditions were improved in both salary and health and safety terms. In companies where senior management had a strong relationship with the ICEM, local bargaining was more successful than elsewhere. Ensuring the participation of local management in most cases required direct communication between the ICEM Secretariat and the multinational's senior management. In these cases, they received unequivocal instruction from international, and in some cases regional, management to participate in good faith. Without this, it is unlikely that local managers would have participated as fully as they did.

The Colombian union movement itself remains both divided and fragile although currently the ICEM unions and their national center, CUT, enjoy the highest level of internal cohesion in their history. Alliances between the ICEM unions involved have proved to be extremely strong, and they represent the most cohesive bloc within CUT. The unions are in regular contact with each other in relation to security for union leaders, contacts which were totally absent in the past. The CUT itself has improved its standing nationally and internationally and is recognized as a serious partner at both levels. All of this has provided a solid base for individual unions and raised their confidence in their capacity to deal with multinationals.

Without the many years of educational programs, it is unlikely that the relationship between the ICEM and its affiliates would have developed sufficiently strongly to sustain a difficult, complex and prolonged process of internationally mediated negotiations. The ICEM's direct role in preparing unions and creating new spaces for dialogue created the only opportunity the unions had to step outside a previously intractable dynamic of threats and local disputes. The Colombian experience of social dialogue was consciously adopted and systematically transferred by the ICEM to other situations such as Thailand and Peru where dialogue between unions and employers had broken down. Several murders of Sintracarbon leaders between 2008 and the present remind us of the continued risks faced by trade unionists in that country.

I.5   Conclusion

The GUF leveraged a 'partnership' approach in one part of the company's operation to enable a revival of distributive bargaining in another. The company was prepared to offset the clear efficiency advantages which it won from raising workers' participation in HIV/AIDS programs in Africa against the costs of revived distributive bargaining in Latin America. The company established a clear reputation as an industry leader in this field that was widely recognized.

The Ghana collaboration deepened relations between the international and the company. The efficiency of company investments was raised by union involvement under the general education umbrella: awareness raising, peer counseling and workplace representative education. The results for workers were also considerable, raising participation rates in the company's HIV/AIDS programs while minimizing risks to individuals. In Colombia, serious political factionalism within unions in an endemically violent situation was overcome and the GUF rebuilt dialogue with AA and other companies.

The ICEM was a major actor in its own right in the two continents that are central to AA's mining operations, taking the initiative and mediating between the company and national unions. The formal collective bargaining that resulted in an IFA with Anglo Gold played a relatively minor role here. The GUF's input was important in taking the initiative with the AA companies and in negotiating significant safeguards for workers, in educating them and their representatives and in generalizing and publicizing the initiative beyond the company. A model was developed that the GUF transferred elsewhere in the world.

The case illustrates the large-scale resources required to form and maintain a relationship between a GUF and a multinational. The resources issue is one factor prompting us to ask how far lessons from the case can have wider significance for the global trade unions, since GUFs have limited capacities to conduct such intensive long-term work. We can only broadly estimate the case's wider significance here and a need exists for more case studies. In this instance, a partnership approach was possible because of the HIV/AIDS issue, which generated an exceptionally powerful business case for working with the GUF. Nevertheless, broadly similar health conditions exist and concern both mining and other companies (Gaunt, 2007). Moreover, AA was predisposed to regard engagement with the GUF positively since it was reconciled to trade unionism, was operating profitably, was accustomed to initiating collaboration with unions to reduce costs, and senior management shared industrial relations experience with the ICEM leadership. These may be unusual features, but they are clearly not unique since the company's federal structure, concern with CSR and raising efficiency through cost reduction are shared by many others.

DISCUSSION QUESTIONS

1 What benefit did Anglo-American and the ICEM respectively gain from these interactions?
2 What lessons can other companies draw from Anglo-American's experience?
3 Do you see alternative ways of dealing with the issues outlined in this case?

NOTE

1 This case study is based on chapter 9 of Croucher and Cotton (2011). It has been slightly modified.

11
Different forms of internationalization and diverse HRM practices: the case of China

Fang Lee Cooke

11.1 Introduction

Compared with their counterparts in developed economies, the internationalization of Chinese firms is a relatively recent phenomenon and has taken various forms and routes. Chinese firms are also faced with different opportunities and constraints in their internationalization endeavor from those encountered by western MNCs. This chapter identifies major forms of internationalization of Chinese firms. It also examines the role of the government and a wider range of institutional actors in shaping these Chinese MNCs' business opportunities and human resource management (HRM) practices. The chapter is divided into four main sections. The first provides an overview of the Chinese economic reform since 1978 and varying speed of development across a number of key industries, in part as a result of the differences in the industrial policy of the government. The second section examines the driving forces for the internationalization of Chinese firms. The third section investigates different routes in which internationalization has taken place. The fourth section then compares and contrasts the diverse HRM practices across Chinese MNCs in various ownership forms and in a number of countries, with particular focus on developing countries.

11.2 Economic reform and industrial development

The development of the Chinese economy since the founding of the socialist China in 1949 can be divided into two major periods. One is the state-planned economy period (1949–1978) in which nearly 80 per cent of the urban employment was provided by the state sector (see National Bureau of

Statistics of China (NBSC), 2011). The other is the socialist market economy period (1979 onward) during which the state sector has shrunk dramatically and the private sector has become the main stake of the economy. By the end of 2010, less than a quarter of the urban employment was provided by the state sector (NBSC, 2011). During this period, market competition has become more intensified, with the rapid growth of domestic firms and the entry of foreign-owned businesses. However, strategic industries such as the IT and telecom industry were protected by the government through favorable policies and resource support. They were able to grow fast and become international players. Similarly, the development of pillar industries such as the automotive industry were facilitated through an industrial policy that forced foreign auto firms who wished to enter the Chinese market to form joint ventures with Chinese (state-owned) auto firms. Foreign auto firms were not allowed to set up wholly-owned subsidiaries in China until the late 1990s. This enabled the Chinese auto firms to acquire the much needed capital investment, technical competence and management skills from their foreign partners, though the forced marriage was not always a happy one (see Cooke, 2008 for more detailed discussion of these industries).

Meanwhile, the transformation of the infrastructure of contemporary China has enabled large Chinese construction firms, many of which are state-owned, to acquire experience, competence and confidence to play in the international market. More importantly, much of China's post-1978 economic growth came from its manufacturing sector that is export-oriented, and the country has become known as 'the World Factory'. The continuous high economic growth of China rendered the country resource-poor, and state-owned energy firms are encouraged by the state to secure natural resources in various parts of the world to sustain the country's development. As China's low labor cost advantage is being eroded due to the skill shortage and rising wage demands, not only are foreign manufacturing firms looking towards other emerging economies such as Vietnam and Thailand as their new production bases, but also domestic Chinese firms have begun to cast their business interests outside China in search of cheaper production sites and new markets. It is within this broader business context that the internationalization of Chinese firms takes place, to which we now turn.

11.3 Internationalization of Chinese firms: driving forces and opportunities

According to Dunning and Narula (2004), there are four major motives for FDI: market-seeking, resource-seeking, asset-seeking, and efficiency-seeking. Exactly where firms can fulfill these motives are often location-specific. Scholars in international business (for example Dunning, 1995; Frost, 2001; Makino et al., 2002) suggest that firms engage in FDI 'not only to transfer their resources to a host country' (asset exploitation), 'but also to learn, or gain access to, the necessary strategic assets available in the host country' (asset seeking) (Makino et al., 2002, p. 405). Strategic assets include, for example, technology, marketing and management expertise. Makino et al. (2002: 404) therefore argue that firms in newly industrialized economies engaged in FDI in developed countries not only to exploit their existing advantage but also to seek technology-based resources and skills 'that are superior or not available in their home countries in a particular product market domain'.

A number of factors are at play in pushing China's outward investment agenda. Some of these motives correspond to those categorized by Dunning and other authors as aforementioned.

Push strategy by the Chinese government

China's outward investment is very much government-backed. As Cai (1999: 870) noted, 'in any analysis of Chinese outward FDI, it is important to point out that political considerations always play an important role'. The Chinese government began encouraging Chinese companies to invest overseas in 1999, initially as part of its strategy to deal with the imminent competitive pressure on the domestic industry which would follow after China's accession to the WTO. Since the early 2000s, the Chinese central government and regional governments have been actively encouraging Chinese enterprises to 'go global' under a broadening set of strategic intents. A number of incentives have been deployed, including tax incentives, subsidies, national bank loans with preferential terms, and better access to the domestic market for goods produced by Chinese overseas affiliates (for example Child, 2001; Buckley et al., 2007; Alon and McIntyre, 2008).

In the government-sponsored 8th China International Fair for Investment and Trade (the sole national event focusing on FDI) in September 2004, equal emphasis was placed on attracting foreign FDI and encouraging Chinese outward FDI (*Asian Pacific Bulletins*, 2004). In particular, state-owned natural-resource companies were under orders from the central government to secure reserves abroad (for example, oil, gas, and mining activities in resource-rich countries) in order to meet the country's booming demand for fuel and other raw materials. In addition, Chinese firms were encouraged to expand overseas to transfer mature technologies in which Chinese firms have a comparative advantage (for example, electronics, textile and garment processing industries). Not only are large enterprises with relatively strong capacities urged to 'go global', but also small and medium-sized enterprises are supported by the government to expand in the international market. The Chinese government's push strategy coincides with the pull strategy by foreign governments, many of which are developed countries, to attract Chinese investment.

Pull strategy by foreign governments

Since the late 1990s, governments from developed countries, such as Australia, Britain, Canada, Demark, Germany and Japan, have been keen to attract Chinese investment to their countries to help revitalize their regional economy and rescue ailing plants. This is evidenced by favorable investment policies, government-led development agencies lobbying, and high-profiled delegate visits to China led by senior government ministers. For example, the First Minister Rhodri Morgan led a 20-strong team from Wales to China in September 2004 to help boost Welsh trade and investment with the Far East (BBC News, 2004). During German Chancellor Gerhard Schroeder's visit to Beijing in December 2004, his sixth trip to China since 1998, more than 38 German business leaders accompanied Schroeder on his trip, and 11 agreements on bilateral cooperation were signed (Zhou, 2004). Recognizing the role of China as an emerging home country of MNCs and the potential for further growth of China's outward FDI, many investment promotion agencies have set up offices in China to court Chinese firms that are potential outward investors (UNCTAD, 2003). The Japanese External Trade Organization (JETRO) is an example of a government-supported organization tasked to attract and assist Chinese firms to invest in Japan to help its economy recovery. JETRO's efforts were initiated by a global five-year plan in which the Japanese government hoped to double its 2001 FDI-level, raising it to a target US$119.3 billion by 2006 (Curtin, 2004). The Chinese companies have responded positively to the incentives offered by foreign governments and other location-specific advantages. For example, a number of Chinese companies were reported to take advantage of investment grants in the United Kingdom (UNCTAD, 2003). Following the 2008 global financial crisis, there was raised expectation from the debt-ridden developed countries for increased level of Chinese outward investment to help their economic recovery.

Financial factors

There are a number of financial factors that motivate Chinese firms to invest overseas. One is that, with growing financial strength, Chinese companies have reportedly been lured into a buying spree abroad to acquire assets whose price may have been negatively affected by the international economic downturn in the early 2000s and then by the 2008 global financial crisis.

Global expansion also enables Chinese firms to make use of overseas fund to finance the expansion on the one hand, and on the other hand secure foreign exchange for China through profit-making. It was estimated that one-third of China's overseas investment was in the form of cash investment, with only 10 per cent of this amount actually remitted out of China (Wu and Chen, 2001). By the mid-1990s an estimated 55 per cent of China's overseas investment enterprises were making a profit, 17 per cent were making a loss, whilst the remaining 28 per cent were breaking even (Shi, 1998). Profit-making companies contribute to the inflow of foreign exchange. An additional financial reason for Chinese firms investing abroad is to avoid trade quotas for exports to developed countries. For example, some Chinese textile companies invested in Cambodia to take advantage of quota-free exports to the United States and European Union. Other Chinese textile companies have also invested in Africa to utilize host-country advantages (UNCTAD, 2003).

Chinese businesses also invest abroad to reduce risk. Since the equity market remains relatively small in size, and is subject to discretionary administrative intervention in China, offshore investments can offer protection against domestic inflation and exchange rate depreciation (for example Alon and McIntyre, 2008). 'China's enterprises have the incentive to set up subsidiaries overseas to achieve a more balanced portfolio, and to evade foreign exchange and other restrictions with which they are saddled at home' (Wu and Chen, 2001: 1251). This is the phenomenon generally referred to as capital flight. It is believed that a relatively large amount of SOE assets have been lost as a result of capital flight in the name of overseas development, although the actual amount is unknown or cannot be precisely calculated.

Knowledge and know-how seeking

It has been recognized that host-country-specific knowledge is a driving force behind international expansion because such knowledge cannot be easily acquired (Inkpen and Beamish, 1997). This is undoubtedly the case for Chinese firms, which have demonstrated a growing appetite in acquiring technological and management expertise through international joint ventures and M&As. High profile cases include: Shanghai Automotive Industry Corporation's (SAIC) acquisition of the Korean SUV-maker, Ssangyong Motor Co. in 2004 and Nanjing Automobile's acquisition of the British MG

Rover in 2005. It is important to note that the former ended up in failure in 2009 in large part due to industrial relations and cross-cultural problems that have been well documented in public media.

Accessing foreign technology also takes the form of establishing R&D centers in developed and/or developing countries that have these competitive advantages. The strongest Chinese firms have started to do this since the early 2000s. For example, Huawei Technologies Ltd, a leading Chinese MNC in the IT/telecom industry, has established R&D centers in Sweden, USA, Canada, India, South Africa and other countries (Cooke, 2012b; also see case study J at the end of this chapter for more information on the company). Guangdong Galanz Group Co., one of the largest household electronic goods manufacturing firm, opened an R&D center in Seattle; Konka (an electronics company) has an R&D facility in Silicon Valley; Haier has an R&D center in Germany and a design center in Boston, United States; and Kelon opened a design center in Japan (UNCTAD, 2003).

Brand name product building and market access

The need to develop brand name products and access to markets to enhance their competitiveness are two related motives for Chinese firms to form strategic alliances or engage in M&As with well-known western firms. For instance, the merger of TCL's television and DVD operations with Thomson (France) has given the former the brand name of Thomson in Europe and RCA in the United States. Other examples include Lenovo with IBM, and Huawei Technologies Ltd's joint-venture agreements with Siemens, NEC, Matshishita and Infineon. There are two important factors that encourage Chinese firms to access these intangible assets from reputable corporations through M&As or strategic alliances. One is the resource and effort needed for brand building; the other is to overcome the relatively poor image of Chinese firms and Chinese products as being low quality. Acquiring brands and selling branded products gives Chinese manufacturers a higher profit margin and raises their corporate profile. Partnership with reputable western firms also provides access to well-developed distribution channels where the distributors are familiar with the local environment and marketing practices. The local partners face few language and cultural barriers and have established credibility and brand image among customers as reputable distributors.

Aspiration to be international players

The success of China in attracting FDI has provided Chinese firms with valuable exposure to international business. Inwards FDI has encouraged

Chinese outward investment through demonstration and spillover effects on domestic firms. As a result, some large Chinese firms have gained confidence and incorporated the ambition to be key international players as part of their corporate strategies. For example, Shanghai-listed SAIC wanted to become a top-six global automaker by 2010, an ambition that did not quite materialize. Similarly, the aspiration of the CEO of Haier, Ruimin Zhang, to compete globally and become one of the Global 500 has played a fundamental role in Haier's active pursuit of international growth. Zhang believed that Haier must go overseas and develop Haier's design, manufacturing, and marketing networks internationally, particularly in the USA, to build Haier's international brand reputation (Liu and Li, 2002). It appears that Haier has been much more successful than SAIC in achieving its global player ambition in that Haier has been ranked the No. 1 brand of major appliances in the world for three consecutive years (2009, 2010 and 2011) and was ranked by *Newsweek* as one of the World's Top 10 Innovative Companies in World's Home Appliance Enterprises (Haier, 2012b).

Increased domestic competition

Since the late 1990s, sluggish domestic demand, intensifying competition from foreign firms in China, and excess industrial production capacity in certain industries, especially in machinery and electronic appliances, have encouraged Chinese firms to look for growth opportunities abroad. This is often achieved by acquiring a portfolio of local assets and transferring mature industries to low-income developing countries, for example, bicycle production in Ghana and video players in South-East Asia (UNCTAD, 2003). Since the mid-2000s, soaring labor costs in developed industrial zones along the eastern coast, and market saturation of daily consumables, have motivated private entrepreneurs to relocate their plants to southeast Asia, notably to Vietnam (Cooke and Lin, 2012; also see Table 11.1).

Expansion and support of export

The majority of early Chinese outward direct investment was in the form of small overseas branch offices set up by trading companies to support their export activities. This trend is continuing at an accelerated rate and on a wider scale. Chinese firms are also adopting other modes of investment to meet their needs, as mentioned earlier and will be further discussed later. They are increasingly investing abroad to support their exports, to service their markets and to expand their market presence. In markets with which China has considerable trade surplus, for example the USA, setting up overseas subsidiaries provides an alternative vehicle to supply those markets.

Table 11.1 Chinese outward direct investment (US$ million)

	Net overseas direct investment		
	2005	2008	2009
Total	12,261.17	55,907.17	56,528.99
Selected sector			
Agriculture, forestry, animal husbandry and fishery	105.36	171.83	342.79
Mining	1,675.22	5,823.51	13,343.09
Manufacturing	2,280.40	1,766.03	2,240.97
Production and supply of electricity, gas and water	7.66	1,313.49	468.07
Construction	81.86	732.99	360.22
Transport, storage and post	576.79	2,655.74	2,067.52
Information transmission, computer services & software	14.79	298.75	278.13
Wholesale and retail trades	2,260.12	6,514.13	6,135.75
Financial intermediation	Not available	14,048.00	8,733.74
Real estate	115.63	339.01	938.14
Leasing and business services	4,941.59	21,717.23	20,473.78
Selected country or region			
Asia	4,374.64	43,547.50	40,407.59
Vietnam	*20.77*	*119.84*	*112.39*
Africa	391.68	5,490.55	1,438.87
Europe	505.02	875.79	3,352.72
Latin America	6,466.16	3,677.25	7,327.90
North America	320.84	364.21	1,521.93
Oceania	202.83	1,951.87	2,479.98

Source: Compiled from *China Statistical Yearbook 2006* and *2010* (NBSC, 2006 and 2010).

Establishing plants overseas also bypasses the technical and other non-tariff barriers imposed by developed countries to restrict imports from developing countries. As part of such a strategy, Chinese firms are also buying local distribution networks (UNCTAD, 2003).

The above interrelated driving forces that fuel Chinese investment overseas suggest that Chinese firms are becoming more sophisticated in their strategic intent to venturing abroad; being selective in locations, types of business and firms they invest in. In addition to investing in other developing countries where they have clear competitive advantages, as conventional wisdom on FDI from developing countries suggests, Chinese firms are buying competitive advantages of a higher order, including technological competence, brand name and recognized distribution channels. They do so through M&As and strategic alliances with reputable firms in developed countries where these intangible assets are more likely to exist. It should be noted that where such competitive advantages are held by local firms in less developed economies, Chinese firms also make efforts to develop business partnership relationships with them. For example, Huawei Technologies Ltd actively seek partnership with elite national IT/telecom firms to access their expertise and other corporate resources (see the case study following the chapter).

The consequence of the combined power of these driving forces has been the steady, albeit somewhat slow, growth of Chinese investment abroad (see Table 11.1). In the next section, we further analyse Chinese MNCs' internationalization patterns, with particular reference to their choice of locations, as issues of why and where to invest have direct implications for HRM.

11.4 Patterns of internationalization, strategic choice and constraints

As discussed in Chapter 3, we commonly refer to four international strategies: simple international, global, multidomestic and transnational strategies. The Chinese MNCs' internationalization strategies similarly seem to fall within these categories.

Choice of locations

Broadly speaking, there are three main types of target countries for Chinese FDI: countries with abundant natural resource endowments; countries with technological leadership; and countries with potential markets (for example Morck et al., 2008; see UNCTAD, 2011 for more detail). Chinese firms particularly seem to have a preference for Germany and Japan for their infrastructure, good engineering base and skilled workforce. By contrast, the United States attracts Chinese MNCs for its markets and brand name. The household electronic appliance manufacturer Haier represents a high profile example of this. Britain has more appeal for its tax relief. Geographic and cultural proximity is an additional factor that encourages Chinese firms to acquire Japanese firms. After more than 30 years of imports of Japanese products, especially household electrical appliances, vehicles and commercial goods, Chinese consumers are familiar with and favor Japanese products for their quality and agile design. With a relatively large number of Japanese firms operating in China, often in the form of joint ventures with Chinese firms, Chinese managers are also relatively familiar with the Japanese management style and business culture. Other developing countries attract

Chinese firms with low production costs, untapped markets and more recently natural resources.

As indicated in Table 11.1, the bulk of the Chinese FDI is in Asia. Geographic closeness and cultural similarity have in particular been key factors for Chinese FDI in Southeast Asian countries (Morck et al., 2008). China's direct investment in this region can enjoy convenient communications and transportation. The relative similarity in the economic development level between China and these countries also to some extent reduces the risk of internationalization. In addition, the Asian region has over 33 million overseas Chinese, by far the largest concentration of overseas Chinese in the world (Wikipedia, 2012). Collectively, these Chinese diaspora enjoy considerable economic power and business networks (Yang, 2003; Hu and Wu, 2011). The common cultural and linguistic roots shared by mainland Chinese and overseas Chinese further reduce barriers often experienced by FDI in a foreign environment. All these factors have been influential in the growth of China's outward FDI in Asian countries.

Forms of internationalization

In general, the internationalization of the Chinese businesses has taken two major forms. One is through outward investment; the other is through the successful bidding of projects or service contracts. The first may take the form of establishing wholly-owned overseas subsidiaries or equity-based strategic alliances, such as Lenovo with IBM PC (US) and Nanjing Automobile Group with MG Rover (UK) (cf. Rui and Yip, 2008). The 2008 Global Finance Crisis has led to the sharp increase of cross-border M&As by Chinese firms, who were taking advantage of the financial crisis to acquire previously valuable firms at bottom prices. For instance, TCL bought the bankrupt Schneider Electronics (Germany) in 2002 for US$8 million, and Huayi Group of Shanghai bought the bankrupt Moltech Power Systems (United States) for an estimated US$20 million (UNCTAD, 2003). There has been a surge in the cross-border mergers and acquisitions (M&As) by Chinese firms since 2008. As Table 11.2 illustrates, not only have the M&A values and number of M&As increased, but also the average size of M&A projects.

According to Li (2011), over 40 per cent of the M&As were carried out by centrally-controlled state-owned enterprises. Despite the growth of cross-border M&As, the majority of enterprises are still at the start-up stage of internationalization with limited M&A capacity and capability. Due to the involvement of the Chinese government (via large state-owned enterprises) and the concentration on the energy and natural-resource sector for M&As,

Table 11.2 Cross-border mergers and acquisitions by Chinese firms (1991–2010)

Year	Value of cross-border M&As*	Number of M&As deals	Average size of M&A deals*	Year	Value of cross-border M&As*	Number of M&As deals	Average size of M&A deals*
1991	185	6	30	2001	73	19	4
1992	1,052	10	110	2002	1,194	34	40
1993	860	22	40	2003	1,590	31	50
1994	731	19	40	2004	917	44	20
1995	−25	7	–	2005	3,653	45	80
1996	09	9	1	2006	12,090	38	320
1997	3,260	30	110	2007	−2,282	61	–
1998	319	24	10	2008	37,941	69	550
1999	−398	10	–	2009	21,490	97	220
2000	−307	12	–	2010	29,201	148	–

Note: *Figures in million US$.

Source: UNCTAD, *World Investment Reports* (1991–2011).

Chinese M&A plans have been met with an increasing level of resistance from the foreign governments and other key stakeholders. As such, Chinese cross-border M&As encounter a paradoxical situation in which super-large state-owned enterprises have far more financial power to invest overseas on the one hand, but also face considerably more obstacles than private firms in acquiring business interests overseas due to their connection with the government (Li, 2011). For example, the proposal of Angang, a Chinese state-owned iron and steel corporation, to acquire a stake in American Steel in 2010 has been met with opposition by a group of US lawmakers, amongst other opponents, over national security concerns (Reuters, 2010). In 2008, after Chinalco acquired 12 per cent of Rio Tinto (Australia), the Australian government issued a policy guide which specifies that foreign investment in an Australian-owned mining firm should not exceed 15 per cent of the share (Li, 2011).

Hu and Wu (2011) observed that many large state-owned enterprises set up or use existing overseas subsidiaries to carry out the M&As in part to minimize the negative impact of their declining corporate image. However, for sensitive industries, this strategy cannot overcome the barriers created by host country institutions that are aimed at preventing the M&As by Chinese firms. In fact, as Hu and Wu (2011) pointed out, the risk of failed attempt of M&As increases dramatically when a sensitive industry is involved, disregarding the ownership nature of the Chinese acquiring firm.

Table 11.3 Turnover of economic cooperation with foreign countries or regions (USD million)

Country (Region)	2008			2009		
	Total	Contracted projects	Labor services	Total	Contracted projects	Labor services
Total	65,116.30	56,611.68	8,056.91	86,617.25	77,706.11	8,911.14
Asia	32,510.25	28,902.66	3,328.89	43,173.81	39,811.17	3,362.64
India	*4,264.04*	*4,208.56*	*0.43*	*5,794.54*	*5,793.96*	*0.58*
Vietnam	*1,982.14*	*1,923.43*	*36.58*	*2,398.85*	*2,371.06*	*27.79*
Africa	20,098.95	19,749.05	244.35	28,436.02	28,098.99	337.03
Europe	3,846.16	3,299.32	518.88	3,406.54	3,174.64	231.90
Latin America	3,047.52	2,995.47	37.90	3,681.72	3,644.18	37.54
North America	645.59	588.25	53.27	977.94	935.95	41.99
Oceania & Pacific Islands	1,098.13	1,068.30	21.41	2,032.12	2,005.78	26.34

Source: Compiled from *China Statistics Yearbook 2010* (NBSC, 2010).

The second form of Chinese internationalization, project contracts, is closely linked to the sharp increase in China's participation in the development of Asia and Africa in the past few years (see Table 11.3). This engagement is strategic and backed by the Chinese government. For example, development aids and loans provided by the Chinese government to beneficiary countries are often linked, explicitly or implicitly, to the award of prestigious projects to the bidding Chinese firms (for example, Corkin, 2008; Cooke and Lin, 2012). As Dijik and Van (2007) observed, China's engagement with Africa is motivated by its multiple objectives: to secure raw material supply for China, to create a market for Chinese products and services, and to provide an alternative to the western model for the regional development and to gain diplomatic support from these countries in supreme international governance bodies such as the United Nations. In other words, the Chinese government has taken a long-term view in pursuing its strategic expansion into Africa (Els, 2009).

Variations amongst Chinese MNCs

Chinese MNCs are not a homogeneous group, and their internationalization strategy and process exhibit characteristics associated with their ownership forms, industrial characteristics, firm history and senior management preference. For example, despite the high level of publicity of Chinese state-owned overseas investment, state-owned firms only made up 13.4 per cent of all

Table 11.4 Ownership forms and characteristics of internationalization

Ownership forms	Opportunities and constraints	Patterns of investment/ internationalization
State-owned enterprises	• Longer firm history and more established • Internationalization a political as well as economic mission • Abundant financial resources • Strong government support (state entrepreneurship) • Lower level of financial risk as loss is absorbed by the government	• Acquisition of (part of) large businesses in the energy and natural resources sector • Joint ventures • Projects (e.g. construction) • Relatively large-scale investment of projects
Privately-owned enterprises	• Generally young firms established since the 1980s • More organizational flexibility and autonomy • Limited financial resources and other corporate capacity (private entrepreneurship) • Higher level of financial risk as loss is internalized	• Small-scale investment in discrete projects • Wholly-owned subsidiaries • Projects (e.g. IT)

Chinese overseas firms in 2009 (Ministry of Commerce of People's Republic of China, 2010). While sharing some similarities, firms with the two ownership forms face different opportunities and constraints; they also have distinct patterns of investment/internationalization, as summarized in Table 11.4.

Industries in China are developing at different paces with different opportunities and constraints due to the varying nature of the industrial policy adopted by the Chinese government (Cooke, 2008). Key industries such as IT/telecom have been well protected by the government and the major beneficiaries of the 'inward internationalization' (Child and Rodrigues, 2005) that characterized the early period of China's economic reform since 1978. During the inward internationalization process, China has attracted a large amount of FDI through joint ventures and original equipment manufacturing (ibid.). Chinese firms have acquired skills, technical know-how and managerial competence from their foreign partners. This has prepared them for their subsequent outward internationalization since the late 1990s. The competitive strengths of leading Chinese IT/telecom firms Huawei Technologies Ltd and ZTE in the global market are the outcome of such state protection.

In other key industries, such as energy, the Chinese government has been the driving force behind their internationalization for the strategic development of the country. The involvement of the government and its agencies in the internationalization of the mining companies, for example, is believed to have led to distinctive corporate behavior (for example Buckley et al., 2007), as well as political resistance from host countries as noted earlier. By contrast, small firms in the manufacturing industry producing non-core products are left to their own devices, as revealed in the study by Akorsu and Cooke (2011) in the African context. In short, industry-based disparities open up new space for Chinese MNCs to develop variant practices within specific institutional context.

The preference of the senior management further affects Chinese MNCs' strategic choice of how and where they develop their global presence. For example, the strategic intent of the Haier Group, a key player in China's drive for globalization, is to build an international brand reputation through establishing its own overseas subsidiaries. Long dominant in China as one of the top five white goods producers and one of the first truly national brands, Haier aggressively pursues a globalization strategy on several international fronts. Founded in 1984 as a small enterprise, Haier employed over 80,000 employees worldwide by 2011, selling its products in 160 countries and owning 13 factories outside China, including the United States, Italy, Pakistan and Iran (Haier, 2012a). Haier chose to enter the USA despite having neither technological nor cost advantage and further disadvantaged by having no brand reputation in the market. Its strategic intent was to gain locational advantage by setting up plants overseas to avoid tariffs and reduce transportation cost. Haier developed its global competitive advantage by controlling services and marketing/distribution, and by developing design and R&D capabilities through utilizing high quality local human resources (Liu and Li, 2002). Haier's strategy is also unique in its preference to be successful in large and developed markets, such as the USA and Europe, before tackling what are considered the easier-to-penetrate developing markets such as Southeast Asia. Haier's success in the US market supports its investment and operations in other countries through the spin-off of technology and corporate reputation/image (Liu and Li, 2002).

By contrast, a different, and perhaps more cautious, strategy has been taken by the leading Chinese PC maker, Legend Group Ltd (now Lenovo), which also decided on a future based on product innovation and overseas market expansion. Legend decided to target the Asian markets first before the US and European markets were targeted. Unlike Haier, Legend accepted that it had a dominant home brand which was little known outside China.

Re-branding – such as by adopting the English name 'Lenovo' – played an important part in its internationalization strategy (Strategic Direction, 2005). Its acquisition of IBM's PC unit in 2004 was the largest cross-border acquisition in China's IT industry (China Business, 2004). The marriage of IBM and Lenovo created one of the world's largest PC powerhouses. It enabled Lenovo to access IBM's strong competitive advantage at the higher end of the product market, distribution channel and high quality customer services.

11.5 HRM of Chinese MNC subsidiaries

Having grown rapidly in recent years, Chinese MNCs share characteristics of MNCs from emerging economies. That is, they are generally young, relatively small in size, mostly deficient in international experience and lack organizational capability to transfer management practices (for example Gullien and Garcia-Canal, 2009; Cooke and Lin, 2012). They encounter not only liability of foreignness but also liability of country-of-origin (for example, Thite et al., 2011; Cooke, 2012b). These institutional and organizational constraints influence the way Chinese MNCs manage their human resources in host countries, including their ability to transfer home-country practices to their subsidiaries. In this section, we examine major differences in the HRM environment between developed and developing countries and what implications this may have for Chinese MNCs operating in different parts of the world. In doing so, some overgeneralization is inevitable.

Labor regulations

A major difference between the HRM environment of developed and developing countries is the provision of employment legislation and its enforcement. It is likely that employment legislation of the former is more comprehensive (for example, working time directives, minimum wage regulations, and equal opportunities acts) and more actively monitored. By contrast, labor rights are less comprehensively legislated and even less effectively enforced in developing countries. Relatively low labor costs that are associated with poor labor standards is commonly the main competitive advantage of developing countries. Issues related to employment rights and labor standards in developing countries are often the focus of criticism by western media and non-governmental organizations. It is important to note that it is not always the case that developed countries have more comprehensive labor regulations. Emerging economies such as India have complicated sets of labor laws that may be difficult for foreign firms to grasp (for example, Saini, 2009).

For Chinese MNCs, one of the most difficult aspects of HRM in an international context is the necessity to manage a diverse workforce, at least as a legal obligation, if not as an effective HRM approach to enhance organizational performance. With over 90 per cent of the population being *han* (汉) race, the majority of domestic Chinese organizations have a homogenous workforce in terms of ethnic origin. Despite the fact that a range of legislation and administrative policy on gender equality is in place, gender discrimination is a common practice in both state-owned and private firms in China (Cooke, 2012a). Chinese managers tend to have a weak understanding of and a lax approach to labor standards; and the enforcement of employment regulations in China is far from stringent (Cooke, 2012a; Cooney, 2007). They are even less aware of the notion of diversity management (Cooke, 2012a). Ageism is widely practiced in China where older workers are more likely to be made redundant or forced to take early retirement and are less likely to be promoted. In both public and private sector organizations, gender discrimination is common in recruitment and promotion, in part because women are perceived by organizational managers to be less productive due to their family care commitment (Cooke, 2012a). These discriminative practices are less likely to be tolerated in countries where the need for cultural diversity management is growing and the employment legislative framework is far more comprehensive and effective compared with that of China. Even in countries where the enforcement of employment regulations is weak, foreign firms may be monitored more stringently, and non-compliant firms are more likely to be punished and more widely publicized, than domestic firms. Poor labor standards and discriminative practices by Chinese firms may be politicized and mobilized to fan national sentiment (for example, Alden, 2007; Nyland et al., 2011).

Recruitment

Firms in developed countries may deploy more sophisticated selection methods for recruitment as a result of the development of advanced HR techniques and tools. There may be a much higher level of transparency in the recruitment process and greater fairness in the outcome due to the relatively more democratic atmosphere in western societies supported by more stringent regulatory procedures and monitoring processes. Since Chinese MNC subsidiaries in developed countries are more likely to be engaged in knowledge-intensive businesses motivated by the asset-seeking strategy of investment, Chinese MNCs may need to adopt a more sophisticated recruitment selection approach to recruit knowledge workers with specialist skills. As the HR competence of Chinese firms is comparatively low, leading Chinese MNCs operating in developed countries, such as Huawei and ZTE, have reported to use recruitment agencies to carry out recruitment and selection (for example, Cooke, 2012b).

While some firms in China are beginning to adopt western methods of recruitment, the majority of Chinese firms are still using traditional and basic recruitment methods with traces of nepotism. In addition, local government intervention may be more common, especially in the staffing issue of foreign-invested firms, in order to reduce unemployment pressure (Ahlstrom et al., 2005). Since a major motive of Chinese MNCs investing in other developing countries is to exploit the host country's cheap labor costs and market, mass production by employing relatively low-skilled and low-paid workers are likely to be the dominant production mode, hence less sophisticated recruitment methods are required, especially where there is a large pool of labor supply in the market.

Performance management and reward system

Performance management is another aspect of HRM where considerable differences may exist between the Chinese approach and that practiced in western countries (for example, Cooke, 2012a). Performance appraisal criteria in the state-owned sector in China have traditionally focused on one's morality, political attitudes, seniority and the need to maintain a harmonious workplace relationship as much as, if not more than, one's productivity-related performance. Even in modern high-tech private firms, as Cooke and Huang's (2011) study found, Chinese managers may lack appraisal skills and are unwilling to provide critical feedback to their subordinates. They may also prefer simple appraisal methods rather than the more complicated ones as recommended in the western HRM literature. Equally, employees may prefer performance assessment to be linked to financial reward more than training and development.

In general, the traditional performance appraisal system in China is reward driven (that is focusing on retrospective performance) and tends to focus on the person's behavior. This is in spite of the fact that Chinese employees in enterprises are becoming more receptive towards performance-oriented rewards and welcome career development opportunities through the implementation of a performance management system (Cooke, 2012a). By contrast, the performance appraisal system promoted in the western HRM literature takes a developmental approach (that is prospective performance oriented) and focuses on the alignment between individual performance and organizational goals. For example, Shen's study (2004) of Chinese subsidiaries in the UK revealed that performance appraisals of Chinese expatriates were more straightforward in these subsidiaries with little emphasis on morality and seniority, but the main purpose of appraisal was on remuneration rather than for personal or organizational development. Such a narrow approach to performance management may not be effective to attract, retain and motivate a western skilled workforce.

Similarly, pay systems between China and host countries may be significantly different. In western countries, wage determinations may involve, for example, trade unions, professional associations, government regulatory bodies, employer associations and so forth. Collective bargaining may be used as an external benchmark to set the pay rates and pay rises. Variable pay schemes, individual performance-related incentives and other work-related benefits, such as occupational pensions, may be used to attract and retain talent. By contrast, pay levels may be determined primarily by the state and the employers in China. Although the trade unions are encouraged by the state to represent the workers in signing collective contracts and wage negotiation, the efficacy of the trade unions, where they are recognized, is relatively low. For workers who are not able to differentiate themselves in the labor market, wage levels may be relatively low and pay rises irregular occurrences. Aggrieved workers may resort to taking self-organized strike actions to secure a pay rise, as was the case in Honda (China) and in a number of other plants in 2010 (Qiao, 2011). By contrast, those who are highly marketable may be able demand favorable terms and conditions, including stock options, from their employers due to the shortage of talent (Cooke, 2012a).

A distinct feature in China's pay system is the extensive use of workplace welfare and benefits to supplement the relatively low wage level. This strategy gives employers more flexibility to control their labor costs in accordance with their financial conditions, labor market situation and productivity needs. Examples of employee benefits include: stock options, transport allowances, canteen and housing subsidies, evening entertainments, birthday parties and short holiday trips for employees and their families. Some firms also provide *ad hoc* benefits to lubricate tense labor–management relations, to relax employees during peak production periods or as a compensation for work–life conflicts due to work intensification (for example, Xiao and Cooke, 2012). The extensive use of voluntary workplace benefits in China is a legacy of its socialist state-planned economy on the one hand, and characteristic of its paternalistic cultural values on the other. Not only is the distribution mode egalitarian, but also many of the benefit programs are of a collectivist nature. These cultural characteristics may be more widely shared in collectivist societies in developing Asia and Africa, and less suitable in developed countries with individualistic culture.

Training and development

In general, firms in developed countries invest more in training their work-force than firms in less developed countries, and the western workforce is generally more highly skilled and engaged in knowledge-intensive pro-duction activities than their counterparts in less developed countries. As Chinese MNCs operating in the developed countries tend to be engaged in more high-tech and knowledge-intensive businesses, it can therefore be argued that Chinese MNCs in developed countries may need a relatively high level of training and development investment and provision, with more varieties of delivery mechanisms. By contrast, the level of training invest-ment in less developed countries is relatively low in general. Training provi-sion often focuses on immediate skill needs rather than on individual career development and HR planning. As many Chinese MNCs in these countries are engaged in labor-intensive production activities, training provision may be less formal and less frequent. It is worth noting that there are also Chinese MNCs that are operating in the high-tech sector, such as the IT/telecom industry, in less developed countries with substantial training investment and provision, not only for their employees but also for customers and local communities (as illustrated in the case study).

Employee involvement and knowledge management

Employee involvement and knowledge management may be HR concepts more familiar to both management and the workforce in developed coun-tries. These initiatives are more widely adopted in workplaces in developed countries, although the motive for and the effectiveness of implementing these schemes have been widely debated elsewhere (Dietz et al., 2009). As the majority of Chinese MNC subsidiaries in developed countries are likely to be engaged in knowledge-intensive businesses, the adoption of these schemes may be more common and necessary to elicit employees' commit-ment and harness their innovativeness. Even though there are manufactur-ing subsidiaries that are engaged in mass production in developed countries, workers in these plants may also be more receptive to the western notions of HRM than their counterparts in less developed countries.

By contrast, the management and workforce in less developed countries may be less familiar with the concepts of employee involvement and knowledge management. Even when they have been familiarized with the concepts, enthusiasm in participating in these schemes may be more confined to the elite employee groups. For example, Cooke's (2004) study of a foreign-owned toy manufacturing plant in China reveals that shop floor employees showed little interest in the employee involvement schemes as they saw little benefit for themselves. Similarly, Hermawan's (2005) empirical study of manufacturing plants (including Japanese-owned and Chinese-owned) in Indonesia shows that shop-floor workers were not familiar with the concepts of employee involvement and empowerment. Nor were they interested in participating in these schemes, believing that they were managerial responsibilities and not the workers'. Likewise, supervisory employees saw these 'western' HR techniques irrelevant to their work environment and were unwilling to implement the schemes in part to avoid doing more work. More broadly, employees in manufacturing plants in less developed countries have been reported to be more used to having specific task instructions, less keen to take their own initiatives in order to avoid risks, and maintain a high social distance between themselves and their firm/manager (for example, Budhwar and Debrah, 2001; Ahlstrom et al., 2005; Elvira and Davila, 2005).

Relationship with trade unions

In less developed countries where job opportunities are scarce and social welfare provision is limited, labor–management relationship may be characterized by management prerogative. Trade union influence may be weak, particularly in the private sector. It has been widely noted (for example, Chan, 2001; Howell, 2008; Warner, 2008) that trade unions in China[1] lack independence and power. They play primarily a welfare role at workplaces and have proved highly ineffective in protecting labor interests in the emerging market economy of China (Cooke, 2012a). In comparison, trade union organizations in developed and some other less developed countries possess far more bargaining power and political networking skills. While trade unions' strengths and functions tend to differ across countries, they generally play a much more influential role than their Chinese counterparts in the labor-management relationship.

In addition, unions' approaches to management-union negotiations may differ. For example, some trade unions may take on a more adversarial stance in certain industries and countries whereas others may be more supportive and take on a more genuine social partnership approach (for example, Bamber et al., 2011; Barry and Wilkinson, 2012). This requires the Chinese MNCs to adopt a very different approach to managing their relationships with the trade unions in host countries. The ability to understand trade union agreements and trade union-related laws and the ability to work with the trade unions effectively are skills that Chinese managers need to develop. Existing evidence suggests that several high profile acquisitions by Chinese firms became costly disasters owing largely to the failure of the Chinese firms to resolve the industrial disputes led by the local trade unions. The aforementioned SAIC-Ssangyong case exemplifies this. Shougang (Capital Steel) Hierro Peru, a wholly-owned subsidiary of a major Chinese state-owned steel corporation (Shougang Group), is another headline catcher for frequent labor strikes on terms and conditions. Having acquired Peru Steel in 1992, the Company's operations have been marred by regular industrial actions. In 2011, the Company had to declare force majeure, following a one-month strike, in order to free itself from meeting contractual obligations on shipments of metal (Reuters, 2011).

Organizational image and identity

To some extent, establishing employees' identification with the new employer/organization is a major but generic challenge in post-M&A integration due to the cultural differences and incompatible corporate identities (Bartels et al., 2006; Cartwright and Cooper, 1993). The severity of this problem, however, could be exacerbated for Chinese MNCs given the relatively poor image of Chinese firms and their products outside China. For firms operating in the high-tech industry, host country employees may be sensitive about the transfer of technical competence and know-how to China, as was the case in SAIC-Ssangyong. Therefore, being sensitive to local cultures and employees' perspectives and values is particularly important for Chinese MNCs that are engaged in joint ventures and post-acquisition integration.

Existing studies have observed how HR practices introduced by expatriate managers of foreign-owned MNCs in China have encountered resistance from the Chinese workforce in part due to cultural differences (for example, Cooke, 2002; Legewie, 2002). The same issues are likely to occur for Chinese managers abroad. Shanghai Electric Group Corp (SEC)'s acquisition of the financially troubled Akiyama Printing Machinery Manufacturing Corp in 2002 is a case in point (Curtin, 2004). What SEC did to revitalize the Japanese operation was in many ways similar to what the Japanese and other foreign-owned MNCs have adopted to enhance the performance of the Chinese subsidiaries. That is, trimming production costs through renegotiating contracts with suppliers, overhauling the entire management system, cutting benefits for senior staff, instituting a merit-based pay system, and encouraging all employees to take initiatives. The Japanese staff adjusted relatively well to the changes, although many found it difficult to come to terms with being taken over by a Chinese company (Curtin, 2004). The above mentioned SAIC–Ssangyong joint venture also went through similar organizational restructuring. But the hasty implementation of the radical change plan failed to get the buy-in from the SUV-making auto workers and their trade unions, and has led to the huge financial and reputational loss for SAIC.

Indeed, how to make employees from a developed country feel proud of working for a Chinese firm is a sensitive and challenging issue for Chinese managers. While most individuals in China see it as a privilege to work for prestigious foreign MNCs, Chinese MNCs abroad may not be in this league yet. This may lead to recruitment and retention problems as well as other HR problems. One possible solution is to employ local managers, adopt local HR practices, maximize employment security and carry out a thorough review before radical changes are made. This will help gain social acceptance in the host countries and avoid turning a business decision into a political and cultural clash.

Existing studies of HR practices in Chinese MNC subsidiaries show that local practices tend to be adopted by Chinese subsidiaries. For example, Zhang's study (2003) found that Chinese managers in their UK subsidiaries adopt British HR practices for various reasons. Some adopted the British practices in order to comply with the British labor regulations while others did so in order to compete for talent. Cooke's (2012b) study of two leading Chinese firms in the IT/telecom industry also reveals that they adapt HR practices from western MNC subsidiaries in the same industry in order to retain local talent.

11.6 Summary

This chapter has analysed major reasons for the internationalization of Chinese firms, both state-owned and privately owned. Cross-border acquisitions have been a main mode of international expansion of Chinese MNCs in developed countries. Guided by the industrial policy of the Chinese government that prioritizes strategic industries such as IT/telecom and energy, cross-border M&As by Chinese firms often focus on these sensitive industries and trigger protectionist behavior from the host countries. Even when the M&A bid is successful, Chinese firms are likely to encounter formidable political and cultural barriers to operating in the host countries. The fact that many Chinese firms lack international management exposure and competence also exacerbates the challenges of managing overseas businesses. It is important to note here that Chinese MNCs are not a homogeneous category, nor do they operate in the same institutional and cultural environment in different parts of the world. Hence, their ability to navigate through institutional barriers and secure support and co-operation from other stakeholders, including key players in the value chain, may differ significantly. These variations in business environment and organizational capability shape the opportunities and constraints in which the Chinese MNCs manage their people, often with broader impact on workers' wellbeing and human capital development in the host country.

Acknowledgement

This chapter draws heavily on Chapter 9 in Cooke (2008: 229–60). The author would like to acknowledge Palgrave Macmillan for granting permission to reuse the material.

NOTE

1 Only one trade union – the All-China Federation of Trade Unions – is recognized by the Chinese government.

Case J

Global expansion and human resource management of Huawei Technologies Ltd[1]

Fang Lee Cooke

J.1 Introduction

This case study examines the motives of internationalization and business strategy of one of the leading Chinese firms in the IT/telecom industry, Huawei Technologies Ltd. It then investigates the Company's HR practices at the corporate level and subsidiary level and highlights a number of challenges to managing people at the subsidiary level due to institutional and cultural differences. The case reveals the deficit of HR capacity at the corporate level to support a rapid international expansion, which has wider implications for other MNCs from emerging economies.

J.2 Background of Huawei Technologies Ltd and its international expansion

Huawei Technologies Ltd (hereafter Huawei) is a privately owned corporation. It is one of the two leading Chinese-owned MNCs in the information and communications technology (ICT) industry. Founded in 1988 as an IT product sales and distribution company based in Shenzhen (southeast China) by an ex-army officer, Huawei has developed into a leading supplier of next generation telecom networks and currently serves 45 of the world's top 50 operators. It prides itself as a leading global ICT solutions provider with end-to-end advantages in telecom networks, devices and cloud computing. Huawei's products and solutions have been deployed in over 140 countries, serving more than one third of the world's population. Nearly three quarters of its sales now come from the international market.

Highly innovation driven, Huawei invests 10 per cent of its revenue in research and development (R&D). Huawei has set up at least 12 R&D centers in different regions round the world to strengthen its position in the region and customize both products and services. These include: Silicon Valley and Dallas in the USA, Bangalore in India, Stockholm in Sweden and Moscow in Russia. In addition, Huawei has set up over 30 training centers worldwide to help its customers and local people to study advanced management and technologies. In 2010, Huawei was selected as one of the World's Top 10 most innovative companies by Fast Company.

Huawei first grew into a strong firm in the home market, a typical growth path for MNCs from emerging economies. It then branched out to other less developed countries to avoid competition with the industry's giants as it built up its capacity, before entering developed economies. Targeting less developed countries initially, Huawei was prepared to take risk in high-risk countries and regions. For example, Huawei entered Russia and its neighbor states in the mid-1990s when western MNCs were stepping out of this region due to political and financial uncertainty. It has grown from being a small representative office in an ordinary neighborhood to having a strong presence in the region with offices in prime locations on a par with prestigious western MNCs. Similarly, Huawei first entered the African market in 1998 and now has representative offices and technical service centers in over 30 countries across the region, including two regional headquarters in Egypt and South Africa. By 2007, Huawei employed over 2,500 people in Africa, of which more than 60 per cent are host country nationals (HCNs). In 2008, Huawei launched a series of corporate social responsibility (CSR) initiatives in Africa, including bridging the digital divide, addressing environmental concerns and contributing to local communities in a practical way.

Huawei's internationalization was achieved mainly by setting up new representative offices and partnerships with prestigious local firms. It has increased its speed of internationalization since 2001, turning its attention in the more developed countries while deepening its expansion in less developed regions. Huawei first established its presence in the UK and Germany in 2001, Sweden in 2001 (R&D center) and 2003 (sales representative office), France in 2003, Italy in 2004, and the Netherlands in 2005 after signing the contract with Telfort to supply the Dutch operator's UMTS network. Huawei expanded its operations in Europe and in other parts of the world rapidly within three years. By 2004, Huawei's overseas sales had surpassed those of the domestic market. In 2010, Huawei's sales revenue was approximately US$29.4 billion. It now has most of Europe's major telecommunication corporations amongst its customers.

Huawei's European headquarters is strategically located in the UK. It is believed that establishing a presence in the UK allows Huawei to tap into this dynamic and innovative telecommunications market and to raise its profile in other European markets. Having won one of the top prizes in the 'Most Globally Competitive Chinese Companies Award' initiated by Roland Berger Strategy Consultants (2007), Huawei is deemed one of the best performing Chinese companies in Europe.

If Huawei's expansion in African and Europe is mainly market-seeking, then its establishment in India is both market-seeking and resource-seeking by tapping into India's IT talent pool. Initially launched as a small software development operation in India in 1999, Huawei opened an R&D center in 2001. Now Huawei's Indian R&D centers hub around Bangalore is its largest and most important outside China, employing over 1,300 staff by 2007. By 2011, Huawei (India) employed more than 2,000 IT engineers, 98 per cent of whom are Indian.

J.3 Corporate business strategy

Huawei's organizational structure is led by its strategy and marketing department. The key components of its business strategy are: innovation, high quality, low cost, and excellent customer service by giving top priority to meeting customers' requirements to enhance their competitiveness and profitability. Huawei has over 20,000 patents and invests relatively heavily in R&D. Customer service is central to its mission statement: 'To focus on our customers' market challenges and needs by providing excellent communications network solutions and services in order to consistently create maximum value for customers' (Huawei, 2012). In addition to a commitment to providing good customer services, Huawei's customer focus strategy is said to be achieved through active engagement with customers. These include setting up training centers globally to provide training courses for customers and inviting current and potential customers to Huawei's headquarters for training and inspection.

According to managers interviewed (see the Appendix for an overview of the research methods for this case study), it is believed that Huawei's per-capita efficiency is much lower than its leading global competitor in the industry. Increasing per-capita efficiency has been Huawei's priority with successive waves of cost reduction drives. In 2006, Huawei launched another wave of cost-cutting initiatives in which all departments were under pressure to reduce costs. A 'Total Efficiency Management' drive was launched company-wide in 2007 to review business processes to cut costs and increase efficiency. According to the managers interviewed, Huawei has been through continuous management process transformation in the last decade in order to establish an efficient process-based organizational operation with high quality end-to-end delivery.

J.4 Human resource management policy and practice

As at the end of 2010, Huawei had over 110,000 employees across 150 countries. About 46 per cent of them were engaged in R&D and 31 per cent in sales and services. Some 69 per cent of employees working in Huawei's overseas offices and operations were locals.

Human capital sourcing

Huawei's overseas subsidiaries typically started with a small team consisting of one Chinese expatriate manager, one or two Chinese expatriate employees and a local administrator. Many grew into a much larger operation within a few years. Chinese expatriates were deployed during the initial set up of the overseas operation. More local employees were hired once the operation was off the ground. For example, in 2002, 335 Indian professionals and 170 Chinese professionals were employed in Huawei's Bangalore R&D center. The Chinese professionals were there for short periods to transfer technology know-how in system design and architecture to the Indian team (*The Times of India*, 2002). It is believed that Huawei (China) is better at system integration and technical architecture, whereas its Indian engineers are better at software design and project management. However, it needs to be noted that the high level of localization of Huawei (India) may be partly the outcome of a political deliberation. It was reported that for nine months in 2006, no employment visa applications from Huawei's Chinese employees were granted due to Indian government security agency's concern of security risk by allowing Chinese IT firms to operate in India. At that time, 50 Chinese employees were working in Huawei's Indian operation, half of whom were on employment visas and the rest on business visas (Rai, 2006). By 2007, only 13 employees in Huawei's Indian operation were said to be Chinese. Leading Indian telecom firms also saw Huawei as a threat initially, although the situation was improved in 2007.

On average, over half of Huawei's employees in its overseas operations are HCNs. In some countries such as India, the localization level is much higher. Compared with other operations in the rest of the countries outside China, Huawei's Indian operations have the highest rate of localization (over 95 per cent). In Asia Pacific, 70 per cent of the employees are HCNs. In the

Commonwealth of Independent States and Russia, over 80 per cent of the employees are HCNs. Similarly, over 80 per cent of Huawei's staff in its UK operations was recruited locally. Many senior managers are HCNs and have grown up with Huawei in their country. They were promoted through the rank. Having HCNs as managers is seen as a more effective way to communicate with local staff. Managers interviewed revealed a number of factors that influence Huawei's decision whether to employ HCNs or send Chinese employees overseas. These include:

- Local government policy in ratio of local and foreign staff (for example South Africa);
- Quality of local labor supply (for example in Africa and the Middle East, the general quality of local labor force may be lower than what Huawei wishes to recruit, so fewer HCNs are employed);
- Huawei's affordability of wage level for local employees (for example wages in developed countries may be too high for Huawei);
- Market needs (locals may be more suitable than Chinese employees for customer interface posts);
- Customer demands (for example in Europe, HCNs are employed in order to satisfy the more demanding customers and use the site as a training base for Huawei);
- Language barriers (for example in Latin America, more HCNs are employed);
- People management (for example HCN managers are employed to look after HR issues).

Since the mid-2000s, localization has been a priority in Huawei's overseas operations and actions were taken to support this move. As noted by a manager interviewed: 'Back in 2000, the level of localization was relatively low because the product support was in Chinese language. But we have improved a lot in the last few years in marketing, R&D and international support. We are now more geared up for our international operations' (Manager 4, Huawei). Other managers interviewed also confirmed that Huawei's long-term staffing intent is localization, with a motto: 'internationalization through localization'. However, key and high-risk positions, such as finance and purchasing, are likely to be staffed initially by Chinese to avoid local collusion. In addition to promoting its HCN employees to managerial positions internally, Huawei's overseas operations have been filling their key managerial and technical posts (for example sales managers, account managers) from the external market in host countries for their skills in the field, knowledge of the industry and customer relationship management experience. Huawei's inclination to deploy HCNs for customer interface positions is perhaps not surprising since the Chinese are well known for giving importance to developing informal social networks in order to benefit their career and/or organization. This finding is in line with previous works, which argue that social capital can lead to enhanced organizational performance and that attention should be given by organizations to develop, maintain and exploit such relationships.

Recruitments in Huawei's overseas operations are carried out by local recruitment agencies. This outsourcing enables Huawei to tap into expertise necessary for effective recruitment of local employees and allows the overseas operations to develop rapidly without having to develop a full in-house HR department. Managers interviewed revealed that some countries, such as India, have more human resources available than others, for example, Nigeria. In their initial days at Huawei, some Nigerian employees did not even know how to use a computer. It was a challenging task to train them up, but they have been trained up and are now training other local employees.

Human resource development

Huawei established Huawei University in 2005 to provide tailored training courses to its employees and customers. New employees receive one to six months' induction training at the university on corporate culture, product knowledge, marketing and sales techniques, product development standards, and so forth. Huawei University is responsible for training and developing workers, technicians, managers and future leaders of Huawei.

Selected local employees and managers are sent to Huawei headquarters for training and development in order for them to better understand Huawei's product and marketing strategy and to internalize Huawei's corporate culture and business process and disseminate it back home. Chinese employees are also sent abroad for assignments to gain wider experience of the product and to understand local customers' needs and technical environment. Cross-functional teams working between design and application help R&D engineers to understand the field situation.

The employees interviewed all agreed that Huawei offers excellent training and development opportunities to its staff, which is a key attraction to job candidates. Managers operating in the African region reported that Huawei offers better training than its prestigious European rivals such as Alcatel and Eriksson. 'They [the competitors] will not teach key technology and skills to the locals, but Huawei does. We have the same expectation of competence for all employees and train the locals the same way as we do to the Chinese employees' (Manager 3, Huawei).

Outstanding performers from one host country may be sent to another to transfer skills. For example, the HR manager of Bangladesh was one of the top three trainees in Huawei's global HR training program in which 20 HR professionals underwent training in 2006. He then went to Huawei's Pakistan operation to provide training and support to the HR team on a range of HR functions (*Huawei People*, 2007).

Financial reward

Huawei adopts a competitive reward strategy through regular benchmarking with its competitors and makes adjustments to its wage level annually based on the market information and Huawei's financial performance. International HR consultancy firms such as the Mercer and Hay Group are used to conduct salary data surveys regularly. An individual bonus system is adopted in which the bonus plan of a Huawei employee is closely linked to his/her level of responsibility, performance and tasks completed in each quarter. In addition, Huawei is privately owned and about 80 per cent of its stocks are held by its Chinese employees who had joined the company in its early years of development. The stock option scheme is no longer available to new employees. It was reported that Huawei has given shares to some Indian employees at its Bangalore facility. It is believed that offering shares to locals would help the company neutralize criticisms that the Chinese army had an influence over the operation of the company and hence a threat to India's security (China Information Industry, 2006). Employee stock options have been advocated by SHRM writers (for example Bhattacharya and Wright, 2005) as one of the mechanisms for firms to retain employees. However, this option, which was initially adopted to boost morale in the firm's early days, had served its function in Huawei. It has become a problem in motivating longer-serving staff, whose profit-sharing income was far higher than their salary income, as well as new employees, who were aggrieved about not being given the options, as disclosed by interviewees (see also *China View*, 2007). In late 2007, it was reported that Huawei made a large number of employees who had worked for the company for more than eight years resign and rejoin the company with a new employment contract. It was speculated that Huawei did so to pre-empt the newly passed Labor Contract Law which requires employers to offer a long-term contract to an employee after two terms of employment. However, Huawei claimed that it did so in order to change the corporate culture of seniority and motivate employees.

Performance management and reward/recognition

At Huawei, performance pressure is internalized. For example, a mentee's performance forms part of the mentor's performance. Long working hours and performance-related pay are the norm. As a long-established corporate culture, Huawei's employees have a tradition of bringing their sleeping cushion to the office and work there for nearly 18 hours a day, catching only a brief nap underneath the desk when exhausted. The sleeping cushion is seen as a symbol of Huawei's hard working culture that is believed to lead to success. Aspired young graduate employees feel the peer pressure to work long hours and achieve results. Huawei's corporate ideology is that those who can endure hardship and are prepared to research hard will get good return.

Each year employees go through their performance assessment, the bottom 3–5 per cent of performers will be dismissed, a similar proportion of managerial staff deemed poor performers would also be demoted or dismissed. There is a general proportion of performance assessment grading: Excellent (top 10 per cent), Good (40 per cent), Normal (45 per cent), and Needing Improvement (5 per cent). Those who are ranked in the last category twice successively will be dismissed. This percentage is adjustable based on the overall performance of the department. Well performing departments can have a higher proportion of people in the top categories while poor performing departments will have a larger proportion of staff in the lower categories. Many new employees feel 'the survival threat', as it is widely known amongst the employees.

In the overseas operations, there is a range of reward and recognition programs that are developed locally, particularly in India and Pakistan where recognition plays an important role, as it does in China. In India, annual recognition rewards include: best team players, best managers, best innovators, best projects, best quality adherences, best mentors, best trainers and so forth.

Employee welfare and engagement with local communities

Huawei provides extra welfare benefits to its employees in addition to the provision of social insurance specified by local employment laws. For example, over 20,000 of Huawei's employees work in its Shenzhen headquarters. Single employees are provided with accommodation, although subject to availability, at a low rate in a holiday resort-like environment on site. The accommodation compound has the capacity to house over

3,000 employees, with comprehensive sports and fitness facilities, hotels, clubs and other social function facilities. It contains three football fields for training and competitions. Chinese food is delivered to overseas sites for Chinese expatriates to improve their living standard, especially for those in 'hardship places' like remote areas of Africa. This is typical of the Chinese paternalistic style of employee care. In addition, Huawei HQ has a wide range of employee clubs that are aimed at enhancing the social life of its employees and achieving a work–life balance. These clubs are responsible for organizing picnics, dancing parties, sport meets, photography, song contests and other activities. Huawei has a 'Family Day' event that enables the families of employees to develop a deeper understanding of and bonding with the company. Huawei's employees' clubs also encourage employees to become the conduit of its corporate social responsibility (CSR) policy implementation through their participation in local community development activities, including donations for relief funds and educational sponsorships

Organizational culture management

Huawei's cultural values include: 'customers first, dedication, continuous improvement, openness and initiative, integrity, and teamwork' (Huawei, 2012). Many of these are typical of the Chinese/oriental social values. Corporate culture training runs through the whole training process. Electronic journals and emails are sent to employees regularly to embed the organizational culture of quality and speed of customer services. There are 'open houses' and 'open days' for each division/business unit for direct communication of any issues of concern between management and employees, although the extent to which these channels are used and with what effect has not been investigated systematically. It is the inspiration of Huawei that corporate culture will drive every part of its business: business strategy, management, the workflows and rules, and operations.

The role of team/project leaders is particularly important. Although a large global company, the management of Huawei at a local level is typically team-based and relatively small. Therefore, the team leader plays a fundamental role in enforcing the corporate culture and management process as well as managing the team members effectively. Each team has its own identity and subculture. In India, many social activities were reported as means for team bonding, work–life balance and employee welfare provision, such as birthday parties and wedding celebrations.

J.5   Challenges to global HRM

Managers interviewed identified a number of HR challenges in managing local and Chinese employees in their overseas operations:

1. The wage level for inexperienced new local recruits may be low as Huawei's remuneration is based on performance levels. This may be difficult for the local employees to accept, particularly those from poor countries. The fact that Huawei is spending resources to train them up may not be sufficiently appreciated and reciprocated with loyalty to the firm. Indeed, retention of competent local staff has been a challenge, as Huawei's wage level is lower than its western competitors in the market (see below for further discussion).

2. Local employment laws are different from that of China and as a foreign firm, Huawei needs to abide by these laws stringently. This can at times cause difficulties in staffing level, especially when overtime is needed at short notice to meet deadlines or to solve customers' problems. It is common for Chinese firms to request their staff to work overtime, paid or unpaid, at short notice. However, some countries do not have the tradition of working overtime. Chinese managers then request their Chinese employees to work the overtime instead. Sometimes HCN employees are moved by their Chinese colleagues and join in with the overtime work. Huawei then pays the HNC employees for the overtime but will not force them to do it. This differential treatment does cause a sense of unfairness among the Chinese employees. Their Chinese managers handle this grievance by 'educating them and giving them reward and recognition' (Manager 3, Huawei). However, managers reported that the reliance on overtime has now reduced compared to the early internationalization stages, as the company is now more established with better professional development and support.

3. Striking a balance between employee development and cost-effective deployment of staff is sometimes a dilemma. In Huawei India, engineers are hungry for new challenges, new projects and new positions to learn different aspects of the industry. Even a new project of a similar nature is seen as repetitious and demotivating. From the firm's point of view, however, frequent job rotation may not be cost-effective as it takes time for employees to get up to speed in their new role.

4. Cultural difference in work values is another difficulty identified. Two managers who have worked in Africa mentioned that African employees have a more relaxed attitude towards work and their efficiency is lower than the Chinese employees. These managers tend to send Chinese employees to work on urgent tasks.

5. Multicultural and diversity management is another challenge. Huawei is perhaps one of the few Chinese firms to have taken on the concept of multiculturalism and diversity management and has developed a formal diversity policy statement. However, cross-cultural team working is not always smooth. Managers interviewed acknowledged challenges arising from cultural differences and misunderstandings, particularly at the initial stages of setting up overseas operations. Potential sources of misunderstandings and conflicts include Huawei's management model, top-down approach to management decision making, communication style, perspectives of thinking, departmental responsibilities, work plans and its relentless implementations, means of handling emergencies, work instruction, workflows and large number of emails and verbal communications in Chinese language amongst Chinese colleagues. Nevertheless, people are working together and trying to resolve and accommodate the differences as best they can. Sometimes the teams try to find compromises or a middle ground when the Chinese and the local employees' views diverge. As far as possible, Chinese and local employees work and live together, mostly in less developed countries, in order to better understand each other's cultures and avoid estrangement. They also have a number of social activities after work for bonding.

6. Local employees' difficulties in identifying with Huawei and its corporate culture represent HR challenges that have led to retention problems. While Huawei is seen as an employer of choice in its home market, offering sparkling career prospects to ambitious engineer graduates, staff turnover is a problem in Huawei's overseas operations, particularly in emerging economies. Local employees tend to join Huawei for the training and then move on to join the operators of western MNCs for higher pay and more prestige. Huawei's subsidiaries have tried different methods to retain staff within the constraint of the corporate HR policy. For example, HCNs are sent to headquarters for training and development so that they can better understand the Chinese culture and Huawei's corporate culture. Good HR practices used by western MNCs are adopted, such as providing African employees with guarantee letters to the bank so that they can raise a mortgage for their house. When allocating bonuses, local employees may receive a favorable share. When local employees have improved their skills and competence levels, they are given higher levels of responsibility and rewards. Local employees are appointed as deputy managers to deal with issues of local staff as they are more familiar with the local culture and customs than the Chinese managers. Huawei also offers higher grades than its western competitors to local employees of the same skill level, even though Huawei's pay level for the same grade is lower than that of its competitors. These HR

interventions are partially effective. Nevertheless, as one manager states, putting on a brave face, 'more trained staff have stayed than those who have left'. What is needed, as identified by the managers interviewed, is greater flexibility in reward and recognition at the local level in order to retain excellent local employees.

7. According to the managers, the company has failed to capture and share experience and knowledge. Organizational learning across subsidiaries is not well managed, although mechanisms are being introduced to harness knowledge developed in subsidiaries. For example, a case study database is now set up for knowledge sharing globally by using IBM's Lotus Notes. This knowledge sharing is between functional departments, such as marketing and R&D. Written case studies have to be sanctioned before they are selected for publication on the network. Important information can only be shared by managers globally through group mail or the database.

8. The uneven development of HR competences at the subsidiary level and the lack of capacity to provide support from headquarters are to some extent contributing to some of the HR problems identified above. This remains a challenge to Huawei's HR function. On the one hand, the HR processes in some subsidiaries such as the Indian operations are believed to be more sophisticated than those adopted at headquarters. On the other hand, some subsidiaries in African countries need more HR support from the headquarters that is not readily available.

When asked if Huawei's HR strategy is adequate in supporting its global business strategy, managers interviewed felt that there is no blueprint available to provide guidance for Chinese MNCs in their internationalization process. As such, Huawei adopted a trial-and-error approach, or what is described by one of the managers as the 'crossing the river by feeling the stones' approach (Manager 5, Huawei). Overseas managers admitted that they have a relatively high level of autonomy in managing their daily activities as long as they conform to the broad regulation of the company. Many of the HR interventions are designed and implemented at the local level. As one manager states, 'Huawei is expanding too quickly. The headquarters cannot cope with all the queries and demands from local operations. They leave it to us how to manage the operations as long as we meet the key performance indicators set by the company' (Manager 1, Huawei).

J.6 Challenges to developing the international market and strategic response

In addition to the HR challenges identified above, managers interviewed identified a number of key challenges during Huawei's internationalization process, particularly in its early stage of internationalization. Lack of presence and brand reputation in the market is perhaps the most significant challenge.

> Huawei's initial stage of internationalization was difficult because we lack brand recognition. Most people have never heard of Huawei. When they heard that it is a Chinese company, their first reaction is that the product quality would be poor, so would be the technology. They were not so open to Huawei's staff when approached for business. (Manager 2)

Huawei has taken a number of strategic actions to overcome this barrier, as summarized below.

Cost leadership

Cost leadership plays an important role in Huawei's business strategy that enables it to win contracts, as interviewees disclosed below:

> We used expos and let customers use our products to develop the market. We also invite potential customers to our headquarters so that they can identify with Huawei as a company. (Manager 1, Huawei)

> We targeted less developed countries first to open the market. They are poor countries and sensitive to price. So Huawei broke into the market with price advantage first. Once we have developed the reputation and brand, we then go for the developed countries through alliances with global giants. (Manager 2)

One ex-employee interviewed also revealed that Huawei's European market has not been making much profit as the products were given to the customers (for example, British Telecom) virtually free in order to develop the market and build up confidence from the customers. It is believed that once the prestigious telecom giants such as British Telecom (BT) use Huawei's product, then it will have a strong market presence and confidence. Profit of Huawei's overseas business comes mainly from product upgrade and maintenance. 'Huawei's strategy is to occupy the market first, even at a loss making, then we will make the profit through product maintenance and upgrading' (Manager 3, Huawei).

It must be noted that the Chinese government's tax refund policy intended to support exports and the growth of strong internationally competitive Chinese firms has played a crucial role in Huawei's low pricing strategy, especially in the early years of its international expansion. While the precise amount of tax refund remains unknown, it is not unusual that up to 30 per cent of the before-tax profit may come from tax refunds. However, the Chinese government has been facing increasing pressure from its trading partner countries and the WTO to reform its tax refund policies that have benefited exporting Chinese companies and Chinese MNCs like Huawei. Interviewees admitted that the cost advantage of Huawei is weakening due to the uncertainty of the tax return policy. Huawei's low-cost success, while providing speedy customer services, is also achieved through the use of excessive overtime of its Chinese employees and internalized performance pressure. These practices are legitimized by the traditional Chinese work ethic that values diligence, humility, perseverance and the paternalistic value of mutual reciprocation between the company and the employees.

Developing and deploying political capital

It was reported that the founding CEO of Huawei was the director of the Information Engineering Academy of the People's Liberation Army that is responsible for telecom research for the Chinese military defense. Huawei's deep tie with the army provides the necessary political patronage and R&D partner that have played a crucial role in Huawei's rapid expansion, first domestically and then globally. When Chinese government leaders visit other less developed countries, they are often accompanied by Huawei's CEO and senior management team. Huawei would use the opportunity to donate its products to the host countries. For example, in 2002, Huawei donated telecom technology to Egypt worth US$6 million. In 2004 and 2005, Huawei donated technology to the Tunisian government worth US$18 million. In 2006, Huawei donated data communication and video conferencing systems to help deploy e-government and e-learning systems in the office of the Kenyan President. Most of these donations coincide with presidential visits involving the nations (Huawei (Africa), 2012).

In 2005, when the Kenyan president visited China, he witnessed the signing of a contract for Kenya's national rural telecommunications network reconstruction between Huawei and Kenya's Minister of Communication which will provide telephony services to thousands of people. The project was funded by the loans provided by the Chinese government. It is in the African continent that Huawei has reaped the most benefit from the Chinese government's longstanding political ties with some of the African governments. By contrast, presidential visits between the Chinese government and those of western governments have been much less frequent and less high profiled. No contractual agreement has been reported between Huawei and western governments. Instead, Huawei targets prestigious western telecom giants for partnership.

However, not all governments of less developed countries are keen to accept Huawei, or Chinese IT firms. India is a case in point as mentioned earlier. Managers interviewed also admitted that relationships with certain African governments still need to be improved.

Partnership with local firms and universities

Huawei makes an effort to develop partnership, for example by being sub-contractors with leading telecom firms in host countries to tap into their technical expertise, networks, customer base, brand reputation and other corporate resources and to minimize competition and resentment from host countries. It also develops joint training programs with universities in less developed countries to help them train people in IT skills. For example, Huawei has established two training centers in collaboration with Moscow Technical University of Communications and Information Sciences and BETO–Huawei.

In addition, Huawei cooperated with South Africa's largest telecoms company TELKOM and South Africa's Ministry of Communication to build the 'Talent Training Centre', which provides telecoms training and offers scholarships to South African college students. Huawei has invested in and cooperated with Angola's Ministry of Post and Telecommunications to build the University of Communication Technologies to increase the number of professional technical talent in the communications field (Huawei, 2007).

Improving management process

Audited by KPMG, Huawei employs prestigious MNCs (for example, Hays Group and Mercer) to improve its internal management system. This enables Huawei to adopt advanced management techniques used by leading MNCs and bring itself closer to the global players' standard. This includes adopting management practices that are not commonly used by Chinese enterprises, such as outsourcing. For example, Huawei India outsources a significant proportion of the projects it gets from its Chinese parent company to its Indian vendor partners like Infosys, Wipro, Satyam, Futuresoft. The outsourcing decisions are part of a strategy to tap into the complementary skills of Indian companies, 'as a complementary approach to developing its innovation capabilities in addition to its internal development' (Fan, 2006: 367).

J.7   Summary

This case study provides empirical evidence on the internationalization process and business strategy of a leading Chinese MNC. It is clear that a

Chinese firm may face many unique as well as common challenges in becoming a global player. Huawei overcomes some of these challenges through the development and deployment of political capital. These include engagement with governments and local communities, CSR activities such as donation and charity events, employment of local employees, sponsoring local education and training of IT skills through the funding of training centers and partnership with universities. Huawei also develops partnership with world leading IT giants to tap into their brand reputation and technical expertise. The mobilization of political capital and alliances with competitors and client firms proves important for Chinese MNCs when their organizational resources, including technical and human resources, are insufficient for them to enter and play in the global arena. At a deeper level, the philosophy underlining Huawei's international business strategy reflects the Chinese traditional value that emphasizes harmony in order to gain local and global acceptance and avoid direct competition.

Internally, Huawei's HR strategy plays an important role in supporting its international business strategy. Huawei's HR system is essentially a high performance work system influenced by western HR techniques such as mentoring schemes and performance appraisal linked to rewards and development. The common characteristics of employees that Huawei seeks in each country – young, ambitious, highly educated and motivated, make it possible for Huawei to implement a high performance system worldwide, albeit with local adaptation. This system is coupled with extensive workplace welfare provisions and non-financial recognition programs typical of oriental societies. Recognition and award is an honor that is highly emphasized in the oriental and collective culture. Huawei's paternalistic style of management is characterized by the involvement of management in its employees' family life, in engaging the employees' families with the organizational agenda and in shaping the local community and moral values.

As Inkpen and Tsang (2005) pointed out, shared goals and shared culture are two important facets of cognitive social capital. Huawei enhances a mutual understanding of different groups of employees and embeds its corporate culture by sending HCN employees to its headquarters for training as well as expatriating Chinese employees abroad. However, expatriation and inpatriation are costly HR practices and not all HCN employees can be sent to Huawei's headquarters for cultural simulation. Indeed, encouraging HCN employees to share Huawei's cultural norms and values remains a key managerial challenge. The high performance and speedy customer response culture practiced by Huawei has so far often been achieved through compulsory overtime for its Chinese employees. The Chinese employees are also sent abroad at short notice and end up staying much longer than the original plan. This managerial prerogative is not readily identified by, and less enforceable on, its HCN employees. As Fleming (2005) noted, paternalistic management style may be resisted by employees for various reasons. Without employees' acceptance of organizational norms and values, the opportunity for firms to leverage employees' cognitive social capital for organizational good remains limited (Taylor, 2007). Nevertheless, Huawei's deployment of HCNs, though contingent upon many factors, gives the company immediate access to local languages, cultures, networks and other resources. This makes it easier for Huawei to win customers, in addition to gaining local authority and community acceptance through the demonstration of its commitment and contribution to the local economy. Huawei's overseas operations make more use of external labor market and local resources (for example, HR outsourcing) than the traditional internal labor market system of China. This is a sign of marketization of Chinese firms that is necessary for those in rapid growth such as Huawei.

DISCUSSION QUESTIONS

1 What is Huawei's internationalization strategy?
2 What are the key challenges to and strategic responses of Huawei in managing its internationalization process, including people management issues?
3 What HR initiatives and organizational support can be developed for Huawei to enhance its host country employees' identification with the company?
4 How can Huawei develop a coherent corporate HR system and HR capacity to support its global operations and expansion?
5 How can Chinese MNCs like Huawei manage their organizational learning to exploit local knowledge at the corporate level, speed up the learning process, and gain competitive advantage?

NOTE

1 Part of this case study has featured in Cooke (2012b).

Appendix: Research method for this case study

A case study approach was adopted for the data collection for this exploratory study. Semi-structured interviews were conducted with a total of 18 employees (12 at the managerial level) of Huawei. Interviews were carried out between December 2007 and October 2009. Two of the informants are of Indian origin based in Huawei's Indian operation. The rest of the informants are Chinese. The Chinese managers were either based abroad at the time of the interview or had worked abroad until shortly before the interviews, as the head of a subsidiary operation or a major business unit of Huawei. These Chinese managers have all worked in three or more host countries, mostly developing countries, where Huawei has subsidiaries. They have worked for Huawei for six to eleven years and were promoted through the rank. This international exposure gives them great insight into the overseas operations of the case study firms. For confidential reason, this study will not reveal in which countries they had worked or where they were based at the time of the interview. No more than two informants were interviewed at each subsidiary operation. The six non-managerial employees interviewed were IT professionals who had worked for the company for at least two years at the time of the interview. Access to all the informants was gained through personal contacts. Interviews were carried out individually over the telephone or face to face by the author. Each interview lasted between 50 and 90 minutes. Detailed notes were taken during the interviews.

Interview information was supplemented by company documents and media reports. This secondary data was drawn from information published on the corporate websites as well as media sources in both Chinese and English language. As Huawei is a high profile Chinese company, there has been a considerable amount of media reporting on Huawei's performance and management decisions in China. Its international expansion move also features regularly in international business magazines and host country media. In addition, Huawei has extensive corporate websites in Chinese and English. It also has an in-house magazine called the 'Huawei People' that is published in both Chinese and English. These sources of information proved useful as they not only supplemented the relatively limited number of interviews, but also triangulate (Yin, 2003) information provided in the interviews.

12

Future challenges

12.1 Introduction

In this closing chapter we will outline some of the challenges that international managers cannot avoid having to pay particular attention to during the coming decade. First, we point out that the increased importance of competencies and networks has meant a shift of paradigm in the conceptualization of managerial challenges in MNCs. One of these challenges is to create agile organizations, that is, companies that can rapidly respond to the evolving needs of customer, employees and other important stakeholders. A second managerial challenge involves the increasingly complex task of developing appropriate structures. The new structures also have personnel implications. They require a 'new' type of individual, who not only tolerates change, but who seeks it out, and who not only is prepared for learning, but who is driven by it. Hence, attracting and retaining new generations of employees represents a third challenge MNCs will have to face. More generally, key issues related to global staffing will have to be handled more effectively along with the managerial challenge of attracting and retaining a more diverse work force that excels in transnational teams. The fourth challenge we emphasize is that MNCs must be able to create meaning and legitimacy in relation to their stakeholders and customers in all of its markets including emerging markets. Finally, we identify a challenge directed at scholars within international management when pointing to the rise of MNCs from emerging markets such as China and the notion that we are now confronted by a multi-polar world.

12.2 Paradigm shift

Over the past decades, we have witnessed the emergence of a new organizational and managerial paradigm that involves a shift from command-and-control structures and working modes to modes that involve motivating highly competent employees to actively engage in knowledge creation and knowledge sharing (Bogsnes, 2009). This reflects a conceptual revolution in the sense that it is no longer financial capital, technology or other physical capital that are the primary determinants of organizational success or failure. Instead the concept of social capital – networks, common mind-sets and mutual trust – is increasingly important for companies as they grapple with the challenge of creating synergies across their operations. The development of social capital is not confined to the MNC but it needs to be developed across steadily more fluid and diffuse inter-company boundaries.

Thus one of the key messages in this book is that the competitiveness of MNCs is dependent on creating knowledge synergies through cross-border knowledge sharing. It is no longer sufficient for MNCs to possess a superior financial and material resource base unless this base is complemented by excellent relations among its employees regardless of geographical location or function, and between the company and other organizations. In the network economy where cooperation both internally and externally is the key factor, much of the MNCs' ability to compete resides within these relations. In other words an analysis of the resource base and competitiveness of an MNC must also take into account its social capital. Learning to develop, utilize and promote social capital will be a key future task for international managers.

Social networking technologies have transformed the potential for achieving connectivity and therefore for developing social capital within complex global organizations. MNCs such as General Electric have rapidly absorbed the e-based approaches pioneered by the 'new economy' enterprises. So while the 'new economy' appears to have lost its initial gloss, its approaches live on within an increasing number of MNCs. Similarly IBM's internal Beehive Web site helps employees to connect and brainstorm with peers they meet on interdepartmental projects or meetings. Virtual work groups have been made possible by the digital communication technology: 'General Electric's Light Speed VST, a state-of-the-art medical scanner, was designed with input from cardiologists around the world. The machine's innards were designed by GE engineers in four different countries, and the software to run it was written by multiple teams working together from India, Israel, France, and Wisconsin' (Bohlander and Snell, 2012: 627). Given the communication technology now available, setting up virtual teams is not difficult. However, international managers must develop the ability to nurture virtual teams in a strategically selective way. Yet less than one-third of the more than 300 global executives surveyed and interviewed by McKinsey believed that their companies were getting the most out of information and communications technology (Gibbs et al., 2012). Clearly this challenge will have to be addressed by future international managers.

The agile MNC

Bogsnes (2009) argues that there is a drive towards less mechanistic and more organic management practices among MNCs. This is not just a product of the new emphasis on intangible resources. There are other, related, factors at work. One factor is the volatility of the external environment of the company that not only makes long-term strategic planning and budgeting challenging, but which also necessitates radically more responsive and agile organizations. Another factor is that relationships with customers are undergoing radical change. Making things or producing services in small batches tailored to a customer is becoming routine (Marsh, 2012). Delivering customized goods and services requires a pronounced degree of agility.

This need for agility means that MNCs need to be able to handle fluid networks, temporary projects, evolving and geographically distant centers of excellence and virtual organizations. The agility required of employees means the abandonment of rigid, hierarchical work structures in favor of more fluid, organic structures and the rejection of the restrictive, controlling management assumptions of Theory X in favor of the self-directed employees of Theory Y (McGregor, 1960). It is simply not possible to compel employees to be agile.

12.3 The dynamics of strategy and structure

In Chapter 1 we indicated that in terms of their assets and sales we accept that the majority of MNCs are still best conceived as regionally integrated. However, there is a significant proportion of MNCs that are not. For these the challenge of developing an appropriate strategy and structure is particularly acute. In Chapter 3 we delineated four generic strategies and corresponding structures. A 'simple international strategy' and 'international division' structure is suitable when domestic business is still dominant and foreign subsidiaries are of little more than marginal significance. Historically, as the importance of MNCs' foreign subsidiaries grew, they adopted strategies and structures in regard to two strategic dimensions: the importance they attached to adapting their products and services in relation to local differences in taste, and the degree to which they believed centralized responsibility was necessary in order to achieve scale-based competitive advantage. The choice appeared to be an either–or matter. If the MNC opted for the former it adopted a multidomestic strategy. If the latter, it adopted the global strategy.

During the 1980s, MNCs became less inclined to regard the issues of local sensitivity and regional or global integration as an either–or trade matter.

Some products could be developed centrally for a global market, whilst others needed to be locally adapted. MNCs recognized the need for internal differentiation (Nohria and Ghoshal, 1994). Furthermore, there was an increasing recognition of the strategic role of foreign subsidiaries, such as the benefits in having multiple centers of technology that could draw on local capabilities. Managers have long grappled with the question of how to design a structure that can address these tensions challenges. The transnational organization based on matrix management as practiced by ABB under Percy Barnevik's leadership was lauded as an example of the MNC of the future. However, the matrix structure proved to be so complex that it was abandoned and ABB reverted to a structure that is predominantly global product based.

ABB is hardly unique. Developing a strategically relevant structure that is not overly complex for those who have to work within it remains a key challenge for international managers. Furthermore, as the SCF case following Chapter 3 illustrates, the management skills required to achieve structural change should not be underestimated.

Generation 'D'

Table 12.1 features the job preferences of the graduating student class of 2010 at elite business schools in Norway and the USA. Although there are national differences – as both cultural and institutional distance theories would predict – it is striking how pronounced the commonalities are. The table indicates that the new generation has a strong preference for working in organizations that offer substantial opportunities for autonomy and creativity and a socially stimulating atmosphere. Bonuses and status are of far less importance. Rather than subscribing to a protestant work ethic they

Table 12.1 Comparative distributions of factors

Factors	Mean	
	Norway	USA
Bonus and company benefits	5.57	6.67
Good social atmosphere	8.07	8.24
Autonomy and creativity	7.53	7.97
Clear goals and feedback	6.79	7.40
High status	6.52	7.46
Career progress	6.86	7.79

Note: 10 = very important, 1 = not important.

subscribe to an intrinsic work ethic in the sense than their work has to be experienced as inherently challenging and interesting. If they are not intellectually challenged or if they are socially discontented they are inclined to look elsewhere (see, for example, Nordhaug et al., 2010; Mayrhofer et al., 2009).

What managerial challenges does this create? Traditionally, HRM has involved systematic efforts to acquire, nurture and retain the carriers of the knowledge resources that are most crucial in relation to the company's goals. This could largely be accomplished through the design and use of traditional rewards, such as salaries, fringe benefits and good working conditions. But in the case of the new generation, Generation D (D for digital), this is far from adequate. In terms of their work style and need for creative activities these individuals are more like artists than 'corporate men'. If they are managed on the basis of bureaucratic, mechanistic managerial practices they will quickly move on to other employers.

A parallel development to the emergence of Generation D is the decline in the opportunity for vertical mobility to managerial positions due to the implementation of flatter organizational forms. For companies in general the challenge is to create meaningful lateral career opportunities and to design rewards that encourage the development of lateral careers. In this respect MNCs have a comparative advantage due to their large and geographically dispersed organizations that yield a wide range of lateral job moves for their employees. As such, MNCs can potentially offer a much greater scope for lateral career development than their domestic counterparts. On the other hand employees have to be motivated to avail themselves of these opportunities particularly if they involve periods of expatriation.

12.4 Global staffing

The way in which multinational companies handle their human capital resources is vital to their degree of success potential (Mendenhall et al., 2003; Noruzi and Westover, 2011; Vance and Paik, 2011). As we have emphasized throughout this book, organizing, mobilizing and utilizing the knowledge and competence resources carried by employees, work teams and networks on an international or global basis, constitute an overriding managerial challenge. An essential part of this challenge is that similar people – whether it be national or functional similarity – are more likely to share knowledge than those who are dissimilar (Mäkelä et al., 2012). MNCs have to act purposively against this bias. Clearly investing in cross-functional teams is important. However, culturally intelligent boundary spanners are also required for the development of networks across the MNC. In other words expatriation or inpatriation, whether it be long- or short-term assignments will not be going out of fashion. However, the 'new' expatriation is increasingly driven by a concern for knowledge sharing rather than control.

Currently, some degree of failure related to expatriation and repatriation remains widespread in MNCs. This is costly and may often lead to loss of key personnel. Likewise, it still appears to be the case that little in the way of resources is spent on repatriation, causing many repatriates to feel underutilized and undervalued, ultimately leaving the firm and leading to lost value for the MNC. As discussed in Chapter 8, MNCs are increasingly focusing on how to improve repatriation and the use of alternative forms of foreign assignments (for example shorter periods and/or more frequent rotation) to enhance knowledge sharing and socialization in the MNC (Bonache et al., 2010). Many MNCs also seek to leverage espoused values to create a shared identity and common culture in the organization. This process of identity construction and socialization enables relationship building internally through a shared understanding of 'who we are' and 'how we do things' in the organization.

12.5 Legitimacy and sources of meaning

Finally let us consider the issue of the existential basis, the very raison d'être, for employees of MNCs to commit themselves to their companies. A fundamental challenge is to be able to provide meaning for employees. Ultimately this can only be accomplished through reputation development and maintenance. Reputation has to be actively created by managers who proclaim the aim of the company through the development of images of the company both for internal and external constituencies. By way of example it is worth considering the effort British Petroleum (BP) invested in developing its 'Beyond Petroleum' image. This paid off to such an extent that in 2001 the company was voted as the most respected company in the world in regard to the of management of environmental resources, by a panel comprising representatives of NGOs and the media (Skapinker, 2002). However, reputations are easily lost. The April 20 2010 BP rig explosion in the Gulf of Mexico badly damaged BP's reputation and with it considerable meaning for BP employees.

Managers in previous eras would probably have perceived the quest for creating meaning for their employees as an unnecessary luxury, but in the era of Generation D it is an important condition for sustaining the type of commitment that is vital for network-based and learning-oriented MNCs. To seek meaning in the sense that one is working at something that does not damage the environment or communities is becoming a core demand of Generation D. This aspiration is articulated in Harvard Business School's Michael Porter and co-author Mark Kramer's (2011) article 'Creating shared value', which argues for the principle of 'shared value' which involves creating economic value in a way that also creates value for society.

Meaning stems from legitimacy in the sense that external stakeholders and other parties view the company in a positive light. Such external legitimacy also impacts the development of a shared organizational identity as employees and managers are influenced by how relevant external actors perceive them (Hatch and Schultz, 2002). In parts of the organization theory literature it is emphasized that companies, particularly large and very visible ones, benefit from actively constructing and maintaining legitimacy. One of the reasons for this is that companies are increasingly exposed to external evaluations of their actions. The visibility of MNCs means that every aspect of their dealings is potentially subject to scrutiny. They must expect their products and services to be scrutinized not just for their quality but also for any possible damage they may inflict on the environment, for any use of child labor and for any maltreatment or exploitation of employees. Because of NGOs including GUFs (see Chapter 10) consumer consciousness about these issues has grown markedly during the last decades. As pointed out in Chapter 9 in this book: Who wants to 'buy' child labor? Who wants to 'buy' pollution of the environment? Who wants to 'buy' brutal exploitation of employees? Who wants to 'buy' violation of basic human rights?

Corruption, even when MNCs are not directly involved, is also an issue that is increasingly subject to scrutiny. In April 2011 Shell and Eni paid $1.1bn to Nigeria's government for a deepwater concession holding up to nine billion barrels of oil. In 2012 it emerged that the Nigerian government had then transferred the exact proceeds, $1,092,040,000, to the Nigerian company, Malabu Oil & Gas. Malabu was controlled by Dan Etete. Etete was oil minister under the late dictator, Sani Abacha, and was convicted of money laundering in France in 2007. Campaign group Global Witness claimed that Etete had arguably abused his public position to obtain ownership of the concession in opaque circumstances during the Abacha dictatorship. Shell and Eni claimed that they only paid the Nigerian authorities and that they had acted at all times in accordance with Nigerian law and normal global industry practice and were not involved in the government's simultaneous settlement with Malabu. However Global Witness says evidence suggests that the two MNCs knew the $1.1bn would flow to the Nigerian company and that a substantial monetary 'reward' ended up being paid to a company controlled by an individual. Indeed Nigeria's attorney general, Mohammed Adoke, wrote in July 2012 that Shell and Eni 'agreed to pay Malabu through the federal government acting as an obligor'. Shell and Eni countered that they had acted at all times in accordance with Nigerian law to which Global Witness responded by arguing that the deal illustrated the need for new EU transparency laws that would require extractive industry companies to report payments to governments on a project-by-project basis (*Financial Times*, 2012b).

Tax avoidance by MNCs is now a particular concern not just for developing nations but also for developed nations. Profit shifting across the operations of an MNC, even when it involves the use of tax havens, is not illegal, but it can be regarded as highly controversial. In November 2012, Amazon, Starbucks and Google were subject to heavy criticism by UK members of parliament (MPs) over what they regarded as elaborate schemes that had resulted in Starbucks paying no UK corporation tax between 2008 and 2011, Amazon paying no corporation tax in 2010 on revenues of £3.3billion, and Google paying just £6m in tax on UK sales of £2.6billion.

Amazon admitted basing its European operations in Luxembourg because of the low tax there, and that all profits were booked there. Its spokesperson claimed that Luxembourg, which employs around 500 people, was the real 'engine' of the business, and that the UK, where it employs 15,000, was no more than a 'service arm'. It also claimed not to know its UK turnover. Starbucks told the MPs that its UK operation 'buys' coffee through Switzerland even though the beans never touch Swiss soil. Its spokesperson revealed that the beans had a mark-up of 20 per cent when being sold to other countries, such as the UK. Starbucks also revealed that it said it had a deal with the Dutch government to minimize its tax bill. Its spokesperson said that the terms of the bargain were 'iron bound in confidentiality'. Google admitted to structuring its affairs to minimize its liability by funneling profits to a company in the tax haven of Bermuda.

One MP said of the three companies: 'It seems to us that you are exporting your profits to minimize your tax' and another MP said, 'We're not accusing you of being illegal, we're accusing you of being immoral.' However, Matt Brittin, Google's UK chief executive, said that it was right to pay the bulk of its taxes in the USA because its crucial operations and technology teams were largely based there. Asked to explain the Bermuda connection, he replied that the island housed the company's intellectual property outside of America (Mail on Line, 2012).

As a result of such external pressures on MNCs, being able to create legitimacy and meaning is becoming a primary task for MNC managers. This is a demanding challenge since managers have to balance corporate social responsibility with the need to generate profits. However, as discussed in Chapter 9, MNCs are increasingly implementing 'triple-bottom-line' reporting that includes assessments of corporate economic, environmental and social performance (Dickson, 2002). We can also observe that an increasing number of companies report on sustainability and matters related to CSR and ethics in their annual reports as well as on their websites (Morrison, 2009: 545–46). However, as Porter and Kramer (2011) argue, creating shared value for multiple stakeholders will continue to challenge future international managers in terms of their thinking and actions. An added twist to this challenge is that in a 'multi-polar' world one should not expect the world to conform to the norms and values of the West. Ethics 'being culturally, historically and religiously bound is interpreted very differently across different countries' (Mail on Line, 2012: 4).

12.6 A multi-polar world

With the rise of the BRIC (Brazil, Russia, India, and China) economies the world is becoming multi-polar rather than uni-polar.

> In business, as well as education, cultural influence has been unidirectional – from the US center to the UK and European semi-periphery, and then to peripheries (that is the rest of the world). With the rise of the BRIC economies we expect the span and direction of such influence to be more complex in the future. (Salmi and Scott-Kennel, 2012: 3)

As new MNCs from BRIC countries emerge no longer will knowledge and capital flows exclusively start in the West. Such changes mean not only new players but also new rules of the game. In particular we should expect new business models to be particularly discernible when the MNCs are first and foremost extensions of government power and operating in institutional voids where regulatory quality and government effectiveness is weak. Thus in the case of MNCs from China, where the 'state remains crucial in shaping firm behavior' (Wang et al., 2012: 665), they are entering poorly regulated countries in Africa on the basis of business practices that are not influenced by Western business culture. In regards to developed economies, in some instances the close ties that Chinese MNCs have to the Chinese state have been viewed as a security issue. For example Huawei's attempts to acquire US companies or the Chinese state-owned CNOOC's interest in buying the Canadian energy firm Nexen sparked intense public debate (*Globe and Mail*,

2012; Olson, 2012). However, in other instances such as Lenovo's acquisition of IBM's personal computer business in 2005, Chinese companies have been able to overcome public concerns.

Across the BRIC countries we can observe distinct national differences in where their outward FDI is directed, thus adding to multi-polarity. Chinese firms are developing ties in the Arab world that may eventually dwarf those of Western firms (Simpfendorfer, 2012), whereas Indian firms are investing in acquisitions of R&D and skill-related business in developed markets (Chen, 2012). However, what many emerging economy MNCs have in common is that they lack the sustainable, intangible firm-specific advantages such as superior technology or brand names that the OLI paradigm we presented in Chapter 1 says is the initial condition for FDI (that is the 'O'). Indeed internationalization for these MNCs is often the means to acquiring the intangible firm specific advantages they lack. Instead of an 'O', what these firms often do have is privileged access to natural resources at home combined with exceptional access to local decision makers (Hennart, 2012). We anticipate that future texts on internationalization and on the management challenges that arise with it may have to adjust some of the field's core theories in order to accommodate emerging-market MNCs. We anticipate that this will particularly apply to those cases where the ties to government agencies are especially pronounced.

References

Accenture (2012). Accenture Fact Sheet. Retrieved July 9, 2012, from http://newsroom.accenture.com/fact+sheet/.

Adamy, J. (2007). 'Steady diet: As burgers boom in Russia, McDonald's touts discipline', *Wall Street Journal*. 16 October.

Adler, N. (1987). 'Pacific basin managers: A Gaijin not a woman', *Human Resource Management*, 26(2), 162–192.

Adler, N.J. and Ghadar, F. (1990). Strategic human resource management. In: R. Pieper (ed.), *Human Resource Management: An International Resource Comparison*, New York: de Gruyter, pp. 426–443.

Adler, P. S. and Kwon, S.W. (2002). 'Social capital: Prospects for a new concept', *Academy of Management Review*, 27(1), 17–40.

Agarwal, J. and Feils, D. (2007). 'Political risk and the internationalization of firms: An empirical study of Canadian-based export and FDI firms', *Canadian Journal of Administrative Sciences*, 24(3), 165–181.

Aggarwal, R., Berrill, J., Huston, E. and Kearney, C. (2011). 'What is a multinational corporation? Classifying the degree of firm-level multinationality', *International Business Review*, 20(5), 557–577.

Ahlstrom, D., Foley, S., Young, M. and Chan, E. (2005). 'Human resource strategies for competitive advantage in post-WTO China', *Thunderbird International Business Review*, 47(3), 263–285.

Akorsu, A. and Cooke, F.L. (2011). 'Labour standard application among Chinese and Indian firms in Ghana: Typical or atypical?' *International Journal of Human Resource Management*, 22(13), 2730–2748.

Alavi, M. and Leidner, D.E. (2001). 'Review: Knowledge management and knowledge management systems: Conceptual foundations and research issues', *MIS Quarterly*, 25(1), 107–136.

Alden, C. (2007). *China in Africa*, London: Zed Books.

Alkhafaji, A.F. (1995). *Competitive Global Management*, Delary Beach, FL: St Lucie Press.

Al Khattab, A. (2011). 'The role of corporate risk managers in country risk management: A survey of Jordanian multinational enterprises', *International Journal of Business and Management*, 6(1), 274–282.

Allen, R., Dawson, G., Wheatley, K. and White, C. (2008). 'Perceived diversity and organizational performance', *Employee Relations*, 30(1), 20–33.

Alon, I. and McIntyre, J. (2008). *Globalization of Chinese Enterprises*, Basingstoke: Palgrave Macmillan.

Andersen, T.M. and Svarer, M. (2007). 'Flexicurity: labour market performance in Denmark', *CESifo Economic Studies*, 53(3), 389–429.

Anderson, E. and Gatignon, H. (1986). 'Modes of foreign entry: A transaction cost analysis and proposition', *Journal of International Business Studies*, 17, 1–16.

Andersson, U., Forsgren, M. and Holm, U. (2007). 'Balancing subsidiary influence in a federative MNC: A business network view', *Journal of International Business Studies*, 38(5), 802–818.

Anglo American (2003). Tony Traher's speech to the AGM, 28 March.

Anglo American (2007). Response to allegations made in War on Want's 'Anglo American – the alternative report' 2007. London: Anglo American.

Anglo American (2008). Sir Mark Moody-Stuart's speech to the AGM, 12 March.

Ardichvili, A., Page, V. and Wentling, T. (2003). 'Motivation and barriers to participation in knowledge-sharing communities of practice', *Journal of Knowledge Management*, 7(1), 64–77.

Arndt, M. (2007). McDonald's 24/7. *BusinessWeek* (4020), 64–72.

Arnold, D. (2000). 'Seven rules of international distribution', *Harvard Business Review*, 78(6), 131–137.

Aron, R. and Singh, J.V. (2005). 'Getting offshoring right', *Harvard Business Review*, 83(12), 135–143.

Arvedlund, E. (2005). 'McDonald's becomes largest corporate land owner in Russia', *The Agribusiness Examiner*, 22 March. Retrieved from: http://www.organicconsumers.org/Politics/russia32205.cfm.

Asian Pacific Bulletins (2004). 10 September.

Bales, K. (2004). *Disposable People: New Slavery in the Global Economy*. Berkeley CA: University of California Press.

Bamber, G., Lansbury, R. and Wailes, N. (eds) (2011). *International and Comparative Employment Relations*, 5th edition, London: Sage and New South Wales, Australia: Allen & Unwin Pty Ltd.

Bamford, J., Ernst, D. and Gubini, D.G. (2004). 'Launching a world-class joint venture', *Harvard Business Review*, 82(2), 91–100.

Barney, J. (1991). 'Firm resources and sustained competitive advantage', *Journal of Management*, 17(1), 99–120.

Barringer, Felicity (1988). McDonald's in Moscow: A 'Bolshoi Mak'. *New York Times*, 30 April. Retrieved from http://www.nytimes.com/1988/04/30/business/mcdonald-s-in-moscow-a-bolshoi-mak.html.

Barry, M. and Wilkinson, A. (eds) (2012). *Edward Elgar Handbook of Comparative Employment Relations*, Cheltenham, UK and Northampton, MA, USA: Edward Elgar Publishing.

Bartels, J., Douwes, R., de Jong, M. and Pruyn, A. (2006). 'Organizational identification during a merger: Determinants of employees' expected identification with the new organization', *British Journal of Management*, 17, S49–S67.

Bartlett, C.A. and Beamish, P.W. (2011). *Transactional Management*, New York: McGraw-Hill.

Bartlett, C.A. and Ghoshal, S. (1989). *Managing Across Borders: The Transnational Solution*, Boston, MA: Harvard Business School Press.

Bartlett, C.A. and Ghoshal, S. (1995). *Transnational Management. Text, Cases, and Readings in Cross-Border Management* (2nd edn), Chicago, IL: Irwin.

Bayer, A. (1995). 'Hugging the bear', *Journal of Business Strategy*, 16(4), 43.

BBC (2009). McDonald's pulls out of Iceland. BBC News, 27 October. Retrieved from http://news.bbc.co.uk/2/hi/8327185.stm.

BBC News (2004). 11 August.

BBC News Online (2006). Published 22 June.

Becker, G.S. (1983/1964). *Human Capital*, New York: Columbia University Press.

Belderbos, R.A. and Heijltjes, M.G. (2005). 'The determinants of expatriate staffing by Japanese multinationals in Asia: Control, learning and vertical business groups', *Journal of International Business Studies*, 36(3), 341–354.

Benito, G., Petersen, B. and Welch, L. (2009). 'Towards more realistic conceptualisations of foreign operation modes', *Journal of International Business Studies*, 40(9), 1455–1470.

Benito, G.R.G., Petersen, B. and Welch, L. (2011). 'Mode combinations and international operations', *Management International Review*, 51, 803–280.

Berger, I., Cunningham, P. and Drumwright, M. (2004). 'Social alliances: Company/nonprofit collaboration', *California Management Review*, 47(1), 58–90.

Berger, P.L. and Godsell, B. (1988). *A Future South Africa: Visions, Strategies and Realities*, London: Westview Press.

Bhattacharya, M. and Wright, P. (2005). 'Managing human assets in an uncertain world: Applying real options theory to HRM', *International Journal of Human Resource Management*, 16(6), 929–948.

Bidoli, M. (2004). 'Beyond the bottom line', *Financial Mail* (South Africa), 7 May.

Birkinshaw, J. (1997). 'Entrepreneurship in multinational corporations: The characteristics of subsidiary initiatives', *Strategic Management Journal*, 18(3), 207–229.

Birkinshaw, J. (2000). 'The structures behind global companies', Part 10 of *Mastering Management*, *Financial Times*. 4 December.

Birkinshaw, J. (2001). Strategy and management in MNC subsidiaries. In A.M. Rugman and T.L. Brewer (eds), *The Oxford Handbook of International Business*, Oxford: Oxford University Press, pp. 380–401.

Björkman, I., Barner-Rasmussen, W. and Li, L. (2004). 'Managing knowledge transfer in MNCs: the impact of headquarters control mechanisms', *Journal of International Business Studies*, 35(5), 443–455.

Black, S.J. and Gregersen, H.B. (1999). 'The right way to manage expats', *Harvard Business Review*, 77(2), 52–63.

Blake-Beard, S.D., Finley-Hervey, J.A. and Harquail, C.V. (2008). 'Journey to a different place: Reflections on Taylor Cox, Jr.'s carrier and research as a catalyst for diversity education and training', *Academy of Management Learning and Education*, 7(3), 394–405.

Bock, G., Zmud, R., Kim, Y. and Lee, J. (2005). 'Behavioral intention formation in knowledge sharing: Examining the roles of extrinsic motivators, social-psychological forces, and organizational climate', *MIS Quarterly*, 29(1), 87–111.

Bogsnes, B. (2009). *Implementing Beyond Budgeting*, Hoboken, NJ: Wiley.

Bohlander, G.W. and Snell, S.A. (2012). *Principles of Human Resource Management* (16th edn), London: Southwestern, Cengage Learning.

Bolino, M.C. (2007). 'Expatriate assignments and intra-organizational career success: Implications for individuals and organizations', *Journal of International Business Studies*, 38(5), 819–835.

Bonache, J., Brewster, C., Suutari, V. and De Saá, P. (2010). 'Expatriation: Traditional criticisms and international careers: Introducing the special issue', *Thunderbird International Business Review*, 52(4), 263–274.

Bond, M.H. (2002). 'Reclaiming the individual from Hofstede's ecological analysis – a 20 year odyssey: Comment on Oyserman et al.', *Psychological Bulletin*, 128, 73–77.

Bouquet, C. and Birkinshaw, J. (2008). 'Managing power in the multinational corporation: How low-power actors gain influence', *Journal of Management*, 34(3), 477–508.

Bremmer, I. (2005). 'Managing risk in an unstable world', *Harvard Business Review*, 83(6), 51–60.

Bresman, H., Birkinshaw, J. and Nobel, R. (1999). 'Knowledge transfer in international acquisitions', *Journal of International Business Studies*, 30(3), 439–462.

Brewer, P. and Venaik, S. (2011). 'Individualism–Collectivism in Hofstede and GLOBE', *Journal of International Business Studies*, 37(3), 285–320.

Brock, D.M., Shenkar, O., Shoham, A. and Siscovick, I.C. (2008). 'National culture and expatriate deployment', *Journal of International Business Studies*, 39(8), 1293–1309.

Brouthers, K.D. (2002). 'Institutional, cultural and transaction cost influences on entry mode choice and performance'. *Journal of International Business Studies*, 33(2), 203–221.

Bruning, N.S., Sonpar, K. and Wang, X. (2012). 'Host-country national networks and expatriate effectiveness: A mixed-methods study', *Journal of International Business Studies*, 43(4), 444–450.

Buckley, P.J. and Casson, M.C. (1976). *The Future of the Multinational Enterprise*, London: Macmillan.

Buckley, P.J. and Ghauri, P.N. (2004). 'Globalization, economic geography and the strategy of multinational enterprises', *Journal of International Business Studies*, 35(2), 81–98.

Buckley, P.J. and Strange, R. (2011). 'The governance of the multinational enterprise: Insights from internalization theory', *Journal of Management Studies*, 48(2), 460–470.

Buckley, P.J., Clegg, L.J., Cross, A.R., Xin, L., Voss, H. and Ping, Z. (2007). 'The determinants of Chinese outward foreign direct investment', *Journal of International Business Studies*, 38(4), 499–518.

Budhwar, P. and Debrah, Y. (eds) (2001). *HRM in Developing Countries*, London: Routledge.

Budhwar, P. and Sparrow, P. (1998). 'National factors determining Indian and British HRM practices: An empirical study', *Management International Review*, 38(Special Issue 2), 105–121.

Buehler, K., Freeman, A. and Hulme, R. (2008). 'Owning the right risks', *Harvard Business Review*, 86(9), 102–110.

Burt, R.S. (1992). *Structural Holes: The Social Structure of Competition*, Cambridge, MA: Harvard University Press.

Business Action in Africa (2007). *Business and HIV/AIDS: What We Have Learnt*, London: Business Action in Africa.

BusinessWeek (2001). 'Confronting anti-globalism', *Business Week*, 5 August, 64.

Cai, K. (1999). 'Outward foreign direct investment: A novel dimension of China's integration into the regional and global economy', *China Quarterly*, 160, 856–880.

Caligiuri P., Lazarova, M. and Tarique, I. (2005). Training, learning and development in multinational organizations. In H. Scullion and M. Lineham (eds), *International Human Resource Management: A Critical Text*, Basingstoke: Palgrave, pp. 71–90.

Calvano, L. (2007). 'Multinational corporations and local communities: A critical analysis of conflict', *Journal of Business Ethics*, 82, 793–805.

Cantwell, J. (1989). *Technological Innovation and Multinational Corporations*, Oxford: Blackwell.

Cantwell, J. (1994). Introduction: Transactional corporations and innovatory activities. In J. Cantwell (ed.), *Transactional Corporations and Innovatory Activities*, London: Routledge.

Cantwell, J. (1996). Transnational corporations and innovatory activities. In *Transnational Corporations and World Development*. Published by Routledge on behalf of the UNCTAD Division on Transnational Corporations and Investment, London: International Thomson Business Press.

Cantwell, J., Dunning, J.H. and Lundan, S.M. (2010). 'An evolutionary approach to understanding international business activity: The co-evolution of MNCs and the institutional environment', *Journal of International Business Studies*, 41(4), 567–586.

Carraher, S.M., Sullivan, S.E. and Crocitto, M.M. (2008). 'Mentoring across global boundaries: An empirical examination of home- and host-country mentors on expatriate career outcomes', *Journal of International Business Studies*, 39(8), 1310–1326.

Carroll, A.B. (1991). 'The pyramid of corporate social responsibility: Towards the moral management of organizational stakeholders', *Business Horizons*, July–August, 42–53.

Cartwright, S. and Cooper, C. (1993), 'The role of culture compatibility in successful organizational marriage', *The Academy of Management Executive*, 2, 57–69.

CBC (2012a). McDonald's to open vegetarian restaurant in India.

CBC (2012b). Quebec parties hailed for plans to end asbestos mining. CBC News, 29 August. Retrieved from: http://www.cbc.ca/news/canada/quebecvotes2012/story/2012/08/29/quebecvotes-asbestos-marois-charest-cancer-society.html.

Cermaq (2006). *Cermaq Annual Report 2006*, Oslo: Cermaq. Accessed at: http://www.nsd.uib.no/polsys/data/filer/aarsmeldinger/AE_2006_19821.pdf.

Cermaq (2007). *Cermaq Annual Report 2007*, Oslo: Cermaq. Accessed at: http://hugin.info/134455/R/1210012/250268.pdf.

Cermaq (2008). *Cermaq Annual Report 2008*, Oslo: Cermaq. Accessed at: http://hugin.info/134455/R/1308872/301995.pdf.

Cermaq (2009). *Cermaq Annual Report 2009*, Oslo: Cermaq. Accessed at: http://hugin.info/134455/R/1409408/362165.pdf.

Cermaq (2010). *Cermaq Integrated Annual and Sustainability Report 2010*, Oslo: Cermaq. Accessed at: http://www.report2010.cermaq.com/.

Cermaq (2011). *Cermaq Integrated Annual and Sustainability Report 2011*, Oslo: Cermaq. Accessed at: http://www.report2011.cermaq.com/.

Chan, A. (2001). *China's Workers under Assault: The Exploitation of Labour in a Globalising Economy*, New York: M.E. Sharpe.

Chang, Sea-Jin and Rosenzweig, P.M. (2001). 'The choice of entry mode in sequential foreign direct investment', *Strategic Management Journal*, 22(8), 747.

Chen, D., Park, S.H. and Newburry, W. (2009). 'Parent contribution and organizational control in international joint ventures', *Strategic Management Journal*, 30(11), 1133–1156.

Chen, S.F.S. (2010). 'A general TCE model of international business institutions: Market failure and reciprocity', *Journal of International Business Studies*, 41(6), 935–959.

Chen, V.Z. (2012). 'Puzzles and truths about Indian outward FDI: Toward a more relevant and nuanced research agenda on emerging market MNEs', *AIB Insights*, 12(3), 11–14.

Child, J. (2001). China and international business. In J. Child (ed.), *Oxford Handbook of International Business*, Oxford Scholarship Online, 1(29), 681–716.

Child, J. and Rodrigues, S. (2005). 'The internationalization of Chinese firms: A case for theoretical extension?', *Management and Organization Review*, 1(3), 381–410.

Child, J. and Yan, Y. (2003). 'Predicting the performance of international joint ventures: An investigation in China', *Journal of Management Studies*, 40(2), 283–320.

Child, J., Faulkner, D. and Pitkethly, R. (2001). *The Management of International Acquisitions*, Oxford: University Press.

China Business [中国经营报] (2004). 13 December.

China Information Industry (2006). Huawei plans esops to gain government's trust. 15 May 2006, Internet source: http://www.cnii.com.cn/20050801/ca351899.htm, retrieved 19 November 2007.

China View, 'Huawei: We're not trying to dodge law', 6 November 2007, http://www.news.xinhuanet.com/english/2007-11/06/content_7019551.htm, retrieved 13 November 2007.

Choi, C.B. and Beamish, P.W. (2004). 'Split management control and international joint venture performance', *Journal of International Business Studies*, 35(3), 201–215.

Chow, C.W., Deng, J.F. and Ho, J.L. (2000). 'The openness of knowledge management sharing within organizations: A comparative study of the United States and the People's Republic of China', *Journal of Management Accounting Research*, 12, 65–96.

Christmann, P. (2004). 'Multinational companies and the natural environment: Determinants of global environmental policy standardization', *Academy of Management Journal*, 47(5), 747–760.

Chung, Sun-Jung (2009). McDonald's Abroad. *Time*, 28 October. Retrieved from http://www.time.com/time/world/article/0,8599,1932839,00.html.

Clarkson, M.B.E. (1995). 'A stakeholder framework for analyzing and evaluating corporate social performance', *Academy of Management Review*, 20(1), 92–106.

Clegg, S.R., Courpasson, D. and Phillips, N. (2006). *Power and Organizations*, London: Sage.

Clouse, M.A. and Watkins, M.D. (2009). 'Three keys to getting an overseas assignment right', *Harvard Business Review*, 87(10), 115–119.

CNN (2009). Big Macs off menu as Iceland's economic crisis bites. CNN, 30 October. Retrieved from http://edition.cnn.com/2009/BUSINESS/10/27/iceland.mcdonalds/index.html.

Collinson, S. and Rugman, A. (2008). 'The regional nature of Japanese multinational business', *Journal of International Business Studies*, 39(2), 215–230.

Companies & Markets (2012). McDonalds to open 45 more outlets in Russia in 2012. *Interfax: Russia & CIS Business & Investment Weekly*, n/a. http://ezproxy.lib.ucalgary.ca:2048/login?url=http://search.proquest.com/docview/1010203133?accountid=9838.

Cooke, F.L. (2002). 'Ownership change and the reshaping of employment relations in China: A study of two manufacturing companies', *Journal of Industrial Relations*, 44(1), 19–39.

Cooke, F.L. (2004). 'Foreign firms in China: Modelling HRM in a toy manufacturing corporation', *Human Resource Management Journal*, 14(3), 31–52.

Cooke, F.L. (2008). *Competition, Strategy and Management in China*, Basingstoke: Palgrave Macmillan.

Cooke, F.L. (2012a). *Human Resource Management in China: New Trends and Practices*, London: Routledge.

Cooke, F.L. (2012b). 'The globalization of Chinese telecom corporations: Strategy, challenges and HR implications for host countries', *International Journal of Human Resource Management*, 23(9), 1832–1852.

Cooke, F.L. and Huang, K. (2011). 'Post-acquisition evolution of the appraisal and reward systems: A study of Chinese IT firms acquired by US firms', *Human Resource Management*, 50(6), 839–858.

Cooke, F.L. and Lin, Z.H. (2012). 'Chinese firms in Vietnam: Investment motives, institutional environment and human resource challenges', *Asia-Pacific Journal of Human Resources*, 50(2), 205–226.

Cooney, S. (2007). 'China's Labour Law, compliance and flaws in implementing institutions', *Journal of Industrial Relations*, 49(5), 673–686.

Corkin, L (2008). 'Competition or collaboration? Chinese and South African transnational companies in Africa', *Review of African Political Economy*, 35(15), 128–133.

Cosset, J.-C. and Suret, J.-M. (1995). 'Political risk and the benefits of international portfolio diversification', *Journal of International Business Studies*, 26(2), 301–318.

Cotton, E. (2011). Contract and agency labor: beyond self-regulation? London: Middlesex University Business School Discussion Paper 134.

Cox, R. (2012). 'The ruthless overlords of Silicon Valley', *Newsweek*. New York: The Newsweek/Daily Beast Company LLC.

Cox, T. (Jr.) (1991). 'The multicultural organization', *Executive*, 5(2), 34–37.

Cox, T. (Jr.) and Blake, S. (1991). 'Managing cultural diversity: Implications for organizational effectiveness', *Academy of Management Executive*, 5(3), 45–56.

Croucher, R. and Cotton, E. (2011). *Global Unions, Global Business. Global Union Federations and International Business* (2nd edn), Faringdon: Libri Publishing.

Curtin, S. (2004). The dragon invests in Japan. Internet source: *Asia Times Online* http://www.atimes.com/atimes/South_Asia, accessed on 15 March 2005.

Curtis, J. (1982). 'McDonald's abroad: Outposts of American culture', *Journal of Geography*, 81(1), 14–20.

Czarniawska, B. and Joerges, B. (1996). The travel of ideas. In B. Czarniawska and G. Sévon (eds), *Translating the Organizational Change*, New York: Walter de Gruyter, pp. 13–48.

Dahlsrud, A. (2006). 'How corporate social responsibility is defined: An analysis of 37 definitions', *Corporate Social Responsibility and Environmental Management*, 15, 1–13.

Davenport, T.H. and Glasser, J. (2002). 'Just-in-time delivery comes to knowledge management', *Harvard Business Review*, 80(7), 5–9.

Davenport, T. and Probst, G. (2000). *Siemens' Knowledge Journey*. In T. Davenport and G. Probst (eds), *Knowledge Management Case Book. Best Practices*, New York: Wiley, pp. 10–19.

Davenport, T. and Prusak, L. (1998). *Working Knowledge*, Boston: Harvard Business School Press.

Davenport, T. and Voelpel, S. (2001). 'The rise of knowledge towards attention management', *Journal of Knowledge Management*, 5(3), 212–221.

Davenport, T., Prusak, L. and Wilson, J. (2003). *What's the Big Idea? Creating and Capitalizing on the Best New Management Thinking*, Boston: Harvard Business School Press.

Davis, L.N. and Meyer, K.E. (2004). 'Subsidiary research and development, and the local environment', *International Business Review*, 13(2), 359–382.

Deci, E.L. and Ryan, R.M. (2000). 'The 'what' and 'why' of goal pursuits: human needs and the self-determination of behavior', *Psychological Inquiry*, 11(4), 227–268.

Denzin, N.K. and Lincoln, Y.S. (eds) 2008. *Collecting and Interpreting Qualitative Materials*, (3rd edn),Thousand Oaks, CA: Sage.

De Long, D.W. and Fahey, L. (2000). 'Diagnosing cultural barriers to knowledge management', *Academy of Management Executive*, 14(4), 113–127.

De Meyer, A. (1995). Tech talk, In J. Drew (ed.), *Readings in International Enterprise*, London: Routledge, pp. 179–195.

Diallo, Y., Hagemann, F., Etienne, A., Gurbuzer, Y. and Mehran, F. (2010). *Global Child Labour Developments: Measuring Trends from 2004 to 2008*, International Labour Office, Statistical Information and Monitoring Programme on Child Labour (SIMPOC), Geneva: ILO.

Dickson. T. (2002). 'The financial case for behaving responsibly', *Financial Times*, 19 August.

Dietz, G., Wilkinson, A. and Redman, T. (2009). Involvement and participation. In A. Wilkinson, N. Bacon, T. Redman and S. Snell (eds), *The Sage Handbook of Human Resource Management*, London: Sage, pp. 245–268.

Di Gregorio, D. (2005). 'Re-thinking country risk: Insights from entrepreneurship theory', *International Business Review*, 14(2), 209–226.

Dijik, M. and Van, P. (2007). The role of China in Africa. Paper for Panel 76, AEGIS European Conference on African Studies, the African Studies Centre, Leiden.

DiMaggio, P.J. and Powell, W.W. (1983). 'The iron cage revisited – institutional isomorphism and collective rationality in organizational fields', *American Sociological Review*, 48(2), 147–160.

Dixon, N.M. (2000). *Common Knowledge: How Companies Thrive by Sharing What They Know*, Boston: Harvard Business School Press.

Donaldson, T. and Preston, L.E. (1995). 'The stakeholder theory of the corporation: Concepts, evidence, and implications', *Academy of Management Review*, 20, 65–91.

Dörrenbächer, C. and Geppert, M. (2006). 'Micro-politics and conflicts in multinational corporations: Current debates, re-framing, and contributions of this special issue', *Journal of International Management*, 12(3), 251–265.

Dunning, J.H. (1981). *International Production and the Multinational Enterprise*, London: George Allen & Unwin.

Dunning, J. (1995). 'Re-appraising the eclectic paradigm in an age of alliance capitalism', *Journal of International Business Studies*, 26(3), 461–491.

Dunning J.H. (1997). The sourcing of technological advantage by multinational enterprises. In K. Macharzina, M.-J. Oesterle and J. Wolf (eds), *Global Business in the Information Age*, Proceedings of the 23rd Annual EIBA Conference, Stuttgart, pp. 63–101.

Dunning, J.H. (2009). 'Location and the multinational enterprise: A neglected factor?', *Journal of International Business Studies*, 40(1), 5–19.

Dunning, J.H. and Lundan, S.M. (2008). *Multinational Enterprises and the Global Economy* (2nd edn), Cheltenham, UK and Northampton, MA, USA: Edward Elgar Publishing.

Dunning, J. and Narula, R. (2004), *Multinationals and Industrial Competitiveness: A New Agenda*, Cheltenham, UK and Northampton, MA, USA: Edward Elgar Publishing.

Earley, P.C. and Ang, S. (2003). *Cultural Intelligence: Individual Interactions Across Cultures*, Stanford, CA: Stanford University Press.

Eccles, R.G., Newquist, S.C. and Schatz, R. (2007). 'Reputation and its risks', *Harvard Business Review*, 85(2), 104–114.

Economist (2001a). Wal around the world. 6 December. http://www.economist.com/node/895888.

Economist (2001b). 'Where is the beef? Face value', *The Economist*, 361(8246), 70.

Economist (2004a). Daring, defying, to grow. 5 August.

Economist (2004b). The opacity index. 16 September.

Economist (2010). A different game. 25 February.

Economist (2011a).Why the tail wags the dog. 6 August, p. 59.

Economist (2011b). The other Asian giant. 6 August, p. 66.

Edelman, L.F., Bresnen, M., Newell, S., Scarbrough, H. and Swan, J. (2004). 'The benefits and pitfalls of social capital: Empirical evidence from two organizations in the United Kingdom', *British Journal of Management*, 15(1), 59–69.

Edstrom, A. and Galbraith, J.R. (1977). 'Transfer of managers as a coordination and control strategy in multinational organizations', *Administrative Science Quarterly*, 22(2), 248–263.

Eells, R. and Walton, C. (1974). *Conceptual Foundations of Business* (3rd edn), Burr Ridge, IL: Irwin.

Eisenhardt, K.M. (1989). 'Building theories from case study research', *Academy of Management Review*, 14(4), 532–550.

Eisenhardt, K. and Martin, J.A. (2000). 'Dynamic capabilities: what are they?', *Strategic Management Journal*, Special Issue 21(10/11), 1105–1122.

Elkington, J. (1997). *Cannibals with Forks, the Triple Bottom Line of 21ˢᵗ Century Business*, Oxford: Capstone.

Elkington, J. (1998). *Cannibals with Forks: The Triple Bottom Line of the 21st Century Business*, Gabriola Island, BC: New Society Publishers.

Els, C. (2009). 'China, Africa and the global recession', *China Business Frontier*, March, 4–5.

Elvira, M. and Davila, A. (2005). *Managing Human Resources in Latin America*, London: Routledge.

Epstein, E.M. (1998). 'Business ethics and corporate social policy: Reflections on an intellectual journey, 1964–1996, and beyond', *Business Ethics and Corporate Social Policy*, 37(1), 7–39.

Ewing, J. (2001). 'Sharing the wealth', *BusinessWeek E.Biz*, 19 March 2001, New York: McGraw-Hill.

Fan, P. (2006). 'Catching up through developing innovation capability: Evidence from China's telecom-equipment industry', *Technovation*, 26, 359–368.

Fenton-O'Creevy, M., Gooderham, P.N., Cerdin. J-L. and Rønning, R. (2011). Bridging roles, social skill and embedded knowing in multinational organizations. In M. Geppert and C. Dörrenbächer (eds), *Politics and Power in the Multinational Corporation*, Cambridge: Cambridge University Press, pp. 101–138.

Figueira-de-Lemos, F., Johanson, J. and Vahlne, J.-E. (2011). 'Risk management in the internationalization process of the firm: A note on the Uppsala model', *Journal of World Business*, 46(2), 143–153.

Financial Times (2006). French poll shows support for corporate protectionism. 9 June, http://www.ft.com/intl/cms/s/0/0dd860f4-f755-11da-a566-0000779e2340.html#axzz1pekxjzEs.

Financial Times (2007). Transcript: Arun Sarin, Vodafone chief executive. 18 November, http://www.ft.com/intl/cms/s/0/04d876a2-95eb-11dc-b7ec-0000779fd2ac.html#axzz1p05lYxvK.

Financial Times (2008a). Siemens too white, German and male, says chief. 25 June, http://www.ft.com/intl/cms/s/0/50925af2-424f-11dd-a5e8-0000779fd2ac.html#axzz1pekxjzEs.

Financial Times (2008b). Löscher puts his finger on a problem for Europe. 28 July, http://www.ft.com/intl/cms/s/0/232b2a8c-5c3d-11dd-9e99-000077b07658.html#axzz1pekxjzEs.

Financial Times (2010). China vows to treat foreign business fairly. 7 September, http://www.ft.com/intl/cms/s/2/0880387e-ba34-11df-8804-00144feabdc0.html#axzz1pekxjzEs.

Financial Times (2011a). China and the world: A chilly reception. 2 September, http://www.ft.com/intl/cms/s/0/a261c6fa-d550-11e0-bd7e-00144feab49a.html#axzz1pHEkhmXk.

Financial Times (2011b). Infosys: include the poor in development, or face the consequences. 30 November, http://blogs.ft.com/beyond-brics/2011/11/30/infosys-include-the-poor-in-development-or-face-the-consequences/#axzz1pf3geUCg.

Financial Times (2012a). 'Stifling' HP under fire in wake of UK deal. 25 May.

Financial Times (2012b). Pressure on Shell/Eni over Nigeria deal. 11 November, http://www.ft.com/intl/cms/s/0/a170f202-2be9-11e2-a91d-00144feabdc0.html#axzz2CBlCBRgZ.

Fleming, P. (2005). 'Kindergarten Corp: Paternalism and resistance in a high-commitment workplace', *Journal of Management Studies*, 42(7), 1469–1489.

Forsgren, M. (2008). *Theories of the Multinational Firm*. Cheltenham, UK and Northampton, MA, USA: Edward Elgar Publishing.

Forsgren, M., Holm, U. and Johanson, J. (2005). *Managing the Embedded Multinational*, Cheltenham, UK and Northampton, MA, USA: Edward Elgar Publishing.

Freeman, R.E. (1984). *Strategic Management: A Stakeholder Approach*, Boston: Pitman.

Frey, B. (1997). *Not Just for the Money*, Cheltenham, UK and Northampton, MA, USA: Edward Elgar Publishing.

Friedman, M. (1970). 'The social responsibility of business is to increase its profits', *New York Times Magazine*, 13 September, 122–126.

Frost, T. (2001). 'The geographic sources of foreign subsidiaries' innovations', *Strategic Management Journal*, 22(2), 101–123.

Furuya, N., Stevens, M., Bird, A., Oddou, G. and Mendenhall, M. (2009). 'Managing the learning and transfer of global management competence: Antecedents and outcomes of Japanese repatriation effectiveness', *Journal of International Business Studies*, 40(2), 200.

Gatignon, E. and Anderson, E. (1988). 'The multinational corporation's degree of control over foreign subsidiaries', *Journal of Law, Economics and Organization*, 4, 304–336.

Gaunt, R. (2007). *Making Disease Management Pay*, London: International Council on Mining and Metals.

Geringer, J.M., Beamish, P.W. and daCosta, R.C. (1989). 'Diversification strategy and internationalization: Implications for MNE performance', *Strategic Management Journal*, 10(2), 109–119.

Ghemawat, P. (2001). 'Distance still matters: The hard reality of global expansion', *Harvard Business Review*, 79(8), 137–147.

Ghemawat, P. (2003a). 'Semiglobalization and international business strategy', *Journal of International Business Studies*, 34(2), 138–152.

Ghemawat, P. (2003b). 'The forgotten strategy', *Harvard Business Review*, 81(11), 76–84.

Ghemawat, P. (2008). 'Reconceptualizing international strategy and organization', *Strategic Organization*, 6(2), 195–206.

Ghemawat, P. (2011). *World 3.0: Global Prosperity and How to Achieve It*, Boston: Harvard Business Review Press.

Ghemawat, P. and Mallick, R. (2003). *The Industry-Level Structure of International Trade Networks: A Gravity-Based Approach*, HBS Working Paper, February.

Gibbert, M., Kugler, P. and Voelpel, S. (2000). Getting real about knowledge sharing: the

Premium-on-Top bonus system. In T. Davenport and G. Probst (eds), *Knowledge Management Case Book. Best Practices*, New York: Wiley, pp. 200–217.

Gibbs, T., Heywood, S. and Weiss, L. (2012). Technology as friend or foe? *McKinsey Quarterly*, June, https://www.mckinseyquarterly.com /Organization/Strategic_Organization/Organizing_for_an_emerging_world_2980#sidebar.

Girotra, K. and Netessine, S. (2011). 'How to build risk into your business model', *Harvard Business Review*, 89(5), 100–105.

Glisby, M. and Holden, N. (2003). 'Contextual constraints in knowledge management theory: the cultural embeddedness of Nonaka's knowledge-creating company', *Knowledge and Process Management*, 10(1), 29–36.

Global Reporting Initiative (2006). *Sustainability Reporting Guidelines (Version 3.0)*, Amsterdam: Global Reporting Initiative.

Globe and Mail (2012). Tougher rules urged for state-owned firms. 15 November: B3, http://go.galegroup.com.ezproxy.lib.ucalgary.ca/ps/i.do?id=GALE%7CA308495941&v=2.1&u=ucalgary&it=r&p=CPI&sw=w

Godoy, M., Kibene, F., Aedo, A., Kibenge, M., Groman, D., Grothusen, H., Lisperguer, A., Calbucura, M., Avendano, F., Imilan, M. and Jarpa, M. (2008). First detection, isolation and molecular characterization of ISA-V in farmed Atlantic salmon (Salmo salar) in Chile. *Salmociencia*, 2, 47–55. Accessed at: http://www.salmonchile.cl/salmociencia/003/archivos/a3.pdf.

Gomes, L. and Ramaswamy, K. (1999). 'An empirical examination of the form of the relationship between multinationality and performance', *Journal of International Business Studies*, 30(1), 173–188.

Gooderham, P.N. (2007). 'Enhancing knowledge transfer in multinational corporations: A dynamic capabilities driven model', *Knowledge Management Research & Practice*, 5(1), 34–43.

Gooderham, P.N., Minbaeva, D.B. and Pedersen, T. (2011). 'Governance mechanisms for the promotion of social capital for knowledge transfer in multinational corporations', *Journal of Management Studies*, 48(1), 123–150.

Gooderham, P.N. and Nordhaug, O. (2003). *International Management: Cross-boundary Challenges*, Oxford: Blackwell.

Gooderham, P.N., Nordhaug, O. and Ringdal, K. (1999). 'Institutional and rational determinants of organizational practices: Human resource management in European firms', *Administrative Science Quarterly*, 44(3), 507–531.

Gooderham, P.N., Nordhaug, O. and Ringdal, K. (2006). 'National embeddedness and HRM in US subsidiaries in Europe and Australia', *Human Relations*, 59(1), 1491–1513.

Granovetter, M.S. (1973). 'The strength of weak ties', *American Journal of Sociology*, 78, 1360–1380.

Granovetter, M. (1985). 'Economic action and social structure: The problem of embeddedness', *American Journal of Sociology*, 91(3), 481–510.

Grenier, J.-N. (2006). 'Local unions and the re-structuring of work within the MNC: Internal solidarity and local context', *Labour Studies Journal*, 31(3), 65–84.

Greven, T. (2006). 'US strategic campaigns against trans national enterprises in Germany', *Industrielle Beziehungen*, 13(3), 1–17.

Grøgaard, B. and Verbeke, A. (2012). Twenty key hypotheses that make internalization theory the general theory of international strategic management. In A. Verbeke and H. Merchant (eds), *Handbook of Research on International Strategic Management*, Cheltenham, UK and Northampton, MA, USA: Edward Elgar Publishing.

Grover, V. and Davenport, T. (2001). 'General perspectives on knowledge management: fostering a research agenda', *Journal of Management Information Systems*, 18(1), 5–21.

Gullien, M.F. and Garcia-Canal, E. (2009). 'The American model of the multinational firm and the new multinationals from emerging economies', *Academy of Management Perspectives*, 23(2), 23–35.

Gupta, A.K. and Govindarajan, V. (2000). 'Knowledge flows within multinational corporations', *Strategic Management Journal*, 21(4), 473–496.

Hahn, E.D., Bunyaratavej, K. and Doh, J.P. (2011). 'Impacts of risk and service type on near-shore and offshore investment location decisions', *Management International Review*, 51(3), 357–380.

Haier corporate website (2012a). http://www.haier.net/en/, retrieved 25 April 2012.

Haier corporate website (2012b). http://www.haierappliances.com.au/about/global-achievements/, retrieved 20 May 2012.

Hakkarainen, K., Palonen, T., Paavola, S. and Lehtinen, E. (2004). *Communities of Networked Expertise: Professional and Educational Perspectives* (1st edn), London: Elsevier.

Hall, P.A. and Gingerich, DW. (2004). Varieties of capitalism and institutional complementarities in the macroeconomy. MPIfG Discussion paper 04/5, Berlin: Max Planck institute für Gesellschaftsforschung.

Hall, PA. and Soskice, D. (eds) (2001). *Varieties of Capitalism: The Institutional Basis of Competitive Advantage*. Oxford: Oxford University Press.

Halpern, Jake (2011). Iceland's big thaw. *The New York Times*, 13 May. Retrieved from http://www.nytimes.com/2011/05/15/magazine/icelands-big-economic-thaw.html?pagewanted=all.

Hambrick, D.C., Jiatao, L., Katherine, X. and Tsui, A.S. (2001). 'Compositional gaps and downward spirals in international joint venture management groups', *Strategic Management Journal*, 22(11), 1033–1063.

Hamel, G. and Heene, A. (eds) (1994). *Competence-Based Competition*, Chichester, UK: Wiley.

Handley, A. (2005). 'Business, government and economic policy making in the new South Africa, 1990–2000', *Journal of Modern African Studies*, 43(2), 211–239.

Hansen, M.T. (2002). 'Knowledge networks: explaining effective knowledge sharing in multiunit companies', *Organization Science*, 13(3), 232–248.

Hansen, M.T. and Løvås, B. (2004). 'Leveraging technological competencies', *Strategic Management Journal*, 25(8–9), 801–822.

Hansen, M.T., Nohria, N. and Tierney, T. (1999). 'What's your strategy for managing knowledge', *Harvard Business Review*, 77(2), 106–116.

Harzing, A.W. (1999). *Managing the Multinationals*, Cheltenham, UK and Northampton, MA, USA: Edward Elgar Publishing.

Harzing, A.W. (2000). 'An empirical test and extension of the Bartlett and Ghoshal typology of multi-national companies', *Journal of International Business Studies*, 31(1), 101–120.

Harzing, A.W. (2001). 'Of bears, bumble-bees, and spiders: The role of expatriates in controlling foreign subsidiaries', *Journal of World Business*, 36(4), 366–379.

Harzing, A.W. (2002). 'Acquisitions versus greenfield investments: International strategy and management of entry modes', *Strategic Management Journal*, 23(3), 211–227.

Hatch, M.J. and Schultz, M. (2002). 'The dynamics of organizational identity', *Human Relations*, 55(8), 989.

Hayes, J. and Allinson, C.W. (1988). 'Cultural differences in the learning styles of managers', *Management International Review*, 28(3), 72–90.

Hayter, S. and Stoevska, V. (2011). *Social Dialogue Indicators: International Statistical Inquriy 2008–09*, Geneva: International Labour Office.

Hedlund, G. (1986). 'The hypermodern MNC – a heterarchy', *Human Resource Management*, 25, 9–36.

Henisz, W.J., Mansfield, E.D. and Von Glinow, M.A. (2010). 'Conflict, security, and political risk:

International business in challenging times', *Journal of International Business Studies*, 41(5), 759–764.

Hennart, J.F. (2007). 'The theoretical rationale for a multinationality-performance relationship', *Management International Review*, 47(3), 423–452.

Hennart, J.F. (2009). 'Down with MNE-centric theories! Market entry and expansion as the bundling of MNE and local assets', *Journal of International Business Studies*, 40(9), 1432–1454.

Hennart, J.-F. (2012). 'Emerging market multinationals and the theory of the multinational enterprise', *Global Strategy Journal*, 2(3), 168–187.

Hermawan, A. (2005). *Analysing Variations in Employee Empowerment in Indonesia*, Unpublished PhD thesis, University of Manchester, UK.

Hill, C.W. (2000). *International Business: Competing in the Global Marketplace* (3rd edn), Boston, MA: McGraw-Hill.

Hillman, A. and Keim, G. (2001). 'Shareholder value, stakeholder management, and social issues: What's the bottom line?', *Strategic Management Journal*, 22, 125–139.

Hitt, M.A., Dacin, M.T., Levitas, E., Arregle, J.L. and Borza, A. (2000). 'Partner selection in emerging and developed market contexts: Resource-based and organizational learning perspectives', *Academy of Management Journal*, 43(3), 449–467.

Hitt, M.A., Hoskisson, R.E. and Kim, H. (1997). 'International diversification: Effects on innovation and firm performance in product-diversified firms', *Academy of Management Journal*, 40(4), 767–798.

Hitt, M.A., Ireland, D.R. and Hoskisson, R.E. (2012). *Strategic Management Cases: Competitiveness and Globalization* (8th edn), Mason, OH: Cengage Learning.

Ho, D.Y. (1976). 'On the concept of face', *American Journal of Sociology*, 81(4), 867–884.

Hodgetts, R.M. and Luthans, F. (2000). *International Management: Culture, Strategy and Behavior* (4th edn), Boston: McGraw-Hill.

Hofstede, G. (1980a). *Culture's Consequences: International Differences in Work-Related Values*, Beverly Hills: Sage.

Hofstede, G. (1980b). 'Motivation, leadership, and organization: Do American theories apply abroad?', *Organizational Dynamics*, Summer, 42–63.

Hofstede, G. (1983). 'National cultures in four dimensions: A research theory of cultural differences among nations', *International Studies of Management and Organization*, 13.

Hofstede, G. (1986). 'Cultural difference in teaching and learning', *International Journal of Intercultural Relations*, 10, 301–320.

Hofstede, G. (1991). *Cultures and Organizations: Software of the Mind*, Boston, MA: McGraw-Hill.

Hofstede, G. (1994). 'The business of international business is culture', *International Business Review*, 3(1), 1–14.

Hofstede, G. (2010). 'The GLOBE debate: Back to relevance', *Journal of International Business Studies*, 41(8), 1339–1346.

Holden, N.J. (2002). *Cross-Cultural Management: A Knowledge Management Perspective*, Harlow: Financial Times/Prentice Hall.

House, R.J., Hanges, P.J., Javidan, M., Dorfman, P.W. and Gupta, V. (eds) (2004). *Culture, Leadership, and Organizations: The GLOBE Study of 62 Societies*, Thousand Oaks, CA: Sage.

Howell, J. (2008). 'All-China Federation of Trades Unions beyond reform? The slow march of direct elections', *The China Quarterly*, 196, 845–863.

Hu Y.Y. and Wu, Z.X. (2011). 'A study on influencing factors of Chinese enterprises' overseas M&A: Empirical analysis from the angle of new institutional economics', *Journal of Finance and Economics*, 37(8), 91–102.

Huawei (2007). Company website: http://www.huawei.com/africa/en/catalog.do?id=543, retrieved 13 November 2007.

Huawei (2012). Company website: http://www.huawei.com/en/about-huawei/corporate-info/vision-mission/index.htm, retrieved 19 April 2012.

Huawei (Africa) (2012). Company website: http://www.huawei.com/africa/en/catalog.do?id=542, retrieved 20 April 2012.

Huawei People (2007). Issue 188.

Huemer, L. (2010). 'Corporate social responsibility and multinational corporate identity: Norwegian strategies in the Chilean aquaculture industry', *Journal of Business Ethics*, 91, 265–277.

Humphrey, J. (1995). 'The adoption of Japanese management techniques in Brazilian industry', *Journal of Management Studies*, 32(6), 767–788.

Husted, B.W. (2003). 'Governance choices for corporate social responsibility: To contribute, collaborate or internalize', *Long Range Planning*, 36(5), 481–498.

Husted, B.W. and Allen, D.B. (2006). 'Corporate social responsibility in the multinational enterprise: Strategic and institutional approaches', *Journal of International Business Studies*, 37, 138–149.

Hutzschenreuter, T. and Voll, J.V. (2008). 'Performance effects of 'added cultural distance' in the path of international expansion: The case of German multinational enterprises', *Journal of International Business Studies*, 39(1), 53–70.

Hyman, R. (2002). The international labor movement on the threshold of two centuries: Agitation, organization, bureaucracy, diplomacy, http://www.arbarkiv.nu/pdf_wri/Hyman_int.pdf.

Hymer, S.H. (1960/1976). *The International Operations of National Firms: A Study of Direct Foreign Investment*. Cambridge, MA: MIT Press.

IBM (2004). *Corporate Responsibility Report*. http://www.ibm.com/ibm/responsibility (accessed 1 August 2006).

Ingebrigtsen, S. and Jakobsen, O. (2007). *Circulation Economics: Theory and Practice*, Bern: Peter Lang.

Inkpen, A.C. and Beamish, P.W. (1997). 'Knowledge, bargaining power, and the instability of international joint ventures', *Academy of Management Review*, 22(1), 177–202.

Inkpen, A.C. and Tsang, E.W.K. (2005). 'Social capital, networks and knowledge transfer', *Academy of Management Review*, 30(1), 146–165.

International Labor Organization (2012). About the ILO. http://www.ilo.org/global/about-the-ilo/lang--en/index.htm, accessed on 25 April 2012.

International Standards Organization (2010). *ISO 26000: Guidance on Social Responsibility*, Geneva, Switzerland: International Standards Organization.

Ishida, H. (1986). 'Transferability of Japanese human resource management abroad', *Human Resource Management*, 25, 103–120.

Ivanov, M. (2000). 'Care for some fries with that reform? *Russian Life*', 43(2), 14–15.

Jakobsen, J. (2010). 'Old problems remain, new ones crop up: political risk in the 21st century', *Business Horizons*, 53(5), 481–490.

Jamali, D. (2010). 'The CSR of MNC subsidiaries in developing countries: Global, local, substantive or diluted', *Journal of Business Ethics*, 93(2), 181–200.

Jassawalla, A.R. and Sashittal, H.C. (2009). 'Thinking strategically about integrating repatriated managers in MNCs', *Human Resource Management*, 48(5), 769–792.

Javidan, M., Teagarden, M. and Bowen, D. (2010). 'Making it overseas', *Harvard Business Review*, 88(4), 109–113.

Johanson, J. and Vahlne, J.E. (1977). 'The internationalization of process of the firm. A model of knowledge development and increasing market commitments', *Journal of International Business*, 8(1), 23–32.

Johanson, J. and Vahlne, J.-E. (2009). 'The Uppsala internationalization process model revisited: From liability of foreignness to liability of outsidership', *Journal of International Business Studies*, 40, 1411–1431.

Johnson, J.P., Lenartowicz, T. and Apud, S. (2006). 'Cross-cultural competence in international business: Toward a definition and a model', *Journal of International Business Studies*, 37(4), 525–543.

Jørgensen, S. and Pedersen, L.J.T. (2011). 'The why and how of corporate social responsibility', *Beta: Scandinavian Journal of Business Research*, 25(2), 121–137.

Jørgensen, S. and Pedersen, L.J.T. (2013). *Ansvarlig og lønnsom: Strategier for samfunnsansvarlig forretningsmodellinnovasjon*, Oslo: Cappelen Damm Akademisk.

Judy, R.W. (2002). 'Where on earth companies choose to do business – and why?' Paper prepared for the World Federation of Personnel Management Associations, Mexico City, 29 May.

Kallman, J. (2005). 'What is risk?', *Risk Management*, 52(10), 57.

Kaplan, R.S. and Norton, D.N. (1996). *The Balanced Scorecard: Translating Strategy into Action*, Chicago: Chicago University Press.

Kedia, B. and Mukherjee, D. (2009). 'Understanding offshoring: A research framework based on disintegration, location and externalization advantages', *Journal of World Business*, 44(3), 250–261.

Kenny, B. (2004). The 'market hegemonic' workplace order in food retailing. In K. Von Holdt and E. Webster (eds), *Beyond the Apartheid Workplace: Studies in Transition*, Scottsville: University of Kwa-Zulu Natal Press, pp. 217–241.

Khanna, T., Palepu, K.G. and Sinha, J. (2005). 'Strategies that fit emerging markets', *Harvard Business Review*, 83(6), 63–76.

Kirkman, B.L., Lowe, K.B. and Gibson, C.B. (2006). 'A quarter century of culture's consequences: A review of empirical research incorporating Hofstede's cultural values framework', *Journal of International Business Studies*, 37(3), 285–320.

Kirkman, B.L., Rosen, B., Gibson, C.B., Tesluk, P.E. and McPherson, S.O. (2002). 'Five challenges to virtual team success: Lessons from Sabre, Inc.', *Academy of Management Executive*, 16(3), 67–79.

Kogut, B. and Singh, H. (1988). 'The effect of national culture on the choice of entry mode', *Journal of International Business Studies*, 19(3), 411–432.

Kogut, B. and Zander, U. (1992). 'Knowledge of the firm, combinative capabilities and the replication of technology', *Organization Science*, 3(2), 383–397.

Kogut, B. and Zander, U. (1993). 'Knowledge of the firm and the evolutionary theory of the multinational corporation', *Journal of International Business Studies*, 24(4), 625–645.

Kogut, B. and Zander, U. (1996). 'What do firms do? Coordination, identity and learning', *Organization Science*, 7(5), 502–518.

Kolben, K. (2011). 'Transnational labour regulation and the limits of governance', *Theoretical Inquiries in Law*, 12(2), 403–437.

Kolk, A. and van Tulder, R. (2010). 'International business, corporate social responsibility and sustainable development', *International Business Review*, 19(2), 119–125.

Kostova, T. (1999). 'Transnational transfer of strategic organizational practices: A contextual perspective', *Academy of Management Review*, 24(2), 308–324.

Kostova, T. and Roth, K. (2002). 'Adoption of an organizational practice by subsidiaries of multinational corporations: Institutional and relational effects', *Academy of Management Journal*, 45(1), 215–233.

Kotter, J.P. (1982). *The General Managers*, New York: Free Press.

Kramer, Andrew (2010). Russia evolution seen through golden arches. *New York Times*, 1 February, B.3. Retrieved from http://www.nytimes.com/2010/02/02/business/global/02mcdonalds.html?_r=1.

Kristensen, P.H. and Zeitlin, J. (2005). *Local Players in Global Games: The Strategic Constitution of a Multinational Corporation*, Oxford: Oxford University Press.

Kuemmerle, W. (1997). 'Building effective R&D capabilities abroad', *Harvard Business Review*, March–April, 61–70.

Kyriakidou, O. (2005). Operational aspects of international human resource management. In M. Özbilgin (ed.), *International Human Resource Management: Theory and Practice*, Basingstoke: Palgrave.

Lampel, J. and Bhalla, A. (2011). 'Living with offshoring: The impact of offshoring on the evolution of organizational configurations', *Journal of World Business*, 46(3), 346–358.

Larsen, M.M., Pedersen, T. and Slepniov, D. (2010). LEGO Group: An outsourcing journey. IVEY case.

Lazarova, M.B. and Cerdin, J.-L. (2007). 'Revisiting repatriation concerns: Organizational support versus career and contextual influences', *Journal of International Business Studies*, 38(3), 404.

Lazarova, M.B. and Tarique, I. (2005). 'Knowledge transfer upon repatriation', *Journal of World Business*, 40(4), 361.

Legewie, J. (2002). 'Control and co-ordination of Japanese subsidiaries in China: Problems of an expatriate-based management system', *International Journal of Human Resource Management*, 13(6), 901–919.

Leontiades, J. (1985). *Multinational Corporate Strategy*, Lexington MA: Lexington Books.

Levenson, E. (2008). Citizen Nike. *Fortune*, 158(10), 165–170.

Levitt, T. (1983). 'The globalisation of markets', *Harvard Business Review*, 61(3), 92–102.

Li, Z.M. (2011). 'The prospect of cross-border mergers and acquisitions for Chinese enterprises under 'Trade deficit'', *Modern State-Owned Enterprises Research*, March, 26–37.

Litvin, D. (1997). 'The discourse of diversity: From biology to management', *Organization*, 4(2), 187–209.

Liu, H. and Li, K. (2002). 'Strategic implications of emerging Chinese multinationals: The Haier case study', *European Management Journal*, 20(6), 699–706.

Lozeau, D., Langley A. and Denis, J.L. (2002). 'The corruption of managerial techniques by organizations', *Human Relations*, 55(5), 537–564.

Luo,Y., Shenkar, O. and Nyaw, M. (2001). 'A dual parent perspective on control and performance in international joint ventures: Lessons from a developing economy', *Journal of International Business Studies*, 32(1), 41–55.

Madhok, A. (1995). 'Revisiting multinational firms' tolerance for joint ventures: A trust-based approach', *Journal of International Business Studies*, 26, 117–137.

Madhok, A. (2006a). 'How much does ownership really matter? Equity and trust relations in joint venture relationships', *Journal of International Business Studies*, 37(1), 4–11.

Madhok, A. (2006b). 'Revisiting multinational firms' tolerance for joint ventures: A trust-based approach', *Journal of International Business Studies*, 37(1), 30–43.

Mail on Line (2012). The 'immoral' tax avoiders: Amazon, Starbucks and Google lashed by MPs over elaborate schemes that deprive Britain of millions. 12 November 2012. http://www.dailymail.co.uk/news/article-2231828/Immoral-tax-avoiders-Amazon-Starbucks-Google-lashed-MPs-elaborate-schemes.html.

Mäkelä, K., Andersson, U. and Seppälä, T. (2012). 'Interpersonal similarity and knowledge sharing within multinational organizations', *International Business Review*, 21(3), 439–451.

Makino, J. and Neupert, K.E. (2001). 'National culture, transaction costs, and the choice between joint venture and wholly owned subsidiary', *Journal of International Business Studies*, 31(4), 705–713.

Makino, S., Lau, C. and Yeh, R. (2002). 'Asset-exploitation versus asset-seeking: Implications for location choice of foreign direct investment from newly industrialised economies', *Journal of International Business Studies*, 33(3), 403–421.

Magretta, J. (2012). Understanding Michael Porter: The essential guide to competition and strategy. *FAQs: An Interview with Michael Porter*, Harvard Business School Publishing.

Margolis, J.D. and Walsh, J.P. (2003). 'Misery loves companies: Rethinking social initiatives by business', *Administrative Science Quarterly*, 48(2), 268–305.

Markus, M.L. (2001). 'Toward a theory of knowledge reuse: Types of knowledge reuse situations and factors in reuse success', *Journal of Management Information Systems*, 18(1), 57–93.

Marsh, P. (2012). *The New Industrial Revolution: Consumers, Globalization and the End of Mass Production*, Yale University Press.

Martin, J.A. and Eisenhardt, K.M. (2010). 'Rewiring: Cross-subsidiary collaborations in multi-business organizations', *Academy of Management Journal*, 53(2), 265–301.

Maslow, A. (1954). *Motivation and Personality*, New York: Harper.

Mayrhofer, W., Nordhaug, O. and Obeso, C. (2009). 'Career and job preferences among elite business students', *Beta.Scandinavian Journal of Business Research*, 24(2).

McDermott, R. (1999). 'Why information technology inspired but cannot deliver knowledge management', *California Management Review*, 41(4), 103–117.

McDonald's Corporation (2011). *Annual Report*.

McDonald's Corporation (2012a). The history of the golden arches. Retrieved from http://www.mcdonalds.ca/ca/en/our_story/our_history.html.

McDonald's Corporation (2012b). Company Profile. Retrieved from http://www.about mcdonalds.com/mcd/investors/company_profile.html.

McDonald's Corporation (2012c). Getting to know us. Retrieved from http://www.aboutmc-donalds.com/mcd/our_company.html.

McFadyen, M.A. and Cannella, A.A. (2004). 'Social capital and knowledge creation: Diminishing returns of the number and strength of exchange relationships', *Academy of Management Journal*, 47(5), 735–746.

McGregor, D. (1960). *The Human Side of Enterprise*, New York: McGrawHill.

McSweeney, B. (2002). 'Hofstede's model of national cultural differences and their consequences: a triumph of faith – a failure of analysis', *Human Relations*, 55(1), 5–34.

McWilliams, A. and Siegel, D. (2001). 'Corporate social responsibility: A theory of the firm perspective', *Academy of Management Review*, 26(1), 117–227.

Mendenhall, M.E., Jensen, R.J., Stewart, B.J. and Gergersen, H.B. (2003). 'Seeing the elephant. Human resource management challenges in the age of globalization', *Organizational Dynamics*, 32(3), 261–274.

Messner, M. (2009). 'The limits of accountability', *Accounting, Organizations and Society*, 34(8), 918–938.

Mezias, J.M. (2002). 'Labor lawsuit judgements as liabilities of foreignness', *Strategic Management Journal*, 23(3), 229–244.

Miles, M.B. and Huberman, A.M. (1994). *Qualitative Data Analysis: An Expanded Sourcebook* (2nd edn), Thousand Oaks, CA: Sage.

Minbaeva, D., Pedersen, T., Björkman, I., Fey, C. and Park, H.J. (2003). 'MNC knowledge transfer, subsidiary absorptive capacity, and HRM', *Journal of International Business Studies*, 34(6), 586–599.

Ministry of Commerce of People's Republic of China, National Bureau of Statistics of People's Republic of China and State Administration of Foreign Exchange (2010), *2009 Statistical Bulletin of China's Outward Foreign Direct Investment*.

Mitchell, R.K., Agle, B.R. and Wood, D.J. (1997). 'Toward a theory of stakeholder identification and salience: Defining the principle of who and what really counts', *Academy of Management Review*, 22(4), 853–886.

Mondi (2007). *Annual Reports and Accounts 2007*. Gauteng: Mondi Group.

Morck, R., Yeung, B. and Zhao, M.Y. (2008). 'Perspectives on China's outward foreign direct investment', *Journal of International Business Studies*, 39(3), 337–350.

Morrison, C., Croucher, R. and Cretu, O. (2011). 'Legacies, conflict and 'path dependence' in the Former Soviet Union', *British Journal of Industrial Relations*, doi: 10.1111/j.1467-8543.2010.00840.x.

Morrison, J. (2009). *International Business. Challenges in a Changing World*, London: Palgrave Macmillan.

Mudambi, R. and Pedersen, T. (2007). Agency theory and resource dependency theory: Complementary explanations for subsidiary power in multinational corporations. Copenhagen Business School. SMG Working Paper No. 5/2007.

Muller, A. (2006). 'Global versus local CSR strategies', *European Journal of Management*, 24, 189–198.

Murakami, T. (1998). 'The formation of teams: a British and German comparison', *International Journal of Human Resource Management*, 9(5), 800–817.

Murillo, M.V. (2001). *Labour Unions, Partisan Coalitions and Market Reforms in Latin America*. Cambridge: Cambridge University Press.

Nahapiet, J. and Ghoshal, S. (1998). 'Social capital, intellectual capital, and the organizational advantage', *Academy of Management Review*, 23(2), 242–266.

National Commission for Scientific and Technological Research – Chile (2007). *The Fishery and Aquaculture Sectors in Chile*. Santiago de Chile: National Commission for Scientific and Technological Research. Accessed at: http://www.embassyofchile.se/espanol/Documentos/Pesca_Acuic_Fishery_Aquac_BD.pdf.

NBSC (National Bureau of Statistics of China) (2006). *China Statistical Yearbook 2006*, Beijing: China Statistics Press.

NBSC (National Bureau of Statistics of China) (2010). *China Statistical Yearbook 2010*, Beijing: China Statistics Press.

NBSC (National Bureau of Statistics of China) (2011). *China Statistical Yearbook 2011*, Beijing: China Statistics Press.

N'Deba, L. and Hodges-Aeberhard, J. (1998). *HIV/AIDS and Employment*, Geneva: ILO.

Nestlé (2011). Annual Report.

Neuhaus, R. (1981). *International Trade Secretariats: Objectives, Organisation, Activities*, Bonn: Freidrich Ebert Stiftung.

Nohria, N. and Ghoshal, S. (1994). 'Differentiated fit and shared values: Alternatives for managing headquarters–subsidiary relations', *Strategic Management Journal*, 15(6), 491–502.

Nonaka, I. (1994). 'A dynamic theory of organizational knowledge creation', *Organization Science*, 5(1), 14–37.

Nonaka, I. and Takeuchi, H. (1995). *The Knowldege-creating Company: How Japanese Companies Create the Dynamics of Innovation*, Oxford: Oxford University Press.

Nonaka I., Toyama, R. and Nagata, A. (2000). 'A firm as a knowledge-creating entity: A new perspective on the theory of the firm', *Industrial and Corporate Change*, 9(1), 1–20.

Nordhaug, O. (1994). *Human Capital in Organizations: Competence, Training and Learning*, New York: Oxford University Press.

Nordhaug, O. (1998). 'Competence specificities: A classificatory framework', *International Studies of Management and Organization*, 28(1), 8–29.

Nordhaug, O. and Gooderham, P.N. (1996). *Kompetanseutvikling i næringslivet* (Competence Development in Companies), Oslo: Cappelen Akademisk Forlag.

Nordhaug, O., Gooderham, P.N and Zhang, X. (2010). 'Elite female business students in China and Norway: job-related values and preferences', *Scandinavian Journal of Educational Research*, 54(2), 109–123.

North, D.C. (1990). *Institutions, Institutional Change, and Economic Performance*, Cambridge: Cambridge University Press.

Noruzi, M.R. and Westover, J.H. (2011). A research agenda for international human resource management: Challenges, developments and perspectives. Paper presented at The 3rd International Conference on Information and Financial Engineering.

Norwegian National Contact Point for the OECD guidelines for Multinational Enterprises (2011). *Joint Statement by Cermaq ASA, Norwegian Society for the Conservation of Nature/ Friends of the Earth Norway and Forum for Environment and Development (ForUM)*, Oslo: Government Administration Services. Accessed at: http://www.regjeringen.no/upload/UD/ Vedlegg/ncp/joint_statement.pdf.

Nyland, C., Forbes-Mewett, H. and Thomson, B. (2011). 'Sinophobia as corporate tactic and the response of host communities', *Journal of Contemporary Asia*, 41(4), 610–631.

Oddou, G., Osland, J.S. and Blakeney, R.N. (2009). 'Repatriating knowledge: Variables influencing the 'transfer' process', *Journal of International Business Studies*, 40(2), 181–199.

O'Donnell, S. (2000). 'Managing foreign subsidiaries: Agents of headquarters, or an independent network?', *Strategic Management Journal*, 2(5), 525–548.

OECD (2009), *OECD Science, Technology and Industry Scoreboard 2009*, OECD Publishing, doi: 10.1787/sti_scoreboard-2009-en.

OECD (2011). *OECD Guidelines for Multinational Enterprises*, Paris: OECD. Accessed at: http:// www.oecd.org/daf/internationalinvestment/guidelinesformultinationalenterprises/.

OFII (2011). www.ofii.org. Organization for International Investment Companies.

Oh, C.H. and Rugman, A. (2012). 'Regional integration and the international strategies of large European firms', *International Business Review*, 21(3), 493–507.

Olson, P. (2009). McDonald's ditches Iceland. *Forbes*, 27 October. Retrieved from http://www. forbes.com/2009/10/27/iceland-mcdonalds-krona-markets-economy-restaurants.html.

Olson, P. (2012). Interview: Huawei's Cyber Security Chief Slams U.S. 'Protectionism'. Forbes. Com, 18.

O'Reilly, C., Caldwell, D. and Barnett, W. (1989). 'Work group demography, social interaction, and turnover', *Administrative Science Quarterly*, 34, 21–37.

Orlitzky, M., Schmidt, F.L. and Rynes, S.L. (2003). 'Corporate social and financial performance: A meta-analysis', *Organization Studies*, 24(3), 119–131.

O'Rourke, D. (2003). 'Outsourcing regulation: analyzing non-governmental systems of labor standards and monitoring', *Policy Studies Journal*, 31(1), 1–29.

Osborn, A. (2011). McDonald's argues it's a supermarket rather than restaurant in Russia. *The Telegraph*, 13 July. Retrieved from http://www.telegraph.co.uk/foodanddrink/foodand-drinknews/8634781/McDonalds-argues-it-is-a-supermarket-rather-than-restaurant-in-Russia.html.

Osegowitsch, T. and Sammartino, A. (2008). 'Reassessing (home-) regionalization', *Journal of International Business Studies*, 39(2), 184–196.

Osterloh, M. and Frey, B. (2000). 'Motivation, knowledge transfer and organizational form', *Organization Science*, 11(5), 538–550.

Parent, M. and Reich, B.H. (2009). 'Governing information technology risk', *California Management Review*, 51(3), 134–152.

Parkhe, A. (1991). 'Interfirm diversity, organizational learning, and longevity in global strategic alliances', *Journal of International Business Studies*, 22(4), 579–601.

Pearce, J. (2004). *Beyond the Perimeter Fence: Oil and Armed Conflict in Casanare, Colombia,*

London: Centre for the Study of Global Governance, London School of Economics, Discussion paper 32.

Peloza, J. and Falkenberg, L. (2009). 'The role of collaboration in achieving corporate social responsibility objectives', *California Management Review*, 51(3), 95–113.

Peng, M.W. (2011). 'The social responsibility of international business scholars: The case of China', *AIB Insights*, 11(4), 8–10.

Perlmutter, H.V. (1969). 'The tortuous evolution of the multinational corporation', *Colombia Journal of World Business*, 4(1), 9–18.

Pfeffer, J. (1981). *Power in Organizations*, Marshfield, MA: Pitman.

Pfeffer, J. (1992). *Managing with Power – Politics and Influence in Organizations*, Cambridge, MA: Harvard Business School Press.

Pfeffer, J. and Salancik, G.R. (1977). 'Who gets power – and how they hold on to it: A strategic contingency model of power', *Organizational Dynamics*, 5(3), 2–21.

Pinnington, A. and Edwards, T. (2000). *Introduction to Human Resource Management*, Oxford: Oxford University Press.

Pistor, K. and Xu, C. (2005). 'Governing stock markets in transition economies: Lessons from China', *American Review of Law and Economics*, 7(1), 184–210.

Polanyi, M. (1962). *Personal Knowledge: Towards a Post-Critical Philosophy*, London: Routledge and Kegan Paul. First published in 1958.

Polanyi, M. (1966). *The Tacit Dimension*, Gloucester, MA: Peter Smith.

Porter, M.E. (ed.) (1986). *Competition in Global Industries*, Boston, MA: Harvard Business School Press.

Porter, M.E. (1990a). *The Competitive Advantage of Nations*, New York: Free Press.

Porter, M.E. (1990b). 'The competitive advantage of nations', *Harvard Business Review* (March–April), 73–93.

Porter, M.E. and Kramer, M.R. (2002). 'The competitive advantage of corporate philanthropy', *Harvard Business Review*, 80(12), 56–68.

Porter, M.E. and Kramer, M.R. (2006). 'Strategy and society: The link between competitive advantage and corporate social responsibility', *Harvard Business Review*, December, 76–92.

Porter, M.E. and Kramer, M.R. (2011). 'Creating shared value. How to reinvent capitalism – and unleash a wave of innovation and growth', *Harvard Business Review*, 89(1), 62–77.

Prahalad, C.K. and Hamel, G. (1990). 'The core competence of the corporation', *Harvard Business Review*, 68(3), 79–91.

Prewitt, M. (2002). 'Global expansion requires world of planning, panelists agree', *Nation's Restaurant News*, 36(42), 58.

PwC (2012). Fact and figures: Geographic coverage. Retrieved 9 July 2012, from http://www.pwc.com/gx/en/about-pwc/facts-and-figures.jhtml.

Qiao, J. (2011). The situation of China's working class in 2010: Calling for the sharing of economic gains and collective labour rights. In X. Ru, X.Y. Lu and P.L. Li (eds), *Society of China Analysis and Forecast (2011)*, Blue Book of China's Society series, Beijing: Social Science Academy Press, pp. 245–260.

Rai, S. (2006). India and China work on building trust. *The New York Times*, 22 November, Internet source: http://www.nytimes.com/2006/11/22/business/worldbusiness/22asia.html, retrieved 19 November 2007.

Raz, Guy (2009). McDonald's closure is latest blow to Iceland. National Public Radio, 1 November. Retrieved from http://www.npr.org/templates/story/story.php?storyId=114376738.

Reed, R. and DeFillippi, R.J. (1990). 'Causal ambiguity, barriers to imitation and sustainable competitive advantage', *Academy of Management Review*, 15(1), 88–102.

Reger, G. (1997). Internationalization and coordination of R&D of western European and

Japanese multinational corporations. In K. Macharzina, M.-J.Oesterle and J. Wolf (eds), *Global Business in the Information Age*, vol. 2, pp. 573–604. Proceedings of the 23rd Annual EIBA Conference, Stuttgart, 14–16 December 1997.

Reiche, B.S., Harzing, A.-W. and Kraimer, M.L. (2009). 'The role of international assignees' social capital in creating inter-unit intellectual capital: A cross-level model', *Journal of International Business Studies*, 40(3), 509–526.

Reuters (2010). Angang sees no setback from US steel firms' objections, 7 July. Internet source: http://www.reuters.com/article/2010/07/07/angang-idUSTOE66604C20100707, retrieved on 20th May 2012.

Reuters (2011). Shougang Peru strike ends after one month. 25 September. Internet source: http://www.reuters.com/article/2011/09/25/metals-peru-shougang-idUSS1E78O06U20110925, retrieved on 20th May 2012.

Richard, O. (2000). 'Racial diversity, business strategy, and firm performance: A resource-based view', *Academy of Management Journal*, 48, 164–177.

Richard, O., McMillan, A., Chadwick, K. and Dwyer, S. (2003). 'Employing an innovation strategy in racially diverse workforces: Effects on firm performance', *Journal of Management Issues*, 28(1), 107–126.

Roberts, P.W. and Dowling, G.R. (2002). 'Corporate reputations and sustained superior financial performance', *Strategic Management Journal*, 23, 1077–1093.

Robinson, G. and Dechant, K. (1997). 'Building a business case for diversity', *Academy of Management Executive*, 11, 21–31.

Roland Berger Strategy Consultants (2007). International champions. Internet source: http://www.news.rolandberger.com/news/content/2007-06-29-International_Champions.html, retrieved 30 November 2007.

Romriell, L. (2002). Bad chain of events said to hamper franchising. *The Russia Journal (153)*, 22 March. Retrieved from http://www.russiajournal.com/node/6020.

Roper, I., Parsa, S. and Muller-Camen, M. (2011). The social audit of MNCs' labor standards: What can it tell us about employer motivation to disclose? Paper to British Journal of Industrial Relations 50th Anniversary Conference, London School of Economics 12–13 December.

Roth, K. (1992). 'Implementing international strategy at the subsidiary level: The role of managerial decision-making characteristics', *Journal of Management*, 18(4), 769–789.

Roth, K. and Ricks, D.A. (1994). 'Goal configuration in a global industry context', *Strategic Management Journal*, 15(2), 103–120.

Royle, T. (2010). 'The ILO's shift to promotional principles and the 'privatization' of labor rights: An analysis of labor standards, voluntary self-regulation and social clauses', *International Journal of Comparative Labour Law and Industrial Relations*, 26(2), 249–271.

Rugman, A. (2001). 'The illusion of the global company', Part 13 of *Mastering Management*. *Financial Times*, 8 January.

Rugman, A. (2005). *The Regional Multinationals: MNCs and 'Global' Strategic Management*. Cambridge: Cambridge University Press.

Rugman, A. and Hodgetts, R. (2001). 'The end of global strategy', *European Management Journal*, 19(4), 333–343.

Rugman, A. and Verbeke, A. (2004). 'Regional and global strategies of MNCs', *Journal of International Business*, 35(1), 3–18.

Rui, H.C. and Yip, Y.G. (2008). 'Foreign acquisitions by Chinese firms: A strategic intent perspective', *Journal of World Business*, 43(2), 213–226.

Ruigrok, W. and Wagner, H. (2003). 'Internationalization and performance. An organizational learning perspective', *Management International Review*, 43(1), 63–83.

Russwurm, S., Hernández, L., Chambers, S. and Chung, K. (2011). 'Developing your global know-how', *Harvard Business Review*, 89(3).

Saini, D.S. (2009). Labour law in India: Structure and working. In P. Budhwar and J. Bhatnagar (eds), *The Changing Face of People Management in India*, London: Routledge, pp. 60–94.

Salmi, A. and Scott-Kennel, J. (2102). 'Just another BRIC in the wall? The rise of the BRICs and educating tomorrow's global managers', *AIB Insights*, 12(3), 3–6.

Saner, R. and Yiu, L. (1994). 'European and Asian resistance to the use of the American case method in management training', *International Journal of Human Resource Management*, 5(4), 955–976.

Schneider, S.C. and Barsoux, J.L. (1997). *Managing Across Cultures*, Singapore: Prentice-Hall.

Scott, W.R. (2001). *Institutions and Organizations*, London: Sage.

Schömann, I., Sobczak, A., Voss, E. and Wilke, P. (2008). *Codes of Conduct and International Framework Agreements: New Forms of Governance at Company Level*, Dublin: European Foundation for the Improvement of Living and Working Conditions.

Schuler, R.S., Dowling, P.J. and De Cieri, H. (1993). 'An integrative framework of strategic international human resource management', *Journal of Management*, 19(2), 419–459.

Schuler, R.S. and Jackson, S.E. (2005). 'A quarter-century review of human resource management in the U.S.: The growth in importance of the international perspective', *Management Review*, 16(1), 11–35.

Schultz, T.W. (1981). *Investing in People. The Economics of Population Quality*, Berkeley, CA: University of California Press.

Schwartz, S. (1994). *Cultural Dimensions of Values: Toward an Understanding of National Differences*. In U. Kim, H. Triandis, C. Kagitcibasi, S. Choi and G. Yoon (eds), *Individualism and Collectivism: Theory, Method, and Application*, Thousand Oaks, CA: Sage, pp. 85–119.

Schwass, H. (2004). *Global Unions and their Regional Structures*, Bonn: Friedrich Ebert Foundation.

Scullion, H. and Starkey, K. (2000). 'In search of the changing role of the corporate human resource function in the international firm', *International Journal of Human Resource Management*, 11(6), 1061–1081.

Seafood Intelligence (2012). *2012 Benchmarking Report of the World's Top 35/36 Salmonid Farmers' Corporate, Social and Environmental Responsibility (CSER) Reporting in English*, Chassignoles, France: Seafood Intelligence. Accessed at: http://www.seafoodintelligence.com/DesktopDefault.aspx?tabid=285.

Sengenberger, W. (2001). 'Decent work: The International Labor Organization agenda', *Dialogue and Cooperation*, 2, 39–55.

Shay, J.P. and Baack, S.A. (2004). 'Expatriate assignments adjustment and effectiveness: An empirical examination of the big picture', *Journal of International Business Studies*, 35(3), 216–232.

Shen, J. (2004). 'International performance appraisals: Policies, practices and determinants in the case of Chinese multinational companies', *International Journal of Manpower*, 25(6), 547–563.

Shi, L. (1998). 'China's investment: The problems and the legal countermoves', *Investment Research*, 5, 33–37.

Shrader, R.G. (2001). 'Collaboration and performance in foreign markets: The case of young high-technology manufacturing firms', *Academy of Management Journal*, 44(1), 45–60.

Simonin, B.L. (1999). 'Ambiguity and the process of knowledge transfer in strategic alliances', *Strategic Management Journal*, 20(7), 595–623.

Simpfendorfer, B. (2012). 'The rise of a new silk road', *AIB Insights*, 12(3), 7–10.

Skapinker, M. (2002). 'World's most respected companies', *Financial Times Survey, 2002 and Beyond*, 1 February, p. 4.

Slywotzky, A. (2004). 'What are the risks you should be taking?', *Harvard Management Update*, 9(10), 3–4.

Slywotzky, A.J. (2008). 'Finding the upside advantage in downside risk', *Strategic Finance*, 90(5), 8–61.

Slywotzky, A.J. and Drzik, J. (2005). 'Countering the biggest risk of all', *Harvard Business Review*, 83(4), 78–88.

Spar, D.L. (2002). 'Hitting the wall: Nike and international labor practices', *Harvard Business School Cases*, 23p.

Spender, J.-C. (1994). 'Organizational knowledge, collective practice, and Penrosian rents', *International Business Review*, 3(4), 353–367.

Spender, J.-C. (1996). 'Making knowledge the basis of a dynamic theory of the firm', *Strategic Management Journal*, 17(10), 45–62.

Spender, J.C. and Grant, R.M. (1996). 'Knowledge and the firm: Overview', *Strategic Management Journal*, Special Issue, 17(10), 5–9.

Stahl, G.K., Maznevski, M.L., Voigt, A. and Jonsen, K. (2010). 'Unraveling the effects of cultural diversity in teams: A meta-analysis of research on multicultural work groups', *Journal of International Business Studies*, 41(4), 690–709.

Stake, R. (1995). *The Art of Case Study Research*, London: Sage.

Steensma, H.K. and Lyles, M.A. (2000). 'Explaining IJV survival in a transitional economy through social exchange and knowledge-based perspectives', *Strategic Management Journal*, 21(8), 831–851.

Stephan, U. and Uhlaner, L. (2010). 'Performance-based vs. socially-supportive culture: A cross-national study of descriptive norms and entrepreneurship', *Journal of International Business Studies*, 41(8), 1347–1364.

Strategic Direction (2005). Inside China, they're looking out: International trade is no one-way route. *Strategic Direction*, 21(3), 1–3, http://docserver.emeraldinsight.com, accessed on 25 April 2005.

Stulz, R.M. (2009). '6 ways companies mismanage risk', *Harvard Business Review*, 87(3), 86–94.

Subramaniam, M. and Venkatraman, N. (2001). 'Determinants of transnational new product development capability: testing the influence of transferring and deploying tacit overseas knowledge', *Strategic Management Journal*, 22(4), 359–378.

Sucher, S.J. and Corsi, E. (2011). Global diversity and inclusion at Royal Dutch Shell, *Harvard Business School Case*.

Suutari, V. and Brewster, C. (2003). 'Repatriation: Empirical evidence from a longitudinal study of careers and expectations among Finnish expatriates', *International Journal of Human Resource Management*, 14(7), 1132–1151.

Szulanski, G. (1996). 'Exploring internal stickiness: Impediments to the transfer of best practice within the firm', *Strategic Management Journal*, 17 (special issue), 27–43.

Tadelis, S. (2007). 'The innovative organization: Creating value through outsourcing', *California Management Review*, 50(1), 261–277.

Taleb, N.N., Goldstein, D.G. and Spitznagel, M.W. (2009). 'The six mistakes executives make in risk management', *Harvard Business Review*, 87(10), 78–81.

Tan, D. and Mahoney, J.T. (2007). 'The dynamics of Japanese firm growth in U.S. industries: The Penrose effect', *Management International Review*, 47(2), 259–279.

Tayeb, M.H. (1988). *Organizations and National Culture: A Comparative Analysis*, London: Sage.

Tayeb, M.H. (1996). Hofstede. In M. Warner (ed.), *International Encyclopaedia of Business and Management*, vol. 2, London: Thompson Press, pp. 1771–1776.

Taylor, W. (1991). 'The logic of global business: An interview with ABB's Percy Barnevik', *Harvard Business Review*, March/April, 91–105.

Taylor, S. (2007). 'Creating social capital in MNCs: The international human resource management challenge', *Human Resource Management Journal*, 17(4), 336–354.

Taylor, S., Beechler, S. and Napier, N. (1996). 'Toward an integrative model of strategic international human resource management', *Academy of Management Review*, 21(4), 959–985.

Teece, D.J. (1998). 'Capturing value from knowledge assets: the new economy, markets for know-how, and intangible assets', *California Management Review*, 40(3), 55–79.

Teigland, R. (2000). Communities of practice. In J. Birkinshaw and P. Hagström (eds), *The Flexible Firm*, Oxford: Oxford University Press.

Telenor (2011). *Annual Report*.

Templeton Global Performance Index (2000). Oxford: Templeton College, University of Oxford.

Templeton Global Performance Index (2001). Oxford: Templeton College, University of Oxford.

The Times of India (2002). 'Cool hand Lu Ke', 15 February, Internet source: http://timesofindia.indiatimes.com/articleshow/1001280.cms, retrieved 19 November 2007.

Theron, J. (2005). Employment is not what it used to be. The nature and impact of work restructuring in South Africa. In K. van Holdt and E. Webster (eds), *Beyond the Apartheid Workplace: Studies in Transition*, Scotsville: University of Kwa Zulu Natal Press, pp. 293–316.

Thite, M., Wilkinson, A. and Shah, D. (2011). 'Internationalization and HRM strategies across subsidiaries in multinational corporations from emerging economies – A conceptual framework', *Journal of World Business*, doi:10.1016/j.jwb.2011.04.012.

Tihanyi, L., Griffith, D.A. and Russell, C.J. (2005). 'The effect of cultural distance on entry mode choice, international diversification, and MNE performance: a meta-analysis', *Journal of International Business Studies*, 36(3), 270–283.

Tomassen, S. and Benito, S.R.G. (2009). 'The costs of governance in international companies', *International Business Review*, 18(3), 292–304.

Trompenaars, A. (1993). *Riding the Waves of Culture: Understanding Cultural Diversity in Business*. London: Nicholas Brealey.

Trompenaars, F. and Hampden-Turner, C. (1997). *Riding the Waves of Culture* (2nd edn), London: Nicholas Brealey Publishing.

Tsang, E.W.K. (2001). 'Managerial learning in foreign-invested enterprises of China', *Management International Review*, 41(1), 29–51.

Tsai, W. (2000). 'Social capital, strategic relatedness, and the formation of intra-organizational strategic linkages', *Strategic Management Journal*, 21(9), 925–939.

Tsai, W. and Ghoshal, S. (1998). 'Social capital and value creation: The role of intrafirm networks', *Academy of Management Journal*, 41, 464–476.

Tung, R.L. and Verbeke, A. (2010). 'Beyond Hofstede and GLOBE: Improving the quality of cross-cultural research', *Journal of International Business Studies*, 41(8), 1259–1274.

UNCTAD (1991–2011). *World Investment Report 1991–2011*. Internet source: http://www.unctad.org/fdistatistics, New York and Geneva: United Nations Conference on Trade and Development (UNCTAD), United Nations, retrieved 12 May 2012.

UNCTAD (1999). *Foreign Direct Investment and the Challenge of Development*, New York and Geneva: UNCTAD.

UNCTAD (2003). *China: An Emerging FDI Outward Investor*, New York and Geneva: UNCTAD.

UNCTAD (2004). *World Investment Report 2004: The Shift Towards Services*, New York and Geneva: UNCTAD.

UNCTAD (2010). *World Investment Report, 2010. Investing in a Low-carbon Economy*. New York and Geneva: UNCTAD.

UNCTAD (2011). *World Investment Report 2011. Non-Equity Modes of International Production and Development*, New York and Geneva: UNCTAD.

UNICEF (1997). *The State of the World's Children 1997*. Oxford, UK: Oxford University Press.

Vagadia, B. (2007). *Outsourcing to India – A Legal Handbook*, Heidelberg: Springer Verlag.

Vahlne, J.-E., Ivarsson, I. and Johanson, J. (2011). 'The tortuous road to globalization for Volvo's heavy truck business: Extending the scope of the Uppsala model', *International Business Review*, 20(1), 1–14.

Valdimarsson, O. (2009). McDonald's closes in Iceland after krona collapse (update 1). 26 October. Retrieved from http://www.bloomberg.com/apps/news?pid=newsarchive&sid=amu4.WTVaqjI.

Vance, C.M. and Paik, Y. (2011). *Managing a Global Workforce. Challenges and Opportunities in International Human Resource Management*, London: M.E.Sharpe.

Venaik, S. and Brewer, P. (2010). 'Avoiding uncertainty in Hofstede and GLOBE', *Journal of International Business Studies*, 41(8), 1294–1315.

Venn, D. (2009). Legislation, collective bargaining and enforcement: Updating the OECD employment protection indicators. www.oecd.org/els/workingpapers.

Verbeke, A. (2003). 'The evolutionary view of the MNE and the future of internalization theory', *Journal of International Business Studies*, 34(6), 498–505.

Verbeke, A. (2009). *International Business Strategy: Rethinking the Foundations of Global Corporate Success*, Cambridge: Cambridge University Press.

Verbeke, A. and Greidanus, N.S. (2009). 'The end of the opportunism vs trust debate: Bounded reliability as a new envelope concept in research on MNC governance', *Journal of International Business Studies*, 40(9), 1471–1495.

Vernon, R. (1966). 'International investment and international trade in the product cycle', *Quarterly Journal of Economics*, 80, 190–207.

Vernon, R. (1998). *In the Hurricane's Eye: The Troubled Prospects of Multinational Enterprises*, Cambridge, MA: Harvard University Press.

Vignali, C. (2001). 'McDonald's: 'think global, act local' – the marketing mix', *British Food Journal*, 103(2), 97–111.

VOA (Voice of America) (2010). McDonald's still thriving in Russia after 20 years. *VOANews*, 1 February. Retrieved from http://www.voanews.com/content/mcdonalds-still-thriving-in-russia-after-20-years-83327327/111887.html.

Voelpel, S.C., Dous, M. and Davenport, T.H. (2005). 'Five steps to creating a global knowledge-sharing system: Siemens' ShareNet', *Academy of Management Executive*, 19(2), 9–23.

Voelpel, S.C. and Han, Z. (2005). 'Managing knowledge sharing in China: the case of Siemens ShareNet', *Journal of Knowledge Management*, 9(3), 51–63.

Von Holdt, K. (2005). Political transition and the changing workplace order in a South African steelworks. In K. Von Holdt and E. Webster (eds), *Beyond the Apartheid Workplace: Studies in Transition*, Scottsville: University of Kwa-Zulu Natal Press, pp. 45–72.

Von Holdt, K. and Webster, E. (eds) (2005). *Beyond the Apartheid Workplace: Studies in Transition*, Scottsville: University of KwaZulu-Natal Press.

Von Krogh, G. (1998). 'Care in knowledge creation', *California Management Review*, 40(3), 133–153.

Von Krogh, G., Ichijo, K. and Nonaka, I. (2000). *Enabling Knowledge Creation: How to Unlock the Mystery of Tacit Knowledge and Release the Power of Innovation*, New York: Oxford University Press.

Vuckvic, M., Mistry, N., Beckmann, S., Lavollay, M. and Girrback, E. (2005). *Making Co-Investment a Reality: Strategies and Experience*, Geneva: GTZ/GBC.

Wang, C., Hong, J., Kafouros, M. and Wright, M. (2012). 'Exploring the role of government involvement in outward FDI from emerging economies', *Journal of International Business Studies*, 43(7), 655–676.

War on Want (2007). *Anglo American: The Alternative Report*, London: War on Want.

Warner, M. (2008). Trade unions in China: In search of a new role in the 'harmonious society'. In J. Benson and Y. Zhu (eds), *Trade Unions in Asia: An Economic and Sociological Analysis*, London: Routledge, pp. 140–156.

Watson, W.E., Kumar, K. and Michelsen, L.K. (1993). 'Cultural diversity's impact on interaction process and performance: Comparing heterogeneous and diverse task groups', *Academy of Management Journal*, 36(3), 590–602.

Weait, M. (2007). *Intimacy and Responsibility: The Criminalisation of HIV Transmission*, London: Routledge Cavendish.

Welch, L.S., Benito, G.R.G. and Petersen, B. (2007). *Foreign Operating Methods*, Cheltenham, UK and Northampton, MA, USA: Edward Elgar Publishing.

Westney, D.E. (2008). 'Challenging the trans-national model', *Socio-Economic Review*, 6(2), 390–394.

Whitley, R. (1989). 'On the nature of managerial tasks and skills: their distinguishing characteristics and organization', *Journal of Management Studies*, 26, 209–224.

Whyte, W. (1991). *Social Theory for Action: How Individuals and Organizations Learn to Change*, Newbury Park: Sage.

Wick, I. (2004). *Workers' Tool or Pr Ploy? A Guide to Codes of International Labour Practice*, Bonn: Friedrich Ebert Foundation.

Wikipedia (2012). Overseas Chinese, Internet source: http://en.wikipedia.org/wiki/Overseas_Chinese#cite_note-81, retrieved on 20 May 2012.

Williamson, O.E. (1985). *The Economic Institutions of Capitalism*, New York: Free Press.

Winter, S.G. (1987). Knowledge and competence as strategic assets. In D.J. Teece (ed.), *The Competitive Challenge*, Cambridge, MA: Ballinger.

Witold, J.H. and Bennet, A.Z. (2010). 'The hidden risks in emerging markets', *Harvard Business Review*, 88(4), 88–95.

World Commission on Environment and Development (1987). *Our Common Future*, Oxford, UK: Oxford University Press.

Wu, H. and Chen, C. (2001). 'An assessment of outward foreign direct investment from China's transitional economy', *European-Asia Studies*, 53(8), 1235–1254.

Xiao, Y.C. and Cooke, F.L. (2012). 'Work–life balance in China? Social policy, employer strategy and individual coping mechanisms', *Asia-Pacific Journal of Human Resources*, 50(1), 6–12.

Yamin, M. and Sinkovics, R.R. (2007). 'ICT and MNC reorganisation: The paradox of control', *Critical Perspectives on International Business*, 3(4), 322–336.

Yan, A. and Louis, M.R. (1999). 'Migration of organizational functions', *Human Relations*, 52(1), 25–47.

Yang, D.X. (2003). Foreign direct investment from developing countries: A case study of China's outward investment, unpublished PhD thesis, Victoria University, Melbourne, Australia.

Yang, X. and Rivers, C. (2009). 'Antecedents of CSR practices in MNCs' subsidiaries: A stakeholder and institutional perspective', *Journal of Business Ethics*, 86, 155–169.

Yaziji, M. (2004). 'Turning gadflies into allies', *Harvard Business Review*, February, 110–115.

Yaziji, M. and Doh, J.P. (2009). *NGOs and Corporations: Conflict and Collaboration*, Cambridge: Cambridge University Press.

Yin, R. (1981). 'The case study crisis: Some answers', *Administrative Science Quarterly*, 26(1), 58–65.

Yin, R. (1994). *Case Study Research: Design and Methods*, Beverly Hills, CA: Sage.

Yin, R. (2003). *Case Study Research: Design and Methods*, London: Sage.

Yip, G. (1989). 'Global strategy – in a world of nations?', *Sloan Management Review*, 31(1), 29–41.

Zack, M.H. (1999). 'Managing codified knowledge', *Sloan Management Review*, 40(4), 45–58.

Zaheer, S. (1995). 'Overcoming the liability of foreignness', *Academy of Management Journal*, 38(2), 341–363.

Zaheer, S. (2002). 'The liability of foreignness, redux: A commentary', *Journal of International Management*, 8, 351–358.

Zhang, M. (2003). 'Transferring human resource management across national boundaries: The case of Chinese multinational companies in the UK', *Employee Relations*, 25(6), 614–26.

Zhou, X. (2004). Singing in tune. *Beijing Review*, Internet source: http://www.breview.com.cn/200418/world-200418(C).htm, retrieved 18 March 2005.

Zsolnai, L. and Ims, K.J. (2006). *Business within Limits: Deep Ecology and Buddhist Economics*, Bern: Peter Lang.

Zuber, A. (2000). 'McDonald's 10th anniversary in Russia brings future confidence despite struggles', *Nation's Restaurant News*, 34(8), 90.

Index